BAZAARS, CONVERSATIONS AND FREEDOM

RAJNI BAKSHI

WITH A FOREWORD BY JOHN ELKINGTON

BAZAARS, CONVERSATIONS AND FREEDOM

FOR A MARKET CULTURE
BEYOND GREED AND FEAR

Greenleaf
PUBLISHING

© 2012 Greenleaf Publishing Limited

Published by Greenleaf Publishing Limited
Aizlewood's Mill
Nursery Street
Sheffield S3 8GG
UK
www.greenleaf-publishing.com

Printed and bound by CPI Group (UK) Ltd, Croydon, CR0 4YY

Cover by LaliAbril.com

British Library Cataloguing in Publication Data:
  A catalogue record for this book is available from the British Library.

  ISBN-13: 978-1-906093-63-1 [paperback]

In Memory of
Sant Dass
Father, mentor, inspiration
and
Dayaji

With untellable *shukriya* to
Pushpa
and
Rohini

CONTENTS

ACKNOWLEDGEMENTS

This journey of ideas and imagination, as well as the actual writing, has been so warmly supported, enriched and guided by a wide variety of friends that my name as the author of this book is primarily an act of taking responsibility for the flaws.

Rohini Nilekani has been fellow-traveller and path-finder as well as midwife and God Mother to this book. Without her constantly sharp challenges, insights, ever-fresh questions and unwavering hopefulness neither the journey nor the book would have come into existence. In addition, she patiently read every draft from start to finish.

It was Professor Daya Krishna who encouraged me decades ago to be both tenacious and faithful to one's own *chintan* (reflection). When the questions that started this exploration first settled upon me I started by seeking Dayaji's guidance. It is to Dayaji and Professor R.S. Bhatnagar that I owe the sheer joy of multifaceted enquiry.

The exploration was materially supported by a Homi Bhabha Fellowship – a manifestation of J.R.D. Tata's visionary social investment which is being steadily maintained by Tata Sons. The wide-open freedom of exploration, enquiry and movement facilitated by the fellowship was an honour and a privilege. Some part of the research was also supported by a grant from the Sir Ratan Tata Trust. A special thanks to Hosi

D. Pajnigar and Dolly B. Nakra of the Homi Bhabha Fellowship
Council, as well as Arun Bannerjee, Suma Chitnis, Professor
S.M. Chitre and Darryl D'Monte – who formed the panel that
selected me for the fellowship.

These grants saw me through half the journey. The rest of
the way was supported by my family. My brother Rajiv made
sure I never wanted for anything while Bobby and Judy provided a steady supply of books and other materials. Above
all they, and my extended family, have helped by believing in
me.

Schumacher College and its entire community provided me
magical periods of study and reflection. A special thanks to
Wolfgang Sachs who first introduced me to the College.

The Centre for Education and Documentation and its ever-
helpful team enabled the search for books, materials and
administered the grant from Sir Ratan Tata Trust.

Nandan Maluste patiently and painstakingly read the earliest raw draft and believed in the book long before it took
shape. I am indebted to him for many insights as well as for
constantly providing a combination of affirmation and coun-
terpoints which were vital to the enquiry.

Anjum Rajabali read a raw version of the manuscript and
lit the path by keeping faith in the journey particularly in the
stormy phases of self-doubt. His guidance on the craft of storytelling was vital: if the outcome is lacking that is due to my
limited learning.

Edgar Cahn, Peter Challen, Amy Domini, John Elkington,
Amartya Sen and George Soros have been beacons – both
through their published works and their generosity in making
time for an ongoing conversation with me.

Arvind Krishnasway, Nick Robins, Nirmal Sethia and Ingrid
Srinath enriched the search by sending me a steady flow of
information, ideas and links.

Titoo Ahluwalia, Arvind Krishnaswamy and Ajay Kumar
read through the last-but-one draft and helped to improve
it. Among those who read and helped with several chapters:

Jairus Banaji, Peter Barnes, Ela Bhatt, John D'Souza, Ram Guha, Walter Mendoza, Sudhakar Murthy, Vineet Rai, Ajit Ranade, Arvind Saxena, Anand Shah, Dorab R. Sopariwala and Wim van der Beek.

Many of the people who feature in the stories, and many more who have remained behind the scenes, were generous with their time and ideas: Peter Barnes, Mashi Blech, Lawrence Bloom, Herman Daly, Frank Dixon, Deborah Doane, Jean Dreze, Paul Ekins, Mary Fee, Edward Fullbrook, Sarah van Gelder, Hazel Henderson, Oliver Karius, Ritu Kumar, Bernard Lietaer, Michael Linton, Amory Lovins, Vijay Mahajan, Raj Mathur, Stephen Marglin, Thomas Moore, Herman Mulder, Nandan Nilekani, Ashis Panda, Ann Pettifor, Ramesh Ramnathan, Jonathan Rowe, Elizabeth Ryan, Michael Shuman, Girish Sohani, Richard Stallman, Nigel Stansfield, Ray Anderson, Tessa Tennant, Sander Tideman, Prashant Varma, Uzramma, Mathis Wackernagel, Atul Wad, Jane Whistler, Ernie Yacub.

Friends old and new kept the sails unfurled, and helped with the rowing when the wind was slack: Aruna Roy, John Michael Byrne, Cornelia Durrant, Ameeta Kaul, Savita Kini, Guy and Kajori Masse, Honey Kripalani, Nita and Achin Mukherjee, Ashis Nandy, Sandra Navidi, Anne Philips, Vijay Pratap, Ritu Priya, Dhirubhai Sheth, R. Sriram, Subbu Vincent, the 'retreat gang' – Venky, Mahnoor, Mary, Bablu, Radha, Walter, John, Leonie, Anjum, Chetna – and my immediate community: Shilpa-Hemant, Saraswati, Mehendales, Basus and Mathurs.

A special thanks to my editor and friend Kamini Mahadevan for her kindness and gentle touch in once again helping me to craft the final draft.

For prayers and ineffable inspiration I bow to Thalia Vitali, Samdhong Rinpoche, Timothy Radcliffe, Vinay Jain, William Thomas and Pervin Varma.

Finally, and above all, my deepest gratitude to my mother
Pushpa Bakshi for inculcating the joy of hard work and the
faith that you can if you think you can.

It is perhaps typical of the world in which Rajni Bakshi lives and works, straddling the traditional and the modern spheres in India and beyond, that I was first introduced to her by Rohini Nilekani – who is both a social entrepreneur address-ing water issues in poorer areas of India and married to a co-founder of one of the giant country's most successful IT companies, Infosys. At a time when so much of our world still operates in silos, to the detriment of the integrated thinking and action we so desperately need, Rajni is a bridge-builder, a connector, a catalyst.

Bazaars, Conversations and Freedom beautifully illus-trates that same ability to move between worlds, to bring the best of the traditional world into the modern, and vice versa. In doing so, however, Rajni is a clear-eyed critic of the worst of both worlds: of the backwardness that traps billions in pov-erty and of the blind faith in markets – the good, which in the words of the Bishop of Durham whom she quotes, has become a God. She also is acutely aware of the dysfunctions of the civil society organisations that have done so much to drive the agenda, but so often lack the ability to move from problems to solutions.

Fundamentally, though, this is a profoundly optimistic book. There is optimism, for example, that we can move beyond what Rajni calls 'autistic economics'. Where Rajni covers bits of the story in which I was directly involved, like The Other Economic Summit (TOES), back in the mists of prehistory, or the evolution of the triple-bottom-line approach to business, I am impressed by the accuracy of her historical research and her ability to link past, present and future.

She asks questions that are tough to answer – but which are fundamental to creating functional, livable, equitable and environmentally sustainably societies and economies. Consider, for example, the first paragraph of her Epilogue:

> Back in the winter of 2001, while the rubble of the World Trade Center was still being cleared and the air was heavy with fear, Edgar Cahn carried a rather basic question into a gathering of the Social Venture Network. He recited T.S. Eliot's poem about the stranger who comes in from the desert and asks, 'What is the meaning of this city?' 'Can we say,' asked Cahn, 'that this is a community; or do we merely dwell together to make money from each other?'

As someone who has spent more of his time than is probably healthy in boardrooms and C-suites around the world, I know how difficult it can be to get the rich and the powerful to consider such questions. And having worked with the wider world of stakeholders around the world I also know how difficult they often find it to frame their demands of business leaders, investors, politicians and policy-makers in ways that encourage immediate, effective action.

But here is a guide to the underlying philosophies that sustain and drive some of the deepest and potentially most transformative leaders of our time. It ranges across very different worlds and very different agendas, but in the process it cross-pollinates and holds out the promise of exactly the sort of hybrid vigour that we now so urgently need. Over to you.

John Elkington
Co-founder, SustainAbility and Volans
Co-author, *The Power of Unreasonable People*

AUTHOR'S NOTE

I cannot pretend that I anticipated the meltdown. But I have spent the last ten years following the trail of those who diagnosed the fatal flaws and are busy fostering a more mindful market culture.

This journey began in the summer of 1998. Thousands of men and women were assembled for a *satyagraha* (peaceful protest), outside Enron's power plant at Dabhol in Maharashtra. Farmers, landless labourers and urban professionals defied blistering heat to squat on the rough country road and block access to the plant. They were protesting the closed-door, possibly corrupt, methods by which that project had been sanctioned by our government on the grounds that it was imperative to make India friendly to international market forces. Those protesters were not just asking for greater accountability from governments and corporations. They were driven by a deeper discontent. We too are producers and consumers, buyers and sellers, the protesters seemed to say. Why, then, do our voices seem drowned out by Enron, the government and 'market forces'?

The defeat of that protest became a turning point for me as a chronicler of struggles where rural communities were demanding control over local *jal-jungle-zameen* (water, forests, land). Suddenly this demand seemed fragile and inadequate.

Greater control over the natural resource base won't necessarily empower people in the prevailing market culture. I now found myself confronted with a question that seemed paradoxically naïve and daunting. Just what is 'The Market'? My curiosity was neither academic nor abstract. I was driven by the need to figure out why so many struggles for economic and ecological justice seemed to be losing out. Could it be that we, the supporters of such struggles, have failed to grasp some fundamental realities? What if economics, and the market, are indeed governed by natural laws? I had been told often enough, by proponents of the free market, that any attempt to curb it is like trying to repeal the law of gravity.

It was just then that George Soros broadcast his passionate critique of market fundamentalism. Soros's life, as one of Wall Street's most celebrated money managers, was a universe away from the village-level struggles I was familiar with. Yet he echoed concerns that I had witnessed and mapped on the ground – that too much competition and too little cooperation can cause intolerable inequities and instability. It is time, Soros argued, to challenge the intrusion of the market ethos in all of society. This inspired me to look deeper and wider for signals of rethinking at the very heart of global markets.

The journey took me from Mumbai to Wall Street, from Schumacher College in Devon (UK), to the City in London and onwards to the Time Dollar Institute in Washington DC, Timbaktu Collective in Andhra Pradesh, the 6th Street Community Center in Manhattan, an old-world investment firm in Boston, a cluttered office at the Massachusetts Institute of Technology where the free software movement was born – on and on, farther and deeper.

At each location I found men and women engaged in a quest for material well-being and values that equate civilisation with good conduct. These are dispatches from a realm of action that lies beyond the familiar extremes of greed and fear, boom and bust. Here is a tentative account of an ongoing adventure, truly a risky undertaking of uncertain outcome.

PRELUDE

A WALK DOWN WALL STREET

It was on 11 September 1609, that the first European set foot on the island we now call Manhattan. Henry Hudson came ashore near about the site where the World Trade Center was later to soar and crash. The explorer and his crew of 20, aboard the ship *Half Moon*, were working for the newly formed Dutch East India Company. Their mission was to find the fabled Northwest Passage which would allow European trade vessels to navigate past the frozen northern coastline of America to reach China.

Sailing into the mouth of the river that was later named after him, Hudson saw scores of native people paddling their canoes between the mainland and an island they called Menatay – 'the place where the sun is born'. The southern tip of Menatay was a summer time gathering place where the Delaware people came to mingle, converse and barter. Hudson and his crew ventured into this gathering with an offering of beads, knives and hatchets. In turn they were given beaver and otter skins. Here was free exchange in an almost pristine form. Hudson's journals glowed with accounts of the loving, generous nature of the indigenous people.

Within a few years, the Delaware gathering place gave way to a rag-tag settlement of Dutch traders and immigrants.

When guns, germs and greed replaced the bonhomie of first contact, the European settlers built a small wood and mud barricade across the narrow southern tip of Manhattan. The walls of Fort Amsterdam were a symbolic representation of collapsed conversations.

Eventually, the Delaware people retreated inland. The expanding population of European settlers now declared Fort Amsterdam to be an 'obstructing nuisance'. So they pulled it down. The short and narrow street that replaced the barricade was named, naturally, Wall Street. A vastly different kind of meeting place and market began to take shape in and around the literal and metaphorical Wall Street. Free exchange gradually morphed into an *idea* known as the 'free market'.

Three hundred and ninety-nine years later, almost to the day that Hudson landed there, Wall Street imploded. From the primitive barter hub of the Delaware tribe to the fall of Lehman Brothers and other giant finance companies in September 2008 we can find a wealth of encoded messages that might be vital to the future of civilisation.

I more or less stumbled upon these codes. My journey was initially driven by rather basic questions which were far upstream of the doomsday machine that has shredded businesses on Wall Street and thus across the world. Can we resuscitate the planet's gasping ecosystems only to the extent that the money bottom line of the market will allow? Why do enough responsible people accept, as a gospel truth, the claim that no further miracle drugs would be invented without the motive of enormous private profit? We all enjoy the freedom of open exchange in a marketplace but is that the same as the 'free market'? To my surprise I discovered that a dazzling variety of people, across the world, are troubled by these questions. Most of them share a firm conviction that the creative freedom inherent to our species is far more powerful than the 'free market' orthodoxy.

Before I could venture further I had to first grapple with my own preconceptions. My training, both at home in India and in the West, urged me to view what I critiqued from up close and with empathy. It was not enough to read about and talk with people who understand, perhaps even worship, the prevailing market culture. It seemed imperative to visit the site of its core symbol. So I went walkabout on Wall Street. The onward journey came to be defined by two sights – Federal Hall and the Trinity Church which crowns Wall Street at its junction with Broadway.

Federal Hall stands on the site of the original New York City Hall where George Washington was sworn in as President and the first federal government of the newly born United States of America was housed. The New York Stock Exchange next door, though it now dominates the image and identity of Wall Street, came up much later. That civic meeting place, and the house of worship nearby, served as a reminder that bazaars and marketplaces have fundamentally been a point of connection and conversation. More importantly, until about 200 years ago, those conversations were as much about civilisation-making values and politics, as about material exchange.

This realisation shaped the onward journey and provided the fundamental premises of this exploration. The bazaar, an ancient mechanism of human society, is quite distinct from what we now call the 'free market'. Bazaar refers to a location; the market is an idea. Bazaars bring together buyers and sellers, eyeball to eyeball, for open and direct exchange. The free market, as it emerged in 18th-century Europe, fostered complex mechanisms of more indirect and distant exchange.

Within the babble and bustle of bazaars buying and selling were tossed together with storytelling, politics and even the framing of moral values. By contrast, the idea of a free market depends on assiduously separating the economic sphere from the rest of life.

As I ventured forth on this journey I found that the bazaar now also serves as a metaphor for those processes that define value, even commercial value, in a deeper and wider sense than price or financial assets. The market culture that is now in the throes of crisis, has depended on keeping the profit motive pure and 'unsullied' by social, moral or ecological concerns – relegating them to family, government and charities.

With a wee bit of licence, the term 'bazaar' can be deployed to allude to a more socially embedded market culture – based on a broader, more well-rounded, view of human nature. This view challenges the notion of 'economic man' as a utility-maximising, or selfish, individual unit. What is now coming apart at the seams is the idea that combining social and moral values with commercial objectives would somehow reduce the reach of 'the market'.

Above all, bazaar is more akin to market economy – that circle of open exchange where producers decipher consumers' will and purchasing power to create goods and services.

What the 'free market' has fostered is a market *society* where virtually all functions of life are seen to be best served by the pecuniary motive.

But now, across the world and at multiple levels, society is fighting back. I found an illustration of this as I stepped off Wall Street and onto a subway train.

'To the best of my knowledge there is no mention of the bottom line in the Hippocratic Oath', said the bold print of an advertisement in the subway car. The copy was accompanied by the photo of a venerable looking male doctor wearing a blue surgical cap. The small print of the advertisement urged New Yorkers to call the Lenox Hill Hospital Physician Referral Service – 'For the surgeon whose only concern is your health.' Even as an advertising ploy, this was a statement. It tapped into deep-seated anxieties.

Back in India, my friend Rohini Nilekani found a more direct and stark expression of this anxiety expressed by a villager in Bihar: 'Once upon a time the natural order of life was that *samaj*, society, came first. Government and market were less powerful. Colonialism changed this. S*amaj* fell to second place and government dominated. Now the market rules, government is in between and *samaj* is a poor third.'

Or, as the economist Jeremy Rifkin has put it: 'Can civilization survive when only the commercial sphere is left as the primary mediator of human life?'

I knew at the outset that merely mapping these anxieties was not my mission. As the walkabout stretched wider, taking me into diverse realms, I found myself recording the quest for ways to redress this imbalance. The stories in this book could be read as dispatches from that journey, an account of scattered initiatives or trends. And, yet, there is a deeper subtext. These tales offer glimpses of how a post-revolutionary era is taking shape.

The people you will meet in these pages are not working for a new order that can come about through a cataclysmic shift of power. However, a host of trends and initiatives are pushing ahead a transformation that may be no less profound. At the heart of this foment is something both simple and demanding – a broader view of human nature. There is a surge of people who are seeking a better balance between competing human tendencies – greed and generosity, competition and cooperation, conflict and conciliation. Most of them are boldly confident that the higher faculties of our species can not only make individual lives better, they can also underpin our interactions in marketplaces.

As this confidence grows, the future is taking shape in the spaces that have opened up since the two dominant, and conflicting, utopias of the 20th century collapsed. While the communist utopia fell dramatically, triumphant free-market fundamentalism has been quietly punctured. The stark choice between State domination and market free-for-all was cleared away along with the debris of the Berlin Wall. But the pulling-down of that Wall may be a greater watershed than we have fully grasped – because barriers to thought and perception are far more stubborn than inanimate bricks and mortar.

That might explain why the wrecking balls bringing down the barrier in Berlin sounded like bells ringing in the victory of 'capitalism'. Many mistook the reaffirmation of free exchange and open society as a victory for 'the market'. And, yet, the process of unbundling these confusions has steadily, if rather quietly, been gathering momentum. So far this shift was restrained by the basic catch that, as Albert Einstein used to say, no problem can be solved from the same level of consciousness that created it. It is now tempting to visualise the meltdown on Wall Street as a forest fire that will clear away not only destructive financial instruments but also a fossilised mind-set – to make way for a healthier culture of commerce in which bazaars are conversations about not just freedom of exchange and material opportunity but also about purpose, and social and moral values.

The memory of the literal wall that once stood at Wall Street is important here. It serves as an invitation to restore collapsed conversations. It is also a reminder that we now live in an age where might is not right. Yes, might still often wins. But after the varied struggles of the 20th century, and above all after Mahatma Gandhi, right has powerful might. More and more people are surging against barriers of thought and ideology to challenge conventional wisdom about what is possible. This is the striving for higher forms of freedom.

Freedom from the dogma of TINA, that 'There Is No Alternative' to the self-regulating market run by a mythical 'economic man'; freedom to foster a culture of commerce based on a fuller, more real, view of human nature; freedom to forge more equitable relations in the marketplace and challenge power structures. But all of this also requires freedom from fear – the fear of wide, uncharted spaces and uncertainties. Writing these stories has taught me to respect such fears of the unknown. Here is an attempt to open a dialogue that is inviting not just to daring innovators but those submerged in business-as-usual.

Then again, not all the premises of this journey challenge conventional wisdom. It is now widely agreed that freedom to exchange and transact is valuable only if it is universally and evenly available to all. Arbitrary controls enforced by unaccountable bureaucracies or distortions created by private power cartels endanger this freedom and must therefore be prevented. This is the theory of even the prevailing market culture.

Yet we find an astonishing variety of 'unfreedoms' persisting. Apart from coining this apt term, Amartya Sen has also shown how the prolonged celebration of utility and wealth has obscured the central value of freedom itself. But just as the walls of Fort Amsterdam had to come down in order to lay Wall Street, the assumptions and baggage associated with the idea of the market are now being unravelled. No pat formulas await discovery, nor do old maps help much. But, as Sen has urged, an overarching concern with *processes* that simultaneously enhance individual freedoms and broad social welfare is a good way to journey further.

Chapter 1 traces the historical and cultural transition that put bazaars and politics in a position of subservience to the market. Chapter 2 continues this journey upstream into the history of ideas to show how the current narrow definition of self-interest came about. It is now being overturned by upheavals within the discipline of economics and other revolts which make *homo economicus* look more like an effigy than a portrait. Chapter 3 delves into multiple dimensions of how the old habit of money is being re-examined, tweaked and recreated to challenge – and perhaps even transform – the ways in which we pass on information about value.

A feral kind of competition has been increasingly endemic in the market. Chapter 4 traces the growing interface between cooperation and competition, particularly the gift culture of the internet and wider implications of the open-source movement. Chapter 5 explores how the terms of engagement between Main Street and Wall Street might be redefined to truly address the needs of those who feel threatened by globalisation. Chapter 6 explores the promise and limitations of changes unfolding within the world of corporations. Chapter 7 grapples with the possibility of creating a new operating system for the market mechanism – one that is founded on the reality that nature bats last and it owns the stadium.

In the tradition of the agora as an open space for philosophical reflection as well as material exchange, these stories are an endeavour to expand conversations in and about bazaars, to explore how far we might stretch the freedom to seek universal well-being. Hence the title *Bazaars, Conversations and Freedom*. True, each of these words evokes a multitude of images and cannot be fixed to any one meaning. And, yet, we can venture forth, carefully, knowing that words serve as tools or signposts for a fluid and multi-dimensional exploration of reality.

The basis of this endeavour is the raw faith best expressed by pioneers of the open-source phenomenon: with enough eyeballs all bugs are shallow. Or, as Marcel Proust said, 'The real voyage of discovery consists not in seeking new landscapes, but in having new eyes.'

1
THE NEED TO GATHER
RESCUING BAZAARS FROM GODDESS TINA

> **The Market is a good that's become a God, and
> that's the problem.**
> *– David Jenkins, former Bishop of Durham*

*After going walkabout on Wall Street I plunged back in time to
the cradles of civilisation, before the earliest forms of buying
and selling. This helped me to distinguish bazaars from the
market. In some form or the other bazaars have been with us
for at least 5,000 years – as gathering places for many different kinds of communication and exchange where value is
expressed in multiple languages. By contrast the market is a
relatively recent human construct that has sometimes been
compared to a computer – a self-regulating machine that can
itself ensure the equilibrium of economic activities.*

*This assumption may not have been vaporised by the
financial meltdown of 2008 but it is more discredited than
ever before. Public clamour for closer, more sophisticated regulation has a new sharpness. But the real story of our times
is taking shape in the innards of what can be visualised as
the global agora. This is a vast, interlinked realm of businesspeople, activists, crafts-persons, software hackers and*

academics fostering bazaar spaces where exchange of goods and services comes second to the need to gather. For exchange of values, reflections about purpose and that most basic question of all: how should one live?

～

Some time in 2003 a retired American admiral, John Poindexter of the Iran–Contra scandal fame, masterminded a futures market in terrorism. This was to be a mechanism through which a wide range of experts could bid on a prediction: for example, that bomb blasts would occur at a particular location. Individual trades were to be kept down to about $100.

When word of this scheme reached Capitol Hill there was outrage across party lines. The idea of a betting parlour on atrocities and terrorism was variously denounced by Senators as 'ridiculous, 'stupid', 'grotesque' and 'sick'. For the promoters of the scheme, at the Pentagon's Defense Advanced Research Projects Agency, it was simply an efficient way to aggregate intelligence information. The scheme was called Futures Markets Applied to Prediction. 'What's wrong with a trading floor for ideas which makes it possible to capture people's collective wisdom in a given area, even if it is terrorism,' asked one of its designers? 'Using such a mechanism will work,' argued another Pentagon expert, 'because markets bring together people with information in a way that blue-ribbon panels of experts just cannot.' None of these justifications sounded convincing to the Senators and Congressmen. The plan for terrorism futures was killed within days of it becoming public. Why? Firstly, as one Senator said, because it would be like trading in death. It's a gross misapplication of the market mechanism. What if traders start investing in a way that might actually bring about a particular terrorist strike? Secondly, markets can go horribly wrong in aggregating information and are known to foster delusions. At that time, a report in *Wired* illustrated this point by reminding people that the idea of terrorism futures was particularly odd after the lessons of the dot-com bust in which many flimsy firms had boasted 'muscle-bound stock prices'.

And yet all this reasoning was merely a thin layer on the surface of public life. The Pentagon's scheme seemed to stir a still darker doubt. Has faith in the market gone too far, become somewhat messianic? The historian Steve Fraser saw the whole episode as a classic example of what he called 'the Wall Streeting of the American mind'. From this perspective, the market is seen not merely as the most efficient processor of information but as the supreme conveyer of *truth* and thus the most reliable basis for organising not only economic but also social life. In the 1990s this view became not only the dominant view of reality but an orthodoxy which held societies across the world in thrall. But disquiet continued to simmer just below the surface. That outrage on Capitol Hill was a rather weak signal of that unrest. Far more creative and robust challenges were being incubated beyond the reach of either state power or money power. For instance, cyber-age iconoclasts pointed out that the internet would certainly end business-as-usual – but not in ways that dot-com boomers imagined. Doc Searls, the editor of the *Linux Journal*, liked to explain why by telling this story about a European tourist at a traditional village bazaar in West Africa.

Wandering through the jumble of stalls the tourist was struck by a particular carpet. With the help of his local friend, an Irish missionary, the visitor asked the merchant for the price of the carpet. Hearing the price, the would-be buyer said, 'That's too much' and walked away.

'You've just offended that merchant,' the missionary gently informed his friend. Immediately, the apologetic tourist turned back and offered to buy the rug at the stated price.

'Wrong again,' said the missionary, 'offering to pay full price is as insulting as refusing to discuss the value of the rug. Why don't you say what you think the rug is worth?'

The tourist made an offer. Finally, here was the conversation that the merchant expected as an essential prerequisite for any sale. The ensuing exchange of ideas and information left the visitor better informed about the rug and threw up a price that both buyer and seller agreed was fair.

Searls enjoys telling this story because it illustrates two elementary truths. One, that markets are conversations, not merely devices for aggregating information. And, two, that value is not the same as price. All value is discovered inside a conversation and price is just one aspect of 'what's it worth to you'. A conversation happens when neither side has the power to dictate a price and walk away. It also has more scope for drawing in questions about purpose and meaning – stuff that is beyond the immediate and momentary transaction.

For almost four millennia bazaars were the seat of such conversation where open exchange of ideas came first, followed closely by exchange of goods and services. How did these multi-dimensional marketplaces, *bazaars*, morph into 'the market' – an idea and a set of assumptions which now rules our lives and has rendered much of society into a veritable auction block? Perhaps the problem began with the birth of mass production and mass markets, about two centuries ago. As direct face-to-face exchange became rare, businesses began to act as though markets are made up of demographic sectors not human beings. This is the premise around which Searls and his buddies crafted their rebellious *Cluetrain Manifesto* in the late 1990s. The 95-point Manifesto, which started as a web-based conversation, argued that the 21st century's *agora*, the internet, can bring the *human* voice back into markets.

The World Wide Web is the latest form of an ancient phenomenon – the need to gather. From the Americas to Mesopotamia, Africa to the far corners of Asia – people first came together by a stream or under a sacred tree not to buy and sell but just to be together. They assembled to celebrate, gossip, play games and also to settle disputes dissolving tensions triggered by anger, fear, suspicion or greed. It was around these community gatherings – somewhat like that summertime hub that Henry Hudson stumbled upon at Menatay – that the earliest buying and selling took place around 5,000 years ago.

In India the *choupal* survives as a traditional forum of the village community. Often located at a *chouraha,* an intersection at which paths from the four directions converge, the choupal has been both a physical and mental space for gossip and politics, even though everyone may not get an equal say. A few centuries before the birth of Christ, the Athenians developed the agora as a place for palaver, long parley or conversation, which doubled as a location for exchanging goods and services. With some variations this pattern repeated itself across the ancient world. From Persia to India, marketplaces came to be known as 'bazaar', derived from the Pahlavi term *vacar* or *baha-char,* meaning 'the place of prices'. And, yet, the bazaar was as much a place for social connectedness as for striking a deal and determining the 'price'. 'Since no man is an island in the market,' said a Medieval European proverb, 'one must not only think of oneself but of other people too.'

On the internet chatting and grouping – for the sake of knowledge, reflection, political mobilisation or plain gossip – is once again ahead of exchanging goods and services. This does not mean that buying and selling are lowly or that commerce is less important. 'Don't worry, you can still make money,' the Cluetrain team assured old-style companies, 'as long as it's not the only thing on your mind.' That's not merely because more and more people can now talk to each other directly and have limitless access to information with a few clicks. The core trait of the internet is that it grows our hunger for democratic *bazaar* spaces which, like the World Wide Web itself, are not owned by anyone, open to everyone and can be improved by all.

Isn't that just what a free market does? Yes and no. Freedom of movement and exchange in marketplaces that are true commons might do that. But the idea and practice of *the market*, over the last 200 years, has been about much more than just this simple freedom of exchange. It is loaded with a heavy baggage of assumptions about human nature and market dynamics that masquerade as laws.

For most of the 20th century a free market could easily be equated with freedom because its opposite was the state-dominated economy of the communist kind. That dichotomy, always a false one, has now faded into history. Details of that process, one of the most well-documented stories of our times, would be out of place here. And yet we need to map the historical context, the backdrop of ideas for the onward journey. The defining moment for our purposes is not, as you might expect, the pulling-down of the Berlin Wall but a juncture in the 1940s.

A TATTERED SOCIAL FABRIC

Londoners once held their breath waiting for, of all things, a government report. On the evening of 30 November 1942 long queues began forming outside the headquarters of His Majesty's Stationery Office, in Holborn. When the office opened next morning it sold all 60,000 copies of its new release within hours. Why? The publication titled *Social Insurance and Allied Services* was, as the historian Peter Watson noted, hardly Christmas-present material. Yet this report eventually sold 600,000 copies and its details were broadcast by the BBC in 22 languages. Better known as the Beveridge Report, this document laid the foundations of the modern welfare state in Britain. The frenzy that attended its release, wrote Watson, was as important an indicator of a shift in public sensibility as the report itself. It was a response to the despair that was rife even 13 years after the big crash.

On the 'Black Thursday' of 24 October 1929, the bottom had fallen out of Wall Street and triggered a global downward spiral. During the subsequent Great Depression, world trade shrank by one-third. At the worst point of the crisis, American farm prices dropped by 51% and the value of some manufactured goods fell by three-fourths. Through the 1930s, on an average about 18.2% American workers were unemployed. Out of the 25,568 banks that existed in the USA in 1929 almost 42% had gone out of business by 1933. In Germany, the number of unemployed swelled from about half a million people in 1928 to over six million people in 1933. In Britain, up to 22% of the workforce was unemployed in the early 1930s.

Beveridge's proposals offered desperately needed relief to people who were exhausted not only by a cascade of economic failures but also two crippling wars within one generation. A government blueprint for social insurance, even the mere glimmer of security, was something to clutch. Curiously enough, Sir William Beveridge's own life captured the crosscurrents of that age. He was born in India, where his father was posted as a judge in the Indian Civil Service. So Beveridge grew up amid the opulence of the British Raj. But as a young man enrolled at Balliol College, Oxford, Beveridge came under the influence of teachers who encouraged students to ask why a rich nation like Britain still had so much poverty.

Like many of his peers Beveridge saw the pre-war form of capitalism as a corpse awaiting burial – hopefully to make way for a more egalitarian and stable economic system. By then it was clear that the communist experiment in the Soviet Union was not a worthy alternative. Beveridge sought ways to patch up Britain's tattered social fabric by getting the state to do what the market was unable to deliver. It was now clear that optimising the generation of surplus would not be enough. Society also needed to check and grapple with the chaotic forces unleashed by the free market.

Beveridge was Master of University College at Oxford when the government appointed him to chair a committee on the coordination of social insurance. All the government wanted was to patch up Britain's social machinery, but Beveridge plunged into a far more ambitious undertaking. Working amid the chaos of Nazi air-raids, his committee brought together written and oral inputs to hammer out the blueprint for a welfare state. Beveridge was not the only one who saw the post-war reconstruction as a revolutionary moment, not to be wasted. He was part of a broad consensus that there was no way back to a laissez-faire order of society which had dominated Western Europe for over a century. The war, wrote Beverige's contemporary, the economist Karl Mannheim, 'is the maker of a silent revolution by preparing the road to a new type of planned order'.

The stage for Beveridge's work had been set a few years earlier by John Maynard Keynes in his seminal work *The General Theory of Employment, Interest and Money.* Proponents of the free market argued that depressions were 'therapeutic' and helpful to remove inefficiency and waste in an economy. Keynes led the brigade that dismissed this argument as immoral and impractical nonsense while pushing for state intervention to help build a more just and egalitarian society.

It was clear that defeating fascism would not be enough. True victory meant building a better world than the one that had been reduced to shambles. A more humane order required among other things a comprehensive social insurance programme and a national health service – with contributions coming from the individual, employers and the state. This social security system was based on Beveridge's conviction that 'minimum should be given as of right and without means test, so that individuals may build freely upon it'. He saw this as essential to attack 'five giant evils' – physical want, disease, ignorance, squalor and idleness – which destroy wealth and corrupt people.

Across the Atlantic, President Franklin D. Roosevelt's New Deal had dramatically increased the role of the state since 1933 by stabilising investment, more carefully regulating financial markets and putting various social safety nets into place. These moves marked a rejection of the 'Let us Alone' philosophy, better known as laissez-faire, that had ruled on both sides of the Atlantic for more than a century. Proponents of this philosophy not only insisted on 'Freedom, Immunity, Liberty' for private business they also insisted that a self-regulating market is the most efficient system for allocating resources and determining the value of everything, including people.

'Enough is enough' seemed to be the signal being sent out by the hundreds of thousands of people who made Beveridge's report a bestseller. The echo of that sentiment circled the globe. Outside the communist bloc most countries opted for a market economy with some form of state planning and welfare measures – because this was considered a practical and life-saving imperative. But this sentiment did not last. In the 1980s and 1990s the free-market 'Let us Alone' thinking re-emerged with such brute force that it was dubbed 'market fundamentalism'.

The story of this peculiar variety of fundamentalism is usually linked to that of the Ronald Reagan and Margaret Thatcher regimes. But this is misleading. The tsunami of market fundamentalism that swept the world in the closing decades of the 20th century had its epicentre in the 1940s – at the very moment when it seemed that the feral variety of market had been tamed. Curiously, the leading actors of this skirmish in the marketplace of ideas were three émigrés from the fading Austro-Hungarian Empire. All three escaped from Nazi persecution and were seeking a reliable basis for freedom. Karl Polanyi, Friedrich von Hayek and Karl Popper were all born in Vienna at the end of the 19th century. Popper, a philosopher of science, coined the term 'open society' which echoes throughout this quest. However, let us defer Popper's appearance until later.

HAYEK AND POLANYI: FREE MARKET VERSUS FREEDOM

Hayek and Polanyi's youthful years were devoured by two world wars, economic depression and ethnic persecution. Both men spent the prime of life trying to figure out why Europe had collapsed into violence and chaos. Why had a century of industrialisation and technological progress based on a free market ended in trench warfare, crashing stock markets and the rise of fascism?

Both Hayek and Polanyi found explanations for this situation that zeroed in on the idea and practice of the self-regulating market. In 1944 both thinkers published books that described such a market as a relatively recent construct but came to diametrically opposite conclusions about its impact. Hayek blamed policies and attitudes that had curbed the proper functioning of the self-regulating market. Polanyi blamed the excesses of that market system. Understanding this sharply divided perception of the same reality is vital for our onward journey.

Hayek was born into a prominent Viennese family in 1899. He studied economics and, like Popper, was a member of the famous Vienna circle of thinkers. After migrating to Britain, Hayek became a professor at the London School of Economics. Loathing Stalinism and fascism with equal intensity, Hayek saw democracy not as an end in itself but as a utilitarian device for safeguarding internal peace and individual freedom. For Hayek the rise of the modern market was one of the great achievements of the Enlightenment

This view had deep roots in Western Europe. Since the mid 18th century, commerce had been celebrated as a gentle and

'civilising' agent that fostered prudence, probity, industrious-
ness, punctuality. This milieu shaped not only Adam Smith's
The Wealth of Nations but also the American Declaration of
Independence – both events occurring in 1776. Commerce
driven by a self-regulating market was deemed to be liberating because it broke free of old power structures closely
controlled by the landed aristocracy and mediæval guilds. By
contrast, the free-market culture had a healthy, invigorating
quality which enabled all manner of people to plunge into the
fray, regardless of status by birth. Yet the cornerstone of this
emerging order was a claim, an assumption that the common
good is ensured not through direct social policies but by everyone seeking their own individual gain.

Therefore, Hayek argued, planning is not only impractical
but wrong in principle. His book *The Road to Serfdom* made the
case that deviating from a self-regulating market erodes both
political democracy and personal freedom leading inevitably
to some form of totalitarian control and abuse of power. Even
Keynes's pragmatic, and for most people desperately needed,
measures seemed to Hayek as a dangerous tilt towards col-
lectivism. Some degree of security is required even to preserve
freedom, Hayek wrote, but security at the expense of freedom will be fatal. The market is a more reliable instrument
for ensuring both dynamism and freedom because it is 'blind'
and impartial, producing effects that no one can predict. All
governments need to do is create the competitive rules of the
game and let the 'invisible hand' of individual profit maximisation operate freely. Of course, Hayek acknowledged, the market is far from perfect and must not be made into a fetish.

The first print run of *The Road to Serfdom* sold out in days.
A few months later, as the general election approached, the
Conservative Party surrendered one-and-a-half tons of their
precious paper ration to publish a popular version of the
book. But it had no immediate impact on policy-making. The
interventionist, mixed-economy approach promoted by Keynes, Beveridge and others became the order of the day while

Hayek's *Road to Serfdom* was dismissed by many academics and policy-makers as 'an intemperate political tract'.

By contrast, Karl Polanyi's book *The Great Transformation: The Political and Economic Origins of Our Time,* also published in 1944, was not an immediate bestseller but went on to earn the status of a classic. Born into a Jewish Hungarian family, Polanyi studied law, philosophy and economic history. After fleeing to England in 1933 he made a hand-to-mouth living as a tutor for the Workers Educational Association, an adult education programme of the Universities of Oxford and London. The more famous Polanyi at that time was Karl's brother Michael, a chemist turned philosopher who taught Sociology at Manchester University and was the first to convincingly propose that much scientific discovery stems from intuition and guesswork. Scientific advances, Michael Polanyi argued, are often made possible not so much by new facts but by new interpretations of known facts. This was essentially what Karl Polanyi did as an economic historian. He looked anew at familiar facts and offered a fresh explanation for why European society lay in a shambles.

First of all, Polanyi's reading of history and anthropology showed that Adam Smith's claim about the human 'propensity to truck and barter' was a narrow Eurocentric view of reality. More importantly, his research showed that the utilitarian individual bent upon maximising his or her material self-interest is a recent construct even in Europe and certainly not a universal constant across the world. Classical economics rested on ignoring the non-economic value systems of pre-modern Europe and other civilisations.

Adam Smith had argued that the division of labour relied on the prevalence of markets. Polanyi pointed to evidence of societies with an extensive division of labour and thriving systems of exchange but no 'markets'. Even in pre-modern Europe no aspect of life was *purely* economic: that is, governed by supply and demand driven by pursuit of individual self-interest alone. Polanyi's *Great Transformation* traced how industrialised 'free market' society had been created through public policies, often pushed through by brute force.

Many of these policies had converted public goods into private. From the 13th century onwards, across Europe, local and traditional codes – which gave peasants inalienable rights over pastures, the fish in a stream or animals in a forest – were replaced by laws based on Roman concepts of private property. This was merely one of the tools by which 'organic society', as Polanyi called it, was liquidated. This was necessary, he added, to 'enable the mighty Market and its selfish value system to trample upon and eradicate the "moral economy" value system of the past which refused to permit the individual to starve'.

When the 19th-century British poet and painter William Blake issued his haunting lament about 'satanic mills' he was not merely repelled by the ugliness of early industrialisation, but how the self-regulating market ground men into masses. Self-interest was now cut off from organic community living with its reciprocal relations extending far beyond the biological family. As work became a commodity human beings found themselves fitted into atomised and individualistic structures. The 'economy' was more and more separated from any expression of social relationships or moral obligations.

Polanyi pointed out that the 'Let us Alone' philosophy, and laws derived from it, were not merely opposed to governmental restrictions. They were equally at odds with a gamut of social and communal concerns. Earlier 'freedom' pertained to freedom from feudal arbitrariness to ensure the activities of the municipality, the guild, the religious order. Now freedom came to mean freedom for private investment, profit and accumulation. Polanyi riled against a bitter paradox at the heart of the laissez-faire philosophy and related policies. While government was exhorted not to interfere in the way industry and commerce treated land and labour, it was required to push through policies that would ensure the destruction of non-contractual relations between individuals and prevent their spontaneous reformation.

Individualism now became the norm. The consequence was a 'great transformation' to a new cultural and economic milieu. Advocates of the new order did not merely believe that the pursuit of individual greed, avarice and lust would balance out to produce common good. They also insisted that all humans in every culture are utilitarian individuals who would maximise their material self-interest if social and religious constraints did not get in the way. It followed that economic improvement is a separate and paramount goal.

Naturally, this was unacceptable to those who were being crushed in the process. Yet even some beneficiaries of the new system were equally outraged. Robert Owen, a successful cotton merchant in early 19th-century Britain, was appalled by the degradation and misery that resulted from turning nature and people into commodities. This was the toll of turning a market economy into a market *society*. Above all, Owen was disturbed by the emergence of a new type of person – cruder and more callous – among both labourers and owners of capital. As a counter to this Owen created a series of cooperative enterprises and is remembered as the father of the cooperative movement, which is still going strong.

These were some of the 19th-century trends that led Polanyi to conclude that socialism is the natural and inherent tendency of an industrial civilisation. By socialism he meant the conscious subordination of a self-regulating market to a democratic and free society not a dictatorship. In a truly open society the market would be a useful, but not all-powerful, tool. It would enable distinctively human relationships by melding the social and economic sphere.

Hayek lamented that the market system that emerged in Europe during the 19th and early 20th century was not free enough. Polanyi argued that the self-regulating market in its pure form was too utopian to be viable because it is dehumanising and inherently unstable. Thus constant political and social intervention, through regulations to ensure basic well-being for all is a practical imperative not an ideological preference.

Half a century later ethical investing expert Nick Robins read Hayek's *The Road to Serfdom* and was struck by its open frustration over people's inability to submit themselves to impersonal economic forces. By contrast, Polanyi's work inspired those who challenge economic systems that demand such submission. Most of them are struck by the question that George Orwell asked when he reviewed Hayek's book at the time of its release. Why, asked Orwell, could Hayek not see that for the great mass of people a return to 'free' competition means a tyranny far worse than that of the state?

This is why Polanyi was confident a laissez-faire regime naturally gives rise to a counter-movement. People, as social and moral beings, inevitably grapple with the pain of dislocation and dispossession. Therefore in the latter half of the 19th century a series of social and political struggles gave birth to norms and laws we now take for granted – such as the eight-hour work-day, protections for workers in hazardous industries and special protections for women and children. Polanyi called this the 'double-movement' between onslaught of a free market and its counter-response by *society*. The Beveridge reforms and the New Deal seemed to validate Polanyi's insight about this tug-of-war of a double-movement.

Between 1945 and the early 1970s the state's share in the GNP of most industrialised countries almost doubled. Throughout that period Hayek passionately campaigned to re-establish the free market. In 1974 he was awarded the Nobel Prize for Economics and his ideas became the foundation of Margaret Thatcher's emphatic assertion that 'There Is No Alternative' to the free market. In 1989, at the peak of her powers, Thatcher wrote a letter to Hayek acknowledging him as the man who had 'set us on the right road'. Thatcher's letter was written at about the time that the Berlin Wall was being pulled down and China was well on its way to a massive course correction away from communism. Hayek's denunciation appeared to be fully vindicated. But in fact it was Polanyi's insight about a double-movement that was validated as societies swung in favour of an aggressively free market – for a while.

It is important to emphasise that this contrast between Hayek and Polanyi is a partial and selective view of ideas and events that shaped our present. It's a keyhole view of the intellectual 'flame wars' and street fights in a complex battle of ideas. And yet even this fleeting glimpse helps to illustrate the point most vital for the onward exploration. A market economy is quite distinct from a market *society*; and it is the latter phenomenon that is now being resisted with renewed intensity. In our times one of the defining episodes of this ongoing conflict was played out by Britain's coal miners.

'THE MARKET 'R' US'

On 12 March 1984 Britain's National Union of Mineworkers declared a strike in all coal fields and plunged into a bitter confrontation with the Conservative Party government of Margaret Thatcher. The crushing defeat of the miners not only set back the labour movement in Britain, it also marked the rolling-back of the welfare state. Across the world, it came to be seen as a crucial battle in which the proponents of a free market claimed victory and marched onwards with renewed confidence. Why was the upsurge of free-market energies, from the late 1970s onwards and particularly in the US, quite so sharp and overwhelming? After all, a combination of factors under a mixed economy had resulted in almost 30 years of unprecedented economic growth that raised standards of living across classes in both US and UK.

In the case of the US it has been suggested that, unlike similar policies in other economically advanced countries, the New Deal reforms never achieved full legitimacy. A.O. Hirschman, professor emeritus of social sciences at Princeton, has noted that these reforms were therefore vulnerable 'to attack from revivalist forces adhering strictly to the aboriginal "colossal liberal absolutism" '. This 'attack' was helped along by faltering economic growth in the mid-1970s which revived faith in the idea that an unencumbered market produces greater efficiency. Simultaneously, there was also a sharp decline of public confidence in the responsiveness and efficiencies of governments.

The economist Milton Friedman, who became the leading proponent of the free market in this phase, argued that the Great Depression was a consequence of government mismanagement rather than market failures. Cheerleading for deregulation was commonplace in the USA by the mid-1970s. Business writer Robert Kuttner has described how organised business that had once been 'tamed and traumatised by the Roosevelt era, awoke from its slumber and began pumping hundreds of millions of dollars into think tanks whose intellectuals would validate and celebrate laissez-faire'. Reagan's election was the culmination of, not impetus for, these trends. Reagan's crusade, as Kuttner put it, was pushing on an open door.

Meanwhile, Wall Street had worked hard for its own rehabilitation. After the crash of 1929 the Street was shrouded in a cloud of suspicion and disgrace for almost four decades. Even John Maynard Keynes had twisted the knife by observing that financial markets attract people of a domineering and even psychopathic nature. That's a good thing, Keynes suggested, because without such an outlet the same energies might well be turned to careers involving open and wanton cruelty. The Nobel Prize-winning economist James Tobin considered this a waste of young talent. But the tens of thousands of aspiring market analysts clearly did not agree.

By the early 1980s pension funds began spinning a bigger share of American savings on the stock markets and Wall Street was attracting hoards of fresh graduates from the best universities. When Michael Lewis quit as a bond trader at Salomon Brothers in 1989 and wrote *Liar's Poker: Rising through the Wreckage of Wall Street,* he secretly hoped that college students trying to figure out what to do with their lives would read his book 'and decide that it's silly to phony it up and abandon their passions to become financiers'. He was amazed to find that it had the opposite effect. Lewis was inundated by fan mail from students seeking further tips about how to succeed on Wall Street. They had read *Liar's Poker* as a how-to manual on getting rich quick.

It helped that the New York Stock Exchange had mounted a public relations campaign encouraging ordinary people to own a share of America by investing in the stock market. Charles Merrill, founder of Merrill Lynch & Company, was among those who promoted the idea of a 'People's Capitalism'. Fraser's account particularly credits Warren Buffett and Peter Lynch for bringing a new respectability to the Street. These legendary investors gave confidence to ordinary folks and small investors, making them feel comfortable about Wall Street in a moral as well as in a practical sense. Such campaigns endeavoured to connect Wall Street with cherished values of the heartland, such as profits based on honest hard work. For instance, Smith Barney ran an advertisement that said, 'We make money the old fashioned way; we earn it.'

Wall Street's rehabilitation did more than revive confidence in stock markets or intensify faith in a particular version of market culture. It gave rise to a mind-set so zealously locked into the certainty of its own assumptions that it came to be known as 'market fundamentalism'. Steve Fraser's history of Wall Street, *Everyman a Speculator*, offered compelling reasons for how this reality took shape: 'In the postindustrial age, where knowledge, not breeding or connections, was king, the Street was reborn as a vessel of revolution. Wall Street, as the quintessential expression of the free market, stepped forward as a twenty-first century utopia.'

Even as market fundamentalism celebrated the collapse of communism, Wall Street's version of utopia became just as evangelical and confident that it had the formula for the path to universal well-being.

The reinvigorated avatar of 'Let us Alone', which gathered strength after the collapse of the USSR, displayed all the old intolerance of governments, plus some new contempt for the moral and ecological concerns of communities. Of course, even a free market needs minimum rules to ensure order. The basis for crafting these rules, for countries across the world, came to be known as the Washington Consensus because it was what the US Treasury, the World Bank and the International Monetary Fund deemed to be economic wisdom.

In essence the 'consensus' was synonymous with the TINA doctrine. It meant that the market, as defined by Wall Street and its related culture of commerce, was not merely the best but the *only* road to progress and growth. This mind-set, sometimes described as 'a form of global financial overlordship' drove the Bretton Woods twins to impose severe financial penalties on countries that stood in the way of free flow of international capital or refused to accept pro-market measures like deregulation and privatisation. This regime also called for cuts on food subsidies, unemployment and other benefits while lowering trade and investment barriers.

The 'Roaring Nineties', as economist Joseph Stiglitz later called this period, also severely distorted checks and balances between Wall Street and Main Street. 'Longstanding wisdom, that there were alternative policies, that different policies affected different groups differently, that there were trade-offs, that politics provided the arena through which the trade-offs were evaluated and choices were made, was shunted aside,' wrote Stiglitz.

By the mid-1990s this mind-set had percolated into the study of law, political science and economic history. Robert Samuelson, economist and *Newsweek* columnist, declared that 'the Market 'R' Us' – meaning that stock markets are an open space empowering ordinary people. In a limited and very qualified way, this is true. But the Market 'R' Us approach was part of a world-view that treated the market as society's only communal gathering place, thus underplaying the role of social and political collectives.

The crux of it, recalls the veteran American social activist Edgar Cahn, was that people had now to be treated as consumers more than as *citizens*. This meant disregarding values and pursuits that could not easily be converted into commodities, taking a more 'tough love' approach. 'Tough Love means withholding help, denying assistance, cutting off aid as the most effective way of motivating people to become productive . . . Within this framework, it is difficult for those who care about social justice to make any headway. Anything which does not entirely further market productivity and wealth is suspect,' wrote Cahn, a pioneer of Time Dollars, a complementary currency system.

A few chroniclers of Wall Street wondered how long this mind-set could last. If nothing else, the growing gap between the incomes of money managers and the returns to shareholders combined with the frequent scandals and scams should bring the structure down, conjectured Michael Lewis. But at some point he gave up. No scandal or reversal seemed to sink the system. Besides, wrote Lewis: 'The rebellion by American youth against the money culture never happened. Why bother to overturn your parents' world when you can buy it, slice it up into tranches, and sell off the pieces?'

Nevertheless, through the 1990s one question slowly inched its way onto centre stage. As Thomas Frank put it in his irreverent book *One Market Under God,* if the market is an ultimate expression of not just free choice but *freedom*, how come Wall Street's version of it is supposed to be the only road to material salvation? Besides, if the market is a level playing field, why is inequity deepening? In the USA, by 1999, the richest 1% of American citizens, about 2.7 million people, held as many after-tax dollars as the bottom 100 million. During the 1960s, the compensation of the average CEO was 25 times that of hourly production workers. By 1999 that gap was 419 to 1. By 2005 the wealth gap in the US was at its widest since 1929 with 21.2% of national income accruing to the top 1%.

A counter-response was due. At this juncture the story takes a fascinating twist – one that inspired the journey of this book. Firstly, there were a wide variety of counter-responses. Secondly, both the state and the market were simultaneously challenged. Thirdly, the most important shift was that the rebels called the bluff of the free market. They challenged how such a constrained a view of human nature and so closed a mind-set could be equated with freedom. What is the higher order of freedom that these diverse counter energies seek? Multiple answers to this question must be left to unfold in the stories that follow. But, for now, a small sample of the challenges and their diverse sources.

GODDESS TINA AND OPEN SOCIETY

Four months into the British coal miners' fateful strike in 1984, David Jenkins was appointed the sixty-ninth Bishop of Durham. Earlier Jenkins had been a professor of theology at Oxford. Now he found himself drawn into the turmoil – at first as witness and then as a combatant. A large segment of his congregation was made up of the striking miners and their families. Moved by their worsening condition Jenkins availed of every opportunity, in his sermons and other public pronouncements, to vociferously criticise Prime Minister Thatcher's harsh treatment of the miners. The iron lady dismissed him as 'a cuckoo in the establishment nest' and urged that he to stick to heavenly matters, leaving the economic domain to those who know better.

Long after the coal miners' fate had been settled, David Jenkins persisted in doggedly challenging the proliferation of policies that had adverse and unfair affects on the poorer members of British society. Jenkins later wrote that he became

> increasingly intrigued intellectually and bothered morally by Mrs Thatcher's habit of calling to her aid what I began to think of as the Goddess TINA – 'You cannot buck the Markets. There Is No Alternative.' . . . Clearly no one who has any substantial faith in a transcendent God, or any deep conviction about the amazing resources of human minds and spirits, or any inspiration from the immense achievement of human inventiveness, passion for freedom and struggling for solidarity and compassion, can accept such fatalism.

These worries resonated within segments of the American establishment as well – for example, Richard C. Leone who was then president of the 20th Century Fund, a major liberal research foundation which funded the research for Kuttner's book *Everything for Sale*. Faith in idealised market structures, Leone lamented, was now a form of 'political jihad' that was stripping away the safeguards against market abuses and imperfections which had been constructed during the Great Depression and after World War II.

Kuttner's investigation in *Everything for Sale* not only challenged the wisdom of putting most of life's arrangements on an auctioneer's block, it also showed how market failures are far more pervasive than market fundamentalists are willing to admit. But most of all Kuttner gave voice to the growing concern that a society that becomes a grand auction block would not be a political democracy worth having. After all, the most vital areas of society are by nature beyond the reach of the market and lie in the province of rights that cannot be alienated or sold. For example, Kuttner pointed out, 'human beings may not be sold, no matter how great their desperation; the prohibition on commercial exchange of one's vote or of public office; of free speech, of professions, of honors and awards'.

Similarly, the source of values such as fairness is *society* not the market. But in the mid-1990s you could not put too much emphasis on fairness without upsetting people who were trained to have absolute faith in the market. Paul Hawken, an American businessman and author of *The Ecology of Commerce*, spoke at countless forums of business and industry during that period. He often found that many people in the audience would go ballistic when he spoke about social justice as fair and equitable distribution of resources. How strange, thought Hawken:

> We are in a country that was founded on 'liberty and justice for all' and if you raise that issue in the business community, some executives will fall off their chairs. Sometimes, I have asked business people who reject the notion of social justice whether they believe in injustice, inequality, lack of opportunity for women, and unfairness. They protest just as vehemently.

This is largely because truly well-meaning people have been trained to believe that the free-market mechanism, within a proper legal structure, will itself deliver justice.

Perhaps the sharpest challenges to this orthodoxy came from yet another Hungarian, an icon of the capital markets who also happened to be a disciple of Karl Popper. Market fundamentalism, said George Soros, is now a greater threat to open society than any totalitarian ideology. Soros's passionate commitment to an open society was not acquired at the London School of Economics where he studied under Popper. The roots of this conviction were in his childhood experiences of dodging first the Nazis and then communists.

Soros was born in Budapest, in 1930, into the family of an affluent Jewish attorney. His father saved the family from the Nazi death grip by adopting false names and a Christian identity. At the age of 17, Soros migrated to England and put himself through the London School of Economics, partly by working as a waiter. Encountering Popper helped Soros to zero in on the fundamental flaw common to fascism and

Soviet-style communism. Both regimes laid claim to an ulti-mate truth and thus became enemies of an open society. Since our understanding of the world is always inherently imper-fect, said Popper, it follows that nobody can have access to the ultimate truth. Therefore, a perfect society is unattainable but we are free to constantly work for successive improvements. This process of ceaselessly striving to improve the social and economic sphere struck a chord in Soros. So what if history has no inherent meaning, he decided. We can give it mean-ing through practical action in favour of more free and equal society.

In 1956 Soros moved to the USA, took up a job on Wall Street and went on to become a billionaire and legendary money manager. Then he set about addressing his social and political concerns by pumping hundreds of millions of dollars into a string of foundations he set up across Europe. In the eastern bloc these Open Society Institutes played a key role first in supporting dissidents and then in the transition out of communism into a market economy. In the mid-1990s Soros reformulated his understanding of open society when he real-ised that excessive individualism and lack of social cohesion are as dangerous as excessive state control. While Popper's critique had been limited to demolishing Marxism, Soros used his insider's knowledge to highlight myths about the free mar-ket. For instance, he repeatedly pointed out that markets do not tend towards equilibrium.

Soros's articulation of the malaise was precise and clinical. Market fundamentalism, he wrote, is a mind-set that holds that

> all social activities and human interactions should be looked at as transactional, contract-based relationships and valued in terms of a single common denominator, money. Activities should be regulated, as far as possi-ble, by nothing more intrusive than the invisible hand of profit-maximizing competition.

How society should be organised, how people ought to live their lives cannot be decided on the basis of market values. Yet this is happening, Soros lamented, as an axiomatic, value-neutral theory has been turned into an ideology by market fundamentalists and come to influence political and business behaviour in powerful and dangerous ways.

Others who had made such arguments had been ridiculed for being sentimental, or worse just stupid. Soros was ridiculed for being a hypocrite and having a split personality. 'He's seen the enemy,' purred a *New York Times* headline, 'it looks like him.' There were many in the corporate world who quietly agreed with Soros even in the mid-1990s. But they were reluctant to speak out for fear of seeming naïve or repulsively 'touchy-feely'. It was not until the opening years of the 21st century that market fundamentalism was more widely challenged for itself being naïve and illogical. This happened only after the Washington Consensus began to lose its lustre and the need for a more healthy balance between politics – the making of rules, and markets – the playing by rules, won greater acceptance. This turnaround was a slow, and at first barely visible, process. The evidence of the shift was diverse and widely scattered. We will review just a few snapshots.

A few weeks after Soros's *Crisis of Global Capitalism* appeared, Japan's leading economist Eisuke Sakakibara joined the ranks. Market fundamentalism, said Sakakibara, is self-destructive since society cannot bear the cumulative strain of allowing the economic system to dictate social relations. The very survival of markets depends on being embedded in social and political institutions. At that time, in 1999, Sakakibara was Japan's Vice Minister of Finance. He was not saying anything new. But it mattered that a man of his stature, a nominee for the top job at the IMF, took a strong public position.

Such voices were partly emboldened by Amartya Sen winning the Nobel Prize for Economics in 1998. For years the Nobel Committee had chosen economists who favoured the 'Let us Alone' orthodoxy. However, Sen, a Harvard-based

Indian economist, had a long track record of showing that the market alone cannot redress poverty or bring prosperity to all without public policy that is committed to those goals. He had also frequently questioned the famous magic of the 'invisible hand' by pointing out that its efficiency is usually exaggerated and misrepresented. In particular, Sen's highly acclaimed empirical study 'Poverty and Famines: An Essay on Entitlements and Deprivation' showed that the market can make a bad situation worse. The Nobel for Sen was widely interpreted as a signal that the domination of free marketers may be on the wane.

Just before Sen picked up his Nobel, the South-East Asian markets went into a freefall. This had been preceded by the meltdown of the Russian market. While these developments rattled the altar of Goddess TINA they did not revive the counter-faith that planning itself could provide all the answers. The command-and-control mode of *both* big government and big private enterprises was now seen as outdated and ineffective. Instead, the quest for a broader, even richer, freedom was growing in a realm out of earshot of high finance and government.

One of the sharpest articulations of this reality came from a leader of what was then still known as, the free software movement. 'The Cathedral and the Bazaar', a paper by Eric Raymond, set out to explain the runaway success of Linux but in the process offered an insight that became a metaphor for a much wider social and economic struggle. Given suitable social machinery, a large and scattered community of software programmers manages not merely to aggregate information but also coheres. Raymond's key insight was that the large pool of peer reviewers, who keep updating Linux, is working in the bazaar mode and its opposite is the domination-oriented cathedral mode. By mid-1998 these stirrings had begun to be noted by mainstream business, with *Forbes* doing a cover story called 'Peace, Love, Software'.

However, the loudest and most dramatic challenge to market fundamentalism did come from an old-style street action in Seattle in the closing weeks of 1999. Over 40,000 protesters blocked the roads and effectively brought the World Trade Organisation's ministerial meeting to a halt. Anita Roddick, the founder and CEO of The Body Shop, was in that surging crowd blinded by tear gas while it dodged rubber bullets. The experience changed her life. It struck Roddick that she was probably the only CEO on that side of the police cordons. She worried, not for the activists facing the armed police but for the business world. 'Being a successful entrepreneur is about imagining the world differently; if the only ones who succeed in doing so side with the powerful, then something is wrong,' Roddick decided.

Inside the WTO conference hall were representatives of governments and private corporations. Surging at the barricades outside were representatives of trade unions and activist groups fighting for virtually every social, environmental and economic cause under the sun. Many reporters of the international media, stunned by the scale and intensity of the protest, offered a simplistic portrayal of free-market forces at the negotiating tables inside and anti-market forces on the streets outside. Not so, thought Roddick, what the governments and the corporations have in common is a fear of people taking their own initiative, 'doing almost anything in the street except shopping or commuting to work'.

A banner by the Rainforest Action Network, floating high on Seattle's skyscape, gave perhaps the most accurate account of what was afoot. The banner consisted of two large arrows pointing in opposite directions. One banner said 'democracy' and the other said 'WTO'. Some protestors might well have been opposed to markets per se. But the bulk of them were just opposed to the unfreedom of the 'free' market. They were challenging the claim that the dominant market model is the *only* way to deliver worldwide prosperity. They were defending the rights of dislocated communities and ecosystems. Many protestors would have agreed with David Jenkins's exhortation that

> If we can make the market our servant, then the possibilities are immense . . . but the present form of market flourishes largely at other people's expense. If you worship the goddess TINA then you may not get mercy but you will get prosperity – for some.

A few weeks before the protest in Seattle, Jenkins, long since retired from the Church of England, had unveiled a book that refuted the charge that Margaret Thatcher had flung at him – that as a priest he had no knowledge or basis to say anything about market matters. I met Jenkins while he was lecturing at Schumacher College in 2001. His book *Market Whys and Human Wherefores: Thinking again about Markets, Politics and People* did not anticipate the Seattle protests and yet it brought the mass action into sharp relief. After all, that globalised protest renewed the power of the most basic biblical commandment – to 'Love Thy Neighbour'. People all over the world, Jenkins gently reaffirmed, are now our neighbours. The view that marketplaces are a good but 'the market' has become a tyrannical God struck a chord in many hearts and minds.

This emerging unity of aspirations moved even those who were beneficiaries of the market. Some of them began asking why the market system wasn't working for everyone and whether the system was ecologically and socially sustainable. Joseph Stiglitz winning the Nobel Prize in 2001 lent further momentum to these questions. A year earlier Stiglitz had quit his job as chief economist of the World Bank and become one of its sharpest critics. He opposed the imposition of a single economic order on the whole world because 'there is not just one market model'. A constructive market model would require that resources are not blindly allocated in favour of private goods at the expense of public goods in ways that undermine social justice, urged Stiglitz. For instance, he criticised aggressive lobbying by Wall Street banks which, in 1999, led to the repeal of the Glass–Steagall Act. This Depression Era legislation had separated investment banking from commercial banking and aimed to protect taxpayers from precisely the kind of expensive public bailouts that had happened in 2008.

Stiglitz's critique was doubly significant because it resonated with a diverse readership – from corporate boardrooms to anti-globalisation protestors – making his book *Globalization and its Discontents* an international bestseller. It was a further signal of the changing times that Stiglitz was invited to speak at St Paul's Cathedral, in the heart of London's financial district, on a platform set up to reflect on the ethical and social dimensions of economic trends. In 2003 this platform took on a question not normally heard in the City: is there an alternative to global capitalism? Leading the discussion was the Archbishop of Canterbury himself. Just what does it mean for the market to be 'embedded' in society, asked Dr Rowan Williams; does this just mean laws and norms that smooth the running of private businesses or does it include rules that ensure wider access, inclusion and democratisation for people at large?

Taking up this lead and running with it was Professor Muhammad Yunus, the micro-finance pioneer from Bangladesh who shared that platform with Dr Williams. Let us explore alternatives to the present form of global capitalism, urged Yunus, because what we have at present is 'a half-done story'. If a market economy means specialisation, then there's been one in Bangladesh for centuries – with basket makers, weavers, farmers, day labourers, rickshaw-pullers, boatmen and so on. These crafts-based 'entrepreneurs' are not poor because they lack initiative or enterprise, said Yunus. They are undermined by the wider market and its institutions. For instance, the mechanisms of the market would even make the Grameen Bank a conduit for flow of rural savings into urban areas. This is prevented only because Grameen's operations

are 'embedded' in a social purpose – the economic enhancement of rural areas.

These are mere glimpses of a transnational restlessness
that is propelling efforts to raise and rally, what David Jenkins
has called 'democratic coalitions of reality, reason, confidence'. From the villages of India to the back streets of lower
Manhattan, groups and individuals are stepping away from a
simplistic, rhetoric-laden, conflict of 'free market' versus 'fet-
tered market' to ask the questions that really matter. 'Free
for whom?' 'Free for what purpose?' Answers to these questions have been quietly incubated by an astounding variety of
people across the world for decades. Some of them counted
on the inevitable crash of the icons of Goddess TINA. But few
anticipated the disasters of 2008. Fewer still can predict what
will rise from the rubble.

POST-MELTDOWN RUMMAGING IN PANDORA'S BOX

On 17 September 2008, ten years after he had famously
declared the 'Market 'R' Us', one of its most admiring chroniclers declared that 'Wall Street as we know it is kaput.' It
is not just that large investment banks have gone bankrupt,
wrote Robert J. Samuelson in *Newsweek*, but rather that 'Wall
Street's business model has collapsed.' Just what does that
mean? At the US Treasury Department it meant admitting
that the financial regulatory system is archaic, inadequate
and requires major reconstruction. This response became
unavoidable as taxpayers demanded to know why Congress
had allowed major institutions like Fannie Mae and Freddie
Mac to run leverage ratios that were estimated to exceed 60
to 1.

Far more significant was the growing acceptance that
markets can not only be wrong but also foolish. A visibly rattled and humbled Alan Greenspan made something close to a

public confession. As Chairman of the Federal Reserve Board for 18 years Greenspan had been an icon for proponents of free markets. In October 2008 Greenspan told a Congressional Committee that he had put too much faith in the self-correcting power of free markets. 'Those of us who have looked to the self-interest of lending institutions to protect shareholders' equity, myself included, are in a state of shocked disbelief,' Greenspan said at a hearing of the House Committee on Oversight and Government Reform.

Greenspan's disbelief was puzzling to at least a few Wall Street insiders who had watched mountains of information being aggregated and ignored. In his diagnostic essay, the 'End of Wall Street', Michael Lewis quoted a hedge fund manager as saying: 'The thing we couldn't figure out is: It's so obvious. Why hasn't everyone else figured out that the machine is done?' Steve Eisman, a money manager at the hedge fund FrontPoint Partners, answered his own question with invectives. It's only justice that Wall Street has gone down, said Eisman: 'They fucked people. They built a castle to rip people off. Not once in all these years have I come across a person inside a big Wall Street firm who was having a crisis of conscience.' Eisman went on to admit that he himself had been simultaneously outraged and opportunistic. The incentives for this are well documented. According to one estimate the 50 highest-paid private investment fund managers in 2007 averaged $588 million in compensation – 19,000 times as much as average worker pay.

Like the triumph of short-term greed, such outrage is not new. Anti-Wall Street feelings have a cyclical pattern. The last such dip came at the end of the 1980s and among the heads that rolled then were John Gutfreund, Chairman of Salomon Brothers, and Michael Milken, the infamous 'junk-bond king'. In retrospect these came to be seen as 'public lynchings' which became an excuse for not cleaning up Wall Street's trading culture. Could it be different this time?

When this question is explored from within the realm of Wall Street, the answers are fairly simple. Since the cycle of greed and fear is viewed as being 'natural', almost in the same way that photosynthesis is natural, it is expected to continue. While the pain remains acute, financial firms are likely to take fewer stupid and wasteful risks. But this is certain to change when the upswing begins. Even as better regulations come into place, it is taken as a given that greed-driven innovation will inevitably stay a few steps ahead of the regulators. Pro-market triumphalism may be over, declared most Wall Street commentators – but only for the moment.

However, the purpose of my journey has been to look at what's happening outside the box which holds these assumptions. Barack Obama's promise to grow the American economy from the bottom up has spread good cheer among those who are cultivating a 'mindful' market culture – one that is more attuned to social, ecological and moral responsibility and thus not *driven* by greed and fear. While there is enormous diversity of approaches among those seeking radical changes they have common ground on two key demands: clean up Wall Street and play by market rules that give primacy to ethical values and are based on a more well-rounded view of human nature.

From this vantage point a 'clean-up' would not stop at tighter regulation of the old game. A serious clean-up would clear the way for a new game. For starters, a new game would prevent predatory lending and asset bubbles of the kind that spawned the sub-prime mortgage crisis. But fundamentally these are efforts to reclaim, or give new meaning to, the concept of 'market freedom' – which has otherwise been commandeered to justify footloose global capital, complex financial instruments with scary leverage ratios and reckless speculation.

Some proponents of a more wholesome practice of market freedom are invoking the 'original' Adam Smith and his vision of a market economy populated by small entrepreneurs, artisans and family farmers engaged in producing and exchanging goods and services to meet the needs of themselves and their neighbours. Thus, there is growing pressure on the US Congress to push through laws to prevent the rise of huge financial conglomerates. The basic principle – that if a company is too big to fail, it is too big to exist – has renewed respectability. Similarly, the assumption that markets tend towards equilibrium and are inherently self-correcting is more widely discredited now – even though academic studies and some market players have known this all along.

However, one of the most quixotic signals of how the times are changing was visible many months before the meltdown. In February 2008 Muhammad Yunus opened a branch of the Grameen Bank in New York and began making micro-loans to some of the tens of millions of Americans who are too poor to have a bank account. Since most people know that one-third of the world's population lives in dire poverty, Yunus usually places more emphasis on pointing out that in the world's freest market, the US, one-fifth of the people lack healthcare and almost 45 million Americans have only limited access to financial institutions.

These inequities have been haunting a wide range of people, including the richest. In 2007 Bill Gates made an interesting confession while addressing Harvard University's graduating class. Some 25 years earlier Gates had dropped out of the same university to go and start Microsoft. Now he was back to say that the years at Harvard had left him ignorant about the appalling disparities of health, wealth and opportunity that condemn millions of people to lives of despair. 'It took me decades to find out,' said Gates, and this raised a further question in his mind. 'Why are millions of children dying of hunger and disease when they could be saved?' The answer, Gates told the Harvard graduates, is simple, and harsh: 'The market did not reward saving the lives of these children, and governments did not subsidise it. So the children died because their mothers and their fathers had no power in the market and no voice in the system.' Seven months later Gates went up on the stage at the World Economic Forum and called for a 'creative capitalism'.

Is such a thing possible? The question evokes images of the Greek Goddess Pandora who opened a box and thus released all the evils of mankind – greed, vanity, slander, envy, pining. For well over two centuries capitalism has been credited with doing just the same. And yet Pandora's Box was not left empty. What remained inside was hope. It is tempting to picture Gates peering within to find and release hope. The bittersweet irony of such an endeavour will undoubtedly elicit both cheers and jeers. Microsoft has well earned its reputation as a competition-quashing monopolist. It is the quintessential command-and-control cathedral in contrast to the bazaar of open-source programming. It is an example of why even proponents of the free market worry about saving capitalism from the capitalists. For instance, Raghuram Rajan and Luigi Zingales, both economists of the Chicago School, have railed against the tendency of capitalism to become 'a system of the incumbents, by the incumbents, for the incumbents'.

At the same time you don't have to be naïve to hear out Gates. That might be worth doing not because of his iconic image but as recognition of the fact that capitalism is horrendously complicated, multi-layered and ever-changing. Many historians have been exasperated by the application of the word 'capitalism' to refer to events, systems and periods that are vastly different from each other. So a few distinctions are in order here. One, capitalism is a much deeper and broader phenomenon than either bazaars or the market. Two, the 'Let us Alone' creed of free-market capitalism with its highly organised corporations, should not be confused with a free and open market economy with its thousands of small and medium proprietors. Large concentrations of resources and capital have been justified for over two centuries as an essential prerequisite for economic expansion and dynamism. That this idea is running out of energy is evident both in actions at the grassroots and in the sphere of ideas – from William Greider's book *The Soul of Capitalism* to Stuart Hart's *Capitalism at the Crossroads* and Jonathan Porritt's appeal for a *Capitalism as if the World Matters*.

Of course the endeavour to foster a healthier market economy is not new. In 1979, the French scholar Fernand Braudel concluded his seminal study of civilisation and capitalism with hope shadowed by a dark question: 'If people set about looking for them, seriously and honestly, economic solutions could be found which would extend the area of the market and would put at its disposal the economic advantages so far kept to itself by one dominant group in society,' he wrote. But the problem is more social than economic, he added. He concluded with a fundamental question: 'how can one hope that the dominant groups who combine capital and state power, and who are assured of international support, will agree to play the game and hand over to someone else?'

And yet a combination of pragmatic compulsions and conscience could, just maybe, alter familiar power structures. Granted, this may seem naïve at first glance, but if we venture forth being fully mindful of contradictions the scenery becomes more and more fascinating. Yes, globalisation of the market still lacks tangible democratising processes. But the pressure for creating such measures is mounting. Yes, the idea of empowering stakeholders, not just shareholders, does not cover the needs of democracy. But it's a start. Yes, the concentration of assets is grotesquely skewed. But new owners of capital and disruptive technologies have triggered processes loaded with both challenge and promise. Old power equations remain in place but challenging pressures are growing in strength. Such energies are a response to fear, of ecological doom, and pain as people feel bruised and shrivelled by unbridled materialism.

Some of this energy is unabashedly of the John Lennon 'Imagine' kind. But let us not be too hasty to add 'dreamy' and turn idealism into a pejorative term. Ten years ago Doc

Searls wrote: 'Imagine a world where what you gave away was more valuable than what you held back ... Imagine a world in which the business of business was to imagine worlds people might actually want to live in someday.' At the time it seemed rather dreamy. In 2007 Gates's last words to a Harvard graduating class were: 'Don't let complexity stop you. Be activists. Take on the big inequities. It will be one of the great experiences of your lives.' Rejecting Gates's statement as hypocrisy or romanticising it is equally futile. By contrast, open exploration with a keenness for dialogue is fertile and fruitful. This empowers us to seek allies in the most unlikely places. But to what end?

To expand our collective imagination on what kind of market system and culture of commerce would allow human civilisation to pull back from the precipice. To foster a healthy and vibrant market economy but not a market *society* – where everything is a deal based on narrow self-interest. At first this may seem like an arrogant or naïve attempt to overturn the flow of history. And yet this quest lies behind multifaceted conversations that are gathering momentum on various frequencies. These are conversations about social transformation based on a broader view of reality – and not merely of the material realm. After all, civilisation has been shaped as much by the babble of the bazaar as by the silence of contemplation.

2
SELF-INTEREST
AND MARKET FAILURE
IN SEARCH OF A POST-AUTISTIC ECONOMICS

It is market fundamentalism, which holds that the social good is best served by allowing people to pursue their self-interest without any thought for the social good – the two being identical – that is a perversion of human nature.
– George Soros

I set out on this journey thinking that those who view conventional economics as a form of brain damage are out on a limb. Even the followers of ignored visionaries like Mahatma Gandhi and E. Fritz Schumacher seemed more well-meaning than effective. But within weeks of my hitting the road, in 2000, there was a student revolt in Paris that turned the story upside down. It alerted me about people and happenings that showed that the striving for 'economics as if people mattered' is throbbing with life. A foray into history became necessary, and exciting, because it explained the roots of contemporary academic firefights, slogan-shouting activism and quieter salvos from the frontiers of research in neurosciences.

The market and classical economics are systems of belief, not a science. Both phenomena have been instrumental in scrambling the radio-signals of the bazaar.

Counter-energies are now rattling the barriers created by conventional economic theory. It's not quite gale-force but the wind is strong enough to clear out the cobwebs. An economics with enhanced cognition will have superior audio-visual tools and might thus be more tuned in to the jumbled babble of bazaars.

∼

In the summer of 2000 there was a bloodless revolt at the Sorbonne in Paris. No buildings were stormed and no slogans were shouted. The quiet event was reminiscent of the legend of Martin Luther nailing his 95 Theses on a church door in 1517. These student rebels posted their challenge to the orthodoxy on the 21st-century equivalent of public space, the internet. On the defensive this time was neither a pope nor a king but an academic discipline – Economics.

'We no longer want to have this autistic science imposed on us,' declared the petition. The signatories, all students of economics, said they were tired of being taught analytical tools that are often out of sync with reality. They went on to protest against the domination of their department's curriculum by neoclassical economic theory with its 'imaginary worlds', disregard for concrete realities and 'uncontrolled use of mathematics'. These handicaps, argued the students, left them ill-equipped to go out into the world and grapple with key challenges like the role of financial markets, globalisation, inequalities and ecological degradation. As though to ward off the risk of being labelled anarchists, who are famously remembered for their slogan 'Demand the impossible', these rebels closed their petition by saying, 'We do not ask for the impossible, but only that good sense may prevail.' In this case 'good sense' was a plea for pluralism, a hunger for other approaches to economics.

Within two weeks the petition had 150 signatures from students at the top universities of France. *Le Monde* immediately widened the conversation with a lengthy article sympathetic to the students. This triggered a heated and acrimonious public debate which soon dashed across the English Channel and, later, the Atlantic. Some of the students and faculty involved in Tony Lawson's Realist workshop at Cambridge drafted their own anti-autism manifesto which soon collected 750 signatures. Similar groups cropped up at various Ivy League colleges in the USA. The result was the Post-Autistic Economics Network which wins new adherents every week.

This was not the first time that neoclassical economics was diagnosed, or accused, as being impaired. But it was news that students, from within the discipline, had turned the ailment into a *cause célèbre*. No shock tactics were used. The term 'autistic' was deployed carefully and precisely. Too much of what they read in textbooks tallied with the characteristics of autism, namely a marked disregard for external reality.

For starters, all the theories were designed around predominantly self-aggrandising individuals. But in real life most people displayed a much richer mixture of motivations. This particular mismatch between theory and reality, though fundamental, was merely the tip of a larger problem.

So let's take a bird's-eye view of some of these stirrings among economists which are taking apart basic assumptions on which 'laws' of the market have been constructed. These fallacies are at the heart of the rupture between society and market, ecology and economy. Efforts to heal this rupture are not new. But the endeavour has now taken on a life-or-death urgency. The partial blindness of the old market culture threatens the survival of civilisation as we know it. An influential British economist, Nicholas Stern, has described climate change as the greatest market failure in history. But is it just that? Is it not rather a failure of the fundamental premise of the prevailing market culture – that if we all pursue our own pecuniary interest, either enlightened or selfish, the common good will unfold naturally.

Governments and businesses alike are now making efforts to account for the value of such essentials as fresh water, biodiverse forests, clean air and healthy communities – stuff that never earlier featured in economic calculations. But the nausea arising within the discipline of economics is not merely a reaction to its inadequate measurement systems or the emphasis of quantity over quality. What we are witnessing is essentially an advanced form of the revolt launched by E. Fritz Schumacher in the early 1970s when he wrote *Small is Beautiful: Economics as if People Mattered*. This was not merely a proposal for tweaking the mechanics of economics. It was a rallying call to create a new system of political economy. As Theodore Roszak wrote in the introduction to *Small is Beautiful*, such an economics would not be 'afraid to discuss spirit and conscience, moral purpose and the meaning of life, an economics that aims to educate and elevate people, not merely to measure their low-grade behavior.'

Above all this rebellion exposes 'economic man', that utility-maximising individual, as a construct of classical economics that became a self-fulfilling prophesy. In some situations this construct does serve as a practical tool. Michael Lewis, one of Wall Street's best-known whistle-blowers, offered the following explanation for why economics graduates are the preferred recruits for investment banks. What the banks want are practical people, willing to subordinate their educations to their careers, wrote Lewis in his exposé *Liar's Poker*:

> Economics, which was becoming an ever more abstruse science, producing mathematical treatises with no obvious use, seemed almost designed as a sifting device. The way it was taught did not exactly fire the imagination . . . [But] Economics was practical. It got people jobs. And it did this because it demonstrated that they were among the most fervent believers in the primacy of economic life.

More recently, Muhammad Yunus has riled against the conceptual restrictions imposed by the dominant market culture. Why do we assume that entrepreneurs must be one-dimensional human beings dedicated to maximising profit? 'This interpretation of capitalism insulates the entrepreneurs from all political, emotional, social, spiritual, environmental dimensions of their lives. This was done perhaps as a reasonable simplification, but it stripped away the very essentials of human life,' Yunus said while accepting the Nobel Peace Prize in 2006.

> We have remained so impressed by the success of the free market that we never dared to express any doubt about our basic assumption. To make it worse, we worked extra hard to transform ourselves, as closely as possible, into the one-dimensional human beings as conceptualised in the theory, to allow smooth functioning of free market mechanism.

As everyday life around us shows, the needs *and wants* of individuals are not only multi-layered they are also paradoxical. Maximisation of individual utility does not even begin to cover the muddled reality in which we make choices. Thus the quest for an economics and a market system with better cognition depends on unravelling the 'doctrine' of self-interest which is virtually a force field blocking out more holistic views of human nature and the place of commerce in society. We will explore why ecology came to be split from economy and how that rupture is now sought to be healed.

It was in 1930 that Lord Keynes made his famous appeal that we continue to pretend for at least another hundred years that 'fair is foul and foul is fair; for foul is useful and fair is not. Avarice and usury and precaution must be our gods for a little longer still.'

Those hundred years are almost up.

~

VIRTUE OF VICE

Dr Mandeville and a brief history of self-interest

The history of self-interest as a doctrine has no definite beginning. But it serves our purpose to enter the story in 1714 with a Dutch physician named Bernard Mandeville who had a penchant for writing satirical verse. 'Do we not owe the Growth of Wine, To the dry shabby crooked Vine?' wrote Mandeville. 'So Vice is beneficial found . . .' Born in Dordrecht, Holland, in 1670, Mandeville lived most of his life in London. He is remembered four centuries later not for the psychological disorders he treated but his poems exalting the utility of vices. Benjamin Franklin, who also spent many years in London at that time, found Mandeville to be 'a most facetious and entertaining companion'.

Mandeville's most famous poem, *The Fable of the Bees: Private Vices, Publick Benefits*, poked fun at 'fools' who strive 'to make a Great and Honest Hive' and exalted the value of 'Fraud, Luxury and Pride'. Mandeville held the view that material civilisation is the outcome of vices gratified rather than the exercise of virtues. The mainspring of commercial and industrial society, the doctor declared, is the self-seeking effort of individuals. He saw all human actions as being equally vicious and motivated by some form self aggrandisement – either the desire for comfort, praise or pride. By contrast, religious and legal restraints were seen as fictions invented by rulers and clergymen to keep the mass of people under their domination.

The Fable of the Bees had a pervasive and lingering influence on both sides of the English Channel. Ordinary folk and professional philosophers alike were fascinated by the proposition that personal vice results in unintended social benefits. Of course, Mandeville did not 'invent' this idea. A receptive climate for such propositions had been building up slowly for some time. Any succour to the poor was now seen as a paternalistic, counter-productive waste. This was the essence of

Daniel Defoe's 1704 pamphlet titled 'Giving Alms no Charity'. Taking the edge away from hunger, Defoe argued, discouraged people from working, while creation of public employment increased the glut of goods on the market. Later, Defoe's novels were populated by solitary characters struggling through life in a manner akin to warfare. Defoe's most famous hero, Robinson Crusoe, became the inspiration for and illustration of the underlying assumptions of the classical economics that took shape later in the 18th and 19th centuries.

Mandeville's celebration of vanity and vice became a cultural landmark in Western Europe's drift towards seeing society as an aggregate of self-interested individuals connected only by bonds of envy, competition and exploitation. Though these claims were attacked by various contemporaries, notably George Berkeley and William Law, *The Fable of the Bees* is said to have had a decisive influence on towering thinkers like David Hume, Jean-Jacques Rousseau, Adam Smith and Immanuel Kant. For instance, David Hume's 1742 essay 'On the Independency of Parliament' accepted it as a given, a maxim, that any system of government must be based on the supposition that every man is a *knave* whose only purpose is private interest. 'By this interest we must govern him, and, by means of it, make him, not withstanding his insatiable avarice and ambition, cooperate to public good.'

Mandeville's writings were also part of a revolution of euphemisms in which terms like 'avarice', 'love of lucre' and 'usury' faded out and were replaced by the word 'interest'. The historian Albert O. Hirschman suggests that, even up to the time that Hume wrote the passage quoted above, the notion of interest was explicitly equated with 'knavishness and insatiable avarice'. But gradually the memory of these unsavoury synonyms of interest was suppressed. For example, the 18th-century French philosopher Helvetius declared that just as 'physical work is ruled by the laws of movement so is the moral universe ruled by the laws of interest'.

It was in this cultural milieu, some 50 years after Mandeville, that Adam Smith crafted the *Wealth of Nations* on the assumption that our suppliers of daily necessities – the butcher, the brewer and the baker – are driven by pure self-interest. Hirschman has suggested that, just as Machiavelli had opened up new horizons for rulers, Mandeville helped to lift a number of restrictions on commoners, particularly about moneymaking. Further, Adam Smith came to believe that the general welfare is best served by everyone pursuing their private interests.

Whereas the Renaissance had celebrated heroism in the public sphere, now direct attempts to attain the public good were mistrusted. It was in the course of the 18th century that the verb 'to meddle' acquired its derogatory connotation. Until then it implied caring for someone outside one's immediate circle. This shift, wrote Hirschman,

> legitimated total absorption of the citizens in their own affairs and thereby served to assuage any guilt feelings that might have been harbored by the many Englishmen who were drawn into commerce and industry during the eighteenth century but had been brought up under the civic humanist code enjoining them to serve the public interest *directly*. They were now reassured that by pursuing their private gain they were doing so *indirectly*.

Above all, this definition of self-interest came to be treated as a 'law' that unlocked secrets of the social universe. This supposedly 'realistic' view of human nature, deemed necessary for creating a stable society, had a profound influence on leaders of the newly born United States of America. Alexander Hamilton declared that 'The safest reliance of every government is on man's interests. This is a principle of human nature, on which all political speculation, to be just, must be founded.'

Naturally, there were challengers who condemned this as a degraded view of the human condition. Edmund Burke famously lamented that the 'glory of Europe is extinguished forever' because the age of chivalry has given way to the rule of sophisters and calculators. Thomas Carlyle bemoaned how finer human values were threatened by 'that brutish god-forgetting Profit-and-Loss Philosophy' and protested that cash payment is not the only nexus of man with man.

Perhaps the most ironic twist to this story is that the man who, above all, is credited with shaping the notion of self-interest spent most of his life preoccupied with emotions such as curiosity, generosity and sympathy.

'INVISIBLE HAND' STEALS SMITH'S THUNDER

> **Adam, Adam, Adam Smith**
> **Listen what I charge you with!**
> **Didn't you say**
> **In the class one day**
> **That selfishness was bound to pay?**
> **Of all doctrines that was the Pith,**
> **Wasn't it, wasn't it, wasn't it, Smith?**
> > *– Stephen Leacock*

A Professor of Moral Philosophy at the University of Glasgow, Smith was profoundly engaged with understanding the origins of our ideas of right and wrong. How, for instance, do we decide which attitudes and actions are morally correct? Smith felt challenged to find a basis of authority that was more solid than the dogmas of theology.

Smith was grappling with these dilemmas at an epoch-shaping moment in history. His contemporary and fellow Scotsman, James Watt, was finalising details on a breakthrough design of the steam engine which later led to the railway locomotive and accelerated the modern industrial revolution. At about the same time an unprecedented revolution for 'equality, fraternity, liberty' was brewing both in France and in Britain's

American colonies across the Atlantic. It is not a coincidence that Smith's *An Inquiry into the Nature and Causes of the Wealth of Nations* was published in 1776 even as leaders of the American Revolution were finalising the Declaration of Independence.

Born in 1723, in Kirkcaldy in Scotland, Smith studied at Balliol College, Oxford. He initially trained to be a priest and later opted for an academic career. Though his ideas shaped commerce in subsequent centuries, Smith himself was considered temperamentally unfit for any kind of trade or business. The empiricist philosopher David Hume was one of his closest friends. Yet, unlike most of his contemporaries, Smith based his moral framework not on utility but on the more Epicurean view that the goal of life is to seek modest pleasures and attain a state of tranquillity as well as freedom from fear.

Smith regarded his earlier book *The Theory of Moral Sentiments,* published in 1759, as his life's work. In this treatise Smith began by conceding the claims made by Hobbes, Mandeville and Rousseau about human selfishness. But Smith was clear that the happiness of others is necessary to us and therefore all freedoms, including those of the marketplace, must be exercised in a way that is conducive to ensuring wider justice. Thus, even when he argued against misguided government intrusions in the marketplace it was within a framework of laws aimed at larger justice. Smith was quite clear that those who wield power have a tendency to abuse it and he hoped that his writings might help people to aspire to virtue, rather than wealth 'and so become members of a truly civil society'. How, then, did this modern humanist end up being enshrined as the father-figure of a market culture that excised commerce from its social and moral anchors?

Curiously enough, Smith made only a passing reference to the invisible hand. How, then, did it come to reinforce the foundations of the doctrine of self-interest? Why was this idea adopted as a gospel truth by those who took *The Wealth of Nations* as the source text of political economy, namely John

Stuart Mill and others who built the cathedral of modern economics? Most answers to these questions are related to the process by which the study of matters economic went from being a branch of moral philosophy to a deliberately 'non-ethical' discipline and a wannabe science.

SEN TO SMITH'S RESCUE

> **John Stuart Mill**
> **By a mighty effort of will**
> **Overcame his natural bonhomie**
> **And wrote 'Principles of Political Economy'**
> *– Edmund Clerihew Bentley*

Two centuries later an Indian-born, Cambridge-educated economist was to win a Nobel Prize partly for questioning if Mill's successful subduing of his good-natured friendliness was a good thing. In a typically British understatement Sen wrote, 'Perhaps the economist might be personally allowed a moderate dose of friendliness, provided in his economic models he keeps the motivations of human beings pure, simple and hard-headed, and not messed up by such things as goodwill or moral sentiments.'

How, Sen asked, did economics come to characterise human motivation in such spectacularly narrow terms? This is particularly extraordinary, he pointed out, since economics is supposed to be concerned with real people, most of whom at some point ask themselves that basic question: How should one live? Surely most people don't go through life with the rudimentary hard-headedness attributed to them in the economic sphere?

The problem can be traced back to how rational behaviour has been defined by much of economic theory. Rationality has been seen not so much as internal *consistency* of choices but rather as maximisation of self-interest. This has led to the counter-intuitive assumption that anything other than maximisation of self-interest must be irrational. 'Universal selfishness as *actuality* may well be false, but universal selfishness as a requirement of *rationality* is patently absurd,' wrote Sen. The attempt to impose this notion of rationality in order to hold up 'the standard behavioural assumption of economic theory (to wit, *actual* self-interest maximisation) is like leading a cavalry charge on a lame donkey'.

Adam Smith himself never claimed that people always act out of pure self-interest. Nor did he view self-interest in itself as a means to ensure efficiency and success. On the contrary, Smith was inspired by the Greek Stoics who saw people not as separated and detached entities but as members of the vast commonwealth of nature. Then each individual's own 'little interest' takes shape within the context of the larger community or commonwealth. Thus Smith insisted on the value of prudence, reason, self-command and self-discipline.

Yet this is not what Smith is famous for two-and-a-half centuries later. He is best remembered for saying,

> It is not from the benevolence of the butcher, the brewer, or the baker, that we expect our dinner, but from their regard of their own interest. We address ourselves, not to their humanity but to their self-love, and never talk to them of our own necessities but of their advantages.

This description of how and why transactions are carried out in the market was blown out of context. Saying that mutually advantageous trades are very common does not imply that self-love can provide the basis of either a good society or economic salvation.

The support that believers in, and advocates, of self-interested behaviour have sought in Adam Smith is hard to find on a wider and less biased reading of Smith, wrote Sen:

> The professor of moral philosophy and the pioneer economist did not, in fact, lead a life of spectacular

schizophrenia. Indeed, it is precisely the narrowing of the broad Smithian view of human beings, in modern economies, that can be seen as one of the major deficiencies of contemporary economic theory. This impoverishment is closely related to the distancing of economics from ethics.

Bringing economics closer to ethics will not be easy, Sen acknowledged, but the endeavour is eminently worthwhile. This view has been steadily gathering momentum. There is more room now for treating economics not so much as a positive science studying 'what is', but rather a normative discipline concerned with 'what ought to be'. Sen won the Nobel Prize partly for showing what the economy would look like when it aimed to promote the welfare of all. Thus the Royal Swedish Academy's Nobel citation credited him with 'having restored an ethical dimension to economics'. Over the last ten years this ethical dimension has gained ground.

At the same time passionate believers have begun to acknowledge the hollowness of 'rational economic man'. For instance, Alan Greenspan now says that human nature appears to be more complex than he thought all his life – based on what he learnt from reading Adam Smith and Ayn Rand's *The Fountainhead*. Of course, the orthodoxy is far from displaced. Bill Gates has to gingerly tiptoe around the old doctrines when he calls for a 'caring capitalism' because it is difficult to shake off the fear that combining sentiment with self-interest might reduce the reach of the market. In order to lend credibility to his appeal for a creative capitalism, at the World Economic Forum in 2008 Gates sought validation from Adam Smith whom he called 'the very father of capitalism'. Gates quoted not from *The Wealth of Nations* but from *The Theory of Moral Sentiments:*

How selfish so ever man may be supposed, there are evidently some principles in his nature, which interest him in the fortunes of others, and render their happiness necessary to him, though he derives nothing from it, except the pleasure of seeing it.

Gates still believes that the genius of capitalism is that it makes self-interest serve the wider interest and the potential of big financial returns is what drives innovation. But he is perturbed by the fact that the prevailing form of capitalism is not benefiting hundreds of millions of people. So he visualises a more 'caring' or 'creative' version of the doctrine of self-interest which marries the drive for profit with people's need for recognition to create profitable businesses that improve the lives of those who are currently left out.

Gates's creative capitalism endeavour may be shot through with contradictions but it does signal stirrings at the core of a market culture that has so far celebrated the virtue of vices. However, these are shallow manifestations of a phenomenon the roots of which lie altogether outside the economic realm. Therefore the quest for an economics with better cognition requires a detour into the realm where science is in conversation with consciousness to explore if our species sense of 'self' might be evolving.

THE SELF AND NOOGENESIS

'Someday after mastering winds, waves, tides and gravity, we shall harness the energies of love, and then, for the second time in the history of the world, man will discover fire.' This passage, from the writings of Teilhard de Chardin, is posted as a mission statement on the site of the Global Consciousness Project (GCP) – a high-altitude tightrope walk by scientists over the vast open territory between physics and metaphysics. The GCP is a fluid re-exploration of that old question: What is real?

Housed at Princeton University since 1998, the GCP involves a multidisciplinary team of scientists and engineers who are using a global network of computing machines to track a 'maybe' global consciousness. One of the guiding inspirations of the GCP is Pierre Teilhard de Chardin's concept of the Noosphere, even though it is more spiritual than scientific. Nevertheless, the concept of a Noosphere provides 'a very interesting interpretive background (one of several that we may consider) for our specific scientific questions,' says the project's director.

Marie-Joseph-Pierre Teilhard de Chardin was born in Auvergne, France, in 1881. He grew up at a time when Darwin's observation about survival of the fittest was taken as a law of nature applicable equally to the biological, social and economic spheres. As a Jesuit monk and a palaeontologist, Chardin dedicated his life to reconciling religion and science, Genesis and Darwin. He embraced the knowledge that we live in a dynamic universe that is constantly evolving. It follows that humans are still evolving.

Jean Houston, author and founder of the Human Potential Movement, has childhood memories of meeting Chardin during walks in Manhattan's Central Park. She recalls Chardin telling her about 'noogenesis', the evolution of a new layer of life that was above the biosphere of Earth's living systems. 'Noosphere' was Chardin's term for a living membrane that was growing in density and complexity, activating the human species to greater consciousness and responsiveness.

For Chardin these were not mystical speculations but revelations now open to science. But in the first half of the 20th century these ideas were a radical departure from both the orthodoxy of modern Western science and the Catholic Church. It took Albert Einstein's work, in the mid-20th century, to establish that we cannot truly know things unless we know the whole from which they originate. Einstein showed that, though we live in a world of seemingly isolated hard-and-fast physical things, underlying these appearances are energy flows continuously interrelating and changing. 'Thus, we are more like intangibles – exactly that which cannot be measured in classic economic models,' says Sander Tideman, one of the founders of the Spirit in Business network.

Chardin, though himself unique, was not alone in rejecting a mechanistic view of the universe or in seeing the Earth
as a living and 'conscious' being with which humans have a
symbiotic relationship. At precisely the same time that Chardin was mapping the unfolding transformation of the human
consciousness, in the first half of the 20th century, Aurobindo
Ghose was exploring the innards of this process within the
Indian spiritual tradition and coming to broadly similar
conclusions.

An award-winning graduate of King's College, Cambridge,
Aurobindo went from being a bureaucrat, to a militant revolutionary opposing the British empire, and then a yogi and
mystic. Aurobindo had an instinctive grasp of the knowledge,
fundamental to India's varied spiritual traditions, that all of
reality is imbued with a spiritual nature. Aurobindo's yogic
practice revealed not only that the human species is evolving to a higher level of consciousness but that this journey
has reached a critical juncture. In the 1970s these teachings
found expression in Auroville, the effort to build a multinational model city of citizens devoted to living by this higher
consciousness.

But why are Chardin and Aurobindo relevant to our journey? Firstly, both contemplatives have energised a counter-
movement to the doctrine of self-interest. Secondly, they offer
us a torch that illuminates the deeply multi-dimensional nature
of reality. Thirdly, work from this vantage point is expanding
and permeating all areas of life and enquiry.

For instance, back in the 1960s, the scientist James Lovelock came up with the Gaia Hypothesis while working for
NASA. The Earth, Lovelock realised, is not an inert stage for
diverse forms of life but rather a self-evolving, self-regulating,
intelligent and living system or *'being'*. Lovelock called this
system Gaia, after the ancient Greek Goddess who represented
the essence of the Earth or Mother Earth. Lovelock is now best
known as one of the first scientists to warn about the scale and
severity of climate change.

Back in the 1970s the science writer Marilyn Ferguson mapped the frontiers of scientific research on the mind and consciousness to report that

> Something remarkable is underway. It is moving with almost dizzying speed, but it has no name and eludes description . . . From science and from the spiritual experience of millions, we are discovering our capacity for endless awakenings in a universe of endless surprises.

Ferguson's book *The Aquarian Conspiracy* was a challenge to cynicism. 'Our most viable hope for a new world,' wrote Ferguson, 'lies in asking whether a new world is possible.' The borderless open space of the internet has put these processes into hyperdrive.

This detour was intended to illustrate that there are rich and varied counter-energies to the concept of the narrow and utility-maximising 'self'. Consequently, the idea of self-interest is being reconfigured and redefined in many different ways. For instance, some European businesspeople welcomed the new millennium by setting up a public platform called Spirit in Business. This is a signal of how the complex interconnectedness of many different levels of reality is now coming to be accepted as a central principle of not merely science but as a basis for interactions in the marketplace. For many, this engagement leads to a richer and deeper sense of 'self' in ways that makes them more creative and ethical.

In a tangential way this connects back to Darwin's key insight about survival of the fittest. It is not the strongest or most intelligent who survive, said Darwin, but the ones who are most responsive to change. But what about the reality of a market culture in which short-term greed often does win? One possible answer is provided by Richard Dawkins, the evolutionary biologist who coined the term 'selfish gene' and has written extensively on the short-term Darwinian selfishness that is built into humans. We are products of Darwinism, says Dawkins, but we are not slaves to it: 'Using the large brains that Darwinian natural selection has given us, it is possible to fashion new values that contradict Darwinian values.'

So the reframing of self-interest is not about trying to eradicate 'lower' human traits or merely fantasising about an idealised higher consciousness but finding its practical applications. A dazzling array of people, working in diverse sectors, are providing evidence of this nascent shift. Among them is Bill Drayton who founded the Ashoka initiative and has succeeded in mobilising hundreds of thousands of young people as change makers and social entrepreneurs across the world. Interestingly, Drayton is deeply influenced by Mahatma Gandhi. As a student at Harvard in the 1960s, Drayton not only read a great deal about Mahatma Gandhi but also spent his holidays in India working with those who were carrying on Gandhi's mission of *sarvodaya* – universal well-being. Above all, Drayton was struck by Gandhi's insight that henceforth ethics must be grounded not in rules but in empathy. After working for some years in the US government and then McKinsey, Drayton went on to found a non-profit organisation to nurture change makers. He named it Ashoka, after the third-century-BC Indian emperor who went from being an aggressive conqueror to a compassionate ruler committed to Buddhist ideals of right livelihood. Ashoka's vastly influential global network is a manifest counter to the narrow and shrunken 'self' of 'economic man'.

However, the onward quest for an economics with better cognition depends equally on recognising and healing the rupture between economics and ecology.

OIKONOMIA VERSUS CHREMATISTICS

Thales of Miletos lived in the sixth century BC and is regarded as the first philosopher in the Greek tradition and the father of science. There is a legend that Thales was sometimes ridiculed by contemporaries for not converting his cleverness into riches. So Thales decided to show them. Knowledge of astronomy enabled him to calculate that there would be a bumper crop of olives one season. Keeping this knowledge to himself, Thales quietly leased all the olive presses in the area at a low price. At harvest time, this monopoly control over the presses gave Thales windfall profits.

Then and now the interpretation of Thales's motives marks the divide between Oikonomia and Chrematistics. The proponents of Chrematistics laud Thales for the innovative concept of a futures option. The proponents of Oikonomia claim that Thales intended this more as a sarcastic parody than as a business venture. The Greek word *Oikonomia* referred to production for one's own use and management of the household in ways beneficial to all members over the long run. This was distinguished from Chrematistics, a branch of political economy dealing with manipulations of property and wealth in the pursuit of short-term monetary gains. This distinction was alive in mediæval European bazaars where subsistence need-based transactions were treated differently from purely for-profit deals.

Today both words, Oikonomia and Chrematistics, have disappeared from most desktop dictionaries. They were revived and reframed by Herman Daly and John Cobb in their influential book *For the Common Good: Redirecting the Economy Toward Community* published in 1989. Since then Oikonomia has often been invoked to represent 'economics for community', while Chrematistics corresponds to 'private–personal preferences'. While Oikonomia is concerned with costs to and benefits for the whole community, Chrematistics is focused on individual profit in monetary terms.

From the vantage point of Oikonomia, Thales's legendary venture is seen as a way of mocking those who value individual, fast-track wealth as an end in itself. After all, wrote Daly and Cobb.

'Thales had planted no olive trees, built no olive presses, discovered no new uses for olive oil, and made no one but himself better off. In fact, he enriched himself at other people's expense. Thales enriched the world with his ideas vastly more than he milked it with his olive press monopoly.

Yet conventional wisdom of the market sees Thales's venture as a role model eminently worthy of emulation. The ability to anticipate or predict the future accurately is itself celebrated as a form of value addition. Wall Street represents Chrematistics of the purest kind largely because it is an amoral realm where, until recently, the only bottom line was monetary returns for shareholders. The need for a balance with Oikonomia is now being driven by threats of ecological collapse and the growing acceptance that monetary wealth does not necessarily ensure *well-th*.

Ecology and economy

The brutal rupture of ecology and economy is, like the market, quite recent. After all, both words have a common ancestor, *Oikos* – the Greek word for 'house' and 'community'. Ecology concerns our understanding of the Earth as our home and our search for appropriate ways to dwell on it. Likewise, economy pertains to how we organise our material relations in this world home. The philosopher and therapist Thomas Moore suggests that therefore the *Nomos* in economics means law, but not natural law. Rather it is the recognition that community is necessary and that it requires rules of participation. Thus, Aristotle's *Nicomachean Ethics* connected economic matters to the nature of human ends and that most basic question: 'How should one live?'

Even Aristotle's Indian contemporary, Kautilya, who articulated the earliest version of the engineering approach to matters economic, did so within a metaphysical framework.

Kautilya's fourth-century-BC Sanskrit treatise *Artha-shastra* was fundamentally concerned with statecraft and the enhancement of material prosperity. But even this text, steeped in the details of accounting systems and logistical arrangements, opens with a discussion of how we distinguish between right and wrong.

The problem lies in the ethically grounded, Oikonomia dimension, having been overwhelmed by the 'engineering' approach. The latter is dominated by logistics and mechanics and has no room for ultimate ends or questions about what may foster the common good. It was the engineering approach that crafted the idea of 'economic man' or *homo economicus* as a creature caught in a brutish existence and driven to maximise individual utility.

Limiting economics to tangible measurable things was necessary to make it look more like a natural science. Concerns about happiness, virtue and institutional reform were then excised from economics and left to the social sciences and statesmen. Mark Lutz, Professor of Economics at the University of Maine, has sympathetically noted that

> Part of the reason for this scientism was that the followers of Ricardo saw their new industrial order as a product of nature, a datum that needed to be understood in the light of natural science. Thus, wanting to reform the status quo was like trying to condemn and banish the force of gravity.

The *idea* of the market stands on the shoulders of such assumptions – including the belief that love and altruism are scarce and thus to be sparingly deployed. It follows that harnessing self-interest is more reliable and efficient. As Robert Kuttner wrote in *Everything for Sale*, the 'market model of human nature has great difficulty comprehending that altruism is worth cultivating; that it is something more than just another arbitrary, self-interested "preference." ' The same model assumes that most, if not all, people are on the lookout for a 'free ride' and happy to let someone else worry about the welfare of society at large. However, game theory experiments have revealed that when people have windfall earnings most of them contribute a portion to the public good. But there's an interesting catch in these findings. The results vary sharply when the experiment is conducted among economics students, who have evidently been conditioned by their training to prize egoist behaviour.

The doctrine of self-interest has nevertheless prevailed, partly due to contortions in the framing of theory. Assumptions, some economists argue, don't have to be realistic since their point is not to mirror the real world's infinite complexity but to abstract from it in order to build a theory that has predictive power. However, economics does not have the equivalent of Newtonian first principles – basic laws on which everyone agrees. For example, it is common knowledge that market fluctuations are haphazard and affected by a plethora of human vagaries. Yet much of economic theory is built on the assumption that humans behave like predictable, rational automata.

What homo sapiens does and what *homo economicus* is supposed to do often don't match. In the natural sciences this would mean that the basic model is wrong. Not so in a great deal of economic theory. Instead much of the discipline has tended to bend homo sapiens into conformity with *homo economicus*. It was through this lens that society came to be seen as little more than functional relations to achieve useful things. Naturally, there has always been internal opposition to this pinhole view of reality. Therefore, before looking at contemporary initiatives it is worthwhile to make a brief foray into their historical roots.

EARLY SIGNS OF AN ECONOMICS WITH BETTER COGNITION

When the leaders of the G7 countries met at London for their annual summit, in 1984, they found a counter-summit happening 200 yards down the road. The Other Economic Summit, also known as TOES, attracted the kind of people who had already spent many years fuming about the flat-earth view of conventional economics. But TOES was not intended to be an anger-venting jamboree. It aimed to offer reality therapy to the leaders of the world's most industrialised countries. Their purpose was to tear away the veil of the G7's glittering affluence and economic 'efficiency' to lay bare what lies behind – waste, ecological degradation and neglect of social and ethical concerns.

The G7 leaders were not impressed. In those days the clamour down the road was easy to overlook as token dissent from a radical fringe. As it turned out TOES was the debut of a sustained phenomenon that has grown in depth and spread. After that, whenever and wherever the G7 met TOES has always been somewhere around the corner. The dissidents knew from the outset that they were in for a long haul. After all, their objective is to address that most daunting and fundamental problem so succinctly articulated by John Maynard Keynes back in 1925 – 'to find a social system which is efficient economically and morally'.

The historical roots of TOES and the diverse global fraternity that gathered around this platform go back at least two centuries. This intellectual and activist legacy has been variedly called Humanistic Economics, Social Economics and even Green or Ecological Economics. These terms are not always interchangeable but these various streams all equate civilisation not so much with technology and modes of production but norms and values for human behaviour.

Historical lineage

One of the in-jokes in these circles is as follows. What happened when Mahatma Gandhi was asked what he thought of Western civilisation? 'That would be a good idea,' replied Gandhi. What Gandhi said is accurately quoted but the question has been sadly distorted. In the actual encounter, recorded on film, the question from a British reporter was 'Mr Gandhi, what do you think of *modern* civilisation?' The malice of our times, Gandhi argued, is not inherent to European culture but derives from the modern model of industry and market which gives primacy to the multiplication of production and consumption rather than good conduct and the quality of humanity's interaction with the rest of nature.

The contemporary search for a 'new' economics is founded on this basic concern. Protagonists of this stream value material exchange and accumulation but only if it enhances welfare in a holistic manner and reaches every last person in society. This approach is anchored in two *a priori* ethical assumptions. One has to do with equality of rights and dignity to all human beings. The other is a rejection of the view that the natural sciences can account for all relevant phenomena. Since the methods of natural sciences depend on mathematical logic they are ill suited for dealing with life as a whole, particularly the realm of self-consciousness. Life, as E.F. Schumacher liked to say, is bigger than logic. So humanist economics is located firmly in the realm of ethics not science.

This view is traced back to the early 19th century. Perhaps the earliest guru of humanist economics was Jean Charles Leonard Simonde de Sismondi, a Frenchman who is credited with originating the business cycle theory. Born in Geneva in 1773, Sismondi was an accomplished historian and thinker who travelled across the rapidly industrialising England and was appalled to observe the consequences of putting things before people, of sacrificing ends to means. Surely, insisted Sismondi, the purpose of an economy is not mere circulation of goods but the actual welfare and happiness of all people. He saw the emerging market culture as a more insidious form of cruelty than any known earlier – because the oppressor is faceless and passionless.

Sismondi was among the earliest voices to challenge the laissez-faire approach and called for government regulation of working hours and employer financed unemployment and accident insurance for workers. He was one of the inspirations for Thomas Carlyle, who famously denounced economics as a 'dismal science', 'pig philosophy' and so on.

However, the sharpest critique of the industrial system as well as the emerging market culture came from the prolific art historian John Ruskin who rebelled against the idea that 'the social affections ... are accidental and disturbing elements in human nature; but avarice and the desire of progress are constant elements'. Wealth should be defined, argued Ruskin, not as exchange value but as the intrinsically life-sustaining quality of goods and services. Some of Ruskin's proposals for reform presaged the welfare state of the 20th century, such as public ownership and management of the economy, a universal system of education, free libraries and museums.

Over a half a century later, reading Ruskin's book *Unto This Last* changed the life of a young Indian lawyer working in South Africa. That man, Mohandas Karamchand Gandhi, modelled his own life on the value of *sarvodaya*, welfare of all, led India's struggle for independence and redefined politics. Freedom from colonial rule was merely one facet of Gandhi's mission. His driving passion was to foster a system of production, distribution and consumption that would ensure plenitude for the very last person – while also ensuring freedom of movement, creativity and dignity.

This, Gandhi knew, cannot be done by concentrating power in the hands of the state, even a socialist one. Instead most power must be vested in a society where individuals enter into mutually reinforcing and creative relations. Gandhi coined the term *sarvodaya,* meaning uplift of all or universal well-being.

Thus his vision for a free India involved revitalising the traditional artisanal base along with use of modern machinery to promote production *by* the masses rather than mass production. His chosen symbol, the spinning wheel, spoke not just of India's struggle for freedom from imperial rule but a system of production that could marry ecology with economy and encourage interdependence rather than feral competition.

More serious work on marrying ecology and economy was done by Gandhi's disciple Joseph Chelladurai Cornelius Kumarappa, a graduate of Columbia University who started out in life as an accountant. Kumarappa fleshed out Gandhi's vision by drawing economic principles from nature half a century before the term 'biomimicry' was coined. Human systems, Kumarappa observed, need to learn from nature where every being fulfils its necessary role in the cycle of life by performing its own primary function. Nature, Kumarappa observed,

> enlists and ensures the co-operation of all its units, each working for itself and in the process helping other units to get along their own too – the mobile helping the immobile, and the sentient the insentient. Thus all nature is dovetailed together in a common cause. Nothing exists for itself. When this works out harmoniously and violence does not break the chain, we have an economy of permanence.

Kumarappa was confident that arrangements of daily life could be 'regulated in accordance with the dictates of our better self'. This was not a utopian fantasy. The reasoning was more logical than moral. If nature's economy and the human economy are to be in sync, then a valid and sustainable basis for determining value has to be detached and independent of personal feelings – be they generosity or greed. Value needs to be based on an objective understanding of the 'permanent order of things' – namely, the interdependence of all species with the biosphere and atmosphere.

These streams of thought remained on the fringes until a German-born Rhodes scholar and economist expanded them in a Western idiom. What Ernst Friedrich ('Fritz') Schumacher had to say was starkly simple. Nothing makes economic sense unless its continuance for a long time can be projected without running into absurdities. A graduate of Oxford and the London School of Economics, Schumacher was chief economist of Britain's National Coal Board for many years. He was also an avid gardener and champion of organic farming.

In the 1950s the British government sent Schumacher to Burma, to advise the regime there on how it might use modern science and technology for development. Wandering about Rangoon's Buddhist monasteries, Schumacher found himself wondering what a Buddhist economics might look like. He concluded that it would be the exact opposite of Western economics because its fundamental premise would be that the individual can and should evolve towards higher levels of being and those material arrangements are best that serve this end. Humanity's critical challenges are no longer technological or economic but moral, Schumacher concluded. Therefore both ethics and spirituality must be put at the centre-stage of the economic discourse. At that time, the 1960s and 1970s, people who wanted to be taken seriously simply did not mention economics and spirituality in the same breath. Certainly the idea of a 'Buddhist Economics' sounded like utter fluff. When colleagues in British academia and bureaucracy asked Schumacher what economics had to do with Buddhism, his reply was simple: 'Economics without Buddhism, that is, without spiritual, human and ecological values, is like sex without love.'

In practical terms this meant finding a middle path of development between materialist heedlessness and traditionalist immobility or, as the Buddhists called it, Right Livelihood. This view showed Keynes to be wrong on both moral and practical grounds: 'If human vices such as greed and envy are systematically cultivated, the inevitable result is nothing less than a collapse of intelligence,' Schumacher wrote in his bestselling book *Small is Beautiful: Economics as if People Mattered*.

> A man driven by greed or envy loses the power of seeing
> things as they really are, of seeing things in their round-
> ness and wholeness, and his very successes become his
> failures. If whole societies become infected by these
> vices, they may indeed achieve astonishing things but
> they become increasingly incapable of solving the most
> elementary problems of everyday existence.

Saying this was hardly original. But Schumacher's articulation inspired ordinary people to have more confidence in their own insights. The counter-economist and futurist Hazel Henderson credits Schumacher with giving her 'and millions like me, the courage of our convictions, even when we were facing the mystifications of legions of brilliant, quantitative specialists and narrow economic rationalizers'.

Similarly, Peter Barnes, a businessman and author of *Capitalism 3.0,* credits Schumacher with helping him to understand why the market utterly disregards the essentials on which all human activity depends – such as air, water, soil and the complex web of nature.

Today Barnes is among those who are creating mechanisms that might morph into a new operating system for the market. Schumacher's work nourished the movement that had been inaugurated by Rachel Carson's *Silent Spring* and later expanded by the Club of Rome's warnings about the *Limits to Growth.*

However, mainstream economics continued to work on the assumption that the majority of people are more interested in economic goods than in psychological or environmental losses. Environmentalists were told not to exaggerate the sufferings caused by industrialisation and to stop underestimating the capacity of capital and technology to keep finding solutions.

But gradually some economists began to challenge these assumptions. Herman Daly, widely acknowledged as the father of ecological economics, exposed the hollowness of *homo economicus* and located the human community in the total web of life. Daly was working at the World Bank while he co-authored

For the Common Good: Redirecting the Economy toward Community, the Environment, and a Sustainable Future. This book outlined the principles of a 'Steady-State Economics' which would allow economies to grow and also be environmentally sustainable.

Daly's tenure at the World Bank, in the 1980s, helped to get environmental concerns woven into the Bank's policies and programmes. But his critique of economics itself found little support. He could not persuade most colleagues that the human economy must be seen as a subsystem of the ecosystem, not the other way around. Most of his colleagues, he realised, were basically 'good-hearted folks out trying to do good in the world, like the missionaries. But they have a bad theology. They went to the wrong seminary.' It has been suggested that, if economics is a religion, then Herman Daly is its arch-heretic, a member of the high priesthood turned renegade who has excommunicated himself from the 'Church of Perpetual Growth'.

Over the last decade, as ecological economics has become a branch of mainstream economics, Daly has been celebrated as a high priest of the rebel church. The International Society for Ecological Economics provides a platform for sharing information and reflection about mechanisms that link ecological, social and economic systems. However, the interrelated streams of humanist and ecological economics are still in a nascent stage. Quantity-oriented measures of progress still dominate – even though emphasis on qualitative criteria has grown. But the main nurturing ground for change has been political gathering places like TOES.

A New Economics

The Other Economic Summit (TOES) offered a platform for a wide range of people to engage in conversations about drafting a new and more accurate map of life and market, ecology and economy. As community currency pioneer Edgar Cahn says, 'The map provided by government and prepared by economists is fatally incomplete. It defines reality exclusively in terms of money transactions. It is a flat earth view.' Many of the people who gathered at the first TOES went on to do path-breaking work in the next two decades.

In 1984, Ela Bhatt's work at the Self Employed Women's Association in India was just coming into full stride. She went on to become a leader of people in the unorganised sector of economies across the world. Herman Daly had just published *The Steady-State Economy*. He went on lead the ecological economics stream of academia and activism. John Elkington was then editing the *Biotechnology Bulletin*. He went on to coin the term 'triple bottom line' and to build the think-tank SustainAbility. Hazel Henderson was then working on the earliest indexes to monitor social and environmental impacts. She went on to spread the new economics through different media, including a television show called *Ethical Markets*. Wangari Maathai, then in the early stages of the Green Belt Movement in Kenya, went on to win a Nobel Peace Prize.

TOES succeeded in building an international citizen coalition for a new economics grounded in social and spiritual values to address issues that the G7 summits, at that time, routinely neglected – such as poverty, environment, peace, health, safety, human rights and democratic global governance. Held in different parts of the world over 20 years, TOES served as a floating 'agora' for those who challenge the dominant ideas and powers of the global economy. It became the precursor for gatherings that brought together diverse NGOs and civil society groups from across the world and led to formation of the World Social Forum, first held at Porto Alegre, Brazil, in 2001.

However, the actual process of crafting a 'new economics' came from the ground up, drawing on both the practical experience of activists and thinkers spread across the world. There were some broad points of agreement within this scattered community. Economic progress must not undermine ecosystems. It must create new wealth, not merely drain resources from the poor to the rich. This new wealth must be created by bringing ethical and spiritual values to the centre of economic life. This means enabling people to foster cooperative self-reliance and self-development. But self-reliance is not to be confused with self-sufficiency or a self-centred isolation.

In the early 1990s the mechanics of these aspirations were spelt out in a series of books – *The Living Economy*, *Wealth Beyond Measure* and *Real-Life Economics: Understanding Wealth Creation* – co-edited by the British musician-turned-economist Paul Ekins and the Chilean economist and environmentalist Manfred Max-Neef. They opposed threats to open society such as centralising, non-participative and potentially authoritarian governments, as well as market fundamentalism. They favoured creation of a complementary equation between the market, the state and society. Community was celebrated but not romanticised.

For instance, as Ekins and other pointed out, the biblical injunction is to love your neighbour *as*, not instead of, yourself. Therefore, sympathy for others is a natural and practical tool because it feeds personal growth and fulfilment. The London-based New Economics Foundation (NEF) has spent the last 20 years translating these broad principles into both policy measures and business solutions. Founded in 1986 the NEF is an offspring of the TOES process. In the mid-1980s mechanisms like eco-taxation, social audits and community well-being indicators, sustainable development indicators and ethical investment were ideas restricted to the circles of radical activism and thus not taken seriously either in academic or business circles.

Defining itself a 'think-and-do tank' the NEF anchored projects that helped to mature these ideas in ways that made them impossible to ignore. For example the NEF has evolved methodologies for mapping the value of social connections, justice, participation and environmental sustainability. This work on social indicators, though largely focused on UK, has fed into similar efforts across the world. Data provided by such indicators now plays a key role in measuring the actual, ground-level impact of economic policies. Citizens then find it easier to hold policy-makers accountable and to generate political opinion to press for changes. Thus well-being and sustainability indicators are simultaneously a means of social engagement as well as a management tool. However, the NEF also points out the limitations of this useful tool. After all, even alternative indicators cannot measure the essence of what is socially and morally valuable.

The NEF also carried out a series of pioneering social audits of companies such as Camelot, The Body Shop, Traid-craft, the Co-operative Wholesale Society, and Ben & Jerry's. Such audits measured and evaluated a company's social and ethical performance, thus making it more accountable to its stakeholders. This work has been instrumental in the forma-tion of the Institute of Social and Ethical Accountability to promote professional standards around social accounting and auditing.

More than a decade before climate change arrived on the top of the G8's agenda, the NEF urged that climate change should become the organising principle of the world economy. When this assessment was dismissed as exaggerated pes-simism, the NEF's director Andrew Simms fumed about the absurdity of 'global governors', namely the IMF, World Bank and WTO, clinging to abstract economic theory as though it was more important than the real world and its vulnerability. It is time, pleaded Simms, for a daily prayer to 'deliver us from the abstraction'. While the NEF, and other such entities, grap-ple with the hands-on tasks of connecting the rebellion within economics to actual mechanisms for community-level prob-lem-solving, the Post-Autistic Economics network has taken the struggle to transform the 'dismal science' into the *sanctum sanctorum* of academia.

Post-Autistic Economics Network

As the George F. Baker Professor of Economics at Harvard, a powerful Washington insider and advisor to two Republican presidents, Martin S. Feldstein was accustomed to being taken very seriously. He taught Ec 10, the introductory economics course at Harvard, for 20 years and this made some of the most powerful people in the USA his former students. So it might have come as a rude shock for Feldstein to be told in Spring 2003, not merely by a bunch of rebellious students but some of his fellow faculty, that his course was not only not good enough, it was misleading.

This disturbance was triggered by Students for a Humane and Responsible Economics (SHARE), a Harvard-based off-shoot of the Post-Autistic Economics Network. But significantly the actual petition demanding changes in Ec 10 was drafted by one of Feldstein's colleagues, Professor Stephen A. Marglin, himself a Harvard graduate and a veteran member of the faculty. If this course is meant to be an introduction to basic economic principles and methods, asked the petition, why is its content limited to the neoliberal variety of economics? Why create the impression that there are no other models in the field of economics? Why isn't there a plurality of approaches adapted to the complexity of objects analysed?

By not providing a truly open marketplace for ideas, Harvard fails to prepare students to be critical thinkers and engaged citizens, alleged SHARE. Its mission statement went on to argue that the standard economic models taught at Harvard are loaded with values and political convictions which inevitably influence, if not define, the students' world-view as well as their career choices. Above all, said the petition, 'by falsely presenting economics as a positive science devoid of ethical values, we believe Harvard strips students of their intellectual agency and prevents them from being able to make up their own minds'.

SHARE's demand for modifications to the content of Ec 10 was firmly rejected. But Harvard did allow Marglin to design and teach a complementary course, titled 'Economics: A Critical Approach'. But the department made it clear that this course was not a substitute for Ec 10, which would remain mandatory. This upheaval at Harvard was an echo of that revolt at the Sorbonne described at the opening of this chapter. The Post-Autistic Economics (PAE) Network is now a web-based platform. 'Sanity, Humanity, Science – Pluralism in Economics' are the words that float across its home page. In 2008, its online journal *The Post-Autistic Economics Review* had 9,590 subscribers in 150 countries. This cyberforum, featuring short essays by well-known economists, is a platform for conversation and debate from a wide range of different perspectives.

In 2000, the French Minister of Education set up a commission to examine the issues raised by the post-autistic economics stream. The commission was headed by French economist Jean-Paul Fitoussi, who is secretary-general of the International Economic Association. Fitoussi recommended that the full range of debates on contemporary economic issues should be integrated into the structure and content of university economics courses. 'Such an open environment would preclude the standard practice of keeping the ideological content of neoclassicism hidden from students,' wrote Edward Fullbrook, editor of the PAE journal. However, such an intellectual shift would have potentially radical implications.

When Cambridge University celebrated the centenary of its economics degree, in 2003, the rebels were at hand. The *Guardian* described it as 'another skirmish in a war that has split the discipline'. However, those who worked to make the centenary conference more multi-disciplinary saw themselves as just expanding conversation. Michael Kitson, a member of the board of the *Cambridge Journal of Economics*, rejected one reporter's description that rebels were parking their tanks on the courtyard of neoclassical economics:

> It's not about a battle, but keeping your eyes open, talk-
> ing and communicating. We want to try to break out of
> the narrow silo that economics is becoming. It's becom-
> ing somewhat sterile, almost a subset of mathematics,
> which gives certain insights, but doesn't provide full
> insights into the way an economy actually operates.

While this anomaly interests many people outside academia, the PAE debates have been largely ignored by both British and US media. This might be partly because, as the *Chronicle of Higher Education*, a weekly newspaper for academics in the USA observed, the PAE endeavour is a bit like trying to start a fire under a huge wet blanket. Nevertheless, the PAE network keeps winning new adherents. The journal often receives emails from academics who say, 'I just discovered the PAE movement. I've been waiting 20 years for something like this. Sign me up.' While neoclassical economists remain firmly in control of economics departments at most major universities, there is simmering discontent within the faculty because dom-ination of the orthodoxy tends to block research into aspects of economic phenomena that do not fit the neoliberal para-digm. The PAE process is counting on the expansion of this discontent.

Meanwhile a steady flow of work challenging the ortho-doxy builds momentum for change. Steve Keen's *Debunk-ing Economics: The Naked Emperor of the Social Sciences* explained why economics is 'intellectually unsound'. Keen's book was aimed directly at the growing band of intellectuals and activists who, according to his own website, 'smell some-thing rotten in the state of market'. Paul Ormerod's *The Death of Economics* explored similar ground. Plus the debates within the PAE network have been brought together by Fullbrook in *A Guide to What's Wrong with Economics*. Addressing the book to students of economics, Fullbrook wrote that it 'is intended to appeal to your imagination and humanity by showing you how interesting and relevant, even exciting, economics can be when it is pursued, not as the defense of an antiquated and close-minded system of belief, but as a no-holds-barred inquiry looking for real-world truths'.

So what would a 'post-autistic' economics look like? First and foremost it would dethrone *homo economicus* or a view of human beings as autonomous self-interested individuals who are rational calculators with unlimited wants. A more well-rounded view of humans, as people in community, would increase space for factors such as gender, class, diverse cultural orientations and various facets of human instinct. It would also shift economic inquiry to a focus on process rather than simply on ends. This would require a new theory of knowledge, perhaps pulling down the division between the positive versus normative approaches in social sciences.

Steve Keen, who is a senior lecturer in economics and finance at the University of Western Sydney, suggests that a post-autistic economics would be based on dynamic modelling and systems theory, not some fantasy notions of equilibrium. Then the history of economic thought would celebrate Schumpeter instead of Walras and Keynes rather than Friedman. The mechanical view of the world would be replaced by a more biological and organic approach. As Keen says,

> A student of mine once commented that the mechanical analogy encourages economists to tinker with the economy as if it were a car; but if the analogy were that of a rainforest, would economists blithely recommend that the forest would work better if we removed some species from it?

This kind of questioning and energy is expressed far and beyond the PAE network. For example, there is the Association for Evolutionary Economics (AFEE), an international organisation of economists and other social scientists who treat economics as the study of evolving, socially constructed and politically governed systems. This branch traces its intellectual heritage to early-20th-century economists such as Thorstein Veblen, John R. Commons and Wesley Mitchell. It is concerned with studying such issues as the role of diverse cultures in economic performance, domestic and international inequalities of income, the role of social, economic and political power in shaping economic outcomes, globalisation and the increasing weight of multinational corporations in the international economy, the urgent need for awareness of the impact of new technology on the biosphere.

Then there is behavioural economics which shows that people often do not act in the ways the economics professors led you to think they should, namely as rational decision-makers. The Nobel laureate Daniel McFadden has described behavioural economics as a fundamental re-examination of the field: 'It's where gravity is pulling economic science.' Richard Thaler, the man who has pioneered this branch, started out by musing over quirky anomalies, including those in the working of stock markets, and ended up challenging several facets of neoliberal theory. For example, Thaler's work showed that people care as much about being treated fairly as they do about the actual value of something they buy. Of course, 'fairness' is not a notion that features in much of conventional economic theory.

Putting his ideas where the money-making is, Thaler went on to co-found Fuller & Thaler Asset Management, which has about $4 billion under management and a long record of beating the market. The company's mission is to capitalise on 'market inefficiencies caused by investors' mis-processing of information'. Thaler's key insight is that better information cannot eliminate market inefficiencies since human behaviour is quirky. This is why, says Thaler, the volatility of stock prices cannot be explained merely by studying changes in earnings, economic trends and related factors. This runs directly counter to the claims of the efficient market hypothesis. Thaler backs up this understanding with evidence that shows how most investors tend to be overconfident. Speaking at the World Economic Forum in 2004, Thaler said many individual investors get into trouble 'by convincing themselves that they're the only ones looking at their Yahoo Finance screens'.

The stirrings of behavioural economics are further rein-forced by the emergence of 'neuroeconomics' – a field in which psychologists, neuroscientists and economists are col-laborating. This line of enquiry employs functional magnetic resonance imaging to look inside the brain and track people's decision-making processes. According to the economist Colin F. Camerer, of the California Institute of Technology, the find-ings of neuroeconomics indicate that for most humans mod-ern economic life is a bit like a monkey driving a car. There is some tentative hope that neuroeconomics might enable economists to describe real people more accurately than neo-classical theory. A report in *BusinessWeek* went so far as to suggest that neuroeconomics may 'finally supply the model that knocks mainstream economics off its throne. The new theory should fit better with reality, but it won't be as math-ematically clean – because the brain is a confusing place, with different parts handling different jobs.'

Significantly, the findings of neuroeconomics tally with emerging research on well-being indicators which shows that after reaching a certain level of material comfort more things do not add to people's happiness. This seems like com-mon sense to most people with a well-rounded view of life. But it runs counter to the view, basic to all marketing and advertising, that people do and *should* indefinitely want more things. In a further assault on the old notion of rationality, neuroeconomics is showing that emotions are conducive, not a handicap, in making sound economic decisions.

Why then, as late as 2007, was Stephen Marglin moved to write a book titled *The Dismal Science: How Thinking Like an Economist Undermines Community*? That is because the excitement at the frontiers of economic theory has still not percolated into the elementary textbooks, Marglin said in my email interview with him. For instance, Harvard does not give credit for 'Economics: A Critical Introduction', the counter-course that Marglin teaches. Yes, there are critiques of markets within mainstream economics, acknowledges Marglin, but they do not question the logic of markets and instead aim to create new markets to solve the problems of markets. However, the damage to human relationships from markets cannot be repaired by more markets.

Of course, there is a case to be made for the market, clarifies Marglin, but at present the discipline is not sufficiently engaged with exploring what limits need to be placed on markets for the sake of community: 'In place of such an investigation, economics substitutes a mantra of market freedom based on assumptions of dubious merit.' However, he adds, writing in *The Dismal Science*, if the research agenda of behavioural economics is carried through unflinchingly, 'the results might well be devastating for the self-interested, utility-maximizing individual who has had the leading role in economics since its emergence as a separate discipline from more general inquiry in ethics, statecraft, political philosophy, and the like'. But that might be a big 'if'. For instance, Marglin's reading is that so far behavioural economists seem 'almost desperate to fit their subversive conclusions into a utility-maximizing framework of calculation'.

This partly explains why the proposition that environmental costs cannot be appropriately calculated in money terms is still not quite respectable in the corridors of power. Therefore, some passionate environmentalists who are convinced that losses of the biosphere cannot be understood or 'valued' in terms of money, feel compelled to go along with creating markets for ecosystem services.

Meanwhile, tectonic pressures are evident at other levels, such as efforts to dislodge the GDP as a measure of prosperity. To look more closely at this trend let us journey to the tiny, landlocked Himalayan kingdom of Bhutan. In the winter of 2004, about a hundred people from across the world gathered there to reflect on what was then a barely known and quirky concept: Gross National Happiness.

FROM GROSS NATIONAL PRODUCT TO GROSS NATIONAL HAPPINESS

In 1972 a handsome teenage prince suddenly became king of the tiny mountain-locked nation of Bhutan. Jigme Singye Wangchuck was 17 years old and had spent some time at schools in India and in Britain but never completed his formal education. Yet in one of his first pronouncements as king, Wangchuck declared that Bhutan would strive for a form of material prosperity which ensured Gross National Happiness.

In terms of modern infrastructure Bhutan was virtually a clean slate at that time. The country's first tar road had been built when Wangchuck was a little boy. The first modern bank was founded in 1968, just four years before the young man became king. Bhutan had little to show for in terms of Gross National Product (GNP) which was then treated as the measure of a country's progress up the ladder of development. Like Ladakh, at the Western end of the Himalayas, the people of Bhutan lived in scattered hamlets, depending entirely on a local subsistence economy. Material conditions may not have met 20th-century standards of 'comfort' but there was a certain harmony and beauty in the quality of life which often led outsiders to see Bhutan as the fabled Shangri-la of James Hilton's novel *The Lost Horizon*.

This immeasurable quality of life was probably what inspired the newly crowned king's statement about Gross National Happiness. It was the kind of formless aspiration that comes naturally to young people, with their unconstrained imagination. There is no known record of Wangchuck being in any way influenced by E. Fritz Schumacher's celebration of Buddhist economics or his exhortations in favour of Right Livelihood. *Small is Beautiful* was not even published until a year after Wangchuck's declaration. His Buddhist upbringing possibly helped Wangchuck to instinctively see that the props of 'development' must be tested against actual, realised human well-being.

For 30 years thereafter the Royal Kingdom of Bhutan quietly tried to live by this concept without making any claims in the world at large. But now that catchy term coined by the King of Bhutan has become a globally reverberating aspiration, a huge area of research and one more way of reconfiguring the parameters of the market. This shift has been driven not by events in Bhutan but by unrest at the pinnacle of material prosperity – the USA. The per capita Gross National Product (GNP) of the United States of America has more than doubled in the last five decades. But the graph of depression, divorce and crime has risen correspondingly. All these forms of social distress actually boost the GNP because they cause money and products to change hands. For example, the sales of anti-depressants put over $10 billion into the US economy annually.

In all fairness the concept of GNP was only ever meant to be a 'brute measure' of total economic activity. It was not designed, or intended, to reflect people's well-being. Attributed to the economist Simon Kuznets, in the 1930s, the GNP was intended to be a mechanism for assessing the annual performance of the economy, measured at the time by the industrial and agricultural output that formally enters the market. Later, Kuznets himself cautioned that the welfare of a nation can scarcely be inferred from a measurement of national income as defined by the GNP. The goal of 'more' growth, Kuznets urged, should specify *of what* and *for what*.

However, the concept of GNP is a kind of cultural artefact of deeper significance. It gained power at a time when it seemed reasonable to assume that more goods must mean more general welfare. Extensive documentation throughout the second half of the 20th century proved that this is a false assumption. There were also more visceral responses. For instance, just months before he was assassinated in 1968, Senator Robert Kennedy lamented that America's GNP was also growing because of the sales of rifles and knives and television programmes that glorify violence in order to sell toys to our children. GNP tells us nothing about the health of children, the quality of their education, or the joy of their play. 'The problem,' said Kennedy, is that the GNP measure 'can tell us everything about America except why we are proud that we are Americans'.

Kennedy's ideas were among the influences that inspired Hazel Henderson to become a counter-economist and a passionate critic of the GNP as a yardstick for judging even material prosperity, let alone well-being. Henderson has documented how conventional calculations of GNP have allowed societies across the world to list the non-renewable 'capital stock' of fossil fuels, as 'income'. By contrast, public-sector investments in construction and maintenance of infrastructure like roads, public buildings and airports are classified as 'spending' instead of being seen as public capital assets that they are. The costs of cleaning up pollution show up as a positive in GNP calculations when, in fact, they should register as a minus. As the head of India's National Dairy Development Board, Amrita Patel, has urged it would be more meaningful to measure a country's Gross *Natural* Product, rather than leaving it unaccounted.

Through the 1970s and 1980s the critique of the GNP as a measure of progress gradually moved from the fringes into the mainstream. This process was pushed along by several activists and intellectuals. For example, Henderson did pioneering work in developing the Calvert–Henderson Quality of Life Index which even incorporates cultural values and opportunities for self-improvement. Similarly, Herman Daly made a seminal contribution, both in academia and as an economist within the World Bank. In 1989 the then President of the World Bank, Barber B. Conable, agreed that GNP figures usually show an income that cannot be sustained because the calculations ignore the degradation of natural resources and erroneously show sales of non-renewable resources as income. A better way must be found to measure the prosperity and progress of mankind, said Conable.

In 1990 the United Nations launched its Human Development Index (HDI) – measuring factors such as education, life expectancy, gender and human rights data. In 1992, at the UN's Earth Summit, in Rio, 170 countries signed Agenda 21 and thus agreed to overhaul their national accounts in order to properly value environmental assets and costs of pollution and depletion. This initiative also took into account the unpaid work of millions of women. In 1995 the World Bank issued a revolutionary 'Wealth Index' which defined the wealth of nations to consist 60% of 'human capital' (social organisation, human skills and knowledge), 20% of environmental capital (nature's contribution) and only 20% of built capital (factories, etc.).

More recently, the New Economics Foundation has designed an index called Measure of Domestic Progress (MDP), which adjusts the conventional economic measure of GDP by subtracting the costs of crime, pollution and environmental degradation. The MDP calculations show that social progress has been decoupled from economic growth in Britain for about three decades. The NEF's study found that for many people quality of life was better when they had less spending power. The MDP is not merely an alternative measurement; it is also a way of focusing attention on a fundamental question:

What is all that economic growth for if it doesn't improve actual well-being?

Genuine progress indicators

In the USA the same concerns have been documented by Redefining Progress, a San Francisco-based think-tank set up in 1994, which calls its alterative index Genuine Progress Indicators (GPI). The GPI analysis showed that the quality of American life has been declining steadily since the 1970s. The GPI looks beyond money and goods exchanged and focuses on time spent with family, fresh air, crime rates, prevalence of depression, among other things. For most Americans leisure time has declined in direct proportion to the rise in GNP. Ever since the early 1970s most Americans have been working harder and longer to stay in the same place.

Then there are the consequences of excess consumption. A $700 billion food industry doesn't necessarily make Americans healthier. Fifty per cent of all Americans consider themselves overweight and about $33 billion is spent every year trying to undo the effects of over-eating. Childhood obesity has been officially declared to be an epidemic. 'We are literally growing ourselves sick, and the resulting medical bills make the economy grow more,' wrote Jonathan Rowe, while he was a researcher at Redefining Progress.

When Redefining Progress set out to evolve the Genuine Progress Indicators (GPI), they began by challenging Paul Samuelson's pronouncement in his famous textbook that 'economics focuses on concepts that can actually be measured'. It is a truism that the value of our family and community life, our oceans and open spaces cannot be measured in the way that cars, diamonds or sacks of wheat can be. The objective of the GPI is not to assign money value to these immeasurables. Instead it seeks to assemble a more well-rounded, and thus realistic, balance sheet of the interface between market and society.

Using mostly US government data the GPI makes an assessment of the factors that the economics orthodoxy ignored. For example, the GNP counts as a plus the money people spend on burglar alarms or repairing damage and losses caused by crime. The GPI lists these on the minus side. Damage to human health, agriculture and buildings from air and water pollution is also listed as a loss. Redefining Progress has also converted the GPI into a set of tools and resources that neighbourhoods, towns or cities can use to check their own GPI status. Essentially, these projects attempted to assess the quality of life in a community by integrating environmental, social and economic well-being

For an endeavour that started out as more of a thought experiment than a scientific measure, the GPI has come a long way in 15 years. Its proponents are not worried that it has holes, for it is a work in progress. They argue that even the holes in the GPI mechanism are less fundamentally 'wrong-headed' than those in the GNP. Further work on the concept is now being done by GPI Atlantic, a non-profit organisation in Nova Scotia, Canada, which is a leader in creating quality-of-life indicators. The GPI Atlantic integrates 22 different components, including work hours and income distribution, population health and greenhouse gas emissions. 'What we measure is a sign of what we value in our society,' says Ron Coleman, director of Atlantic GPI. 'If you measure the right things, you change the whole policy agenda.'

The outcome of these altered measurements can be eye-popping for even money bottom-line number crunchers. For example, GPI Atlantic has shown that solid waste recycling saves Nova Scotia taxpayers $31 million per year in energy use and landfill replacement. Old accounting methods focused on basic operating costs and neglected even obvious outlays like the $10 million paid to one town's residents for landfill-related quality-of-life losses. Atlantic's work has inspired a wide array of regional studies on quality of life within Canada. Naturally, such efforts find a powerful resonance with the term *Gross National Happiness*.

Gross National Happiness (GNH)

For almost three decades after their monarch set the goal, Bhutan made quiet statements about its commitment to GNH. For instance, it strictly controlled the number of tourists allowed in every year – to protect both its natural and cultural ecosystems. But then, in the late 1990s, King Jigme Singye Wangchuck began a transition towards democracy and opened up the country to satellite television and the internet. This also brought more international development agencies and researchers into contact with the country's rare endeavour.

As the mood of introspection in the West deepened, Sander Tideman, one of the founders of Spirit in Business, played a key role in urging Bhutanese officials and scholars to speak about the concept of GNH in international forums. When Bhutan's Prime Minister Lyonpo Jigmi Y. Thinley travelled abroad, he found more and more people asking questions about what humanity has actually achieved. What have we sacrificed at the altar of material advancement to appease insatiable wants that do nothing to further human civilisation? Have we become less refined and less capable of peaceful co-existence in a world that compels us to live together within diminishing space and time?

All that Bhutan has to offer you, Thinley said at several international gatherings, is a simple belief in the primacy of happiness and an unshakable faith that 'given an enabling environment, each citizen will find the wisdom to engage in the quiet but infectious pursuit of happiness rather than being trapped in the jungles of supposed means'.

It was with some trepidation that the Bhutanese hosted the first international conference on Operationalising Gross National Happiness, in February 2004, in Thimphu. That gathering attracted not only researchers in quality-of-life indicators but people working in the field of Socially Responsible Investing. Frank Dixon, then with Innovest Strategic Value Advisors on Wall Street, participated because he had a hunch that the concept of GNH could be the most significant advancement in economic thinking over the last 150 years. That's because the GNH is not merely an alternative yardstick. It is also a mindset that could enable human systems to emulate the infinitely greater sophistication of nature. That is, bring ecology and economy in sync.

For instance, at present individual companies and national economies are compelled to keep growing indefinitely. The only parallel for this in the natural world are cancer cells, which by growing exponentially destroy the host body and themselves. It is now accepted that the human economy cannot keep growing at the cost of its habitat. A GNH *mind-set* would redesign production systems and consumption patterns to stay within the carrying capacity of the planet.

So has GNH helped Bhutan to do this? Answers to this question are mired in controversy because of limited and conflicting data. Bhutan's average household income is still among the lowest in the world. The poorer people's access to better food, housing and healthcare has not sufficiently improved. And yet between 1984 and 1998, life expectancy increased from an average of 47 years to 66 years. Bhutan also has the remarkable achievement of having expanded its network of roads and simultaneously increased its forest cover. About 26% of Bhutan's area is managed to protect its astonishing biodiversity and 72% of the country is under forest cover, much of it pristine.

Of course Bhutan has its grim political problems, including ill-treatment of its Nepali-speaking minority. So its endeavour to foster a GNH model of development is as complicated and fraught with challenges as most other countries. A *New York Times* writer, who compared the GNH ideal with the pursuit of happiness as enshrined in the American Declaration of Independence, expressed the challenge quite precisely: 'The "happiness" of GNH is a ceaseless striving to cohere individual and community interests – not a point of arrival.'

Growing international interest in GNH has also drawn attention to the numerous studies that show that, beyond a certain basic level of material comfort, increases in income do not translate into greater happiness. For instance, in China, life satisfaction declined between 1994 and 2007, a period in which average real incomes grew by 250%. Simultaneously there is an explosion of professionals who measure the links between material goods and actual well-being in countries as diverse as Costa Rica, Canada, Iceland, Netherlands, Sri Lanka, Mongolia and Britain. It is important to note that the indices they develop are not intended to do away with the GNP measure. Their purpose is to provide a closer understanding of what fosters well-being and thus helps policy-makers in making better legislation and regulations.

But that still leaves unanswered one basic question: how does the idea of GNH connect with the pliable nature of people's wants? For instance, how does the GNH ideal match the steadily rising material aspirations of Bhutan's younger people?

Letting in global influences has meant that Bhutan's teenagers are now exposed to a culture that connects happiness with brand-name shoes and clothes. Those who are passionately committed to living by the ideals behind GNH hope that those values will continue to be inculcated through the education system and the national media. Will this work? The answer will take a decade or more to surface.

Meanwhile, at the other end of the world there are campaigns to redefine consumption in more holistic terms. For example, the Center for a New American Dream works to help Americans consume responsibly to protect the environment, enhance quality of life, and promote social justice. The traditional American dream was about security, opportunity and happiness. The seekers of a New American Dream are concerned about how these fundamentals have been supplanted by an extraordinary emphasis on acquisition with all its hidden costs for the environment and quality of life. A 'new' American Dream would not be about denial or deprivation. It would be about 'getting more of what really matters – more time, more nature, more fairness, and more fun'. Such initiatives are a creative response to some stark realities. If each of the planet's six billion inhabitants consumed resources at the level of the average American, we would need four additional Earths. Americans consume 40% of the world's gasoline and more paper, steel, aluminium, energy and meat per capita than any other society on the planet.

Concepts like GPI and GNH are vital supplements for rectifying distortions in the prevailing patterns of economic activity and the functioning of markets. A more well-rounded report card of the economy could alter how the market intersects with society. However, a radical application of these concepts would imply some fundamental change. The more nuanced grasp of reality provided by Genuine Progress Indicators or a Gross National Happiness mind-set would be rendered meaningless if the GNP measure, with its pure money bottom line, still remains the basis of measuring growth and such growth remains the main motive force.

FAILURE OF MARKET IDEA OR JUST ANOTHER MARKET FAILURE

In December 2006 ecological economists and social activists from across the world gathered in New Delhi for the ninth biennial conference of the International Society for Ecological Economics. Just a few weeks earlier there had been two dramatic announcements about the toll of rupturing ecology from economy. The former chief economist of the World Bank, Sir Nicholas Stern, submitted a report to the British Treasury which said that business-as-usual cannot tackle climate change. At about the same time the Intergovernmental Panel on Climate Change declared that climate change is now set to accelerate exponentially. A decade earlier the same panel had arrived at a consensus that climate change is largely human-induced and can be stemmed only by rapid reductions in the emission of carbon and other greenhouse gases.

The 'revenge of Gaia' is no longer a bizarre prediction by the scientist James Lovelock. It is a reality. These developments have turned the search for a post-autistic economics into a bit of a cliffhanger. So how close are we to an economics as if people and planet mattered? Stern's somewhat bold declaration that climate change is the biggest market failure in history is a mixed signal. The good news is that more policy-makers and businesspeople now accept that the market alone cannot reverse the factors causing climate change. Plus, Stern explicitly called for *collective action*, rather than individual self-interest, to set things right. These are important advances.

But none of this even begins to address the critical question that, if left unanswered, could destroy civilisation as we know it. What is the optimal scale of the human economy in relation to nature's ecosystems? The theory of the self-regulating market, where supply and demand ensure optimum allocation of resources, does not have the tools to address this question at the speed that is now required. Even public policy has no ready template on which to address that question and thus frame the optimum 'rules' for the market.

Are skirmishes within the discipline of economics helping substantially to nudge along the transformation of the market culture? Only moderately, says Steve Marglin, because 'economics is nurtured by politics and the mainstream of the profession will hardly venture beyond the mainstream political spectrum'. This view is echoed by Paul Ekins, musician turned economist, who pioneered much of the literature on a greener and more humane economics in the 1990s. But now Ekins feels it's a waste of time to critique conventional economics since it reflects, more than creates, the dominant mind-set. The fundamental challenge is moral, according to Ekins: 'we will only get a "post-autistic" mainstream economics when most people buy into a "post-autistic" value system'.

The good news is that challenges to the orthodoxy have created a lively tension and forced a conversation where there was none. Wall Street's meltdown in 2008 has infused these conversations with energy, urgency and money.

Precisely ten years after the student rebels issued their rallying call for a post-autistic economics, King's College, Cambridge (UK), played host to a congregation that reflected this gradual shift. In April 2010, 200 of the world's most reputed and powerful economists assembled to ponder what's wrong with economics and how it can be fixed.

They were invited by the Institute for New Economic Thinking (INET), founded in October 2009 by George Soros and economists who share his critique of market fundamentalism – such as Robert Johnson, Joseph Stiglitz, John Kay, Paul Romer, Jeffrey Sachs and others. This initiative is based on the assessment that even the meltdown has not led to a serious rethinking within economics departments at most leading universities. Ideologists of unfettered markets are still in command.

INET is counting on a shift in demand from students. Soros is hopeful that more and more young people will now avoid studying the 'wrong kind of economics'. By supporting a wide range of research which explores the fallacies of old economic theories, INET aims to help change the curriculum at economics departments – eventually. Under scrutiny are some of the central pillars of the orthodoxy, such as, the efficient market hypothesis and rational expectations theory.

More mainline economists than ever before now acknowledge that the study of economics, particularly in graduate studies, has been manipulated by the marketplace. Charles Ferguson, the director of *Insider Job*, a searing documentary on the causes of the meltdown, has documented the deep conflicts of interest between academic research and financial sector.

Newsweek magazine described the conference at Cambridge as an opening shot in what will inevitably be a bitter and long-drawn-out war. Stiglitz was quoted as saying that the conference was intended to 'energise the troops'. Soros has committed $50 million over a period of ten years and INET hopes to raise more funds to support its research agenda. Whether this new research will break through the barriers of old dogma-controlled academic journals is another matter. But pressure for change is mounting.

For example, a decade ago *The Economist* magazine may have dismissed a gathering of this kind. But it chose to describe the Cambridge conference as 'a coming-out party for misfits, mavericks and pioneers, as well as open-minded members of the mainstream'.

Meanwhile, the Post Autistic Economics network has tweaked its focus, from hard critique to an emphasis on positive alternatives. Its journal, now called *Real-World Economics Review*, is a space for a wide range of fresh thinking as well as skirmishes in the battle of ideas.

In February 2010 the *Real-World Economics Review* held a poll among its 11,000 subscribers to select winners for two contrasting awards – the Dynamite Prize in Economics and the Revere Prize in Economics.

The Dynamite Prize marks the general failure of economists to warn of the approaching global financial collapse. This failure, said the *Review* team, has once again demonstrated that the economics profession's 'competence at real-world economics is grievously less than what society requires'. Even worse, they added, 'the economics establishment has attempted to evade all responsibility for the global financial collapse by calling it an unpredictable, "Black Swan" event. Such statements are plainly untruthful.'

Alan Greenspan, Chairman of the Federal Reserve System from 1987 to 2006, was voted the winner of the Dynamite Prize both for leading the over-expansion of money and credit that created a bubble, and for aggressively promoting the view that financial markets are naturally efficient. Runners-up for the Dynamite Prize were Milton Friedman and Larry Summers.

By contrast, the Revere Award for Economics honoured those economists who have pointed out fundamental flaws and warned about the financial collapse. The award is named after Paul Revere, a hero of the American Revolution. Steve Keen won the poll hands down – being judged as the one economist who first and most cogently warned the world about the coming global financial collapse. Keen has been in the public eye since 2005 when he registered a web page, www. debtdeflation.com, dedicated to analysing the 'global debt bubble'. Nouriel Roubini, of New York University, came in second with Dean Baker of the Center for Economic and Policy Research in third place.

There is now a broad, and growing, consensus about the preferred values of a new market culture, namely: interdependence, empathy, equity, personal responsibility and intergenerational justice. Whether you regard these as rare and scarce human traits or innate and potential to all human beings depends on how far and wide you are willing to look for solutions. But attitude, rather than aptitude, holds the key to the onward journey.

For instance, in the 19th century, those who thought of life as short, nasty and brutish read Darwin and found confirmation for perpetual conflict and selfishness. Peter Kropotkin, the Russian geographer and anarchist philosopher, read the same writings by Darwin and came away with a different view. He was struck by details, like Darwin's account of a blind pelican that lived because the other pelicans caught fish for it.

3
CAN MONEY WORK DIFFERENTLY?
COMMUNITY-CREATED CURRENCIES

> ... the notion that it [money] is a reliable arti-
> fact to be accepted without scrutiny or ques-
> tion is, in all respects, a very occasional thing
> – mostly a circumstance of the last century.
>   – *John Kenneth Galbraith*

*Of all the areas in this book that challenge conventional wis-
dom this one may seem to be the most counter-intuitive of all.
Other than its uneven distribution, what is there to rethink
about money itself? And yet an assortment of groups and
individuals, coming at life from divergent vantage points, are
trying to reclaim power that they feel has been handed over
to money.*

*While appreciating the convenience of money, they ques-
tion why it should be the predominant tool for communicating
about value? Besides, if money serves as a kind of language,
why shouldn't there be a diversity of languages?*

*Yes, this might well be the farthest frontier of creative val-
our. How can local communities just create their own money?
Isn't that the road to economic chaos? In this chapter we will
meet those who are travelling that road in the hope of better*

balancing bazaars and the market. They are troubled by the uneven spread of money but don't see it as the core problem. How money actually works, how its mechanisms might now morph, is what excites the innovators.

Attempting to reform the functions, and thus effects, of money is neither an act of brazen hubris nor stupidity. Protagonists of this sphere can be admired for sheer daring, though they are more often ridiculed as cranks. We venture into this realm not to dissect and determine which ideas are 'workable' but simply to expand our imagination.

~

The American vaudeville star Jack Benny was famous for a routine in which an armed robber accosts him with a gun and a somewhat rhetorical question.

> 'Your money or your life,' says the robber, sticking the gun in Benny's face.
>
> There's a long pregnant pause.
>
> 'Hey! Your money or your life!' shouts the impatient mugger.
>
> 'I'm thinking, I'm thinking,' replies Benny calmly.

Benny's indecision echoes dilemmas that afflict people across the poverty-to-affluence spectrum. It evokes memories of ancient folk-tales – from the ill-fated Greek King Midas to Indian myths about beings who chose wealth over well-being. This partly explains why *Your Money or Your Life* became a bestseller in the US during the mid-1990s. Written by two social activists, Vicki Robin and Joe Dominguez, this self-help book offered people advice on how they could grapple with questions like: Does making a living feel more like making a dying? Does money *own* you? On the surface, these may seem like concerns of people in rich societies. Yet, in some form or the other, these questions now strike a chord in diverse cultures and income groups – from impoverished African or

Asian villages, to affluent suburbs of New York, New Delhi or Rio de Janeiro.

Benny's comic persona was so attached to money that he was tempted to cling to his wallet rather than his life. Perhaps money, like sex, has a numinous quality. It is filled with fantasy and emotion in ways that resist rational judgement. Thomas Moore, the American philosopher and psychotherapist, has suggested that this is why money can become a fetish when it is actually just a medium of exchange. This may seem absurd since most people experience money as an instrument of power. And, yet, money is wealth only as long as it gets you the goods, services and experiences you need or want.

A wallet thick with cash and credit cards becomes useless if you are marooned in a wilderness. You need other people to trade in those tokens for what can actually be consumed. Even that is possible only if the people you encounter value your paper notes and share your trust in the credit card company. This brings home the reality that money is nothing more than an agreement. Currency notes work because we all agree to trust the governments that issue them as a token of exchange. Similarly, credit cards or cheques are an agreement between the user and the bank that issued them.

Across the world some communities are now forging new kinds of agreements to make money work differently and on their own terms – not those set by governments, banks and other big players in the market. Why do this? What is the problem with conventional money? After all, conventional currencies seem to do a good enough job in facilitating the conversations that are basic to the marketplace. Most of us enjoy the mobility facilitated by the widespread acceptance of a national currency. So what are the motivations for experiments where communities create their own complementary currencies?

First, mobility has some disadvantages. 'We printed our own money because we watched the Federal dollars come to town, shake a few hands, then leave to buy a rainforest and fight wars. Ithaca's Hours, by contrast, stay in our region to help us hire each other,' says Paul Glover who is co-founder of the Ithaca Hour local community currency which circulates in a small town on the east coast of the USA.

Second, conventional currencies create a strange monoculture of value, partly because the agreement implicit in them is with distant and amorphous entities. Take, for instance, the reasoning offered by the founders of the Bia community currency in Thailand. Not too far back in time their local bazaars were closely intertwined with community relations and there was a wider variety of modes of exchange. Value was not determined entirely by money. Over the last 50 years, as the local economy became more and more monetised, community bonds gave way to purely commercial relations dominated by distant traders who deal in powerful global currencies. Eventually, even within the local community, mutual aid declined. So in 1999 some of the locals got together and created the Bia Kud Chum currency in the hope of reducing 'destructive dependence' and strengthening both local economy and community.

Third, 'normal' money just can't fulfil some of the most crucial needs in life, such as friendship. So in Western countries community currencies partly serve as an antidote to loneliness. 'Often you can't buy what you really need,' says Mashi Blech, who set up the Time Dollars programme at ElderPlan, a health maintenance organisation in Brooklyn. 'You can't hire a best friend. You can't buy somebody you can talk to over the phone when you're worried about surgery.' Yes, you can buy the services of a therapist but that is no substitute for the sense of belonging found within a community.

Fourth, such currency innovators are empowered by the awareness that money is a human artefact. Since money is a device humans created, we can alter it. This confidence is based on the knowledge that the prevailing money system is the product of multiple influences and historical trends. So isn't it logical, then, that money should morph still further, taking different forms that cater to far more needs than the monoculture of government and bank-generated money. The real cost of money, argues Edgar Cahn, the creator of Time Dollars, is not interest but the imprisonment of our imagination:

> We invest money with magical powers that in truth belong to us . . . We have to find a way to value the contribution of those for whom the market has no use for ultimately, people, all people, are the true wealth of this society. We cannot cede to money or market the power to determine value.

If money communicates information about value and serves as a kind of language, why shouldn't there be multiple languages? This is the crux of increasingly intense global conversations among those who anticipated the cascading failures of conventional financial institutions. So far this monetary innovation and rebellion at the grassroots seemed like rumblings of a radical fringe. This is partly because it seems to attempt the impossible – separating the function of money as a token of exchange from its function as a store of value. But the meltdown of 2008 has reminded all of us about an elementary truth. What we think of confidently as value stored in our bank account is little more than a fragile promise – made by either a government or a private bank.

The bulk of money is an accounting entry which depends entirely on trust and confidence. As virtually every report on the meltdown pointed out, what has evaporated is not actually money but confidence. And confidence was vaporised not by events in the nuts-and-bolts economy but by a fatal garbling of information – due to opaque and complex financial instruments. Innovations of a vastly different kind, at the grassroots, offer no direct solutions for the malice in the financial markets at the top. But they do draw attention to a fundamental truth. Since money is essentially information it can, potentially, be held and circulated in more fair, stable and creative ways.

Community currencies are merely one facet of a much wider foment which has a rich lineage.

MONETARY INNOVATION: MUTUAL AID AND FREE MONEY

Money as a symbol, or token, to facilitate exchange has been around for more than 5,000 years. The earliest such tokens were backed by the most basic of all resources – food. The Sumerian word for money, *shekel*, referred to one bushel of wheat. Ancient Egypt created one of the earliest banking systems based on stores of grain. The word 'capital', from the Latin for head, carries memories of the time when all wealth was counted in tangibles like food and heads of cattle. A variety of useful objects have served as tokens of exchange – shells, wood, cloth, metals, salt and even dried fish.

Money in the shape of precious metal coins appeared around the sixth century BC almost simultaneously in Greece, Mesopotamia, India and China. Like other forms of money, coins were a convenience. It was easier to carry a token to the bazaar rather than lugging a bushel of wheat to exchange it for oil or incense or cloth. As metal coins became the dominant form of money throughout the world, more and more value was stored in things that could not themselves be consumed – as salt or fish could. But interestingly the word 'money' is derived from the Latin verb *moneo*, 'to remind', perhaps because it was initially just a memory-link to reproductive goods and services that people actually consume.

Gradually, money shifted from being a mere convenience, a pure trading instrument, to an asset in its own right. But throughout that journey two elements remained constant – meaning and trust. Whether it was coins minted by a monarch or promissory notes issued by merchants, the value depended on a sufficient number of people trusting the issuer. The birth of the Bank of England in 1694 marked a watershed point in the evolution of money. What the Bank did on a day-to-day basis was quite simple. Depositors brought their coins to place in its coffers and in exchange got a receipt for the deposit. Banks had handled deposits and transfers for centuries but not loans and advances. The Bank of England did something new. It not only issued receipts for gold deposited, which circulated as money, it began to issue credit notes in excess of the gold it actually held. This is what all banks did henceforth.

'The process by which banks create money is so simple that the mind is repelled,' wrote John Kenneth Galbraith.

> Where something so important is involved, a deeper mystery seems only decent ... The original deposit still stood to the credit of the original depositor. But there was now also a new deposit from the proceeds of the loan. Both deposits could be used to make payments, be used as money. Money had thus been created.

Creation of money in this manner was a key element in shaping commerce as we know it today.

This creation of money eventually morphed into the complex web of financial mechanisms that are now commonplace. One consequence was an unprecedented expansion of business opportunities. But disquiet simmered alongside from the beginning. It was sharply manifest as a bitter dispute that divided the founding fathers of the American republic – most notably Thomas Jefferson, the first Secretary of State, and Alexander Hamilton, the first Secretary of the Treasury. On one side were land-anchored farming folk and on the other an entirely new breed of financial wizards. The farmers feared a new complex financial system that allowed private banks and players in the stock market to spin agreements that, for the most part, only they understood. Jefferson had such a deep mistrust of emerging financial institutions that he considered banking establishments to be more fearsome than standing armies.

This mistrust became a persistent element of American politics. At the end of the 19th century it was a major plank in the repeated attempts of the populist leader William Jennings Bryan to become president of the US. Bryan saw himself as Main Street's 'David' standing up to the 'Goliath' of Wall Street banks.

Since then, three major anxieties about money have remained constant. Firstly, there is a moral disquiet about making money just by juggling money, mostly through speculation. The counter-view, that the risk-taking ability of the speculator is itself a form of value-addition, which helps in price discovery and provides liquidity, does not address the core concerns of those outside the 'money market'. It was not the amassing of wealth, even in paper form, that disturbed 18th-century farmer-folk in America. What frightened them, says historian Steve Fraser, were 'newer, shadowy forms of moneymaking, the darker commercial arts' which seemed to release 'animal passions, pandering to man's baser desires'.

Secondly, as money became more powerful as a commodity, it seemed to have less and less of a link to tangibles of actual utility, such as fertile land, food, metals and other raw materials needed for production. This is now the predominant concern of those trying to unravel how the logic of money inherently undermines ecological sustainability. For instance, if you cut down a forest, sell the timber and put that money in a bank, money earned as interest is likely to outstrip what you could have earned annually by harvesting the standing forest in a sustainable manner. That's an additional twist to 'your money or your life' since it is the standing forest that stores value essential to the survival of our species.

Thirdly, financial wizardry created money flows and instruments that became both distant and unintelligible. This meant a greater gap, and mismatch of power, between those issuing the instruments and the rest of society. But more critically it complicated how value is defined and measured even within the money markets. The term 'derivatives' is thus quite eloquent. These are financial instruments the value of which is *derived* from the underlying asset which in turn depends on trust between those evaluating the asset and those accepting the derivatives. However, this trust becomes increasingly fragile in direct proportion to the complexity of the financial jugglery. Testifying before Congress, at the peak of the sub-prime crisis, one Wall Street insider put the matter in a nutshell: 'Complexity cloaks chaos.'

Proponents of the free market have defended a variety of misadventures as a necessary price for innovation which in turn ensures growth. Most of the global discourse on these issues tends to see 'innovation' in a small and familiar box and then plays around with combinations of government regulation and self-regulation by private financial institutions – in their existing form. Money in itself is rarely re-examined. Yet over the past century a variety of out-of-the-box innovators have built on the elementary insight that money is a convenience, a public good that has run amuck. They have thus sought to free money so that it may work more creatively for what we actually seek – dynamic production and exchange of goods and services.

In the early 19th century the French anarchist philosopher Pierre-Joseph Proudhon argued that since money is not itself wealth but a public convenience it ought to be produced, issued, lent and handled on a no-profit, no-loss basis. Under such a system bankers would revert to their original role as professional money handlers, charging a professional fee, rather than creators of money.

Proudhon's British contemporary Robert Owen went ahead and acted on these principles. The founder of the cooperative movement in Britain, Owen launched an interest-free complementary currency in 1832. This scheme, anchored at a National Labour Exchange, was based on Owen's definition of wealth as the 'combined manual and mental powers of people called into action'. Workers who joined the National Labour Exchange were invited to deposit the products of their labour and in exchange collect promissory notes valued at the hours of labour put in. For this purpose the Exchange printed its own National Equitable Labour Notes in denominations ranging from one to eighty hours. A Labour Exchange Bazaar was set up for this purpose at Gray's Inn Road in London. These Labour Notes helped many unemployed workers to earn a livelihood.

Owen's experiment was short-lived but the local authorities in Guernsey, an island in the English Channel, had a longer innings with their experiment in issuing local notes from 1815 until about 1835. As elsewhere, the notes served the purpose of reviving a flagging local economy. The memory of that endeavour perhaps survived in some form because it was suddenly revived in 1914 and is still operational today in the form of Channel Island Notes. These notes are used as parallel currency in the Channel Islands. However, it was the Great Depression that gave a big boost to locally created complementary currencies.

One example of radial innovation is tucked away in the small and otherwise obscure Austrian town of Worgl. A commemorative plaque at a bridge in Worgl proudly declares that the structure was built with locally created interest-free money during the Great Depression. That bridge is the remnant of a short-lived but successful experiment in 'free money' inspired by Silvio Gesell – a German-born economic philosopher who ran a prosperous business in Buenos Aires at the end of the 19th century. Initially, Gesell's interest in the workings of money was a response to the hassles of running a business with a highly unstable currency. Gesell went on to study the phenomenon of interest in detail and spent the last 20 years of his life living in Europe – lobbying extensively for the creation of what he called 'Free Money'.

Gesellian 'free' money would be a perishable commodity so there would be no incentive to hoard it. A Free Money note is designed to lose one-thousandth of its face value weekly, or about 5% annually, at the expense of the holder. Gesell's

objective was to break the unfair privilege enjoyed by money
over all other goods. Producers of material goods, whatever
their shelf-life, have to contend with storage and decay. By
contrast the possessor of money has none of these hassles and
the added advantage of waiting power – except in a period
of runaway inflation. So why not make those who have more
money, than they can immediately use or invest, pay a user
fee? A demurrage charge on money is not a new idea. The
grain-based banks of ancient Egypt operated on this basis –
both for the natural reason that stores of grain tend to deplete
but also to encourage rapid circulation of the deposit receipts.
In *The General Theory of Employment, Money and Interest* Keynes described Gesell as a 'strange, unduly neglected
prophet' whose intuitions contained profound and original
insights. According to Keynes, future generations would learn
more from the spirit of Gesell than from that of Marx. Though
Gesell died in obscurity in 1930, his ideas inspired the creation of WIR, a complementary currency system of businesses
in Switzerland which is still thriving.

Throughout the 1930s many different models of complementary currency sprang up all over the USA, Canada,
Denmark, Ecuador, France, Italy, Mexico, the Netherlands,
Romania, Spain, Sweden, Finland, Switzerland and even
China. According to one estimate such systems sprang up
in 127 cities across the US and involved more than a million
people. In most cases a locally cobbled together entity issued
tokens, either as interest-free loans or in payment for services
rendered. This was a risky mechanism since it was easy to
issue more tokens than the value of goods produced, which
would lead to inflation and a loss of confidence in the value of
the currency. Contemporary initiatives have learnt from and
are correcting these flaws.

This buzz about different mechanisms for money has not
been restricted to radical idealists or anarchists. It grabbed
both the intellectual interest and political engagement of Irv-
ing Fisher, one of the most influential American economists

of the early 20th century, whose theory of money and prices became the foundation for much of contemporary monetary economics. Fisher studied the experiments in complementary currency and also looked closely at Gesell's writing. He went on to conclude that the interest-free locally created forms of money could be used to lift millions of Americans out of the miseries of the Depression. Fisher then approached the US Treasury Department with this proposal. Treasury officials in turn consulted the economics faculty at Harvard. In principle the professors could find no argument against the issue of stamp scrip for the purpose of creating jobs. But, said the dons, the proposal had far-reaching implications. If implemented on a sufficiently large scale it would end up restructuring the American monetary system and lead to a profound decentralisation of decision-making. At just about the same time President F.D. Roosevelt was in the process of launching the New Deal. When Fisher's proposal for a stamp scrip reached the Oval Office it was not merely rejected. F.D.R. issued an executive decree prohibiting local currencies. Soon the massive flow of federal grant money released by the New Deal swept local currencies off the scene. Within a generation local currencies faded from popular memory.

Central authorities have repeatedly blocked local currency experiments because they threaten the state's monopoly on determining what the universal meaning of money should be within its own territory. Such control by the state in turn bolsters the power of private banks to create money. So far the public discourse has overlooked challenges to both monopolies while voices calling for a more democratic alignment of money and bazaars remained on the fringe. But they don't give up. Therefore, local currencies have been proliferating again in the USA, Canada and Australia since the 1980s.

Meanwhile, in a related stream of action, those who seek to reform conventional currency now expect to gain momentum. American Monetary Institute, a non-profit organisation, is lobbying in Congress for a new legislation called the American

Monetary Act. Under this legislation the Federal Reserve System would be incorporated into the US Treasury and dollars would be created by the federal government, as interest-free loans put into the economy for infrastructure spending, including healthcare and education. Reformers promote this as a means of eliminating 'commodity money' based on credit and debt to what many of them call 'real' money – that is, a more accurate and stable mechanism for circulating information about value.

On both sides of the Atlantic such monetary reformists are also deeply critical of the US dollar's hegemony and convinced that its rapid decline is inevitable. After all, since the US dollar ceased to be based on gold its value has been entirely faith-based – or rather dependency-based since producers all over the world have counted on ever-expanding consumption by Americans. As James Grant, the editor of *Grant's Interest Rate Observer*, put it: 'That a piece of paper of no intrinsic value should pass for good money the world over is nothing less than a secular miracle.'

Grassroots innovators see the chaos in the global financial system as a huge opportunity. They hope the crisis will clear the way for a more decentralised, democratic and sustainable system. The impetus for this shift is provided both by pragmatic compulsions and political pressures for greater justice. Hazel Henderson, author of *Politics of the Solar Age,* offers a compelling logic for the shift. Just as the gold standard failed to provide enough 'bandwidth' for growth, innovation and transactions in the 20th century, similarly existing money circuits lack bandwidth for the full potential of exchange possible in the information economy. As most reformers will be the first to admit, there are few ready-made answers on the details of how money should morph. It is the aspiration, the raising of challenge that is more significant. Community currencies are but one facet of this emerging work in progress.

Interestingly, the idea of non-governmental complementary currencies was supported by F.A. Hayek, as part of his shrink-the-state agenda. He opposed the government monopoly on money and favoured a role for private issuers of competing currencies. Today corporations are issuing Digital Value Contracts (DVCs), which virtually function as money. But these forms of private money, which smooth the flow of trade within corporations, are not designed to redefine the market culture in the way that we are concerned with here.

Community currencies are proliferating across the world on quite a different grid. In 1994 there were an estimated 500 communities with local currencies, spread across North America and Western Europe. There are no precise figures available but by 2008 there were estimated to be over 2,000 community currencies of different forms and levels of efficiency spread across the world, including Asia and Australia.

A community currency comes into being when people of a town or a village, or even those with a virtual linkage, get together and create their own token of exchange. Like conventional money, such currencies are a credit instrument, or IOU. But unlike conventional national currencies these IOUs circulate only within a particular network or community. This could be a geographical locality, a town, or it could be a group of software developers scattered around the world.

Many of these are mutual credit systems through which the participants empower themselves to do the same thing that banks have done for years. Communities create their own money in the form of credit but save the cost of interest and distribute the money themselves according to their own needs. Thomas Greco, a prominent proponent of such currencies, argues that without such 'monetary transcendence' it is impossible to have government of the people, by the people and for the people, since the fundamental structures of economics and finance are monopolised by a few people.

This quest for economic democracy is also an expression of the urge to assert the primacy of society over the market – to have markets that are embedded in society rather than ruling over it. Community currency innovators see modern money as being 'disembedded' from community values and preferences because it serves the interests of distant state bureaucracies and elites.

Creators of such currencies essentially ask us to imagine a money system that simply enables people to trade equitably and efficiently. They are seen as a mechanism for enabling connections – person to person, business to business. 'Imagine money that circulates in communities and networks so that what you spend always comes back,' says Michael Linton. On that note, let us delve into the details of the two most common kind of community currencies – Time Dollars and Local Exchange Trading System or LETS.

'What's up doc?' How Michael Linton created LETS

In September 1997 The Other Economic Summit (TOES) network organised a workshop of activists and innovators working on community currencies. Introducing himself, Michael Linton said, 'I've been involved in this since 1982 when I ran out of money. It's been a fascinating process for me . . . and none of it is about running the system or even starting a system. It's all about propagating the system.' This propagation is an ambitious effort to re-form patterns of social behaviour which Linton likens to 'a new dance step or a new way of saying "What's up doc!" . . . that's copied and moved on.'

Linton's gusto may have something to do with his Scottish lineage. Our everyday life is dominated by things and ideas that were originated by Scotsmen – logarithms, steam engines, rubber tyres, telephones, antibiotics, radar, television and, of course, modern economics. It was Linton's reputation as a legend in the sphere of community currency that inspired me to make the trip to his home in Courtenay on Vancouver Island, Canada. Linton studied natural sciences at Cambridge University and briefly worked for Shell before migrating to British Columbia and becoming a jack of many trades – from chemical engineer, computer programmer, research psychologist to truck driver, ski instructor, school teacher, fisherman, logger and retailer. Today he describes himself as a systems designer who works on systems for an open society.

In 1979 Linton was working as an Alexander Technique therapist when the local economy went into a tailspin, taking with it most of his clients. At about the same time, Linton came across E. Fritz Schumacher's book *Good Work* and was riveted by the Buddhist ethic of Right Livelihood. Above all, he was struck by Schumacher's ability to be benign and devout without being devotional. This helped Linton to integrate his own life with a moral stand on political and economic justice that was grounded rather than being lofty: 'I like my wine, women, [and] fun and want a good living, beer and bread and occasionally a good movie. And most people are like this.'

Meaningful change, Linton knew, depends on what seems 'doable' to ordinary folks, not the exceptionally talented and committed. At that point, a local exchange system being run in another part of Vancouver Island caught his attention and Linton plunged into unravelling how money works. If money is essentially a measuring device, he asked himself, how can a community be short of measures? It's like saying you just ran out of inches. But the exchange system was too small and not spreading. So Linton set about designing a computer-run system and called it 'Lets', by which he meant 'let's do it'. But when people asked, 'Let's *what*?' he came up with 'Local Exchange Trading Systems' – a form of local bazaar activity that requires no conventional currency.

LETS is designed as a self-regulating system that allows communities to stabilise their local economy without diminishing their participation in the national or international economy. This is how it works. First you need a bunch of people, or even just one person, who takes the lead by acting as account-keeper. Then any number of residents of that town or network can join the LETS. Each member starts with a zero balance. Then as people exchange goods and services, they earn and spend credits through their LETS account. For example, the car mechanic pays his or her barber in LETS credits. The barber then uses those credits to buy bread or groceries at the local store. The grocer then uses those credits to have his car fixed and so on. For example, the LETSystem's directory in Totnes, UK, goes by the motto 'Let's do it well' and lists 21 different categories of services. These range from baby-sitting, food catering, dog-walking, gardening and health therapies to business and office services, as well lessons on a wide variety of subjects including sports, creative arts and spiritual disciplines.

At first sight LETS can seem like a slightly evolved form of barter with a suspicious whiff of tax evasion. But LETS has far more convenience and flexibility than barter allows and sales tax can be woven into LETS-based commerce if and where required. The essential purpose of LETS is to create a locally anchored line of credit that energises the frequency and volume of exchange within a community – the local multiplier of a town's economy. This is done not by attempting to replace the national currency but by complementing it. But what if some members take goods and services on LETS credits and then abandon the system? In the conventional monetary system it hurts when a person who owes you money jumps town. But not in the case of LETS since the credits are not a store of value.

LETS has had a rough childhood. The first LETS began in Comox Valley on Vancouver Island, in 1982, and soon spawned seven schemes in that region. Encouraged by this initial success, Linton launched Landsman Community Services in 1984, as a for-profit private limited company for the purpose of promoting both for-profit and non-profit models of community currencies. It was through Landsman that Linton designed and launched the computer software for operating LETS.

Interestingly, this software worked on principles similar to the GNU GPL though Linton had no contact with the then infant Free Software movement. 'We felt that you can't ask money for this software, that is as profit,' Linton wrote later.

'It would completely contradict what we're trying to do. But, later the intellectual property rights for the software were conferred on the LETS System Trust, to be held in the public domain. This was done to ensure that no one could misrepresent LETS by using the name to mean anything else.' Linton sees community currencies as having an inherently Chaordic quality, a term coined by Dee Hock the creator of the Visa system. Community currencies are a form of social organisation where individual self-interest is married to the larger community interest.

This is possible because no higher authority, either government or bank, 'issues' the currency. Instead it is a credit system created by the same people who will be using it – local residents and businesses. In this case a negative balance means you have issued money to others, not borrowed it from them. As Linton and his colleague Ernie Yacub wrote:

> It's not debt, it's commitment, and you honor it at your own rate – usually some LETS and some normal money, enough to cover your cash costs. My commitment, in a debit position, is a general one to the community as a whole. A temporary or even permanent inability to recompense hardly restricts the rest of the community, who are still perfectly able to continue trading with each other, using my issued money. My inability to meet commitments in the cash economy is often a result of the scarcity of money. In the LETSystem the money I issue never leaves the community. It's always available for me to re-earn, and since it is not in short supply, it is less likely that competition for it will exclude me from earning.

With smart cards a LETS system becomes even easier. One smart card can carry many independent virtual community moneys, just as a wallet can hold several different national currencies. Such smart cards can then be hooked into an online network linking not only geographical but virtual communities. In such open money systems, as Linton calls them, money would both be free and in sufficient supply. Since the promise to redeem is not by a central authority but among members of a community it means that 'our money is our word'. While conventional money flows erratically in and out of the base of the economy, creating dependencies, open money recirculates and thus empowers business and trade close to the grassroots. Conventional money essentially creates conditions of the zero-sum game. It is money that neither knows nor cares who you are – because it is intended to work anywhere for anyone. On the other hand, Open Money is meant to *connect* people more fruitfully. 'Since there's no competition for this money,' says Linton, 'it can't be used as an instrument to buy or bully anyone.'

Since Open Money concentrates on being an information system, it can be programmed to serve different purposes. This makes it is far more flexible and helps foster a robust market – which after all is a networking system for the flow of goods and services. Linton even sees it as a new skin for communities:

> An organism is defined by its skin, a boundary layer that selectively allows the free transfer of some materials while retaining others. The more complex the organism, the more is its activity related to internal processes than to transfers across the skin. The only skin possessed by a community in present circumstances is geographic and is related to transportation costs. Since the last half-century has seen transport costs steadily decline, most of our communities have been reduced, by excessive dependence on imports and exports, to extremely primitive economic processes. LETSystems are a way to give local communities new skins.

This new skin is created by the chemistry of individuals within a community making a promise to other community members.

Thus, reciprocal exchanges in LETS happen in a socially embedded bazaar whereas the conventional money facilitates purely transactional exchange. Eric Helleiner, professor of international political economy at Trent University, has observed that LETS promoters are not the first to recognise that currency reforms can alter transaction costs to promote new conceptions of economic space. After all, nation-builders in the 19th and 20th centuries saw the creation of an exclusive and homogenous national currency as a key element of constructing a national economy.

Over the last two decades LETS schemes have sprung up in far corners of the world. Most of these schemes do not follow the letter of the design offered by Linton and that's how it is meant to be. Besides, other such systems have sprung up entirely independent of Linton's innovation. For example, in the mid-1980s, David James, a Quaker, launched the Whangarei Exchange and Barter System (WEBS) in New Zealand. Australia has many LETS communities. In some cases the currency is called Green Dollars. In 1993 a French organic farming specialist named Claude Freysonnet initiated the *le Grain de Sel* network, also known by the acronym SEL – for Système d'Exchange Local (Local Exchange System). Soon the television network France 2 was telecasting a programme every Saturday called *Troc Moi Tout* (Barter Everything).

In 2002 the Institute for Public Policy Research (IPPR) in London initiated a programme to create SchooLets and Time Banks for schools. This was an action research project for encouraging schools to start their own community currencies. SchooLets are a way of getting greater involvement from parents in school activities and for linking the school with the wider community. Schools are then treated as social capital banks, where families and the wider community can invest, deposit and withdraw various forms of support – using the community currency as a medium of exchange. There is also scope for currencies to be organised across neighbouring schools, thus fostering cooperation and interdependence. For instance, a student can earn Time Credits, or LETS credits, by being a tutor for a younger student and then use those credits to acquire coaching in some other area. This activity also fits in with the fact that Citizenship Education and Financial Literacy are now compulsory in the British school curriculum. SchooLets ensures that children are not given a one-sided view of financial literacy and also know about complementary currencies.

LETS was not the only type of community currency to take off in the early 1990s. Ithaca Hours was another model that emerged, in the town of that name in upstate New York. Hours are actual currency notes which carry the imprint 'In Ithaca We Trust', as a variation of the Federal Dollar's logo 'In God We Trust'. Paul Glover, the designer and coordinator of this system, calls it a way of bringing into the marketplace time and skills not employed by the use of conventional money. Unlike LETS, Ithaca Hours is not a membership organisation. The Ithaca Hours system is run by a 'Municipal Reserve Board', which consists of Hours members, and this Board decides on the amount of new notes to be issued. Often when new notes are issued some are given as grants and loans to communi-ty-based organisations which are then able to acquire local goods and services in exchange for those Ithaca Hours. A key function of the Ithaca Hours is to create a sense of coopera-tive community rather than winners and losers scrambling for a scarce resource. The Bia Kud Chum scheme, operating in the Pomprab District of Thailand since 1999, also uses locally printed currency notes which are valid within the community – equal in value to, but not exchangeable with, the Thai baht.

According to the Schumacher Society of USA, such Hours programmes spread to over 50 communities through the 1990s. For example, the Berkeley campus of the University of California has the Berkeley Bread currency, which works along similar lines. The Bread notes carry the logo 'You Knead It'. Such Hours systems require fairly vigorous coordination and a group of people that must periodically decide the quantity of Hours to be kept in circulation. By contrast, a mutual credit system like LETS operates through a chequebook system, or now smart cards, and the 'money supply' is left to the natural flow of debits and credits lodged in the systems register.

LETS schemes have not enjoyed an up-up-and-away growth pattern. Those engaged with this innovation must necessarily live with bursts of enthusiastic energy, sharp declines, periods of lull and slow revivals. This is true of the very first LETS initiated by Linton himself on Vancouver Island. An analysis of LETS on Vancouver Island reveals the following flaws. There was an over-reliance on the coordinator and insufficient participation by the members. Though the rules allowed any member to check the credits balance and turnover of another member at any time, in practice no one ever did this since an ethos of 'trust' was advocated and this created a strong social disincentive for people to check each other's accounts. Businesses that participated in the LETS scheme wound up with far more credits than they could spend. So why persist?

Mary Fee, who has been closely involved with LETS Link UK, describes it as 'a mission, a train you can't get off'. Fee is otherwise an activist in the sphere of natural healing. We met at a festival of alternative health systems in London, where Fee had a stall. Her work with LETS Link consists of helping people who want to set up a LETS scheme anywhere in London. She spoke at length about various technical problems in running LETS, including excessively high balances of credits, which the holders cannot find avenues for spending. But from Fee's perspective the main problem is that LETS coordinators tend to be volunteers who eventually get tired and worn out.

So why does she persist in that role? 'Because I'm quite obstinate,' Fee said happily. 'And its one way of educating people. We must pursue it, *make it* work through experience because it is part of the answer to globalisation. It's important to support new LETS to make sure they don't repeat the same mistakes. I concentrate on people who are trying to use LETS to work for refugee groups and other disadvantaged sections.' Users and promoters of other forms of community currency, such as the 'Chiemgauer' operating around Munich and the 'Berliner' in Berlin, seem to share this motivation.

Linton's benchmark for a LETS to be make a significant impact is that at least 10% of the people in a community should be on board, with at least 10% of their income and expenses circulating through the complementary system. Few, if any, LETS schemes at present meet this benchmark. And yet Linton and hundreds of others in the field are not discouraged. They treat the performance so far as merely indicative of possibilities yet to be realised.

For Linton, two decades of ups and downs have strengthened both resolve and confidence because it is becoming more evident that open money is merely one facet of a much larger phenomenon. The open-source phenomenon has arrived powerfully at the centre-stage of the software business. More and more people are talking about open accounting, open participation and open organisation and so on. The homepage of Linton's open money website explains that open money is 'an invitation to come inside and play, as in open door and open house; collaboration as in open hand and open for all; attitude as in open mind'.

Proponents of complementary currencies are growing more confident as people across the world gain access to the internet and enter the Information Age. The Net naturally lends itself to many forms of non-bank currency – many of them created by the traders themselves in the act of buying or selling. Eventually, Greco anticipates, credit clearing will supplant *all* political currencies and money as we know it today will become obsolete.

Of course, all endeavours of this nature are work-in-progress. Glitches in implementation seem less important than the motivation that drives innovators. Veteran American political activist Ralph Nader offers an explanation for why people are keen to give even seemingly far-fetched possibilities a chance – they are fed up of being told by the media, congressmen and economists that there isn't enough money to ensure the well-being of all babies, homeless people and old people who are alone. Community currencies offer people at least the hope of breaking what Nader calls 'a moral, fiscal, political grid-lock'. So how does the 'core' or 'love' economy fit into this excitement?

Time Dollars: Edgar Cahn's vision of co-production

Holding his new-born grandchild was a moment of revelation for Edgar Cahn. He was struck by the realisation that our species was not designed to survive. The baby in his arms felt just too frail and helpless. All the little fellow had going for him was the ability to cry, grimace and grasp as much as tiny fingers allow. Yet, thought Cahn, 'we of all species have survived, adapted, dominated, largely because of mother love'. Awe and wonder in the presence of a new-born life is not rare. The remarkable thing about Edgar Cahn is that he anchored a different kind of economics in this heightened awareness of the bonding energies that ensure human survival and make society possible. The result is Time Dollars, 'an inflation-proof currency that can provide as constant, as powerful, as reliable a reward for decency as the market does for selfishness,' says Cahn's old friend Ralph Nader.

Edgar Cahn is a dapper and elegant man whose very presence exudes gentleness and leaves no mystery about why he is so deeply engaged in healing. Cahn has spent almost half a century working shoulder to shoulder with people who are left out of the American Dream of prosperity for all. Over two days of leisurely reflections at his home-cum-office in Washington DC, I discovered that in the course of a fiercely hectic life Cahn has converted the outrage he experiences into a form of renewable energy. Taking up a strategic position in the battle of ideas he has concentrated on forging practical solutions.

To begin with Cahn was appalled to find that most economists and virtually all of economic policy were oblivious to that realm of life that functions without money. Why, he asked, is money always seen to be in the driver's seat? Conventional economics says this is because it takes money to activate time. But what if money no longer defined all of what society can do? What if, Cahn thought, one person's time could activate the time of another – through a form of exchange that was not dependent on personal favours or even barter. What if time itself could be turned into a medium of exchange? 'Super' was the answer from Dolores Galloway and others like her who were part of the pioneering Time Dollars scheme, which finally answered many of these 'what ifs'!

Dolores's story takes us to Anacostia, a few blocks away from the White House, where survival is threatened by poverty and crime. People from the more affluent side of town avoid even driving through these parts and wouldn't dream of stopping there – unless they are looking for a down-market drug dealer or are not averse to being robbed at gunpoint. Yet for more than a decade now the use of Time Dollars by Youth Courts has helped hundreds of young people to say no to a potentially life-long career in crime.

In 1990 Dolores Galloway was 48 years old, confined to a wheelchair, living alone and dependent on various government social service programmes. Galloway, like many other disabled or elderly and impoverished residents of Anacostia, lived in dread of the next budget cuts in public services. Then, with the help of Cahn and his team, Galloway and her neighbours in a federally subsidised building turned time into money.

The members of this money system simply do things for each other and chalk up Time Dollar credits which then keep going round and round in more and more services and even self-made products. One of the members, in this case Galloway herself, kept a computer record of the credits each member spent or earned. The beauty of Time Dollars, as Nader says, is that 'Government does not control it. It does not need new laws to make it happen. It can spring up tomorrow in a thousand places.'

Much of this has been possible because Edgar Cahn has a finely nuanced understanding of how bazaars and money have worked in the past. It is quite recently that the market was allowed to decide all value for people. The DNA of money and DNA of the human species are not one and the same, says Cahn. Yes, we are a competitive species, but that is only part of who we are. Cahn is a realist driven by the need to rebuild what he calls the core economy. When I asked Cahn to explain 'core economy', he preferred to do so by narrating how his friend Alvin Toffler, the author of *Future Shock,* sums up the Time Dollar perspective for executives of Fortune 500 companies. Toffler asks them, 'How productive would your workforce be if it were not toilet-trained?' Cahn's point is that family, neighbourhood and community rather than market are the home base of our species. Family and community, the incubators for democracy, work ethic, as well as values like trust and reciprocity, are the *core economy*. Hazel Henderson has called it the Love Economy.

Unless this non-market sphere provides the fundamental substratum, there is nothing on which to build a market economy. This may seem absurdly obvious yet it needs reiteration. That is why Cahn has chosen to place himself in the no man's land between these two spheres and attempts to rework their interaction. A Washington DC veteran from the opposite side of the power track, Cahn has spent most of his life 'raising hell and suing the government on behalf of poor people'. Fresh out of Yale Law School in the early 1960s, Cahn investigated the not so visible problem of persisting hunger in the USA. This work fed into a controversial documentary on the CBS network. After a stint as speech writer for Robert Kennedy, Cahn and his wife set up one of the first neighbourhood law offices in the USA, aimed at giving the poor access to the legal system. They also got intensely involved in struggles for the rights of Native Americans and helped to design the Navajo Department of Justice Economic Recovery Program.

In 1980, this hectic life was abruptly interrupted by a severe heart attack at the age of 44. As Cahn lay in hospital recovering from this traumatic close encounter with death, he had another shocking experience. He felt useless. It was then that he was first struck by the possibility of a new kind of money, where the medium of exchange would be *time*. He saw it as a way to ensure that no one need experience the sense of being useless as he had felt lying in that hospital bed.

It was just about then that market fundamentalism was on the ascent. As the Reagan administration settled in, Edgar found that *privilege* now had more protection and moral sanction. Whereas homelessness once seemed like an outrage, now it was deemed to be the homeless people's fault. The withdrawal or weakening of state-funded social services was now presented as not merely a necessary evil but an indirect social good, regardless of the pain inflicted. These trends fuelled Cahn's passion for refining the concept of time-based money.

At just that point, in 1986, he received an invitation to be a Distinguished Visitor and Fellow at the International Centre for Economics and Related Disciplines, at the London School of Economics (LSE). England was familiar territory: he had been here in his youth as a Fulbright scholar at Cambridge University. It was during this study year at LSE that Cahn fine-tuned the details of the Time Dollar concept. He began by studying the nature of money more closely and seeing how every form of currency has built-in characteristics that both measure and shape our social structures. Money's invisible hand of price does indeed help us to deal with scarcity; it also signals quality, frames preferences, and thus modulates choice. But, on the other hand, if conventional money is the only kind we deal in, then tax dollars set limits on public expenditures for solving social problems.

The economists and political scientists at the LSE listened to Cahn and conceded that his ideas were theoretically feasible. 'The first breakthrough came when I understood their language enough to be able to put Time Dollars through a simple, litmus test. Did the *benefit* of earning Time Dollars equal or exceed the *cost* of earning them?' Cahn wrote later in his book *No More Throw-away People*.

> I learned that *cost* didn't just mean money and *benefit* didn't just mean monetary gain either ... Once I understood that personal satisfaction and self-esteem can count in the benefit column, I was home free ... The LSE gave me one other important gift: the imprimatur of legitimacy. It published a paper I had written. That, together with what I had learned, gave the idea of Time Dollars critical momentum.

That nod of academic approval was not surprising. The four core values of Time Dollars readily find universal agreement. One: the real wealth of any society is its people and every human being can be a builder and contributor. This later became the basis for Cahn's rallying call – 'No more throw-away people'. Two: work must be redefined to include whatever it takes to rear healthy children, nurture families, ensure that the frail and elderly are cared for, neighbourhoods are safe and enable democracy to work. At present all of this work is either taken for granted or undervalued. Three: there is need to celebrate reciprocity, the universal impulse to give back. This means that one-way acts of largesse need to be replaced with two-way relations. Or, as Cahn puts it, 'You need me' becomes 'We need each other'. Four: there must be proper valuation of social capital, that essential social infrastructure without which the roads, bridges and other utility lines become worthless. What kind of investments will renew trust, reciprocity and civic engagement?

This was the basis on which Cahn set up the Time Dollar Institute and began experimenting with a new medium of exchange 'designed to reward altruism, to turn strangers into extended family, to rebuild community and to empower persons discarded as useless to define themselves as contributors helping to meet critical social needs'. Time Dollars do this by enabling people to both convert personal time into purchasing power along with helping others in ways that empower both the 'giver' and 'taker'. Cahn explains this with graphic illustrations:

> Leave aside Mother Teresa and Mahatma Gandhi. Ask your mother if she would accept market wages to go next door and clean a sick neighbor's house. Then ask her if she would accept Time Dollars which she could give to Granny across town so that she could get a ride to the doctor. Subtle issues of self-respect are involved. Money can deter action as well as bestir it. One teenager from Anacostia section of Washington, DC, was earning Time Dollars doing yard work for elderly home-owners. The Time Dollars were important, he said, because otherwise his buddies would think he was a chump. Earning something he could give away was a token of status; market wages for the same work, by contrast could have subjected him to ridicule, especially from acquaintances who could make much more by dealing drugs.

Co-production is the term that best explains why Time Dollars work. It enables erstwhile 'dependents' to see themselves as producers and contributors who provide vital help to others. Then the ill are not merely 'consumers' of medical services; they can be 'co-producers'. This approach simultaneously challenged the to-each-his-own market culture as well as conventional charity or social work. As a social work professional, Cahn knew that many efforts fail because they can't elicit participation from the very people they are trying to help. Cahn elaborated this concept in *No More Throwaway People: The Co-production Imperative*, a book he wrote in 2000 'for those who want to do something about the vast disparity between what could be and what is'.

The prefix 'co' connotes a relationship, a partnership that is not necessarily equal; 'production' implies that the consumer is no longer to be regarded as a passive, invisible factor to be taken for granted.

> Just as our body needs its autonomic system and our
> post-industrial civilization requires the environment,
> so too the market economy needs a healthy non-mar-
> ket economy . . . Co-production generates the dynamic
> needed to build those bridges, restructure those rela-
> tionships, restore and preserve the functioning of those
> infirm, impaired, and fragile elements in the non-market
> economy . . . The core values embodied in Co-production
> move in logical progression, from individual to society,
> in expanding concentric circles. They convert individual
> capacity into contribution to others, contribution into
> reciprocal obligation, and reciprocal engagement into
> social capital.

Time Dollars took off in a big way in the early 1990s, with favourable stories appearing in the *New York Times*, *Newsweek* and other leading publications. The US Administration on Aging recommended that public agencies use Time Dollars. The federal government committed $400,000 to pilot projects in different parts of the USA. The Internal Revenue Service declared Time Dollars as tax-exempt – on the grounds that these are non-market transactions.

Time Dollars have continued to grow and produce what Cahn calls 'Numbers with a Heart'. For example, a Health Maintenance Organisation (HMO) in Virginia created a support network for its clients using Time Dollars and thus reduced Emergency Room visits by 39%, and hospital admissions by 74%. This meant not only better quality of life for its members but also lower costs for the HMO. Youth Courts are run by teen jurors who earn Time Dollars. Such courts handle more than one-third of all non-violent first offenders among juveniles in Washington DC. Sentences include community service, restitution, jury duty and an apology. Jurors can cash in Time Dollars for a recycled computer, among other things. Chicago public schools are using Time Dollars to run one of the largest after-school peer tutoring programmes. TimesBanks.org now serves as a link for such programmes spread across 22 countries on six continents.

In the UK the New Economics Foundation has worked with various public agencies to set up a string of Time Banks all over London. In Japan, Time Banks and Time Credits have become central to the Japanese social service and volunteering policies partly through a healthcare currency called Hureai Kippu or 'Caring Relationship Ticket'. Volunteers who help older or handicapped persons in their daily routines earn credits on a 'Time Account' which works like a savings account where the unit of credit is hours instead of the conventional yen. These Time Credits can then be used to receive similar services either by the volunteers themselves or those to whom the credits are gifted. Many of the volunteers simply gift away the credits. The recipients of the care, the elderly, are reported to prefer these Hureai Kippu arrangements since the quality of care turns out to be better than what they usually get from yen-paid social service workers. These time-unit-based services also seem to provide a more comfortable emotional context since most people are embarrassed about accepting anything completely free. This makes the Hureai Kippu both cost-effective and more compassionate than conventional commercial services.

So what do Time Dollars and LETS have in common? Both eliminate interest on money and endeavour to strengthen local economies by empowering community. Yet they also serve entirely different, though complementary, functions. While Time Dollars operate more in the grey zone between the core economy and market economy, LETS aim to strike roots within the market economy and widen its scope. Time Dollars work on the basis of an hour for an hour of any person's time, regardless of the service provided. By contrast LETS more closely mirrors market pricing, even though the value of each exchange is determined more at the community level.

Time Dollars primarily reject the hierarchy of values. They work on creating the external benefit of purchasing power and the internal benefit of personal satisfaction. 'The more you intensify the second power the lower the value of the first,' says Cahn. LETS provides more ready access to essentials like plumbers, electricians and gardeners by, as Cahn says, turning commerce into the cause of promoting local trade and skills. In this sense Time Dollars seem like a weaker alternative since they are rooted in altruistic behaviour. LETS has the ambitious goal of creating a niche for community-based market exchange within the global market economy. Time Dollars are not trying to create an *alternative* market culture. They are 'designed to rebuild a fundamentally different economy, the core economy of home, family, neighbourhood and community – by conferring both purchasing power and psychic reward'.

Thus Time Dollars tend to attract people who are socially, or economically, challenged and unlikely to make use of the LETS system. By contrast, LETS seem to empower those who already have some marketable skills and services. Both systems could well work in a complementary manner. Cahn, characteristically, wants to raise the bar much higher. These currencies are not merely about making money work differently. They are about raising our empowerment to a level where we, as individuals and in communities, try to answer two basic questions: Why are we here? And, what kind of world do we want to leave behind?

Another question hovers in the background. If these concepts are so attractive and workable, why have Time Dollars not flooded the world? Cahn's answer is that this is largely because proving it works is not enough. Wider, all-pervasive application calls for a more radical shift of thinking and Cahn is hopeful even about this: 'We are essentially spiritual forces housed in material bodies ... There are planes of being we don't understand, currents of energy that exceed anything that we are capable of comprehending.' That is why Cahn is certain that we can create social impulses that harness both the long-term interests of the species and the demand for immediate gratification of desires.

Cahn's hopefulness has a powerful, magnetic quality. It is backed equally by dogged determination, attention to detail and unabashed *caring*. It was on this note that our discussions concluded as Cahn drove me to the nearest Metro station – to save me from being drenched in a torrential summer shower.

A GREAT INNOVATION OR CRAZY IDEA?

Community currencies might now be at the same stage that aeronautical engineering was on 17 December 1903, when the Wright brothers first managed to make their contraption airborne. Flying machines were a crazy idea in those days. Even on that historic day at Kitty Hawk, the Wright's contraption stayed in the air for just about three seconds. Yet that mere glimmer of success gave the inventors the confidence to continue their experiments, leading eventually to the prototype that inaugurated the aviation age.

This is a thought worth hanging on to when trying to decide if the excitement about community and other complementary currencies adds up to anything. Some of the greatest innovations tend to first appear in a muddled and confusing form. In the natural sciences there is often little hope for a speculation that does not at first glance look quite crazy. Bernard Lietaer, perhaps the most multi-dimensional promoter of complementary currencies, has clung to this conviction to survive ridicule.

When I met Lietaer at London in 2001 he had just published *The Future of Money* – a book in which he forecast an unprecedented planetary crisis caused by the convergence of four interrelated trends: financial instability, climate change, unemployment and an ageing population in the developed world. While his analysis of alarming trends found some takers in the financial press, Lietaer's projection that complementary currencies would become imperative in the near future was dismissed as absurd. But this Belgian-born former money trader and banker held his ground. It helped that he has an MBA from Sloan School (MIT) and three decades of business experience – including a stint at the Belgian Central Bank. Plus he has closely studied both the tenacity of the conventional money system and the ingenuity of complementary systems. So when his worst predictions began to come true in 2008, Lietaer chose *not* to highlight the insights of LETS or Time Dollars.

As more people became keen to hear Lietaer, he concentrated on a story that global businesses could relate to – the success of a 74-year mutual support circle that has enabled Swiss businesses to weather innumerable recessions and other forms of market turmoil. This mutual credit system, *Wirtschaftsring* (WIR), was initially inspired by Gesell's free money theory and enables members to conduct business with each other using a book-keeping system that serves as a complementary currency. The WIR has approximately 60,000 companies, mainly small and medium business, whose combined turnover in 2007 was 1,640,700,000 WIR francs.

Information technology now makes such business-to-business (B2B) systems even more attractive. At first this seems untenable because multiple currencies would make price formation more difficult and inefficient. That's true, acknowledges Lietaer, but the prevailing currency systems have in any case proved to be fatally complex and brittle. Economists at the IMF have counted 124 systemic banking crises between 1970 and 2007. So why not deploy B2B schemes to offset the instability inherent to the prevailing monetary system?

Similarly, Greco visualises community currencies becoming more mainstream and overlapping with a variety of other complementary currency systems which draw in different types of businesses – retailers, wholesalers, service providers, and even manufacturers. So far community currencies seem to work best in situations where local resources exist but the medium of exchange is scarce, so it helps to have more than one currency in your pocket. But in much of the global South communities are so poor that they must have an input of resources from the outside. That is why micro-credit and the 'credit without collateral' concept pioneered in Bangladesh and India are proliferating across the world. Myrada, a major micro-credit institution in India, has tied up micro-finance with the establishment of community resource centres which enable people to be more effectively involved in village-level government. For many resource-poor communities, community currencies are a relatively more challenging concept.

This could change as increasing access to the internet and mobile phones fosters more self-organising, decentralised, non-controllable networks. This is likely to boost complementary currencies that work for people who are geographically dispersed but virtually linked. Linton visualises a wide variety of money cultures and technologies rapidly co-evolving as more people are able to transfer funds using mobile phones: 'Systems that can support "real" money can readily support other currencies in parallel – how long before we have chips with everything?' As these trends gather momentum, complementary currencies could be deployed to bring resources from outside into severely deprived areas.

'You are doing things that theoreticians haven't got the theory for yet,' Lietaer says to grassroots innovators. 'So go on doing it. Don't be afraid of experimenting with something new, while learning from other experiments around the world.' Mashi Blech has lived this truth for almost 20 years as she grappled with the details of using Time Dollars to facilitate healthcare for the elderly in various neighbourhoods of New York City. There is no direct and simple way to link the hopefulness of Blech's daily work with the *big* events that shock and rattle us – be it the financial meltdown of 2008 or the terrorist strike of 9/11 which temporarily displaced Blech from her apartment since she lives next door to the World Trade Center.

Looking out of her apartment window, the site of ground zero is a stark reminder for Blech that Time Dollars are a barely visible dot on the map of a grotesquely complicated world. Yet the spirit behind the actual Time Dollars is a powerful and elemental force. It draws on a rather simple dictum that innovators have followed through the ages. Mahatma Gandhi put it like this: 'Hesitating to act because the whole vision might not be achieved, or because others do not yet share it, is an attitude that only hinders progress.'

~

That's all well and good, the sceptic might argue, but how does this address the opening questions about challenging money as the predominant tool for communicating about value? Does any of this creative foment really give back the power that reformers feel has been handed over to money? The questions themselves seem fragile when faced with the tenacious power of money to define value and self-worth even if individuals can become indifferent to it.

For instance, George Soros has consistently maintained that money is not to be taken too seriously. You don't have to be a cynic to think that it's easy for a billionaire to underplay money. But Soros is not in denial about the power that money brings him. One part of my conversation with Soros took place as we moved through Bangalore's snail-pace traffic in a chauffeur-driven Mercedes Benz along with Soros's friend Sandra Navidi. At one point in the discussion Soros mentioned that it is his money-making ability more than his ideas that allow him to be taken seriously. When Navidi suggested that Soros's insights and political engagements evoke respect on their own merit, he gently but firmly disagreed. The respect, he knows, derives largely from his money-trading achievements and his ability to back political mission and moral values with big money. Soros sounded neither cynical nor rueful.

It was simultaneously a dispassionate description of a reality that he simultaneously lives within and dissents from.

Money, value and self-worth are not easily untangled. The lure of the innovators is that they tug our imagination to the edge of the possible and beyond. Edgar Cahn's appeal is somewhat visceral when he urges us to remember that restricting the measure of value to money is like seeing reality merely in feet and inches while leaving out time.

4
COMPETING COMPASSIONATELY
THE FREEDOM TO COOPERATE

> As long as we treasure the freedom and oppor-
> tunities that the market economy provides, we
> will have to find a way to live with competition
> . . . But competition without a moral dimension
> is like an elephant gone wild – it will destroy
> the very earth it depends on.
>
> *– Amartya Sen*

A month before the anticipated frenzy of Y2K, a group of Euro-
pean business leaders met with the Dalai Lama in Amsterdam
to consider if 21st-century enterprises have to choose between
compassion and competition. Some time in 2000 I received
a transcript of that discussion from a young activist of the
Tibetan-Indian community. At the time it seemed like a stray
and rare reflective exercise. It was not enough to make coop-
eration and compassion a major focus of this exploration.

The decisive impetus was provided by the free software
and open-source movement and its acceleration into a per-
vasive phenomenon. Linus Torvalds's confident declaration,
'with enough eyeballs all bugs are shallow', gave words to the
instinct with which I set out on this journey. Eric Raymond's

evocative metaphor of 'The Cathedral and the Bazaar' became virtually a lodestar. Richard Stallman, the founding guru of the movement, agreed to meet me for an interview but warned in advance that he had nothing to say about markets for the common good. Yet that meeting with Stallman, in his cluttered office at MIT, became one of the defining moments of this journey. My mission, said Stallman, is the freedom to cooperate.

So I went down various by-lanes to ferret out the possibility of a contemporary gift economy – which had otherwise seemed like the dreamy preoccupation of idealists. In retrospect, I realised that the Amsterdam dialogue with the Dalai Lama was a signal of doubts that trouble those at the core of the prevailing market culture. This section explores some facets of this nascent shift which, as it matures further, could rewrite the operating system of the market.

~

Sander Tideman, a Dutch lawyer, spent many years working for ABN AMRO Bank. Amid the daily preoccupation with stock market listings, mergers and acquisitions it seemed blasphemous to even mention compassion. You just didn't display the softer, kinder side of yourself at a deal-making table, or even openly before colleagues. You had to leave these dimensions of life at home or reserve them for friends. A 'winner-takes-all' variety of competition was the fundamental norm of the trading floor and in striking deals.

Tideman traced this feral variety of competition to a misinterpretation of Darwin's observation about survival of the fittest, which has shaped how we understand 'winning'. For instance, few of us are aware that tennis was once pure play – shared fun with no losers. The ball would be bounced back and forth for the sheer thrill of seeing how long the cooperative exchange could be maintained. Today a game in which a fitter or cleverer person does not win over another is considered boring if not utterly absurd.

Competition, per se, like markets is not the problem. The question is which kind comes to dominate – an individual life, social institutions and the market culture. One dimension of competition pushes us to do better than our best. This is what drove a brilliant young Bill Gates to drop out of Harvard and build a company that led the desktop software revolution. But this creative aspect of competition is quite distinct from the drive to win by obliterating others or dominating over them. It is in the latter respect that a Microsoft finds itself crushing competitors and then running rings around anti-trust laws. And, yet, this is only superficially a *choice* that Microsoft exercises. It is essentially driven by a survival imperative dictated by the market culture within which it operates.

Maximising shareholder value means that a company must stay ahead of the competition in perpetuity. The fact that even a mega-corporation like Microsoft has to constantly do some fancy footwork to stay ahead is offered as evidence of the dynamism of the market. Microsoft's future is no more assured than its predecessor giant IBM's was, or Google's could be. In this context competition is celebrated as an antidote to complacence or laziness. But there are growing concerns that these strengths have a vulnerable underbelly. Is there perhaps something seriously amiss with a culture of commerce in which, across the spectrum, everyone must perpetually scramble for survival either of sheer existence or for positions of power? In his crusade against market fundamentalism George Soros has frequently argued that too much competition and too little cooperation inflicts intolerable inequities and instability which undermine an open and free society as much as complete absence of competition. How, then, is the creative element of competition to be balanced with the pursuit of the common good?

We could start by considering how the Dalai Lama views different kinds of competition. The negative kind is when you want to reach the top, and because of this you actually create obstacles for others. Alternatively, says the Dalai Lama, 'one simply accepts that just like oneself, others also have the right to reach the top, and if one works hard and determinedly with that attitude, then there's nothing wrong'. But even more significantly, he adds, the desire to be the best can be applied to many things, not just to profit. 'One could be the best at bringing the most benefit to people . . . Therefore, I think the desire to be the best is absolutely right. Without that kind of determination there's no initiative, no progress.'

At the worldly end of the spectrum, George Soros has demonstrated another vital distinction. One should distinguish between competing by a given set of rules and the process of making and improving those rules. 'When it comes to making the rules, I'm guided by the common interest,' says Soros. 'And when it comes to competing, I'm guided by my self-interest.' This might be a practical basis for learning, as Amartya Sen has urged, to compete compassionately.

A fine ideal, but can it form the basis of action in the real world of the market as it exists? Let us look for possible answers by exploring several seemingly unconnected trends – starting with the credit card in your wallet. Compassion, as we are concerned with it here, is not an ideal on a spiritual pedestal. It is practically manifest in everyday life through many different kinds of cooperation, such as the kind that makes the Visa credit card system possible.

A brief history of cooperatives is important as reconnaissance for how the necessity of profit can be honoured while pursuing a larger purpose. Cooperatives have done much more than give an edge in market competition to poor or otherwise disadvantaged producers and consumers. They represent a socially anchored business model that has continued to thrive amidst even a feral market culture. And, yet, while the experience of cooperatives is important, this is not the cutting edge of the changes now unfolding which promise to expand bazaar spaces.

Technological evolution has made cooperation a practical and *creative* imperative more than a moral 'choice'. Every time you log on to the internet you are not merely part of a technological revolution but a social and political leap. In order to understand the deeper implications of this transformation we will first make a seemingly tangential foray into the realm of gift culture. The story of gift economies takes us outside the parameters of the market and yet also delves into the complementary nature of gift and commodity exchange.

With this backdrop we can approach the Source War, the story of how free and open-source software could well be the definitive battle in the contest of freedom versus control, creative cooperation versus combative competition, inclusive conversations versus closed-in systems which limit the elbow room for haggling over *value* in a wider sense. All these varied trends are a counter to what Soros has identified as the flaw common to market fundamentalism, geopolitical realism and vulgar social Darwinism – namely, a disregard for altruism and cooperation.

COMPASSION OR COMPETITION: A DIALOGUE WITH THE DALAI LAMA

'I want to have the biggest company. I want to have the most powerful company, and so on. It generates greed. We want to have more employees, more assets, and the shareholders demand that. It doesn't generate sharing at all. The rules of the game are wrong in the Western economy – that's our problem,' says Eckart Wintzen, a co-founder of the European Social Venture Network. Wintzen gets a hearing from business people because he built up the Dutch software services company BSO/Origin into a multinational with an annual turnover of $500 million. Having spent over two decades in decision-making positions where it would have been professional suicide to decry competition, Wintzen is not now being hypocritical. Here is someone with intimate knowledge of how vital competition is to the marketplace. It is the nature and extent of 'having and getting' that he is questioning.

Wintzen is among those who are re-examining how Darwin's observation about survival of the fittest has been misapplied. In reality, the web of life tells a different story. From the cellular level to the interaction between different life-forms we find an intricate overlapping of competition and cooperation. How, then, can our species expect to survive on the basis of competition and a sense of achievement that is anchored in a narrow and limited 'self'?

One of the most compelling incentives for this line of reasoning is the growing realisation that like the oceans, atmosphere, satellite orbits or the internet, the interconnected global economy is a commons. Like earlier, pre-modern, commons the global economy and its market culture require win–win agreements – rules and standards applicable to all users. Otherwise, as the futurist Hazel Henderson points out, if the win–lose variety of competitive behaviour remains dominant the outcome will be lose–lose as most players make suboptimal choices pushing the system over the edge since it cannot absorb risks indefinitely and will eventually break down.

There is another powerful incentive for various kinds of cooperation – which has to do with what really makes us happy. Our physical survival requires food, clothing and shelter but *enrichment* of life depends on freedom, dignity, love, beauty, family, community and compassion. The self-renewing abundance that comes from generosity and a broader definition of 'self' is neither a secret nor rocket science. Yet much of economic theory is based on sweeping assumptions about scarcity and competition without properly acknowledging the human instincts of coordination and cooperation.

In the commercial sphere compassion need not mean boundless generosity or charity. If compassion always meant giving, the Dalai Lama points out, then any company that acted compassionately would soon go bankrupt! Presiding over a dialogue between business people and activists in 1999, he went on to elaborate the Buddhist viewpoint:

> What we actually need to do if we want to help others is *empower* them to stand on their own feet. It's not a question of limitlessly giving without any kind of initiative on the part of the recipient. So I feel this idea of empowering others through one's own help could have direct relevance in the business world as well.

That dialogue on 'Compassion or Competition: Enterprise and Development in the 21st Century', organised by Sander Tideman at the Nieuwe Kerk cultural centre in Amsterdam, brought together those who were keen to step back from the daily life of business to undertake a more ambitious reflection. The Dalai Lama shared that platform with Jermyn Brooks, the global managing partner of PricewaterhouseCoopers, Ruud Lubbers, the former Prime Minister of the Netherlands, Hazel Henderson, Eckart Wintzen and others. Brooks opened the discussion by reminding everyone that it was quite recently that Milton Friedman convincingly argued that 'the business of business is business'. The mere fact that such a dialogue was being convened indicated a decline of Friedman's 'gospel'. Enlightened companies, Brooks observed, are moving on and 'stepping up to the challenge of ethical behaviour without embarrassment'.

This does not mean that the world of business has found a more effective way of ensuring efficiency other than by allowing competition between businesses. But there is growing awareness about the need to go beyond the short-term bottom-line objectives which drive capital markets. The shift has partly been driven by data that shows that a longer-term approach to shareholder value is bringing in dividends. Significantly, this dialogue of business leaders with the Dalai Lama happened within weeks of the first international gathering of triple-bottom-line investors.

These trends validated Hazel Henderson's prediction that the world would now see a greater interdependence between the Four Cs – Competition, Cooperation, Compassion and Creativity. These went on to become the foundational principles of the Spirit in Business (SIB) network which was born out of the dialogue at Nieuwe Kerk. The SIB describes itself as a response to a deep crisis of leadership and business ethics which has resulted from a legalistic interpretation of norms. This degrades both consumer and investor confidence. SIB's mission is to counter this by fostering an alternative business culture. This is done partly by celebrating those companies and individuals who encourage compassion and an ethical culture that is driven from within and goes far beyond compliance with laws.

Those who are tempted to dismiss this striving as do-gooder efforts on the margins of the 'real' business world may, however, relate to Dee Hock's post-Visa mission.

DEE HOCK AND THE PROMISE OF 'CHAORDIC' ORGANISATIONS

Most people who use a Visa card don't know that it is a small part of a radical vision for more humane organisational structures. The story goes back to the early 1960s when the credit card business was in infancy. As the innovation caught on, there was an explosion of banks issuing credit cards, many of them sending out pre-approved cards to just about anyone, including children and pets. Chaos and rampant fraud ensued and the banks soon began to haemorrhage with losses.

In 1968 the Bank of America called its licensees to a meeting in Columbus, Ohio, to find a solution. Dee Hock, then 38 years old, attended that meeting as vice president of a licensee bank in Seattle. He wound up heading the committee that was constituted to sort out the mess. The challenge was to create an organisation that could globally guarantee and clear electronically transmitted monetary information across a web that involved millions of customers and thousands of banks.

At the very outset it was clear to Hock that no existing form of organisation was up to this task. Instead, there was need for a 'transcendental organization linking together in wholly new ways an unimaginable complex of diverse institutions and individuals'. But just how would such an unprecedented organisation be created? Through a slow and painful exercise Hock and his team found a startlingly simple answer: strengthen the foundations with cooperation and then build an edifice that facilitates competition but naturally discourages command-and-control behaviour.

In detail this meant the following principles:

- Participation must be open to all relevant and affected parties

- Power and function must be distributive to the maximum degree

- Decisions must be made by bodies and methods representing all parties, yet dominated by none

- It must seamlessly, harmoniously blend both cooperation and competition

- It must be durable in purpose and principle while infinitely malleable in form and function

- It must release the human spirit and human ingenuity

Activating all these principles seemed impossible to most participants. Yet Hock could see that there was no other way to reconcile the fundamental tension between the member banks' need to compete with each other in the open market and the, even more basic, need for a shared clearinghouse – the glue of cooperation that would make all the links cohere.

It was equally clear that cooperation could not be *enforced* by restricting what members could do. So instead members were encouraged to remain free in how they create, price, market and service their own products under the Visa name. But, says Hock, 'At the same time, in a narrow band of activity essential to the success of the whole, they engage in the most intense cooperation.'

This harmonious blend of cooperation and competition enabled the Visa system to expand worldwide transcending language, currency, politics, economics and culture – connecting over 20,000 financial institutions, 14 million merchants and 600 million people in 170 countries and territories. The annual volume of business is well over $1.25 trillion and grows steadily at the rate of 20% compounded annually.

Visa is only a partial representation of what Hock calls a chaordic organisation – where all relevant decision-making mimics the natural world and flows through the entire system rather than only from the top. The parts of a whole might compete furiously, generating 'chaos', while the whole runs on cooperative mechanisms providing 'order'. Hock coined the word 'chaord' by borrowing the first syllable of two opposites 'chaos' and 'order'.

Long before he found himself in the driver's seat at Visa, Hock was already convinced that command-and-control organisations are archaic, irrelevant and destructive. He became obsessed with three questions that have continued to dominate his life. Why are organisations everywhere, whether political, commercial or social, increasingly unable to manage their affairs? Why are individuals everywhere increasingly in conflict with and alienated from the organisations of which they are part? Why are society and the biosphere increasingly in disarray? Some answers emerged from observing how human systems of hierarchy are out of sync with the web of life. For instance, says Hock, 'Show me the Chairman of the Board of the forest, show me the chief financial fish in the pond, show me the Chief Executive neuron of the brain.' Hock's concept of 'Chaordic Commons' builds on this realisation by marrying individual self-interest with that of community and society as a whole through new forms of leadership and responsibility.

Adulation for his successful leadership of Visa did not alter Hock's own dissatisfaction with the fact that he managed to implement only 25% of the chaordic vision. For example, in his book *Birth of the Chaordic Age*, Hock described how he tried to get the bank owners to keep the partnership open for customers and merchants to join, so that they too would share in the profits. The bank owners refused. Eventually, Hock got tired of beating his head against a stone wall. So in 1984 he quit and disappeared completely from public life to come back ten years later as a crusader of chaordic organisations. 'The concepts of chaordic organisations will take a century or more to mature. The idea is a baby, like a daughter or a son,' says Hock. 'We can have a vision of what it will eventually be. But we won't see that in our lifetime. That's the fun of it, the mystery . . .'

Initiatives like Spirit in Business and the Chaordic Commons play their own vital role, but the biggest push for cooperative behaviour is coming from the cutting edge of technology, where cooperation is emerging as an attribute, not a choice. In *Smart Mobs: The Next Social Revolution* (2001) Howard Rheingold showed how communication and computing technologies amplify human talents for cooperation. This has partly to do with how internet-linked mobile communication devices are facilitating conversation and collaboration of the kind that was not previously possible.

At the core of this technological revolution is a gift culture with profound implications for shaping the future of human civilisation. How we see 'having' and 'owning' is central to the quest for evolving creative forms of competition and cooperation. But, before we venture into the realm of Gift Economy, here is a brief glimpse at the tradition of cooperatives and some of its thriving inheritors.

EARNING EMPOWERMENT: ARE COOPERATIVES STILL RELEVANT?

On a bright spring day in April 2000, Mirai Chatterjee found herself sharing a platform with Bill Gates and World Bank President James Wolfensohn at the East Room of the White House. Chatterjee, then secretary of the legendary Indian women's trade union SEWA, was Bill Clinton's guest at a day-long conference on 'The New Economy'. Just before Chatterjee spoke, Wolfensohn had reminded the gathering that half the world's six billion people live on less than $2 a day and out of this 1.2 billion people live on less than $1 a day. The women Chatterjee works with are in that latter group – some of them earning as little as 40 cents a day by selling vegetables at a street corner, or foraging to collect forest produce or doing some manual work.

The Self Employed Women's Association, better known as SEWA, has over one million members – a small fraction of the 93% of India's workforce that is self-employed or seeks its livelihood in the 'informal sector'. This is a realm where most labour laws do not apply and most institutions of the formal economy do not reach. This overwhelming majority of India's working population accounts for 63% of the nation's Gross Domestic Product and 55% of national savings. Yet this vibrant, dynamic, growing sector of India's economy is faced with many disadvantages. Back in 2000 SEWA's presence on the table at a high-powered White House meeting indicated a higher profile for humanitarian non-profit organisations. But increasingly SEWA's work demands attention as a demonstration of a market culture beyond greed and fear.

SEWA, which is also the Hindi word for service of a volunteer nature, employs cooperation to give a competitive edge to women who were otherwise struggling against impossible odds. Three decades after it was registered as a trade union in 1972, SEWA offers its members a presence in the bazaar and, in some cases, even a toe-hold in global markets. Members include urban vegetable vendors, forest-dwelling gum-collectors, rural-based embroidery artisans and seamstresses who turn crafted fabrics into fine garments.

Behind this success lies a simple cardinal principle: 'Empowerment has to be earned and not given'. This has meant grappling with markets on the basis of collective strength and the confidence that such action can level out the playing field more than does the unfettered pursuit of profits. This is the foundational principle of the cooperative movement worldwide of which SEWA is a more recent and currently better-known success story. That movement began in Britain, at just about the same time that its colonial empire was reaching its peak.

Robert Owen, the founder of the cooperative movement, was a Welshman who had made a fortune in the cotton trade in the first half of the 19th century. He realised that a system that turns everything, including people and nature, into commodities will foster great evils. Owen's answer was to promote villages of cooperation where workers could overcome poverty by growing their own food, making their own clothes, and operating in self-governing communities. Ironically, the two such communities that Owen founded, one at Orbiston in Scotland and another at New Harmony, Indiana (USA), both failed.

Yet the values that Owen promoted had a far-reaching influence. One of his contemporaries, Dr William King, published a monthly journal called *The Cooperator* which offered practical instructions on how the working class could benefit by setting up cooperatives. King's prescription for the woes of the poor was that they cooperate to create their own niches within the larger market. 'We must go to a shop every day to buy food and necessaries – why then should we not go to our own shop?' urged King.

These ideas found a willing audience among impoverished Britons. For example, when the traditional cotton textile industry in the North of England collapsed, the wages of handloom weavers fell from around 150 pence to less than 20 pence.

So 28 impoverished weavers in the small town of Rochdale came together and created the Rochdale Equitable Pioneers Society in 1844 – little knowing that they were destined to be remembered in history as the inspiration for a global cooperative movement

Rochdale was not the first cooperative initiative. But none of the earlier ones had worked quite as well or grown and lasted as long. Each member of Rochdale started by buying one share worth a pound. So the Rochdale Equitable Pioneers Society began with a capital of £28, which was first invested in a cooperative grocery store. The initial stock of this store was so meagre it could fit in a wheelbarrow. From this modest base the cooperative's business grew rapidly because it offered members pure quality, honest measure and the comfort of buying and selling without fear of fraud. Within six years, the cooperative had a membership of 600 people and capital of more than £2,299 – a growth rate that most private companies would envy.

This cooperative eventually expanded to include other enterprises. Its success was attributed to values that became the basis of the cooperative movement across the world and are now known as the Rochdale Principles – open, voluntary membership; democratic control; net surplus going to owner-users; honest business practices; aiming for the common good; cooperation among cooperatives. Throughout the 19th century cooperatives emerged in many fields – agriculture, industry, services and more. In 1895, this momentum led to the formation of the International Cooperatives Alliance (ICA) in London. In 1917 the cooperative movement in Britain formed the Cooperative Party in order to work for its principles in parliamentary and local government. This party is still active and now functions as a sister organisation of the Labour Party.

The fundamental premise of the cooperative movement is a faith in people's natural capacity to improve themselves, economically and socially, through mutual self-help in democratically controlled economic organisations. Until recently, these values were not considered viable on the fast track of the globalised economy but the buzz about 'social entrepreneurship' might now change that. In the heyday of market fundamentalism many cooperatives did feel vulnerable. Some found themselves in direct competition with large transnational firms which have much greater access to capital as well as increasing support from legislative measures. Over the last two decades both media and educational institutions have glamorised businesses which make it big within the frame of Wall Street. By contrast, democratically controlled cooperative enterprises have been seen as do-gooding entities in the 'also ran' class. Cascading failures and scandals of enterprises in the Wall Street mode may change this.

In 1995, when the ICA celebrated 100 years of existence, the cooperative sector confidently reaffirmed that it is uniquely placed to help in harmonising the interests of people in their different capacities – as consumers of goods and services, as savers and investors, as producers and as workers. 'As nation states lose their capacity to control the international economy, cooperatives have a unique opportunity to protect and expand the direct interests of ordinary people,' according to a declaration by the ICA.

Of course, cooperatives, like any other institution, are not immune to corruption or abuse of power by management. And, yet, the vast number of credible and efficient cooperatives constitutes one of the many ways in which commerce can be anchored, or embedded, in social concerns and ethical values. The story of cooperatives is too vast, and well documented, to cover in detail here. By way of illustration let us take a brief look at two of the most famous success stories of this sector – one in Spain and the other in India.

Mondragón

Shortly after World War II, a young priest named Don José Maria Arizmendiarietta settled in the impoverished Basque region of Spain where most youth were compelled to migrate in search of a livelihood. Don José started a technical trade school which included a social and ethical education for the youth. Along with some graduates of the technical school, he set up a small stove factory in 1956. In order to raise capital for the business this team established a cooperative bank, the Caja Laboral Popular, which sought the savings of local people. The founders of the new bank appealed to the people of Basque saying that here was one way to build local industry and keep the youth at home. This enterprise became the flagship of a string of cooperatives founded on Don José's conviction that a humanistic cooperative business could succeed within the capitalist world. More than half a century later Mondragón's thriving cooperatives are a major example of democratic worker-owner industrial enterprises.

For Don José Maria commerce was incidentally a means for amassing wealth and primarily a way of living together in society – of putting Gospel values into the marketplace and factory. Inevitably, this push for a new and reformed social order drew opposition from fellow clergy who preferred not to engage with the economic sphere. 'If the Gospel does not apply to the economy, then to what does it apply?' Don José asked them. Profits from the Mondragón cooperatives flow partly to individual worker-owners, partly into a capital fund and the rest into social funds that provide community benefits. The trade school eventually grew into a polytechnic institute offering high-tech training. The Mondragón network now includes high-tech industrial firms, agricultural networks, schools, a university, retail stores, housing complexes, a cooperative bank, research and development institutes, and a cooperative that provides welfare benefits.

In the late 1990s these units reorganised themselves as the Mondragón Cooperative Corporation (MCC) which describes itself as a business-based socioeconomic initiative created for and by people and inspired by the basic principles of cooperative experience. The MCC is now among the largest and most successful Spanish firms competing in the European Union. In 2009 MCC employed about 85,066 workers and its total revenues were €14,780 million. MCC's assets are valued at €33,334 million. MCC cooperatives annually invest 10% of their profits in activities of a social nature, channelled through the Education and Cooperative Promotion Fund.

Naturally, the MCC too struggles with many of the ecological and social problems that afflict industrial society the world over. According to some observers, the MCC is now more a corporation than a cooperative. However, the MCC attributes its ongoing success partly to the lingering impact of Don José Maria's influence. The cooperatives have reportedly retained a personal nature, where people are given priority over capital and they work in an atmosphere of consensus and collaboration. Terry Mollner of the Trusteeship Institute in the US admires the Mondragón structures because they reinforce trusteeship behaviour while allowing the freedom to go against it.

While Mondragón is internationally the most famous network of cooperatives, two of the other widely celebrated success stories are from India – Amul and SEWA, both based in the state of Gujarat. The story of Amul began in 1946 with just two dairy cooperatives and 250 litres of milk per day. This led to the formation of the Gujarat Cooperative Milk Marketing Federation which by 2008 had a capacity to collect and process over 10.21 million litres of milk per day. This milk is then marketed as cheese, butter, yoghurt, ice cream and chocolates under the brand name Amul.

The Amul network, covering 13,141 village cooperatives and about 2.7 million members, had a turnover of US$1.3 billion in 2007–2008. As in the case of Mondragón, the Amul units consist of producers who now function from a position of strength. However, SEWA has pioneered many ways of enabling the poorest and most disempowered to benefit from cooperative solidarity.

Self Employed Women's Association (SEWA)

The raw energy evident in the workings of SEWA is drawn from India's rich tradition of social and political activism. Yet the actual birth of SEWA was inspired by Israel's cooperatives. In 1970 a young Gandhian trade union leader from India earned a three-month fellowship at the Afro-Asian Institute of Labour and Cooperatives in Tel Aviv. Back in her home town, Ahmedabad, Ela Bhatt was convenor of the women's wing of the Textile Labour Union, which organised workers in the city's textile mills. For many years before that study time in Tel Aviv, Bhatt had been restless about the limitations of the union work. It bothered her that such unions offered no protection or assistance to those who laboured outside the factories and mills regulated by labour laws.

The Israeli experience fascinated and energised Bhatt. There she studied the cooperatives of bus drivers, construction workers, banks and health services. 'I came back wanting to start a union of self-employed women,' Bhatt recalled three decades later. She had no blueprint for how to proceed but two things were clear: 'Unless the self-employed are in the mainstream of the labour movement there is no *movement* worth its name. And since women produce so much they must play a leading role.'

SEWA was created as a unique 'union' since all members are self-employed women, initially the street vendors. In 1974 SEWA set up its own cooperative bank which now has 300,000 members. SEWA has a dispersed network of 98 cooperatives which serve the needs of dairy farmers, artisans, vendors, traders as well as other service providers and manual labourers. The driving energy for this work still draws on Bhatt's fundamental conviction that 'If the poor are organised and build up their strength then social marketing can strengthen the local economy.'

Grappling with markets has been central to SEWA's mission, since its members are the smallest entrepreneurs in the local bazaar. SEWA's growth has been a journey of discovering ways by which these self-employed women can hold their own in a marketplace. At one level, SEWA facilitates exchange of goods between its members: for example, handloom weavers supply fabrics to embroidery artisans, who in turn supply the crafted fabrics to women tailors. At another level, SEWA has helped its farmer members to sell grains directly to big buyers in the national markets, bypassing several middlemen.

Reema Nanavaty, a senior SEWA staffer, says that their activities have been guided by the awareness that when markets are controlled by a few, market fundamentalism tends to flourish. Thus, SEWA's answer has been to create greater access to credit, as well as more equitable meeting grounds where sellers and buyers can meet and negotiate terms. The focus has been on building institutions that can deal with the market process, says Nanavaty, who quit a government job in the prestigious Indian Administrative Service to come and work at SEWA.

For example, here is one of the stories that made SEWA famous among international development agencies. In India the sale of forest produce is regulated by state governments. In Gujarat the state gives licences to merchants for the collection of gum in forests. Tribals and others who live in or near the forest areas do the actual collection and then sell the gum to the licence holders. The licensee then turns over the gum to a state corporation which auctions it to traders. Under this system, most gum collectors were paid as little as Rs.2 or Rs.3 a kilogramme.

With SEWA's assistance women gum collectors formed a cooperative and themselves became a licensee. Suddenly their earnings tripled. But the traders, who were losing business because of this spread of opportunity, formed a cartel which bid down the price of gum at the public auctions, thus wiping out the gum collectors' gains. SEWA responded by pushing for transparency and accountability. It demanded that the state-owned corporation, which auctioned the gum, should set the prices based on open-market research and the gum-collection licence holders should be allowed to sell directly in the open market. It took five years of relentless struggle for SEWA to get the permission to sell in the open market, thus securing enormous benefits for its members.

Then there is the case of SEWA's venture at the Jamalpur Municipal market for wholesale vegetables in Ahmedabad. Here is a classic bazaar at work with the incessant babble of price negotiations, and the bustle of trucks and hand carts ferrying the green goods virtually round the clock. Vegetables and other farm produce keep pouring into Jamalpur from the surrounding villages and are then taken up by retail vendors who supply the fresh vegetables across the city. SEWA members have carved out a niche for themselves here, running a wholesale vegetable business which offers better rates both to sellers and buyers.

SEWA's venture into this wholesale market was initially jeered by established traders – all male. 'Go home, they said to us, this selling is not women's work,' says Labhuben Thakkar, one of the SEWA members who ran the operation. The hostility was not merely gender-related. SEWA's shop did business on a much lower commission of 4%, compared to the 6–10% charged by most other traders. Plus at the SEWA shop the vegetable farmer is treated as an equal, whereas the conventional traders, who are higher up in the caste hierarchy, tend to talk down to the farmers. After an initial daily turnover of about Rs.500 the shop soon had a turnover of Rs.20,000-worth of business every day.

SEWA has also ventured into services like running shops that supply low-cost drugs to the general public, not just its members. This is an enormous benefit for low-income households who spend a big chunk of their monthly budget on medicines. This initiative was supported by an interest-free loan of half a million rupees from the Gujarat Government. SEWA's medical stores are able to supply drugs cheaply by sourcing directly from manufacturers and eliminating many layers of middlemen. While the average retailer has a 15% profit margin, SEWA's shops work on a margin of about 5–6%. The revenue from these shops in turn helps to pay for SEWA health workers, also known as barefoot doctors. SEWA has also worked with *dais*, traditional midwives, helping them to upgrade their skills.

In 1992, SEWA registered the Gujarat Rajya Mahila Sewa Sahakari Sangh which trains women in how to set up and run cooperatives. The Sangh also has an export licence which enables its members, mostly in the sphere of fabrics and crafts, to access markets globally. As fairtrade awareness has grown in the northern countries, products marketed through networks like SEWA have found a sizeable clientele – since buyers know that a good part of what they pay is going to reach the craftswomen.

The successful running of SEWA is the joint achievement of highly trained middle-class professionals and working-class women working in a multi-tiered organisational structure. Combining democratic processes with efficiency has not always been easy. For example, in its initial stage one of the crafts cooperatives was faced with serious problems in how to maintain quality control. Sales were low and stocks piled up. 'So we stopped the work for three months,' recalls Nanavaty. 'Then the craftswomen all got together and themselves came up with a system for ensuring quality control. They also found fair ways of eliminating bias of judgement in the quality assessment process.'

At SEWA efficiency is viewed not as an end in itself but as a by-product of rising self-confidence. This happens when artisans and other producers no longer feel powerless and see themselves as owners and managers. The collective engagement not only sharpens their craft it also creates contemporary business skills. SEWA has played a crucial role in facilitating skill enhancement. It has run full-fledged schools that have taught its members to read and write in Gujarati and English. Some have become computer-literate and learnt to make their own video films. For these purposes SEWA has drawn on the services, often voluntary, of the staff and students of the prestigious Indian Institute of Management in Ahmedabad.

SEWA now consists of more than 26,000 groups, which are organised in nine local economic federations. This network gives the members better information about pricing norms, the prevalent market rates, and market demands – all of which lead to a better bargaining position. The result is rise in income, access to education, better health and education for the members and their children. This is possible because SEWA fosters a work environment and a market culture where self-interest is aligned with collective interest not merely market share. Therefore, SEWA has found that globalisation and liberalisation is a mixed bundle. As Ela Bhatt says, 'I am for privatisation but not the kind of privatisation which is only for MNCs and big companies. The street vendor and milk producer are also private sector.' So far globalisation has very selectively expanded opportunities. Most small producers are left feeling more vulnerable and insecure in the globalised economy. Plus the wages and productivity of the unskilled are lagging far behind. The increased mobility of capital and skilled labour has further reduced the bargaining power of unskilled workers.

Looking back on the last three decades, Bhatt notes with satisfaction that SEWA's work has been widely recognised on the global scene. 'At least there is now visibility for the fact that the poor are bankable,' says Bhatt who has retired from the day-to-day functioning of SEWA but remains active as mentor and ambassador. She has served on the board of the Rockefeller Foundation and headed a global financial services network called Women's World Banking. An optimist by nature, Bhatt is also a realist. The political visibility needed to effect macro change is still lacking not merely for SEWA but the cooperative sector. 'What we need to create is a countervailing force and this hasn't happened yet,' she says.

> For this we need political action of the kind that changes
> the balance of power in favour of those left out or dis-
> advantaged. But challenging Wall Street culture is not
> easy because the whole atmosphere has been Wall Street
> oriented. And now look who has ruined the entire world
> economy – from financial crisis to economic crisis to
> now employment crisis which hits the hardest those who
> have not contributed to creating the crisis – whether it is
> financial or climate change.

For all its success, SEWA remains on the fringes of the economy. Bhatt and her colleagues are still told that coopera- tive and unselfish work is unrealistic for society at large, while maximisation of individual utility is a more realistic basis for participating in the global economy. However, Bhatt enjoys seeing SEWA's ground experiences further validated by a growing body of literature on altruistic behaviour and forms of utility maximisation that are not narrowly selfish.

Besides, SEWA's members are bolstered by a sense of inter- national solidarity: for instance, with the 'social economy' phenomenon in Europe. 'Social economy' refers to activities of associations, cooperatives and foundations that are driven not by the profit motive but the need to serve the community. The European Union's social economy is estimated to consist of 900,000 enterprises and represents 10% of GDP and employ- ment. Then there is the 'third sector' of voluntary work and other forms of civic engagement in most societies. An esti- mated 89 million Americans volunteer at least five hours a week in community service. This sector contributes about $16 trillion annually to the economy but this value does not feature in GDP calculations.

In Japan the Seikatsu Consumers' Club Co-op started out as a consumers' cooperative set up by housewives and has become a formidable commercial enterprise serving over 230,000 households. Cooperative entities are estimated to employ more than 100 million women and men across the world. They are spread across a wide range of economic activities – agricultural marketing and supply, finance, whole-sale and retailing, healthcare, housing and insurance, information and communication technology, tourism and cultural industries. So are cooperatives an alternative to the production system dominated by a maximisation of individual profits? Both at SEWA and in the Mondragón cooperatives the answer is sober and unpretentious. As the MCC's website says:

> We simply believe that we have developed a way of making companies more human and participatory. It is an approach that, furthermore, fits in well with the latest and most advanced management models, which tend to place more value on workers themselves as the principal asset and source of competitive advantage of modern companies.

Manifestation of these values is not limited to such famous giants of cooperation – they are evident in the phenomenon of socially responsible investing. On the more radical edge is an entity like the Trusteeship Institute in the US which unabashedly seeks to bring the spirit of love into economic institutions. Drawing on Mahatma Gandhi's economic ideas, the Trusteeship Institute offers consultancy services to companies that want to convert to employee-ownership based on the Mondragón model. Terry Mollner, who founded the Institute, is also part of a wider movement for Community Land Trusts – a mechanism for democratic ownership of land by local communities developed by the Schumacher Society, based in Great Barrington in Massachusetts. Interestingly, the concept and design of Community Land Trust is traced to an American activist who worked with Gandhi's disciples, Jaya Prakash Narayan and Vinoba Bhave. In the 1950s and 1960s, Bhave walked across India urging large landowners to voluntarily hand over some of their surplus land to those who had none or too little.

Contemporary initiatives draw on Gandhi's ideas about democratic and cooperative control of resources and economic activities. At the heart of these processes is a challenge to the empires of commodity. This is a reminder that in essence no one really owns anything. Sooner or later we all die but many things, particularly land, live on. Since a person's life is a short span of time relative to the potential future of the planet, says Mollner, it follows that the proper relationship of the human being to anything is that of a trustee. This was the basis of the movement Bhave led and called Bhoodan, literally Land Gift. Bhave, then, and assorted people in the cooperative movement today, are drawing on an ancient awareness that was alive in societies across the world until the industrial revolution and the rise of free-market culture turned bounty of nature into commodity: 'What is given away feeds again and again, while what is kept feeds only once and leaves us hungry.'

GIFT ECONOMY

Varkari yatra

As the monsoon goes into full swing over western India, in June every year, a singing river of pilgrims unfailingly flows towards the temple town of Pandharpur. It has been this way for about 700 years. Over a million men and women of the Varkari community set out from their homes, scattered over that region, to walk hundreds of miles in countless little processions that take two to three weeks to reach their destination. They are brought together by love of community, shared values of generosity and devotion to Lord Krishna – the deity who stands akimbo in the form of a small black-stone statute in the inner sanctum of the Pandharpur temple. On *ekadashi*, the 11th day of lunar cycle, of *Ashad*, the sixth month in the Hindu calendar, this stream of humanity flows into the temple town in a glorious celebration.

Tar roads, motorised vehicles and the countless distractions of modern life have irrevocably altered the terrain traversed by these pilgrims. Yet the Varkari *yatra*, or journey, retains most of its traditional form and spirit as a decentralised, self-managing mobile gathering of people from all classes and castes. For centuries the residents of towns and villages en route to Pandharpur have been hosts to the pilgrims of the Varkari yatra. Some of these host families still feed hundreds of pilgrims every year. Here is a living gift culture that can trace its roots back for millennia, in virtually all cultures, based on the precept that what is given away feeds again and again. This is not altruism as the modern mind understands it. Rather it is acknowledgement of a natural law. Just as the planted seed multiplies, so unconditional generosity replenishes goodwill, well-being and thus can secure material plenty.

It is vital to note that the Varkari yatra has always co-existed with market exchange. An annual mobile retreat, the yatra allows everyone from landless peasants to urban rich to temporarily withdraw from daily family obligations and market relations. The vast majority of pilgrims now organise themselves in groups where individuals pool their own resources, or accept contributions from family and friends, to make collective arrangements for food, tents and other essentials required for the journey to Pandharpur. Since the number of pilgrims has swelled from thousands to over a million some buy food along the way. But it is commonly said that even today a pilgrim can set out on this journey without a single paisa and yet not go hungry all the way to Pandharpur.

It is significant that this grand annual event and other such phenomena are barely visible to most residents of metropolises. The Varkari's world has few points of intersection with modern India and its efforts for a place on the world stage. Many of the Varkari probably see their own experience of the yatra as being in an entirely different domain from their job or businesses or livelihood. The marginal farmer merrily singing along in the procession to Pandharpur would look agape at anyone who suggested that he carries the DNA of a gift economy, a way of life that is not merely a link with the past but could also shape the future.

What is a 'gift economy'? Today this term crops up in a wide variety of endeavours for more creative and just economic systems. It features prominently in speculations about how we might have a market economy but not a market *society*. Yet isn't the proposition that 'what is given away feeds again and again' merely romantic idealism? Can the material and economic arrangements of the 21st century be influenced by this ideal?

Gifts, even when they are material things, emanate from the realm of spirit and essentially fulfil our need for connection – not just with other humans but with nature and a possible hereafter. Gifts are not to be confused with charity or philanthropy, which is a one-way giving often based on pity or benevolence. The distinction between commodity, charity and gift rests on an awareness of the *spirit* which imbues a gift. Here is a small story that illustrates how cultivating such awareness has been a challenge across the millennia.

As Jesus was preparing for crucifixion a woman devotee came with the finest oil to anoint his head. Some of the disciples were quick to suggest that it might be better to sell the expensive oil and give the money to the poor. This is when Jesus said 'Ye have the poor always with you' – a loaded statement which has often been interpreted to mean that someone or the other will always remain poor.

It is much more likely, suggests LETS pioneer Michael Linton, that Jesus was referring to those who are poor in spirit. In his classic book *The Gift: Imagination and the Erotic Life of Property*, Lewis Hyde concurred with this view and offered a beautiful interpretation of that biblical story:

> They (the disciples) are thinking of the price of oil as they sit before a man preparing to treat his body as a gift of atonement. We might take Jesus' reply to mean that poverty (or scarcity) is alive and well inside their question, that rich and poor will be with them so long as they cannot feel the spirit when it is alive among them.

By focusing on the commodity value of that oil, the disciples have failed to be moved by the sacramental spirit of the oil and the woman's gesture of love and reverence. That oil represents the purest kind of gift there is – a giving that asks for nothing in return and is ever abundant. The 'poor' referred to by Jesus are those who cannot feel this spirit of ever-renewing bounty. Such gifts are not *lost* by being given away or shared. Thus it has been suggested that the gift is an emanation of Eros: 'to speak of gifts that survive their use is to describe a natural fact: libido is not lost when it is given away', wrote Hyde.

Of course not all gift-giving is an expression of unconditional love. Gifts have also been an expression of power and prestige from before the beginning of recorded time. The Queen of Sheba's visit to King Solomon 3,000 years ago is still remembered for the competitive gift exchange between the two monarchs. There was a practical reason why status and gift-giving were closely tied together in the ancient world. A person's standing within the community depended not on what he or she could personally consume but on how much they could give away. Hoarding earned the worst kind of disrepute. Even in the 20th century the Maori lived by the view: 'Give as much as you receive and all is for the best.'

Long before the dawn of history, when our ancestors lived by hunting and gathering, the status of a hunter was determined not by how much of the kill he ate himself but rather by what he brought back for others. Thus, once again we are drawn back to the opening scenes of our journey – that summertime gathering place on Menatay before the arrival of Henry Hudson. The natives of the Americas were still rooted in a gift economy while the Europeans came from a culture that had come to be dominated by commodity exchange. That is why Christopher Columbus and others who followed were baffled by the initial generosity of the natives. Later European settlers exhorted the natives to switch to commodity exchange in order to become 'civilised'.

Marrying gift culture with commodity exchange

Our journey into gift culture has two major guides: the early-20th-century French scholar Marcel Mauss and Lewis Hyde, a professor of creative writing at Kenyon College in Ohio, USA. Mauss drew on both ancient texts and anthropological research to show that elaborate gift-based systems of exchange were also a form of economy even though they bore no resemblance to what Adam Smith and his inheritors understood as 'economic'.

The notion that commodity exchange is a higher form of civilisation was a key element in the rise of the market from the 18th century onward. It followed that progress in the world would now be measured by the ability to accumulate material goods and money, even if some of the wealth is later given away through philanthropy. This partly explains why Bill Gates as a billionaire philanthropist is treated as a folk hero and Tim Berners-Lee, who gifted us the World Wide Web, is not a household name.

This does not mean that premodern societies managed without a sense of property, or lived entirely by gift exchange. Even ancient tribal societies had a clear sense of property but made a sharp distinction between gifts and capital. According to Hyde, they lived by the code that one man's gift must not be another man's capital. This meant that if one clan transferred wealth to another clan, usually in the form of cattle or grain, these goods had to be consumed by the recipient and not invested for growth. Turning the gift into capital meant that the recipient clan became indebted to the gift-giving clan. The key element about the gift spirit was continuous flow and circulation – so that 'A' gifts to 'B' who then gifts to 'C' and so on. Such a system not only kept goods and services in circulation it also defined political relationships and ranking.

Long after surplus accumulation became a way of life in the ancient world, wealth was more a matter of prestige than utility. Power and self-importance were very much at play but consolidated more through gift-giving than hoarding which brought dishonour. So there was accumulation but no maximisation of individual utility as the modern economist understands it. Mauss's research revealed fairly enlightened societies in a state of 'perpetual economic effervescence', where, in some cases, goods and services circulated without sale, purchase or speculation.

Many cultures described gifts as property that perishes. Gifts are perishable in the sense that they are given away without a 'deal' to get something directly in return. And, yet, in all gift economies something inevitably did come back to the giver, even though this was not an explicit condition. This made gift exchange emphatically different from barter. Barter involves lots of talk, haggling, to strike a bargain. A gift is given in silence.

Since such premodern systems of surplus accumulating societies were imbued with religious elements, classical economics either failed or refused to recognise them as 'economic' systems. The seminal contribution of Mauss and other 20th-century scholars was to show that there have been *economic* systems based on gift exchange that served multiple functions without the commodity culture that came to dominate in Europe from the 18th century onwards. More importantly, this demonstrated that the commodity exchange of the modern market system was not a universal truth.

For instance, civilisations on the Indian subcontinent evolved intricate and sophisticated mechanisms of gift exchange which were not merely religious rituals but a mechanism for exchange and distribution of goods and resources. These systems co-existed with commodity exchange – the latter involving individual contracts, a money-market with coins, fixed weights and negotiable prices. India's particular mixture of gift and commodity exchange was defined by the system of *varnas,* or castes.

Quite another kind of gift culture was alive among the Trobriand Islanders of the South Pacific right into the 20th century.

The Trobriand culture was based on elaborate rituals of gift exchange, in which the ceremony and meaning attached to the act of giving was more important than the intrinsic value of the item itself. The gifts, many of them ceremonial artefacts made out of shells, moved not only from person to person but from island to island. Today the Trobriand culture is taken as an inspiration for a paradigm of wealth in which 'to possess is to give', where the owner of something automatically becomes a sharer, a trustee.

On the other side of the Pacific Ocean the natives of north-western America, from Vancouver to Alaska, lived by a good-will ceremony known as Potlatch – a Chinook word which originally meant both 'to nourish' and 'to consume'. In the 19th century the word was adopted into the English language as meaning 'gift' and 'giving'. The potlatch is a ceremonial practice in which the individuals hosting the gathering give away most, if not all, of their material goods in a show of good-will to the rest of the tribe or visiting tribes. As the gifts pass from hand to hand they become an instrument of social cohesion. Since this sense of collective is highly valued, generosity in the potlatch was also a way of maintaining social status. The practice is still alive among Native Indian communities of the Pacific Northwest.

Most of these societies saw market exchange as a necessity but as a relatively base activity. This is because reciprocal exchanges tended to nurture community life, with its guarantees and security, while market exchange is potentially alienating. That is why many cultures evolved market exchanges but kept them at arm's length. For example, even the Trobriand islanders simultaneously operated through commodity exchange, known as *gimwali*, and a gift-based reciprocal system known as the *kula*. These two systems co-existed but the *gimwali* was kept peripheral. Commodity exchange was a necessary way of engaging with the world outside the tribe: that is, the world beyond the periphery of the gift circle with all its intricate obligations and rights.

In some form or other these traits persisted in most societies even while commodity exchange gathered greater importance and momentum. The domination of commodity culture in Western Europe coincided with the Protestant revolt. After that everything from land and labour to culture came within the fold of pure commodity exchange with its compelling lure.

The no-strings-attached benefits of pure commodity exchange allowed the individual freedom and mobility that were often not possible within the traditional tightly knit community. But there was a catch. It was accompanied by the rise of the detached, self-made person who must carefully compartmentalise his and her spirit from the realm of material exchange. The 'bleeding heart' now became a pejorative term referring to the person who lacked the ability to limit compassion. And yet, as Hyde says, 'the sentimentality of the man with the soft heart calls to us because it speaks of what has been lost'.

This sense of loss finds expression today in a wide range of efforts, mostly in northern countries, to recover and rebuild community. And yet the demise of gift culture has implications far beyond the quality of community and family life. The cutting edge of efforts to reclaim gift culture is in the realm of knowledge and information. Virtually all progress in knowledge has depended on ideas and insights contributed by individuals as a 'gift' to the wider society or a fraternity of scholars. In this sense the term 'academic freedom' refers not merely to the freedom of individuals but to the freedom of *ideas*. But what happens when the flow of ideas and insights is governed by mechanisms of the market, expressed partly through tighter and tighter patent regimes? The free flow of ideas is constrained when they are treated more as commodities.

So are gift and commodity exchange irreconcilable? All possible answers are subjective and ideologically coloured. For example, in the 1960s, a stream of New Left thinking called anarcho-communism argued that tribal gift economy systems are an ideal worth recreating. This utopian vision has few takers today. Most creative energy is concentrated on trying to marry gift and commodity exchange. Interestingly, Hyde's inquiry into gift culture began on the assumption that it was utterly irreconcilable with the cold market culture. However, having journeyed through time, cultural history and contemporary developments he came to a different conclusion.

After all, Logos, or Reason, which is the seat of market culture, is as much a part of the human spirit as Eros – the principle of attraction and union which is the source of the gift spirit. So what is the middle ground between gift and commodity? This question excites a wide range of people – from political activists who are battling excesses of the dominant market culture to computer software 'hackers'. There appear to be broadly four trends.

One: there is a struggle to recover those areas of life and work that are better suited to gift culture but have been taken over by commodity exchange and relations. Edgar Cahn's efforts to win more space and respect for the 'core economy' and 'love economy' are part of this struggle.

Two: there are efforts to save and nurture parallel spaces and institutions where reciprocity, mutuality and cooperation are still the norm. The Varkari yatra described at the beginning is an example of such a phenomenon thriving on its own.

Three: there is the hope that a widening of gift culture spaces could make the commodity exchange culture more humane, more socially responsible than it is at present.

Four, and most significant of all: some areas on the cutting edge of technology have given a new twist to this ancient phenomenon. In some cases information gains rather than loses value through sharing. So forms of exchange and notions of commodity that worked in the industrial age may not suit the information age.

The internet has an inherent gift-oriented, potlatch mentality since people create whole sites to give away ideas, information, links and so on.

Internet and open source as gift culture

Howard Rheingold made the full text of his book about electronic democracy, *The Virtual Community*, available online.
The opening page carries the following message: 'I put these
words out here for the Net without charge because I want
to get as much good information distributed as possible right
now about the nature of computer communications.' But, he
went on to urge those who like his writing to go out and buy
the ink-and-dead-trees edition selling in stores since that
'support will help me spend more time cooking up cool stuff to
post here'. Rheingold is one of the foremost authorities on the
social implications of technology and among the first to see the
link between digital communications and gift exchange.

Clearly this kind of gift exchange is vastly different from the
ritualised systems we observed among the Trobriand Islanders
or the traditional Hindus of India. Yet from email to listservs
and online conferences the key elements of gift culture are
alive – it's open, unconditional exchange in which no direct
return is demanded but reciprocity is inbuilt. Besides, the bulk
of servers that make up the internet run on Apache and Linux
programs – open-source software created by a hi-tech gift
economy that thrives on cooperation and peer-approval as the
basis of competing for prestige and social status.

While market exchange is premised on scarcity and defines
social status in terms of what a person can own or control, the
open-source fraternity is based on abundance since there is
no shortage of its survival necessities – disk space, network
bandwidth and computing power. Gaining prestige through
cooperation is not so much a moral preference but a practical
necessity in this realm since that is what secures the attention and collaboration of peers. Being known for generosity,
intelligence and fair dealing opens opportunities for more free
and open exchange which in turn leads to better and better
programs.

Curiously, this modern phenomenon of prestige as motivation for creativity works much like the primitive gift culture. This is a milieu that frowns upon explicitly seeking or claiming esteem as a reward and honours those for whom the creative task is an end in itself. That also makes it egalitarian. As open-source guru Eric Raymond points out, there is a critical difference between saying 'I'm giving you this reward because I recognise the value of your work' and saying 'You're getting this reward because you've lived up to my standards.'

Few people are aware that this ethos was crucial to many of the inventions that came out of Xerox PARC and are now part of our daily life. In 1970 the Xerox Corporation brought together a team of world-class researchers to work in a climate of free enquiry with the mission to create 'the architecture of information'. The Palo Alto Research Center, or PARC as it came to be known, was a place where genius could flourish without pressure to produce. Over the next two decades, PARC gave the world the prototype of the personal computer, the mouse, the window and icon style of software interface, the laser printer and the local-area network. Partly by omission and partly by commission, all these era-defining inventions went out from PARC in the form of gifts. The inventions were then turned into multi-billion-dollar businesses by companies like Apple and Microsoft.

In conventional business circles PARC became the butt of ridicule for incubating brilliant ideas for everyone else but the host company. But the output of PARC made nonsense of the assumption, basic to the old market culture, that technological innovation is driven by big-buck returns. Inventors of the world-transforming technologies that came out of PARC did not become public figures but they exerted a pervasive influence on 'hackerdom' and on an emergent hi-tech gift culture. Thus the source war could potentially define much more than market culture.

SOURCE WAR

It's not really about access to the source code of computer software. For instance, a part of Eric Raymond's inspiration has come from the 19th-century Russian anarchist philosopher Pyotr Alexeyevich Kropotkin, who was brought up in a serf-owner's family and entered active life with a great deal of confidence in the necessity of commanding and ordering. 'But when at an early stage, I had to manage serious enterprises and to deal with (free) men, and when each mistake would lead at once to heavy consequences, I began to appreciate the difference between acting on the principle of command and discipline and acting on the principle of common understanding,' wrote Kropotkin in *Memoirs of a Revolutionist*. 'The former works admirably in a military parade, but it is worth nothing where real life is concerned, and the aim can be achieved only through the severe effort of many converging wills.'

This 'severe effort of many converging wills' is precisely what a project like Linux requires because, says Raymond, 'the "principle of command" is effectively impossible to apply among volunteers in the anarchist's paradise we call the internet. To operate and compete effectively, hackers who want to lead collaborative projects have to learn how to recruit and energize effective communities of interest in the mode vaguely suggested by Kropotkin's "principle of understanding"'.

The source war is a contest between open creativity and repressive control, between the freer conversation of bazaars and the relatively restrictive ownership patterns of the dominant market culture. Yes, there are shades of the anarchist, hippie culture of the 1960s. But a decade after *Forbes* magazine noted the rise of Linux with a cover story titled 'Peace, Love, Software', it is clear that the challenge to the status quo is far more substantial. Even the caricature of David-like hackers slinging it out with the Goliath-Microsoft has worn thin. What we have here, as Linux coordinator Linus Torvalds says, is 'a more organic way of spreading technology, knowledge, wealth, and having fun than the world of commerce has ever known'.

Eric Raymond's evocative metaphor of the *cathedral* alludes to the command-and-control model of old-style commerce, particularly corporations. The *bazaar* represents the free and open mingling of minds and wares. The analogy struck Raymond because he found that 'the Linux community seemed to resemble a great babbling bazaar of differing agendas and approaches'. For example, thousands of scattered programmers send submissions for inclusion in the ever-evolving Linux programs and from this emerges a coherent and stable piece of software. Hackers explain this coherence out of cacophony by invoking what has come to be called Linus' Law: 'Given enough eyeballs, all bugs are shallow'.

This is how it works. 'In the cathedral-builder view of programming, bugs and development problems are tricky, insidious, deep phenomena. It takes months of scrutiny by a dedicated few to develop confidence that you've winkled them all out,' wrote Raymond. By contrast the bazaar approach is based on the assumption that bugs are generally shallow phenomena or 'they turn shallow quickly when exposed to a thousand eager co-developers pounding on every new release'.

But how is Linus' Law applicable outside the world of computer code-writers and designers? How and why does this pertain to the wider struggle to build 'bazaar' spaces? The quick and short answer is that it's all about *freedom*. A more thorough explanation requires familiarity with the history and impetus of the community where 'hacker' is an appellation of honour. This has not changed because many journalists loosely use the term 'hacker' to describe cyber-criminals or vandals who break into other people's computer systems. In the words of their first historian, Steve Levy, hackers are computer programmers who are 'adventurers, visionaries, risk-takers, artists'.

Richard Stallman and the freedom to cooperate

For Richard Stallman, the founding guru of the free software movement, it all began in 1982. That was when MIT's Artificial Intelligence (AI) lab installed a new PDP 10 computer which worked on a non-free timesharing system. Stallman was appalled. He had worked in the AI lab since 1971, when he was still a sophomore studying physics at Harvard. He thrived on being part of a software-sharing community that was as old as computers, just like sharing recipes is as old as cooking. But now the rules at the AI were changing:

> The first step in using a computer was to promise not to help your neighbor. A cooperating community was forbidden. The rule made by the owners of proprietary software was, 'If you share with your neighbor, you are a pirate. If you want any changes, beg us to make them.'

Proprietary software had arrived in a big way. Stallman's opposition had little to do with the fact that copyrighted software was becoming a multi-billion-dollar business. His anger and frustration stemmed from practical obstacles and points of principle. At the most mundane level, for example, one of the printers at the AI lab lacked certain features which made its operation extremely frustrating. But the required modifications were virtually impossible to execute because the manufacturers of the printer refused to hand over the source code for the printer's control program.

Above all, Stallman, and scores of other hackers, felt their creativity stifled by the walls and controls that accompanied the rise of proprietary software. Over 15 years later, when I met Stallman, he recalled it as a challenge of making a stark moral choice. He could go along with the emerging trend, amuse himself writing code and make money as well. 'But I knew that at the end of my career, I would look back on years of building walls to divide people, and feel I had spent my life making the world a worse place.'

So instead he made a life-mission out of asserting the freedom to cooperate and became the leading philosopher of a community of hackers writing *free* software. Free as in *freedom* not 'free lunch' or 'free of cost'. Any software is deemed free if the user has four freedoms. One is the freedom to run the program for any purpose. Two is the freedom to modify the program to suit his or her needs. In order to make this freedom effective in practice the user must have access to the source code, without which making changes is either difficult or impossible. Three is the freedom to redistribute copies, either gratis or for a fee. Four is the freedom to distribute modified versions of the program, so that the community can benefit from your improvements.

In 1985 this emerging free software community, under the leadership of Stallman, set up the Free Software Foundation (FSF) as a charity for the development of free software. This Foundation became home to the GNU project and the GPL or General Public License. The purpose of the GPL was to *Copyleft* the freeware. As Stallman explains it copyleft flips the copyright law and instead of privatising software ensures that it remains free. Copyleft protects the four freedom-values and makes them 'inalienable rights'.

This reasoning lies at the heart of why this movement enriches bazaar energies. It challenges the most basic assumptions which advocates of proprietary software assert as 'rights'. Firstly, that software companies have an unquestionable natural right to own software. But copyright is a privilege created by law not a natural right like the right to life or freedom of movement. Secondly, it is assumed that software is a value-free utility. Not so, asserts Stallman. Helping others people is the basis of society and thus preventing people from freely sharing and collaborating in the design of software lowers the quality of life and society. Thirdly, it is assumed that high-quality software would not be designed if the company did not have complete control over its sale and use. The free software movement demonstrated that computer users can share and come up with software of the highest quality.

Hackers tend to scoff at a romantic projection of their reputation-based gift economy. This culture works not because it occupies a higher moral plane but because it serves a technological *need* – to prevent barriers to invention and research. Stallman evokes admiration even from people who don't like him because the GPL model played an important role in the creation of the best technology. A licence system that prevents hoarding of technology naturally ensures that anyone who wants to work on the project won't be excluded from its development. 'The GPL is wonderful in its gift of letting anyone play,' says Torvalds.

Thus, Stallman has been feted as 'the prophet' of the free software movement. Almost two decades after he quit his job at MIT's Artificial Intelligence Lab, Stallman still had a two-room office there. This is a recognition of his stature by an establishment with which he is mostly at odds. Stallman works in a room overwhelmed by stacks of files, loose papers, books and old-style music records. A delicately crafted gold-leaf image of Saraswati, the Hindu Goddess of learning and wisdom, embellishes the wall beside his desk. With his long beard and below-shoulder-length hair, Stallman may look like a hippie but he doesn't relate to that particular era of counter-culture. He found it anti-intellectual and anti-rational. There is just one aspect of the hippie era that appeals to him: the idea that personal success is not worthy of being a prime motivation in life. It's too small an ambition. While Stallman is the founder and torch-bearer of the free software movement, it was Linus Torvalds from Finland and Tim Berners-Lee from Britain who played the decisive role in making it a global and mainstream phenomenon.

Linus Torvalds and the largest collaborative project in history

The theory behind open source is starkly simple. When the source code is free anyone can improve it, change it and deploy it for new purposes. But the improvements, changes and exploitations must also be made freely available. 'Think Zen,' says Torvalds in explaining the logic of open source. 'The project belongs to no one and to everyone. When a project is opened up, there is rapid and continual improvement. With teams of contributors working in parallel, the results can happen far more speedily and successfully than if the work were being conducted behind closed doors.'

Torvalds floated the bare bones of the Linux kernel on the internet while still a university student at Helsinki in October 1991. The program was so raw, he called it version 0.01. By January hundreds of hackers scattered across the world were in regular contact with Torvalds, to create the best operating system around. Some pointed out the bugs, others sent back debugged versions and others made radical improvements. As a workable programme took shape, they decided to call it Linux.

Gradually the hackers cottoned on that Torvalds was a student making a meagre living as teaching assistant with some support from his single mother. Many of them asked Torvalds if they should send him some money for all the work he was doing as their coordinator. No, said Linus, he would rather they sent postcards. He wanted to see just where on Earth each hacker lived. So cards poured in from New Zealand, Japan, the Netherlands, the United States and so on.

Did Torvalds have something against earning money? Not at all. But he had strong reasons for not wanting his fellow hackers to send him money. For one thing he knew he was just following in the footsteps of centuries of scientists and other academics who built their work on the foundations of others. Besides, what he most wanted was feedback and some praise.

So, wrote Torvalds, 'it didn't make sense to charge people who could potentially help me improve my work . . . (being brought up under the influence of a diehard academic grandfather and a diehard communist father had something to do with it as well).' Selling the fledgling Linux might also have moved it into the proprietary realm and locked up the source code.

Above all, Torvalds and fellow hackers wanted to have full and open access to all future improvements. 'It made sense to me that the way for Linux to develop into the best possible technology was to keep it pure. If money was to get involved, things would get murky. If you don't let money enter the picture, you won't have greedy people,' Torvalds wrote years later. While Torvalds insisted on calling himself an accidental revolutionary, he clearly had more innate political conviction in him than he was keen to broadcast. By the time he wrote his youthful biography in 2001 he was quite emphatic about his conviction that 'Greed is never good.'

The first-generation free software hackers were themselves a bit stunned by the success of Linux. 'Who would have thought,' wrote Raymond, '. . . that a world-class operating system could coalesce as if by magic out of part-time hacking by several thousand developers scattered all over the planet, connected only by the tenuous strands of the Internet?' Eventually, Torvalds himself called it 'the largest collaborative project in the history of the world'. What started out as an anti-copyright ideology became instead a superior method for the continuous development of superior software.

Why not a Berners-Lee Web?

In the same year that the kernel of Linux was first floated on the internet, a young British software engineer unveiled a program that made the World Wide Web possible. The emergence of the internet itself has been a vast collaborative effort. But it was the crafting of the Hypertext Mark-up Language (HTML) and the Hypertext Transfer Protocol (HTTP) that brought order to cyberspace and gave us the easy-access internet that we now take for granted. Tim Berners-Lee created these protocols and released them as a global commons. He did not patent them. It might have helped that he was based at an academic research institution rather than a company.

Berners-Lee's driving motivation was to ensure that the fundamental value of the Web would be created by its users. He designed the hyperlink protocols to serve this purpose. As the language of web pages, HTML encouraged participation by ordinary users, not just software experts. Tim O'Reilly, the leading publisher of open-source literature, has observed that it is odd that HTML is generally not thought of as open-source technology. However, its openness was vital to the explosive spread of the Web. 'Barriers to entry for "amateurs" were low, because anyone could look "over the shoulder" of anyone else producing a web page",' wrote O'Reilly.

In 1999, *Time* magazine listed Berners-Lee as one of the 100 Greatest Minds of the 20th century. In its profile *Time* wrote:

> He designed it. He loosed it on the world. And he more than anyone else has fought to keep it open, non-proprietary and free . . . You'd think he would have at least got rich; he had plenty of opportunities. But at every juncture, Berners-Lee chose the non-profit road, both for himself and his creation.

Refusing to patent the protocols he crafted, or build a company around them, was for Berners-Lee both a technological and ethical imperative. This was the only way to ensure its universality, as opposed to various competing webs. In any case cyberspace makes old notions of copyright somewhat absurd. Every time you access material in cyberspace, when it appears on your computer screen, it has already been transferred, if not actually copied, from one computer to another! Thus, conventional concepts of intellectual property don't quite match the abstract information space.

Berners-Lee is now based at MIT where he runs the World Wide Web (W3) Consortium which coordinates Web development and establishes technical standards for its infrastructure and applications. It was not until 2004 that Berners-Lee was bestowed a British knighthood. He accepted the honour as 'an endorsement of the spirit of the Web; building it in a decentralised way; of making best efforts to keep it open and fair; and of ensuring its fundamental technologies are available to all for broad use and innovation, and without having to pay licensing fees'. And then he raised the bar a bit higher, asking both creators and users of the internet to share a responsibility. Precisely because information technology changes the world, said Berners-Lee, 'its practitioners cannot be disconnected from its technical and societal impacts. Rather, we share a responsibility to make this work for the common good, and to take into account the diverse populations it serves.'

Open source burst upon the corporate world in 1998 when Netscape released the code of its Navigator 5.0 Web browser. At this juncture some hackers adopted the term 'open source' as a more accurate reflection of their purpose. 'Free software' left many people with the impression that such software was hostile to all patents and also anti-commercial. By the end of the 1990s, Linux was the operating system for the vast majority of Web servers and Linux-based companies having successful IPOs. Microsoft's toughest competition in the field of Web servers comes from the Apache program, which is open source. BIND (Berkeley Internet Name Daemon), a critical facilitating program for the internet, runs on open source. The Internet Engineering Task Force which sets standards operates on an open-source ethos. The participatory nature of the exercise is reflected by the term used for proposed internet standards – Request for Comments (RFCs).

But how do the insights and innovations of the open-source phenomenon truly energise bazaar energies in a wider sense? After all, sceptics have alleged that open source destroys value.

Does open source destroy value and other questions

Hackers tend to be more fun-inclined rather than anti-money. Where survival is more or less assured, passion beats money as a motivator. This is as true for playwrights and sportspeople as for entrepreneurs or software engineers. Above all, what seems to drive the open-source hackers is the chance to work with the world's best programmers, not the few who happen to be employed by their company. Many are driven by the need to earn the esteem of their peers. But this may not be a life-defining mission for everyone. For some hackers open source is just a convenient tool, devoid of any ideological passion. In *The Cathedral and the Bazaar,* Raymond identified 19 lessons of good hacking. The first lesson is that all good software starts by scratching a developer's personal itch. By contrast, Raymond observed, in the corporate world many 'software developers spend their days grinding away for pay at programs they neither need nor love. But not in the Linux world – which may explain why the average quality of software originated in the Linux community is so high.'

Creative effervescence is well and good but what about money? Are the proponents of open source indifferent about making money? Not at all. A piece of software is not 'free' because it is given away for nothing or at a low price. Stallman has frequently urged his followers to charge a substantial fee and make some money since redistributing free software is a good and legitimate activity. 'I'm not against making money,' says Stallman, 'I only say don't make money by ways that hurt other people.'

Similarly, Torvalds is clear that money is a good reward for hard work and 'it certainly is handy when it comes to filling up the gas tank in my BMW'. Torvalds could drive around in a BMW, within a few years of leaving college, not only because he took a job at Transmeta Corporation in Silicon Valley but because he happily accepted the stock options that Red Hat, an open-source company, offered him as thanks. And, yet,

Torvalds turned down a $10 million offer from a London-based entrepreneur who wanted him to lend just his name to a fledgling Linux company: 'He [the entrepreneur] couldn't fathom that I would turn down such a huge amount for such little heavy lifting. It was like, "What part of ten million dollars don't you understand?" '

Similarly, many of the stars of Silicon Valley called Torvalds when he first moved to live there, among them Steve Jobs. It was not much of a conversation. Jobs's pitch to Torvalds was that if he wanted to capture the desktop market he should join forces with Apple. Torvalds's answer: 'Why should I care? . . . And my goal in life was not to take over the desktop market. (Sure, it's going to happen, but it's never been my goal.)'

Why, then, does the open-source movement seem utopian to outsiders? Perhaps because open-source culture is perceived as disrespecting the profit motive. After all, attaching more value to creative freedom rather than to monetary returns is a different kind of 'profit' motive. This is partly why Microsoft gets to play the role of imperial bully in the Source War. In the 1990s, Microsoft waged war against the GPL, dubbing it a 'dangerous' and coercive licence, since it insists that even modified versions must be free. But, as Stanford University's Lawrence Lessig, an authority on cyber-law, pointed out, a condition is not itself coercive: 'If it's not coercion for Microsoft to refuse to permit users to distribute modified versions of its product Office without paying it (presumably) millions, then it is not coercion when the GPL insists that modified versions of free software be free too.'

Lessig illustrates what is at stake by offering an analogy from the legal realm. Laws control society justly only when there is transparency – the terms of the law are knowable and controllable by those it regulates. In the sphere of law creativity and incentives do not depend on perfect control over the products created. 'Like jazz, or novels, or architecture, the law gets built upon the work that went before,' wrote Lessig. 'This adding and changing is what creativity always is.

And a free society is one that assures that its most important resources remain free in just this sense.'

Therefore, the world governed by computer code must operate on the same values as modern democracy – liberty, equality and fraternity. For instance, Torvalds has pointed out that if the logic that's used against open source were applied to government, then there would always be one-party rule:

> With one party you don't have to worry about getting agreement with other people. The reasoning would follow that government is too important to waste on the give-and-take of openness. For some reason people see the fallacy of this argument as it applies to politics and government, but not as it applies to business. Ironically, in business it makes people nervous.

Of course, change is scary. Staying with the status quo seems a safer way of deciding where a company can or will go. Provided, adds Torvalds, playing it safe is more important than being hugely and unpredictably successful. So why, then, does free and open software appear anti-commercial?

Stallman has persistently insisted that freedom of software is important first and last. 'If it's bad for business that's tough; in general what business wants is not that important,' Stallman said when I met him. But then, as our conversation deepened, I realised that in essence what Stallman is saying is this: give primacy to social needs and let business fit itself around what is good for community and secures other people's freedom.

But all hackers do not share Stallman's, and the Free Software Foundation's, anti-hoarding zeal nor do they see cooperation as a supreme value. Raymond, Torvalds and others represent a less confrontational, more market-friendly strain in the hacker culture. The emergence of Linux from the mid-'90s onwards gave the pragmatists a definite edge. Today countless hackers work for commercially successful open-source companies like Red Hat. Yet, interestingly, many of them remain firmly opposed to direct-revenue-capture licences. This is largely in order to preserve the advantages of peer review and the gift culture that feeds it.

Senior Microsoft executives have been known to denounce open source as 'an intellectual property destroyer'. It is trade legend that, back in the late 1990s, when one of Microsoft's senior engineers suggested that the company should give away its Web browser and make it open source, Bill Gates accused the man of being a 'communist'. From Gates's point of view the accusation is valid. Open source does seem to destroy value in conventional Wall Street terms. Even though Linux now dominates the server market and the largest Linux distribution company Red Hat had an annual revenue of $523 million in 2008, that is dwarfed by Microsoft's $60 billion revenue for the same year.

Advocates of open source argue that it eliminates inefficiencies rather than destroying value. But open source rattles business-as-usual in ways that go deeper than the familiar business cycles with their phases of radical innovation, creation and destruction. Rishab Aiyer Ghosh, managing editor of the internet journal *First Monday*, has coined the term 'cooking-pot markets' to express what is afoot here. This metaphor is taken from the tribal past when individuals contributed different items to the communal cooking pot and then shared the stew with no guarantee that what they got was a 'fair' exchange for what they put in, which is a kind of altruism. To some extent the internet is a cooking pot but it does not require any deliberate altruism. Value accrues from the sheer fact that the internet enables continuous interaction of ever-increasing numbers of people at light speed with both flexibility and freedom to trade tangible and intangible goods and services – without any need to keep account of inputs and takeouts.

Thus open source and the internet have brought non-monetary forms of defining *value* onto the centre-stage of both contemporary technology and business. Naturally, those who are steeped in a market culture that swings between greed

and fear view the hacker culture – with its focus on peer recognition rather than how to make a million bucks – subver-
sively anti-business. But gradually more and more people are
beginning to recognise that reputation is itself a form of *value*
which, though quite different from money, works somewhat
like a currency and greases the wheels of the economy. There
was a time, some 30 years ago, when Bill Gates ridiculed the
free software movement – saying why would anyone write
code if not to make money. While Gates does not, as yet, seem
ready to embrace the open-source world-view in its entirety,
he now acknowledges that reputation is as powerful a motivation as monetary gain.

To the extent that Gates is a bit of a weathervane for trends
in the dominant market culture, this is a significant shift. It is
another facet of the 'value' generated by free and open-source
programmers. Back in 2003, during an email conversation,
Raymond had expressed the hope that 'perhaps enough people will learn from us how to organise without coercion that it
will begin to make a political difference'.

Is it a paradigm shift?

Is the open-source phenomenon a sufficiently profound break
from existing knowledge and attitudes to be dubbed a 'paradigm shift'?

Technologically, it is clear that open source and the emergence of the World Wide Web are a multi-dimensional paradigm shift. The natural architecture of participation that they
enable is a radical break from the era of one-way broadcast
communication and other centralised and control-oriented
technologies. How deeply the values and benefits of this shift
will percolate throughout society is an open question.

Torvalds has spoken about feeling a bit like the early scientists whose work was viewed as dangerous, subversive and
anti-establishment. That is how proponents of proprietary
software have tended to view open source. After all, open

source and the internet do restore and widen the primacy of conversation between widely scattered producers and consumers who are independent of big business, government, and other control-oriented institutions. As the *Cluetrain Manifesto* argued, 'Conversation may be a distraction in factories that produce replaceable products for replaceable consumers, but it's intimately tied to the world of craft, where the work of hands expresses the voice of the maker.'

For instance, 'Creative Commons', a US-based non-profit organisation, has been inspired by the Free Software Foundation's GNU General Public Licence to create a middle ground between copyright laws that lean towards total control and a complete 'copyleft' approach. Creative Commons' free tools enable authors, scientists, artists and educators to use the 'CC' logo to indicate 'Some Rights Reserved'. Since it was founded in 2001, Creative Commons has been adopted by millions of users across the world. The best-known illustration of the open-source ethos is the Web encyclopaedia Wikipedia, also launched in 2001, which operates on a GNU Free Documentation Licence issued by the Free Software Foundation. Wikipedia is collaboratively written and constantly improved and updated by some of the over 600 million people who were visiting its site in 2008.

Don Tapscott, author of the book *Wikinomics*, has warned corporations about the folly of fearing these massive online communities since they are here to stay. Such networked communities are engaged in activities as diverse as sequencing the human genome, remixing music, designing software, finding cures for diseases, editing school texts and much more. For instance, an online group of 150 Indian engineers and other professionals has used Yahoo groups to pool ideas on how India can achieve energy independence by 2022 and published the outcome in a book.

Then there is the xigi, pronounced 'ziggy', network, which enables the online world to 'discover the capital market that invests in good'. Xigi.net is designed as a set of open-source market formation tools that capture the zeitgeist of how the investor mind-set is shifting towards a hybrid capitalism. It does this through a creative commons, an open meeting place, which investors and entrepreneurs can tap for information, about risks and opportunities.

Then there are hybrid applications of the open-source approach in the commercial realm. For instance, low-cost, open-source software has been important to the success of Amazon though it does not share or distribute the software that makes it the world's largest internet bazaar for books. And yet Amazon has created a structure of participation that has far-reaching implications since it has connected millions of people buying, reading, rating and reviewing books in an open space. Even more interestingly, as Tim O'Reilly wrote, 'Amazon realizes some of the incongruity between its closed, proprietary code and the many benefits it has received from open source, and it has become a leader in thinking about how to redress the balance.'

Torvalds has noted with satisfaction that what started out as an ideology has proved itself in the marketplace, 'Think of how this approach could speed up the development of cures for disease, for example . . . As the world becomes smaller, as the pace of life and business intensifies, and as the technology and information become available, people realize the tight fisted approach is becoming increasingly outmoded.' And, yet, the success of open-source software cannot be literally applied to other realms. But it certainly poses a creative and moral challenge to intellectual property regimes in other fields that promote secrecy and private control.

However, Torvalds's views are aspirational and not to be taken literally. Open-source champions are cautious about casually or sweepingly applying their principles. For example, most medical research involves resources and infrastructure of a magnitude that cannot be compared with the realm of software design. Raymond urges that the stakes are too high for a frivolous application of the open-source approach, which might undermine the substantial successes of the movement. Why weaken the winning argument for open-sourcing software by linking it to other areas in any manner that lacks rigour?

It is now almost a decade since the open-source phenomenon burst upon the mainstream business world. The free and open-source movement has made its point and yet the wider 'source war' may have just begun. The future of the internet itself is far from secure. For instance, a battle is being waged to protect net neutrality; essentially this means that those who provide connections to the internet should not be allowed to favour some over others. Such neutrality is considered essential to innovation because it ensures that a good idea can compete regardless of where it originated – in a corporate lab or from an amateur working out of a garage. David Weinberger, one of the co-authors of the *Cluetrain Manifesto*, gives examples of how one Canadian company blocked access to a site supporting workers with whom it was negotiating. Just as democracy is about all people being equal and no institutions become too powerful, argued Weinberger, Net neutrality is the essence of what makes the internet a great equaliser. Therefore SavetheInternet.com is a coalition of more than a million people – including businesses and non-profit organisations – working to protect internet freedom. The battles in this realm are likely to intensify as the 'war' over internet freedom is unlikely to be settled anytime soon.

Towards the end of 2010 India's open-source community won a three-year battle to secure Open Standards. The Indian government's Department of Information and Technology finalised a national policy on Open Standards which was welcomed for balancing the interests of business and the rights of the people. Open standards that are royalty-free allow anyone to create applications without seeking permission or payment and are thus more conducive to innovation.

Ironically, at the same time – a few weeks short of the 20th anniversary of the day when the Web first went live on his desktop – Tim Berners-Lee issued a dire warning on the various ways in which internet freedom is being endangered. In an article for *Scientific American*, published in November 2010, he described how some of its most successful inhabitants have begun to chip away at the foundational principles of the Web:

> Large social-networking sites are walling off information posted by their users from the rest of the Web. Wireless Internet providers are being tempted to slow traffic to sites with which they have not made deals. Governments – totalitarian and democratic alike – are monitoring people's online habits, endangering important human rights.

At stake is not merely freedom of speech and thus democracy but the right to cooperate versus the power of command-and-control business models. As Berners-Lee wrote, the Digital Economy Act in UK allows the government to order an Internet Service Provider to terminate the internet connection of anyone who appears on a list of individuals suspected of copyright infringement. What is even more disturbing is that people can be disconnected from the internet or their websites blocked without due process of law.

'The goal of the Web,' wrote its creator, 'is to serve humanity. We build it now so that those who come to it later will be able to create things that we cannot ourselves imagine.'

~

Thorstein Veblen, an American economist, knew back in the 19th century that the ruthless pursuit of self-interest, with its erosion of reciprocity and cooperation, poses more of a practical than moral danger. He feared that reckless self-aggrandisement would deny humanity the advantages that can accrue from advances in science and technology. A hundred years later, millions of people continue to suffer from ailments that could be cured but are not because the afflicted cannot afford the required medicines or medical procedures. In the closing decades of the 20th century, patent regimes across the world tilted away from emphasis on common good to the profit-maximisation of the patent holders, who are now mostly companies, not individual inventors. Philanthropic programmes offering relief to those who cannot afford the market rate for those medicines can alleviate some of the suffering. But these cannot undo the still more serious damage of patent regimes that prevent open access knowledge sharing and thus stifle creativity.

While the free software and open-source movement has been advancing, ancient common knowledge has been claimed under patents. In perhaps the most quixotic case of this kind, the University of Mississippi Medical Center took out a patent on turmeric. The healing properties of turmeric, which the university claimed to have 'discovered', have been common knowledge in Indian households for centuries. The patent was challenged by the Indian Council of Scientific and Industrial Research and later struck down. Similarly, Jeremy Rifkin's Foundation on Economic Trends forged a global coalition of more than 200 organisations from 35 nations to legally challenge the granting of a US patent to W.R. Grace Company for exclusive use of a pesticide extract from India's neem tree – another long-standing and common Indian practice. The larger battle against 'biopiracy' continues.

Impending threat of ecological collapse is inducing some shifts. The World Business Council for Sustainable Development (WBCSD) is collaborating with leading corporations to set up a mechanism for sharing environmentally friendly technologies. 'Eco-Patent Commons' is an online space available to the public. Nokia and Sony, among others, have pledged to release patents into this commons which will enable individual researchers and companies to access knowledge that would facilitate further advances in energy conservation or fuel efficiency, pollution prevention and use of renewable materials, etc. The private equity company Kohlberg, Kravis

& Roberts has taken a creative commons approach to sharing the green business tools it is innovating. Interface, a large American floor tile manufacturer, has set up a consulting arm to share its innovations and help other companies to shorten their learning curve.

However, in many spheres – particularly medicine and agriculture – social groups are in a tough fight for more balanced patent regimes which would give due credit and monetary benefit to the inventor but retain the primacy of common well-being and creative commons. Such movements emphasise that all invention draws on the 'gift', the legacy, of existing knowledge that is already in the public domain. Thus a fruitful model of patents must both acknowledge that gift element and nourish the creative commons, while rewarding the creator of new idea or invention.

This is not a mistrust of the profit motive. For instance, Eric Raymond trusts the drive for profit to do more good and less harm than any other social organising principle: 'Not because I think the drive for profit always has good results, but because the political alternatives normally have evil ones . . . The only alternative to the market is the use of force, whether in its obvious form as private crime or its thinly-disguised from as political interference in markets.'

Essentially, this is a variation of a view that has been expressed repeatedly – from 19th-century cooperatives to Gandhi, and formations as diverse as Mondragón, SEWA, Open Source Institute and Open Society Institute. People are constructive and creative when they are free to join together to help each other in fulfilling the multi-layered needs and wants of life. Therefore, Stallman's critique of global business is not that it is committed to profit-making but that this drives it to secure markets by preventing people from helping each other:

> The Wall Street culture is a form of collective insanity that has won over a bizarre number of people and it closes people to many possibilities. They believe that

> profit motive drives all, when in their own lives they
> know it's not true.

So Stallman is not opposed to patents as such, just those that obstruct further creative development and hurt the users.

From this vantage point 'trusteeship' and 'stewardship' look as natural and inevitable as the desire for personal success and wealth. From the registered cooperatives of SEWA and Mondragón to those hacking away at open-source software we find rich combinations of these traits. American activist Terry Mollner sees these developments as a vindication of Mahatma Gandhi's confidence in cooperation and non-violence as the basis of democracy. Mollner has further enhanced the Sanskrit word *ahimsa* (non-violence) by paraphrasing it as 'loving struggle to agreement'. Or, as Kropotkin said, 'the severe effort of many converging wills'.

That's all well and good but these energies are playing out to a dark backdrop. For instance, Dee Hock is confident about the potential for chaordic organisations but he also cautions that a cataclysmic failure of social institutions and ecosystems cannot be ruled out. For instance, pure supply and demand is turning grains into fuel because that pays better than selling the harvest as food. If this happens on a large enough scale, millions more will starve than are already going hungry. In 2007 and 2008 food riots broke out in countries across the world. If pain on the ground leads to open chaos, there could well be a sharp swing towards centralisation of power and control, with widespread loss of liberty and freedom.

And yet Hock is still hopeful. Why? Because, as he often says while speaking in public: 'I'm a sort of command-and-control-a-holic. I may never get it out of my system.' But Hock finds more and more people attempting to overcome their own tendency to command and control. For instance, the growing emphasis on 'emotional intelligence' within the corporate world has brought basic cooperative values to the fore as companies find that a work environment of fierce competition fosters mistrust and leaves people feeling bruised and isolated. By contrast, a culture of cooperation fosters free exchange and mutual well-being.

Those who take these trends seriously are not deluded utopian seekers, in denial about the warts-and-all reality of the human condition. They merely pay closer attention to the reality that human traits manifest themselves in startling combinations – compassionate *and* competitive, cooperative *and* selfish.

Ancient dilemmas of the human condition are not being wished away. But they are now being playing out on a stage where the stakes are higher than ever before. Are we, as a species, sufficiently evolved in humility, intelligence and spirit to balance chaos and order, cooperation and competition, compassion and brutality? No one knows. But, as Hock says, 'It is far too late and things are far too bad for pessimism. One must try!'

5
COSMOPOLITAN LOCALISM
WALL STREET, MAIN STREET AND BEYOND

My backyard is this fragile planet.
– Amy Domini

The gigantic multinational protest outside the WTO's ministe-rial meeting in Seattle made the cover of most international magazines in the concluding weeks of 1999. More than the protest itself, the way the story was reported set the coordi-nates for this journey.

Some of my friends and colleagues were in that crowd surging against the barricades at Seattle. I knew that they were not anti-market or anti-trade in quite the way that many reports depicted them. But then just what kind of markets and commerce will work for those who feel run over by its prevail-ing form? No one seems to know for sure; yet a wide variety of possible answers are blowing in the wind.

Following some of those clues, I've realised that the image of two clear opponents facing each other across the barricades is a distortion of reality. Local and global, bazaar and the market are interlocked in a four-dimensional puzzle, some-what like a Rubik's Cube.

~

When the first aircraft struck the World Trade Center on 11 September, the greenmarket farmers at the base of the twin towers had just got into full gear for the day. A couple of hours earlier, they had unpacked their trucks to set up roadside stalls displaying piles of farm-fresh fruits and vegetables. Some of the early-morning regulars, mostly stockbrokers, bankers and secretaries, were briskly picking apples, or a pint of fresh orange juice when the explosion overhead shook the earth.

As the lethal debris came raining down like mortar fire, farmers and customers dived into the trucks. Only two of the farmers managed get their trucks out. Others just ran, leaving their vehicles and goods to be crushed under the rubble of the collapsing towers. It is not surprising that this little farmers' bazaar barely found mention in the media blitz that followed. Compared to the global businesses on Wall Street, the fate of that roadside *haath*-like space did not seem to be linked with the lives of people across the US, let alone around the world.

That farmers' market in the shadow of the WTC brings alive the imagery of a pyramid with a few big and powerful entities towering over a mass of dispersed, relatively unorganised, energy at the base. It brings the tussle between local and global, small and big into sharp focus through the most basic of all needs – food. Those roadside stalls are also a reminder that the term 'market forces' should never be accepted without closer examination. 'Pure' market forces had deemed hundreds and thousands of family-run farms to be unviable. But, given that tiny bit of space on the pavements and public squares of New York City, hundreds of such farms have become profitable.

Millions of farmers and other small producers across the world do not get such a break. They feel done in by an amalgam of trends that crowd under that all-purpose umbrella-word 'globalisation'. Their howls of pain can sound like a rejection of global interdependence and markets. Actually the angst and frustration is caused by dwindling of spaces – spaces for fair exchange, for combining community and business, for defining value through more than money – or even other than money.

Like the gatherings of the Native Americans centuries ago, possibly at that very spot, the farmers' bazaar below the WTC was not just about buying and selling. It was more fundamentally a point of human connection. For weeks after 11 September, customers and farmers who did not even know each other's names scoured other greenmarkets of Lower Manhattan desperately seeking the reassurance that the familiar faces were still around, still alive. As one farmer recalled, 'I can't tell you how many people searched us out at other markets to find out if we were all right, when all we wanted to know was whether they were all right.'

However, this need for human scale face-to-face exchange pales in comparison to the still more basic need for sheer survival. The realisation that business-as-usual cannot meet the world's food needs over the next half-century inched closer to a consensus in 2008 when the United Nations-sponsored International Assessment of Agricultural Science and Technology for Development (IAASTD) released its report. This assessment, done by hundreds of scientists from 60 countries, concluded that industrial agriculture controlled by large private companies cannot ensure food security. Suddenly, innovations in spheres like that greenmarket in Manhattan seem more significant than a quaint niche phenomenon. Such bazaar spaces are now seen as incubators of vital food solutions, part of a global movement that is simultaneously political and commercial – which treats food primarily as a gift and secondarily as a commodity.

Conversations outside the market have been buzzing with anxieties about our dwindling food security for well over a decade. Networks of scientists, activists, farmers and just plain citizens have thus been forging solutions that challenge globalisation in its present form but celebrate global interdependence as a kind of 'cosmopolitan localism'. Ethical investing pioneer Amy Domini's picture of the fragile planet as her backyard is expressed in innumerably diverse ways. One small example of this can be observed in New Delhi every year on Mahatma Gandhi's birthday. An Indian organic agriculture group Navadanya, or Nine Seeds, celebrates the day by holding a memorial lecture to honour a British botanist, Sir Albert Howard – whom they regard as the founder of modern organic farming. The lecture is usually delivered by activists of food-related issues from across the world, such as Carlo Petrini, an Italian, who is leader of the Slow Food phenomenon – also known as a global 'eco-gastronomic movement'.

Such gatherings illustrate that the clash is not essentially between local and global. It is more a contest between different levels of the economy, globally and within each nation – from grassroots to enterprises housed in towers like WTC. There is more here than an obvious contest between the small, who crave a more level field, versus the big who benefit from sheer size and sharp asymmetries in access to information and resources. Size matters but in essence this is a conflict of mind-sets – of values and priorities which determine how individuals and companies define and pursue self-interest. Even if the global marketplace were a more level field from top to bottom, what kind of social energies, public policies and business culture will broaden conversations and help secure our species' future on this planet?

There are no easy or rapid-assembly solutions. Even those plunged deep into the fray are not sure precisely how to foster more equitable relations – among humans and between our species and the natural world. But one thing is clear. What we venture into is a global *agora* where commerce, though vital, need not be dominant.

MASS SUICIDES: WHODUNIT?

On a blistering summer day a procession of handloom weavers poured through the main street of Chirala. The protest march was part of an eloquent tableau. In the background was a large signboard of the 'Hollywood Shoe Centre' with a black and white image of Charlie Chaplin but made-in-India footwear inside. The pervasive littering of Pepsi signs was backed by actual products. Tiny tea shops displayed 'Pepsi' emblazoned mini-refrigerators stocking the cheaper small-size bottles in search of cash-poor consumers in this small town of Andhra Pradesh in southern India.

Outside these *pucca*, or fixed, shops was the ebb and flow of roadside vendors – potters with their piles of earthenware, others with steel and aluminium pans, some hawking ripe mangoes and others selling mounds of fragrant, heat-defying flower *venies* which women wear in their braided hair. The variety and vibrancy of this scene is common from Chirala to Cuernavaca in Mexico. Amy Domini, a financial innovator from Boston, visited one such bazaar in Cuernavaca and marvelled at how it all comes together without corporations, shareholders, a central purchasing office to negotiate prices or a marketing department. Not only do consumers find the goods they desire but millions of individuals – across the world – depend on such bazaars to make their living.

The ancestors of the handloom weavers have been buyers and sellers in such bazaars for at least 2,500 years. Their craft and its ever-changing business models have gone through all kinds of ups and downs. But there is no communal memory of a spate of suicides. The immediate trigger for that protest march was the excess of funerals. More than 300 weavers, in and around Chirala, had killed themselves in less than a year. From a distance this could seem like a bizarre form of *choice* – opting out of the struggle to find affordable raw materials and then markets for their products. For those actually locked into that reality, it was a preference for death at one go, rather than the tortured ebbing of life on less than Rs.50 ($1) a day.

This pain propels multinational protests against globalisation on the streets of major world capitals. Since the mid 1990s 'Globalise Liberation, Not Corporate Power' has been the common rallying call at the barricades. Most of the protestors are striving to level the field between the small and the big, the local and global, our species and the rest of life on this planet. This is pressure for not merely free but also fair exchange. Otherwise, as Professor Muhammad Yunus of Grameen Bank says, globalisation looks like a 'highway for the big guys who can have their heavy trucks to go through but the Bangladeshi rickshaws will be blown away'.

Some media reports have tended to denigrate the protestors either by over-simplifying and romanticising their story or flatly condemning them for being anti-market. For example, after the landmark protests against the WTO at Seattle in 1999, the entire cover of *The Economist* was cast in mourning black. In the centre was a tiny picture of a malnourished Indian child. The editorial inside ridiculed the agitators for questioning the superior wisdom of 'the market' and held them responsible for that child's starvation. The editors of *The Economist* saw no need to substantiate or explain their allegation. They relied on readers to share their conviction that markets = freedom = plenitude.

This line of reasoning did not work for the 100,248 Indian farmers who killed themselves between 1993 and 2003. Presenting this staggering fact to the Indian Parliament the minister for agriculture made some vague connection with severe indebtedness. Similar reasons were cited by friends of Lee Kyoung Hae, a Korean farmer who stabbed himself to death in the midst of a protest rally at the WTO's Cancun meeting in 2003.

Where do we pin the culpability for these mass suicides?

The scene of the crime is strewn with multiple, overlapping clues. It might help if we venture forth by resisting easy, but futile, anger. This is hard to do when you are confronted by the stunned silence of the farmers' orphaned children. But the truth is indeed multi-shaded since the links between cause and effect are arranged in concentric circles.

Our leading clue is embedded in the opening scene of farmers below the WTC. It alerts us to an uneven contest which emerged about two centuries ago. The Americans call this quarrel Wall Street versus Main Street.

This conflict runs to the very roots of the American republic – from Alexander Hamilton versus Thomas Jefferson onwards. Those farmers at Manhattan's greenmarkets are direct descendants of the losing side, the one led by Jefferson. Diverse and diffused forms of the tussle are manifest in countries across the world. It holds the key to most of the other clues.

In their most literal form, Main Street and Wall Street are places we all know. Main Street is that local hub where we go to buy what we need in everyday life. Wall Street is the location of finance capital – a narrow lane at the southern tip of Manhattan, The City in London, Dalal Street in Mumbai and so on. Even their metaphorical form is globally familiar. Main Street's 'David' to Wall Street's 'Goliath'; the local shopkeeper or even manufacturers of goods or services versus the Wall Street speculator or feral raider of the kind immortalised by Gordon Gekko in the film *Wall Street*.

Manhattan's greenmarkets represent the primaeval and sustained base of the market economy. Below them is what Fernand Braudel called the 'lowest stratum of the non-economy', or, as contemporary activists calls it, the Love Economy of community-based structures of cooperation and mutual care. The rising sun of the market has universally dehydrated and shrunk this base of both non-economy and most basic local economy – casting a darkness which has driven many, like those farmers and weavers, to desperation.

Of course, Main Street encompasses much more than those greenmarket farmers in New York or the simplest vendors in bazaars like Cuernavaca and Chirala. It's also more than the millions of small and medium producers who join in the dance of supply, demand and prices. Main Street is traditionally associated with a *mind-set* embedded in a respect for sufficiency and stability – even if that means moderate returns.

In sharp contrast to this the Wall Street culture values speculation and worships the ability to take big risks and make windfall gains. The proliferation of this culture to the very base of the economy is one of the whodunits. Yes, the farmers 'chose' to shift from subsistence to commercial farming for higher payoffs. From the vantage point of Wall Street this is the only road to progress and thus a good thing. If the farmers miscalculated their own ability to manage the risks, that's their individual problem. The same view point also isolates, and ridicules, the farmer who turns his back on windfall profits to stick with diversified cropping systems, ecological sustainability and relatively modest returns.

'It is a choice between the classical values of stability and sufficiency and the modern drive for bigger and larger and quick riches. With each choice there are costs involved,' says Girish Sohani, a senior manager at the BAIF (Bharatiya Agro Industries Foundation), a non-profit organisation in western India. Thus, champions of bazaar spaces now also equate Main Street with a culture that makes a distinction between needs and wants, emphasising actual well-being and *'well-th'* over just paper wealth. The popularity of a triple bottom line may now be growing but the realm of Wall Street remains firmly committed to money as the primary, if not exclusive, bottom line.

Reliance on money as the most reliable criterion of success and the only rational modus operandi is another accused whodunit.

The essence of this view was expressed by Lawrence Summers when, as US Secretary of the Treasury in the Clinton administration, he declared that 'Financial markets don't just oil the wheels of economic growth; they are the wheels.' It follows that what keeps Wall Street happy is good for Main Street, not the other way round. This has openly been the conviction behind the globalisation of the market. The reasoning is that benefits trickle down and add to vibrancy on Main Street. But does this happen on a sufficiently large scale? And what is the social cost? The distribution of power from Wall Street to Main Street is an old failed promise. People on main streets across the world know this by instinct and experience. Even the growing presence of small individual investors in stock markets does not remove the inherent anomalies.

Main Street is not merely a metaphor but a more robust model of market economy. Wall Street pushes for deregulation of both domestic and global markets with unfettered flow of capital and trade. It equates a rising stock market with good health of the economy. Thus any policies that constrain the accumulation of paper wealth, in the form of stock value, are deemed bad. By contrast the Main Street model is identified with investments in public infrastructure and human capital, fair trade based on labour rights, employment security and corporate social responsibility.

Lee Kyoung Hae, the anguished Korean farmer, experienced globalisation as the opposite of all this. It was after Korea joined the WTO that Kyoung Hae could not even recover his cost of production. The WTO became, for him, the prime accused whodunit. Shortly before his bizarre protest suicide at WTO's Cancun meeting, Kyoung Hae wrote about feeling traumatised and helpless ever since his neighbour, another farmer, gave up by drinking a toxic pesticide.

Thus farmers and small producers from virtually every nation surge against the barricades – from Seattle to Cancun to Hong Kong and on – riling against multinational corporations, the WTO, the IMF and the World Bank. But the source of the problem is what Fernand Braudel identified as the anti-market zone which he described as the real home of capitalism where 'the great predators' roam. These are not just monopolists or cartels but others powerful enough to bend the rules and undermine fair play in the market place. However, in our times the story has become still more complicated.

Take the case of Billy Tiller, a cotton farmer in Texas, who is hardly a capitalist in that predatory sense. But if you ask Mama Idrissou, a farmer in West Benin, then Tiller is certainly a creature of the anti-market zone. Both farmers grow cotton. Back in 2003 Tiller was spending about $860 per hectare to harvest 825 kilos of cotton. Idrissou was spending just $380 per hectare to reap 1,400 kilos. This should have made Tiller uncompetitive, compared to farmers like Idrissou. Instead, Tiller made much more money than Idrissou. That is because the Texan got a share of the $3.9 billion that the US government gave in subsidies to its cotton farmers.

An investigation by James Meek of the *Guardian* estimated that Africa lost $301 million in just one year, 2001–2002, as a result of US cotton subsidies. Benin alone lost 9% of its export earnings, which far outstripped what it got as debt relief from western nations. *Such manipulation of global commodity prices illustrates yet another element of whodunit.* This injustice is extensively documented and has been the core area of disputes in the WTO. And yet the superpower versus small nation conflict can easily draw attention away from the fact that within their own context individual farmers like Tiller are also struggling to make ends meet. As one American cotton farmer told the *Guardian*, 'We are not trying to beat up someone overseas here. In one sense we have more in common with these people in Africa than their government and our government will ever have.'

How can this be? The problems of small and medium farmers in the US are quite different from those of their counterparts in Benin or India or Mexico. Yet they have a binding agent – an unrest about how subsidies actually work. Ironically, the raw idea of subsidies is anchored in the value of socially embedded bazaars. It is part of Main Street's preference for levelling the field rather than allowing the weak to perish. In practice, subsides have become an instrument for distorting the equation between different levels of each economy and even between Main Streets in different countries.

Vijay Jawandia, a farmer in central India, expresses his angst with a twisted jest. After this life, says Jawandia, he would like to be reborn as a European cow. With a subsidy support of Rs.90/– ($2) a day, that cow is better off than many farmers Jawandia knows – both in India and abroad. But Jawandia also knows that the privileged cow is probably on a corporate farm not a family-owned farm like his own. For example, the European Commission's data shows that 18% of Europe's farms cornered 85% of subsidy payments that EU nations gave in 2005. These were also the largest farms.

In the US, the 2002 farm bill handed out a $125 billion package of state support funds. It is estimated that two-thirds of this package will benefit the top 10% of farms over a 10-year period. These subsidies to large farms on both sides of the Atlantic don't just unlevel the field for farmers like Jawandia all the way out in India, they add to the volume of people in the Western nations who are part of the global South. *This process thus becomes culpable in the suicides of many of Jawandia's neighbours.*

Yet agricultural subsidies are the tip of a much larger trend which unlevels the field between the small and the big of the global economy. For example, The Green Scissors Coalition and Friends of the Earth have identified $33 billion of annual government subsidies in the USA to mining, logging, fishing, farming, arms and energy-production industries. Nearly all the beneficiaries of these subsidies are large-scale, export-minded corporations. The US Public Interest Research Group has found that, between 1991 and 1996, Congressional candidates received more than $89 million in contributions from polluting industries. During that period Congress bestowed $19 *billion* in subsidies on the same industries. This comes to a return of $213 for every dollar 'invested' in campaign donations. The Cato Institute has estimated that the US government annually gives corporations $51 billion in direct subsidies and another $53 billion through various tax breaks.

Therefore, the Geneva-based Global Subsidies Initiative (GSI) tracks and analyses not only how subsidies transfer public money into already well-endowed private hands but how this is slowing the shift towards sustainable modes of development. The GSI pushes for full transparency and public accountability in subsidy programmes across the world – to ensure that subsidies are deployed with precision to deliver public goods to those who have otherwise been deprived. Such efforts enter into the murky terrain where the corruption of public officials, as well as misjudgement of policy-makers, colludes with abuses by 'predators' of the anti-market zone. The decisive role here is played by the state and not just through direct subsidies. It happens through a wide variety of state supports – such as tax-breaks, legal provisions, intellectual property rights regimes – which work to make large-scale production and distribution artificially cheap while rendering much of small-scale production artificially expensive. This not only undermines local economies, in many cases it also damages the environment. Thus American advocates of Main Street rile against 'corporate welfare'.

For example, Michael Shuman, an American lawyer and the author of *Going Local*, argues that

> Depletion allowances and insurance liability limits that benefit the oil, gas, coal, and nuclear industries slow down the transition to community exploitation of renewable energy sources. Below-market sales or leases of publicly-owned land, forests, and minerals encourage overexploitation for export rather than sustainable use for local consumption.

This phenomenon is fairly universal. For instance, in India, BAIF's Girish Sohani says, 'Give us a real market and we can compete. What this means is that prices should not be artificially influenced, such as cheap bamboo for pulp companies, or low contract prices enforced even in buoyant markets.' *The absence of such a 'real', or level, market is another element of the muddle that is driving the farmers to suicide.*

For example, subsidies for fertiliser and pesticide inputs have essentially bolstered the manufacturers while raising input costs of farmers and driving them deeper into debt. Moreover, excessive use of chemical inputs has done extensive damage to soil quality and lowered productivity in the long run. In India virtually all studies on farmers' suicides have identified the overuse of pesticides as a whodunit. Again, this pesticide overkill is due to a combination of misinformation by some manufacturers, or their sales agents, failure of public education services and the anxiety-cum-greed of the individual farmer – the delusion that just a shovel more of pesticide may secure a bumper crop and windfall profits.

However, if you ask veteran organic farmers the overuse of pesticides, or even mono-cropping, are so far downstream in the flow of causes that it is almost frivolous to include them in a list of the 'accused'. *The source of the problem lies about four decades back when the definition of land productivity was taken away from sustained soil-animal-human nutrition and attached solely to annual output that could be sold.* This conversion of agriculture from being an act of husbandry to pure commerce also made it capital-intensive and drew millions of small farmers into credit systems that were either inadequate or corrupt or both. The result: large-scale indebtedness and negligible risk mitigation services. *Again, the whodunit is both public policy and a particular kind of market culture.* The jury is still out on whether this was the only way to feed India's rapidly multiplying population.

The woes of handloom weavers we saw in the bazaar of Chirala at the beginning are broadly similar. The weavers are caught in the twilight zone between a time when traditional technologies, with socially embedded business models, worked well and an era dominated by technologies of mass production organised by the market. What matters to our investigation is that the twilight zone emerged over the same two centuries in which the current tussle between Main Street and Wall Street took shape.

The first blow to craft-based industries was dealt not by superior technologies but by colonial conquest – the most brutal way to unlevel or completely destroy bazaar spaces. Even today not all craft industries are naturally withering away because their time is up. Many, like handloom textiles in India, have the field tilted against them. The mechanisms of finance, credit, research and, above all, of generating raw material are designed largely to serve the interests of mass production. Treating the craft-based industries as cripples requiring humanitarian aid pushes them still further out of the bazaar. Some of those who switch to other forms of livelihood are pulverised by their own lack of experience and missing or inadequate infrastructure. At least one major study into the farmers' suicides in Andhra Pradesh found that many of the dead farmers were earlier artisans who had little or no experience of cash crop cultivation and its risk management. Again, there are no clear fingerprints at the scene of the crime – only the wreckage of a historical process aided by the dysfunctional mechanisms of both state and market.

And, yet, even this does not explain why millions of people at the base of the market economy feel locked into a space with severely limited options. To examine this part of the mystery we have to again visualise Main Street, or local economy, in a literal sense. The 'local' can be variedly defined – as a village, a town or even a region. Now visualise this local economy as a tank that has in inflow and an outflow. A healthy, brimming tank ensures that the people in and around it have sufficient resources to fulfil basic needs – food, shelter, clothing, healthcare, education – and then something more. If the outflow channels of this tank are draining resources out much faster than inputs, then there is less to go around within the ecosystem of the tank. If, however, the inflow and outflow is so balanced that money and resources keep multiplying locally then most, or all, inhabitants of the ecosystem should thrive.

The single largest cause for distress of local economies across the world is not that they are resource-poor to start with but that the surpluses they do generate drain out. This need not be to another country, but just from the base to other levels of the market economy. This is the main reason why those who are struggling to empower local economies in the US and Europe clash with the large chainstore conglomerates. And why there is a hole at the heart of the idea that world poverty can be solved just by large corporations going to the 'Bottom of the Pyramid'. For example, a joint study in UK by The Countryside Agency and the New Economics Foundation collated data from the annual reports of various retail chains to map how much of their gross earnings are then put back into the local area. The highest local plough-back was found in pubs and restaurants, which re-spent 20.6% of their incomings locally. The next best were clothing stores and they ploughed back just 12.9%. From there it is steeply downhill, with supermarket chains ploughing back 10.2% and banks a mere 1%. A poor 'multiplier effect' imperils the economic health of a town or village in much the same way that a poor 'balance of trade' hurts a nation.

The challenge of improving local multiplier links back to the distressed farmers in a bizarre way. More and more farmers now depend on hybrid seeds which are sold under patents that alter the most fundamental practice of agriculture. These patents make it illegal for a farmer to replant a part of his harvest. A large chunk of the surplus generated by the farmer thus gets moved out of the local economy, or out of Main Street and onto Wall Street, since the seed manufacturers are large corporations. The Monsanto Corporation is sitting on possibly the most powerful technology in this sphere – the terminator seed. The technology is designed to prevent 'theft' of its genetically modified plants by rendering the next generation of seeds sterile.

In the villages and small towns of India there is an egg-and-chicken relationship between a poor local multiplier and desperately few non-farm employment opportunities. One study of the farmers' suicides in the western India state of Maharashtra found that through the 1990s hundreds and thousands of farmers found themselves caught in a pincer movement. From one side they were squeezed by declining productivity of soils that had been depleted in the quest for higher and higher annual returns. This led to ill-informed use of chemical inputs which further deepened indebtedness. Plus, the dependence on external inputs further depleted the local multiplier which in turn worsened the shortage of non-farm livelihood opportunities. This was happening in precisely the same decade when those parts of the national economy that worked in the Wall Street mode began bursting at the seams with prosperity. For many farmers there was no mystery to their suffering. They saw themselves as victims of 'market-driven globalisation'.

Consequently, there is now a global demand for greater localisation. Many of the multinational protestors, who surge against the barricades outside WTO or G8 summits, argue that, if production and distribution were more in local control, the terms of exchange would improve and the worst forms of economic distress would wither away. American 'Going Local' advocates like Michael Shuman urge communities to keep their economic multiplier strong by hiring local, buying local, saving local and investing local. The objective is not parochial isolation but interaction with the global market from a position of strength.

However, the lines between Main Street and Wall Street are blurring and shifting in various ways. Let us map a few aspects of the struggle to reframe conversations between different levels of the economy. Remnants of old dogmas, people power versus 'Let us Alone' capital, are not irrelevant. But they mostly mark the points of departure from which contemporary initiatives are taking off. We will examine two broad areas – food and entrepreneurship that grows the local multiplier.

'LOCAL FOOD, GLOBAL SOLUTIONS'

From Sixth Street Manhattan . . .

'We will not have to wait for the last wheat plant to shrivel up and die before wheat can be considered extinct,' Cary Fowler and Pat Mooney wrote way back in 1990. 'It will become extinct when it loses the ability to evolve and when neither its genetic defenses nor our chemicals are able to protect it. And that day might come quietly even as millions of acres of wheat blanket the earth.' Winners of the Right Livelihood Award for sustainable agriculture, Fowler and Mooney were saying what is now widely accepted. If enough diversity is lost, crops will lose their ability to adapt and evolve.

Long before global food scarcity became headline news in 2008, the Sixth Street Community Center in New York and Timbaktu Collective in southern India were engaged in warding off this nightmare scenario. The Sixth Street Community Center serves a middle-income neighbourhood on the Lower East side of Manhattan, not far from Wall Street. Timbaktu Collective works with farmers on the undulating, water-scarce fields of Andhra Pradesh. There is no contact between the two groups and yet they are part of a dispersed sub-surface process that is only slowly becoming visible in the mainstream media. Both entities are in the business of salvaging soils, reviving biodiversity, expanding livelihoods and doing all this by revitalising local bazaar spaces.

Such initiatives are a response to harsh facts. Every sixth person on Earth is chronically malnourished. Poor agricultural practices have depleted one-quarter of the world's soil and the damage continues. One way of not being overwhelmed by these trends is to take a worm's-eye view of efforts to counter them. Let's start with the American end of the story.

If you walk into the one-time synagogue that houses the Sixth Street Community Center, a private non-profit organisation, you will find prominently displayed pale green pamphlets about their Community Supported Agriculture (CSA) link with the Catalpa Ridge Farm nearby in rural New Jersey. The brochure is an open invitation to residents to insure their food future by joining the CSA scheme and promote local food-plant diversity while also enjoying fresh, sometimes organic, fruits and vegetables.

Members of the CSA are somewhat like 'shareholders' of the Catalpa Ridge Farm, which plants over 200 varieties of vegetables and herbs. This is how it works. The city-dwelling consumers purchase a share in the farmers' harvest at the start of the growing season, which then becomes the farmer's running capital. This makes the members of the CSA somewhat like venture capitalists, rather than just customers, because they share both in the farmer's risks as well as the bounty of a good harvest. These 'investors' put down anywhere between $300 to $600 to get a weekly bag of fresh organic produce throughout the growing season. This strengthens the local market and gives the members something that the overwhelming majority of Americans lost decades ago – a direct link with and knowledge about the food they eat. As the CSA brochure says, 'We recognise that obtaining food means much more than standing in line at the supermarket!'

Put like this, it can easily seem like a fringe activity of extraordinarily dedicated people. But both CSA schemes and urban street-side farmers markets are growing. To understand why let us look at the phenomenon from two different perspectives – that of the Sixth Street Community Center's director and food visionary Howard Brandstein, as well as a mainstream Manhattan professional, the journalist John Cloud.

Brandstein, an engineer by training, was drawn into the politics and 'business' of food back in the early 1990s when he tried to get to the bottom of why so many of the young people he encountered at the Community Center were unhealthy. He traced most of their ailments, both physical and psychological, to poor nutrition and a diet laced with toxins. Linking the youth with local organic farms improved their nutrition.

Cloud, who is a writer at *Time* magazine, is one among the 25% of Americans who now buy organic products at least once a week. But he got interested in local food when he found that, even when not organic, it tastes better than what he can get from the supermarkets.

More and more people now prefer fruits and vegetable plucked just a day or two ago, rather than those that have spent weeks in the supply chain of supermarkets. Long periods of storage, they believe, diminish the vitamin content of many fruits and vegetables. Plus, many customers of local farms feel enriched by an even fleetingly visceral link to the land and those who tend it. The US organic chainstore Whole Foods, an over-$5-billion company with 190 locations, now has a strong focus on local foods. This is partly because many of their customers are disturbed by the fact that organic food is spuriously eco-friendly when it has travelled thousands of miles and acquired a large 'eco-footprint'.

For example, Cloud was impacted by the knowledge that a strawberry that gives him five calories consumes 435 calories of fossil fuel when it is transported from California to New York. 'Local' can be variedly defined. Columbia University nutritionist Joan Dye Gussow suggests that 'local' is any place that is within a day's leisurely drive of your home. Yes, that's an entirely arbitrary definition, Gussow adds: 'But then, so was the decision made by others long ago that we ought to have produce from all around the world.' Google's campus at Mountain View, California, has a restaurant called Café 150 which serves only that food which can be sourced within a 150-mile radius.

Since all of this is standard 'market' behaviour involving a jumble of consumer choices, what is its relevance for our quest? Firstly, we need to note that both organic and local foods were incubated in purely civic spaces. They are the outcome of social concerns being expressed through a combination of volunteer effort and the most basic level of bazaar. The market, driven purely by a money bottom line, could neither track nor respond to the fact that in the course of the 20th century the Earth lost about 75% of its agricultural diversity.

Creative problem-solving responses have also initially come from socially and ecologically motivated groups not businesses. For example, the New York-based network Just Food is essentially an activist endeavour. Since 1994 Just Food has promoted a holistic approach to food, hunger and agriculture issues. Their bottom line is not money but the creation of a strong regional food system that preserves ecosystems, reduces pollution, ensures social justice and invigorates the regional economy. Money is an instrumentality but not the driving force. And yet the CSA network makes money for otherwise endangered family farms while also enabling low-income New Yorkers to access high-quality fresh food at affordable prices.

Even the engagement of culinary experts in local food issues is essentially a cultural, rather than commercial, phenomenon. For example, the pioneering Chez Panisse gourmet restaurant in Berkeley, California, dedicated itself to using only fresh, high-quality seasonal and local foods back in 1971. It was not just a clever marketing device to create a unique selling point. Chez Panisse became an inspiration for professional chefs, home cooks and diners who now count themselves as part of the Slow Food Movement, a global network that has been growing since the late 1980s. The founder of the Slow Food concept, Carlo Petrini, defines it as a form of resistance to fast food, fast life, unsustainable farming and the erosion of local economies. Members of the network lobby governments to save endangered foods. Plus the movement finds expression in everyday life through the commercial enterprise of restaurants.

Such concerns first surfaced about half a century ago. The earliest CSAs were formed in Germany, Switzerland and Japan in the early 1960s when groups of consumers and farmers came together in cooperative partnerships to pay the full costs of ecologically sound and socially equitable agriculture.

Some of these partnerships are still thriving across Europe. In Japan, similar schemes known as *teikei* supply food to about 11 million people. The *teikei* system, which also began in the early 1960s, is often cited as a major inspiration for community-supported agriculture around the world. Many of these initiatives have been driven by people who got into it primarily to build and nurture communities. For instance, Brandstein grew up in New York at a time when the city was decaying and so he became involved in a non-profit formation called Community Land Trust Homesteaders which revitalised entire neighbourhoods of Manhattan. Engagement in the politics of food followed from this work within the community.

Wander about Britain and you are bound to run into similar people getting together at a farmers' market be it in London or a small town. FarmersMarket.net estimates that there are 500 farmers' markets across UK offering a wide range of local 'ethically-retailed, reared or produced, foods'. The same markets are also a hub for political action and lobbying to take WTO agreements away from the agenda set by agribusiness. British food activist Colin Hines has called this the mobilisation for local food and global solutions!

Growth of CSA schemes in the US has been exponential, going from two in 1986 to anywhere between 1,200 to 1,700 schemes at present. But half the food sold in the US is now produced on just about 2% of its farms which are owned by corporations and operated more by machines than human workers. There are now approximately just 3 million people working on American farms, while there are 2.2 million in its prisons. The Pulitzer Prize-winning journalist Timothy Egan has consistently documented how pockets of hard poverty have taken shape in rural America 'amid large agribusinesses supported by taxpayers'. Of course, poverty in rural America cannot be traced back entirely to the dwindling of family farms. But the long food chain has created structures that put much less of every dollar spent on food in the pocket of the small farmer. An estimated 67 cents of every food dollar goes to marketers and the extensive chain of storing, packaging, branding and hard-selling farm produce.

All that packaging, refrigeration, advertising, trucking, supermarket fees and so on is great for the GNP. But now people as diverse as Brandstein and Cloud are asking why the quality of their food should suffer in order to grow the GNP. They are also asking if large feedlot-based cattle farms, with their large volumes of pollution, are indeed efficient? True efficiency would come from ensuring that the richly multi-purpose cow dung is fully utilised rather than being rendered a form of waste and pollution.

CSA answers some of these questions by fostering modes of food production which respect the land as a living, breathing entity whose cooperation the farmer elicits. Then all operations – pest control, tillage, fertilisation – are undertaken with close concern for how it will affect the health of the soil, rather than focusing purely on immediate monetary returns. But this requires a radical leap in consciousness. It means accepting that food is not a mere commodity but an outcome of multi-layered relations between the soil, animals, humans and within society.

On the surface, CSA can easily pass off as a conventional market-driven idea. The roots, however, reach into fairly radical ground. Their ideological nutrients include influences like Rudolf Steiner's concept of a world economy based on more equitable forms of ownership. While many CSAs are on family farms, some are on land held by a community through a legal trust. The trust then leases its property long-term to farmers who use the land to grow food for the community. This inherently replaces the employer–employee relationship with an equation of co-ownership. Those influenced by Rudolf Steiner call this an associative economy in which the guiding principle is not increase of profits per se but rather identifying and meeting the actual needs – not just of the people involved but also the land.

Thus activist groups like the UK-based International Society for Ecology and Culture (ISEC) are calling for a bottom-up review of the gridlock between the money bottom line, technological innovation and the crisis of farming across the world. From the earliest factory-made farm equipment to the mammoth grain combines and tomato harvesters in evidence today, says an ISEC report, 'technologies were invariably designed to reduce investors' and industrialists' expenditure on human labour, rather than to improve the well-being of farm laborers and their communities'.

The success of CSA and farmers' markets, even as a niche, broadens the space for some vital questions. For instance, what is truly efficient when it comes to growing food not just for people now alive but generations yet to come? In that context, what kind of farms are 'naturally' viable? What form of agriculture produces better-tasting, more nutritious and non-toxic food? Do some of these objectives clash? Phenomena like CSA illustrate that the conversations of the socially embedded bazaar encompass much more than supply, demand and price negotiations. Above all, such initiatives take the quest to an arena beyond any single power centre – be it a government department, ideological vanguard, a politburo or even a 'best and brightest' kind of liberal elite.

... to Timbaktu

Towards the end of 2006 a few hundred people gathered quietly for a candlelight protest one evening in the heart of Hyderabad, a city known globally as India's second largest hub for information technology companies. The people carrying the candles were mostly urban professionals and activists. They were paying homage to farmers who have committed suicide across India – now estimated to be about 200,000 over the last 15 years. The organiser of the protest was a CSA with a difference. In India the acronym refers to the Centre for Sustainable Agriculture, a non-profit lobbying group that links a wide variety of initiatives to save both farmers and food plant diversity.

Timbaktu Collective, a non-profit group in Anantapur District of Andhra Pradesh, is one such endeavour. Bablu Ganguly, one of the founders of Timbaktu, is an erstwhile city-dweller who has chosen to husband the land. Over 20 years Ganguly has watched a steady and painful decline in the nutrition to the land, the animals and the human beings. He has mapped the acceleration of a process by which nutrition is leaving the area.

About 25 years ago, the farmers in Anantapur switched almost entirely to growing groundnut (peanuts), since the crop thrives in the dry, sandy soil there. Government policies and market forces worked in tandem to facilitate and promote this mono-cropping. Cash incomes rose since groundnut fetched a much higher price than the native crops earlier grown – which included a wide variety of millets. Meanwhile, both the social importance and market price of millets plunged as government policies promoted a predominantly two-staple diet of rice and wheat. The end result is an ecological, economic and nutritional crisis.

The most obvious reason is that relentless mono-cropping depleted the soil and yields declined. Plus groundnut became more vulnerable to pests and diseases. This meant higher input costs and lower net returns for farmers. The resulting indebtedness and depression is one of the reasons that 758 farmers have committed suicide over ten years in Anantapur District alone. Ironically, the millets, which farmers earlier grew and ate, were nutritionally richer than the polished rice which is now the main staple.

Earlier, when groundnut was grown as one among several crops, much of it was either consumed locally as nuts or pressed for oil, at traditional oil-presses. Local crushing of peanuts threw up several by-products, including cattle feed and biomass for renewing the soil. But, when the scale of production rose dramatically, virtually the entire crop was taken

up by traders who supplied the peanuts to large-scale oil manufacturers in other parts of the country. Local value-addition
mechanisms somehow failed to morph to the new levels of
production. Sale of raw peanuts, husk and all, meant an influx
of money but a drain of nutrition for the animals and soil and
of business opportunities for humans.

There was a period in which the Timbaktu community
felt helpless in the face of these circumstances. What could a
tiny non-profit entity do about such large trends? But a group
committed to the motto 'Life We Celebrate You!' and the philosophy of Perma-Culture could not remain aloof to the suffering of neighbouring farmers. Perma-Culture is a way of life,
popularised by Australian activist Bill Mollison, which designs
land management and production in tune with the rhythms of
nature and its ever-renewing bounty. Over 20 years, Timbaktu
Collective has turned its 40 acres of undulating land from a
wasteland to forest by following the principles and methodology refined by Mollison.

Timbaktu's engagement with other farmers in the area
first focused on seeds. Since hybrid varieties of seeds cannot
be replanted after a few seasons, farmers become dependent
either on government seed programmes or companies that sell
seeds. To begin with Timbaktu acted in a social and cultural
domain. It organised seed melas (fairs) and a Dharti Utsav or
Earth Festival. These celebrations, somewhat like the ancient
agora or *haath*, brought farmers together to exchange traditional seeds which some of them had saved over the years. In
some cases the exchange was reciprocal but in others it was
a pure gift.

It was clear from the outset that such symbolic gestures
were not sufficient. Gradually, Timbaktu forged links between
the different kinds of local initiatives, including the credit
lines within women's self-help groups and other cooperatives.
But they knew that the crisis could not be fully addressed by
non-profit initiatives. It was clear that some form of market
incentive had to be found for implementing a wide range of

solutions. So Timbaktu Organic was born as a hybrid of social activism and commerce. The venture started in 2005 with 360 smallholder farmers in 11 villages, covering just 1,100 acres of land. Its immediate aim was to enhance the farmers' income by at least 20%, over three years, and do this through sustainable forms of agriculture. This venture built upon the Collective's various strengths. These include its substantial experience in regenerating wastelands and watersheds as well as its successful promotion of the Mahasakthi cooperative, a women's thrift society network with over 8,023 members spread over 119 villages.

Timbaktu Organic provided marketing support by raising public awareness about the importance of millets. This task was made easier by a higher incidence of diabetes across India and the growing awareness that most millets are a natural antidote for the ailment. Timbaktu Organic floated its own version of a socially responsible investing scheme inviting individuals to invest in the venture at an interest rate of 5% per annum, with a lock-in period of five years. Many, but not all, of these investors are existing supporters and admirers of Timbaktu itself. Once the links had been set up, marketing became simple. By the second business cycle, in 2006, orders far outweighed the production estimate for the next two seasons.

In conventional market terms, Timbaktu Organic would probably be listed under charity or philanthropy not business. But this is social venture capital at work. How else can you set up production systems that benefit the disadvantaged and nurture the environment while also being financially viable? Most of Timbaktu Organic's investors are neither looking for massive financial returns nor wanting to give out grants. Timbaktu Organic aims to meet the demands of its different stakeholders and work on the basis of 'returns'. This ensures scalability, says Ashish Panda, a young graduate of the Institute of Rural Management, who led the team that set up Timbaktu's organic business.

Timbaktu's key innovation has been linking individual investors with such business innovations at the grassroots. Otherwise, a wide range of non-profit organisations have pumped millions of dollars of grant money into creating livelihoods and regenerating the environment. For instance, the BAIF (Bharatiya Agro Industries Foundation) Development Research Foundation has helped transformed thousands of acres of wasteland and enabled thousands of families to live and eat better. Working largely with grant funds, some of them from Western foundations, BAIF has provided inputs of knowledge and marketing infrastructure that increase the yield from the land while enriching, rather than depleting, the soil.

Founded by a Gandhian social worker almost half a century ago, BAIF is now run by highly qualified technical and management professionals. Even though BAIF is essentially a social organisation, the processes it facilitates are anchored in the bazaar. The Gram Vikas Mandals, or Village Development Committees, through which BAIF's schemes are implemented, are a cross between a cooperative and business association. Thus, the endeavour is not just about planting and profitably harvesting trees and crops. It is fundamentally about harvesting an overall prosperity, says Girish Sohani, executive vice-president of BAIF. However, even the most successful of such initiatives seem to shrink in significance when placed in the wider context of India. Meanwhile, organisations representing large and medium farmers are still relying largely on direct support from government. Even the Rs. 60,000 crore loan waiver granted by the Indian government in 2008 is expected to largely help this segment of farmers.

However, efforts as diverse as Community Supported Agriculture in the USA and Timbaktu in India have made a seminal contribution in widening the conversations about food security, good health and sustainability. For instance, the Gates Foundation and the Kellogg Foundation are funding a project called Community Food Enterprise which is a response to worldwide evidence that the shift in favour of local food offers small farmers and other entrepreneurs an opportunity to strengthen food security. This project aims to locate the best examples of community-owned food enterprises world-wide, analyse why they work and identify lessons that can be applied elsewhere.

Meanwhile, as the scale of the impending global crisis of food security threatens to outstrip the worst fears of food activists, the need to build upon all positive clues is escalating dramatically.

In 1996, the FAO convened a World Food Summit at which 180 countries pledged to halve the number of malnourished people by the year 2015. A mid-term review by FAO showed that this goal is unlikely to be met and that's not the worst of the news. Those who have been eating well for decades may now find that their food security is in peril. International conversations facilitated by the FAO are throwing up a consensus about what needs to be done – a global transformation of agricultural methods and their environmental impacts. Food security depends on policies and institutions that empower farmers to revive ecosystems through sustainable agricultural practices. And this, FAO officials have said often enough, depends more on political will than markets.

At the same time pure supply and demand forces are pushing both agriculture and commerce in the opposite direction – with continued mono-cropping of select crops and diversion of a staple grain like corn to produce lucrative biofuels. This not only takes land away from food production; it also further accelerates erosion of biodiversity. In addition, there is the spectre of catastrophic disruption of food production due to climate change. To overcome these crises the FAO has, among other things, stressed the role of local food in improving nutritional quality, as well as empowering producers and consumers. While the potential of organic agriculture in providing complete food security is still under study, the lessons it offers for sustainable food systems have been acknowledged. Even more significantly, the FAO has called for policy initiatives that would help farmers to access technology that complements local knowledge. But this would mean reworking the equation between public policy, farmers and 'proprietary crops' controlled by agribusiness.

The International Assessment of Agricultural Science and Technology for Development (IAASTD) might tip the balance, to put people and planet before profits. This three-year effort by experts from 60 countries concluded that the emphasis of industrial agriculture on food productivity has taken a dangerous toll on biodiversity, environmental sustainability and also increased the gap between rich and poor farmers. It also cautioned that current intellectual property legislation restricts poor farmers' access to technological innovations because it inhibits the saving, free exchange and sale of seeds.

Therefore the IAASTD report, released in April 2008, called for more public investment in research and asserted that food security cannot be left to the private sector since agribusiness focuses on those food crops that make the largest profits. The view that food systems cannot be left to the market alone is likely to keep gaining ground. Even a market fundamentalist would find it unacceptable that so much of agriculture is diverted to produce profitable biofuels that food becomes scarce. In the time that it took for the market to correct itself, millions could die of starvation. And yet food cannot be kept entirely outside the market. Centralised government systems have shown mixed results and tend to be afflicted by chronic corruption.

So what is the answer? CSA in the USA and Timbaktu in India are only glimmers of partial solutions. Interestingly, the British local food advocate Colin Hines himself cautions that farmers markets and local food networks don't come even close to addressing ecologically crises triggered by industrial agriculture. Finding technologies that nurture land, water and food plants to feed the 9 billion people expected to inhabit the Earth by 2050 is also just one part of the challenge. The bigger challenge is what kind of free trade of food is sustainable?

Apples from New Zealand and the USA are now commonly sold in India where there is no shortage of good native apples. Indian apples are in turn exported to other countries. Britain both exports and imports milk in almost equal measure. This trade is viable largely because producers and consumers are not paying the real costs of environmental damage, unsustainable production methods and long-distance transportation. Hines argues that eco-taxation would make some of this trade unattractive and also pay for the costs of fading out damaging agricultural systems and replacing them with more benign ones. But even this may not be enough. Hines also favours import controls to protect those agricultural goods that can be produced domestically. The core objective would be to restrict the power of major food retailers through new competition laws while simultaneously encouraging rural regeneration and employment.

Curiously, while efforts for more holistic agriculture are deemed to be 'social pressures', corporations lobbying for trade regimes that promote long-distance food chains tend to be treated as 'market forces'. The same contrast is manifest in the struggle of open marketplaces where all shape and sizes of buyers and sellers can meet freely.

STREET VENDORS, PUBLIC MARKETS AND SUPER STORES

Twice a week Elizabeth Ryan wakes up at 2 am, packs a truckload of fruits, veggies and other produce of her Breezy Hill Orchard in upstate New York and heads for Manhattan. It's usually still dark and quiet as Ryan and a few assistants set up shop at the Union Square farmers' market. In the first light of day, before the crowds arrive, Ryan has a clear view of the statue of Mahatma Gandhi, which stands at the other end of the Square. It was here, over 30 years ago, that farmers first began making direct kerbside sales to the city folk. 'You develop relationships with people whose name you may not know. Direct contact with the customers is very stimulating, even addictive. Your customers treat you like a folk hero. It's not just about an apple for $1,' says Ryan.

New York City's greenmarkets are the brainchild of Barry Benepe, an architect and urban planner. Back in the 1970s, Benepe noticed that many apple orchards and family farms in upstate New York were on the verge of bankruptcy. Most such farms were too small to enter the sphere of large wholesalers. They were also cultivating varieties of fruits and vegetables that the supermarket system did not favour – either because of shorter shelf-life or their unattractive appearance. Benepe realised that he was not alone in craving the taste of precisely those not-so-attractive but delicious varieties grown by the smaller farms. The result was the birth of New York City Council's Greenmarket programme in 1976.

Greenmarket farmers are simultaneously a community based on cooperation and a space where individual sellers compete. Ryan calls it the purest form of market: 'You keep fine-tuning your understanding of what customers want. Then you know what to bring for sale and how to price it.' Yet the farmers' market is distinctly different from all the other branded businesses that are thriving around it at Union Square because it has an artisanal quality.

While such marketplaces have continued to thrive in the developing world, from Cuernavaca to Chirala, in the US and Western Europe most such markets became virtually extinct as the economy and urban spaces came to be dominated by larger more organised businesses. For example, in 1994 the City of Chicago dismantled its historic Maxwell Street open-air market which once served as an entry point into the economy for the poor and immigrant communities. It was also known as one of the incubators for the Chicago style of blues music. That open and sprawling marketplace has since been replaced by a much smaller, more strictly regulated and structured shopping area with branded products and exotic stores that cater to the city's more affluent consumers.

Public Markets, the American term for such bazaars, are now being revived by civic groups and local authorities. Some of the people who opposed the closure of the Maxwell Street market went on to set up a volunteer-based research and educational project called Open-Air-Market Net. This is a worldwide guide to open-air marketplaces, farmers' markets or other kinds of street vendors around the world. Such bazaars are vital as gathering places for a wide assortment of traders and consumers of different scale.

They also serve as a safety net for people at the bottom of the economic ladder. Here consumers can easily access low-cost goods and services, while even the smallest vendors get a chance to start an enterprise. In affluent countries where email, telephone banking and impersonal superstores have become commonplace, such bazaars allow people the pleasures of a gathering and meeting place.

Revival of Public Markets is part of a larger struggle between small entrepreneurs, on or below Main Street, and corporate giants. In the West this is not only a contest of local versus distant, small versus big, but also a desire for diversity versus the monotony of chain stores. In UK the New Economics Foundation campaigns against 'Clone Towns', with an estimated 42% of towns in UK already having lost their distinctive character as high-street shops are replaced by a monochrome strip of global and national chains.

The need to preserve local identity is not hometown jingoism. It is a long-standing struggle within most countries. In the US, an activist group called Sprawl Busters, campaigns against the 'doughnut effect' of a ring of big-business-dominated malls flourishing on the outskirts of towns while the downtown area decays from lack of business. Back in the 1950s, Senator Hubert Humphrey urged Americans to choose between a marketplace dominated by a 'few Frankensteins and giants' and one made up of 'thousands upon thousands of small entrepreneurs, independent businessmen, and land-holders who can stand on their own feet and talk back to their Government or to anyone else'.

Ironically, Sprawl Busters' enemy number one is a company that was started by a Main Street entrepreneur who set out to serve the one-horse towns that were otherwise ignored by big retailers. Sam Walton's Walmart is now the biggest corporation in the US and spreading fast to other parts of the world. Between 1980 and 2000, Walmart's outlets grew from 275 to 3,500. In 2010 Walmart's 8,747 retail units across the world employed more than 2 million people and had total sales of $405 billion. These superstores are a one-stop shop for 'lowest ever prices' on everything that people traditionally bought on Main Street plus things that were never available at the local store.

Since the big national retailers buy directly from manufacturers and operate through their own in-house distribution systems, their spread has displaced vast networks of wholesalers and distributors. The number of grocery wholesalers in the US declined from 400 in 1981 to just 97 in 2000. Independent pharmacies now account for less than 17% of retail pharmacy sales in the US. This trend has already spread across Europe and is now percolating to other parts of the world. In UK, the five largest food retailers now hold over 50% of the total market share. Supermarkets on the whole control 70% of food retailing, while the total number of grocery stores in that country went down from 147,000 to about 28,000 in the last 40 years. Tesco alone now controls over 30% of the grocery market in the UK and a rising share of the convenience store sector. In Italy the opening of superstores resulted in the demise of about 370,000 family-run businesses.

It has been argued that the well-oiled machinery of these retail giants offers consumers wider selection, better services and lower prices. But the cost efficiencies are not merely due to economies of scale and often derive from greater muscle power. For example, the sheer size of Walmart's operations makes it difficult, or impossible, for most suppliers to have a conversation with Walmart. Charles Fishman's book *The Wal-Mart Effect* documents how the business ecosystem Walmart has created allows it to control the tempo, the rules and economic climate, making it a dominating presence even for others in the anti-market zone.

Other giant chains exercise similar advantages. For example, the bookseller Barnes & Noble gets price breaks from publishers that go far beyond the discount justified by their larger orders. Thus Barnes & Noble enjoys an advantage over local bookstores that is not only unfair but illegal under US anti-trust statutes, claims Stacy Mitchell in her book *The Home Town Advantage*. Moreover, chainstores are also not consistently cheaper for consumers. At times, chainstores sell certain items below acquisition cost, just to gain market share. Once rivals have dropped out of sight, the prices at the chainstore sometimes rise. Studies have also shown sharp price variations at different outlets of chains like Walmart and Home Depot, depending on the competition around that particular outlet. 'Again, consumers were blessed with lower prices, but likely at the expense of a competitive market over the long-term,' says Mitchell.

Advocates of local economic empowerment are also disturbed by the fact that national and provincial governments alike vie with each other to offer lavish incentives for corporations to set up shop. The inducements include tax cuts and other infrastructure subsidies that add up to tens of thousands of dollars for every job created by the incoming corporation. Cyber-age responses to these trends include CafePress, an online marketplace that links a wide variety of sellers and buyers – to exchange every kind of merchandise. Launched in 1999, CafePress.com is a network of over 2.5 million members who have 'unleashed their creativity to transform their artwork and ideas into unique gifts and new revenue streams'. But what about those who are not yet part of cyberspace and still operate in the old world of face-to-face markets? Of course, the jumble-tumble of this somewhat chaotic bazaar never withered away in most countries that Wall Street lingo describes as 'emerging markets'. Let us take a glimpse of how some of these trends are taking shape in India.

'The early morning flower seller, fruit vendor, coconut seller, idli maker, peanut vendor, the *chatwallah* are all part of our public culture,' writes Renana Jhabvala of SEWA. 'To drive them away and replace them by supermarkets would destroy a part of our own being and certainly stunt the growth of our collective psyche and self-definition . . . Open markets, street corner markets, weekly *haaths*, door-to-door service are a part of our tradition and culture.'

From the smallest weekly *haath* in a remote tribal village, where there are no fixed shops, to this jumble of vendors and hawkers outside a commuter train station in Mumbai – this direct, lightly regulated and multi-layered bazaar has been a central feature of Indian life for at least two and half millennia. Even today in most Indian cities and towns there are marketplaces where fixed shops inside buildings are complemented by vendors squatting with their wares on the pavement outside or roaming about carrying goods in their hands or in bags hanging from their shoulders. Renana Jhabvala, a scholar and senior manager at SEWA, has referred to these as 'natural markets' which have a life of their own, despite being suppressed by police and municipal authorities. Now the mall is a major presence on the landscape of urban India with large corporate houses entering the retail sector on an unprecedented scale. So what happens to those who depend on the open public markets?

On the face of it, the Indian context seems vastly different from anything that an entity like Sprawl Busters is dealing with in the US. There are far more layers here between Wall Street, Main Street and beyond. There is the dwindled, but still living, presence of traditional craftspeople seeking outlets. There are urban street vendors who sell everything from fruits and vegetables to clothes, shoes, toys, brooms, books and so on. Then there are the estimated 12 million independent, mostly family-owned, retail shops of all shapes and sizes.

The biggest difference is that in India the urban areas are the stage for a much more stark interaction between different classes, communities and interest groups. Underlying the disparities of urban India, says Jhabvala, is a dialogue through which different classes and communities seek opportunities: 'The street vendors in many ways represent this dialogue and interaction within the city, with all its successes and in all its cruelty.' Urban vendors, many of them women, provide goods and services to such a wide range of people that they symbolise the interdependence between the rich, middle classes and poor.

Yet these 'natural markets' are constantly under pressure from government agencies, main-street shop owners and now superstores. For instance, in the city of Ahmedabad alone hawkers and vendors are estimated to annually shell out up to Rs.5.5 crore in illegal fees after being denied licences by corrupt local officials. Those vendors and hawkers are part of that majority segment of the urban population, anywhere from 45% to 65%, who are either self-employed or work in the 'informal' sector. In Mumbai alone it is estimated that the annual turnover of the street vendors is over \$1.5 billion (Rs.6,000 crore) and this provides direct and indirect employment to more than 4,00,000 persons.

This face-off between the 'natural' spontaneous bazaar and one that is regulated in favour of more formal structures is not new. It is part of the rise of 'the market', which in India overlapped with colonial rule. When Ela Bhatt, the founder of SEWA, set about organising vendors in the late 1970s she began by studying the Police Act, which is a hand-down from the British Raj. She was shocked to find that it perceives vendors as criminals and denies them any legal status. Since then SEWA has been working with government authorities to create licensing and other legal structures. Much later, when Bhatt served on India's Planning Commission, she still found it hard to convince her colleagues that vending is a legitimate activity which adds dynamism to the economy. In her travels to all corners of the world Bhatt has found vendors similarly disadvantaged everywhere.

Now, thanks largely to successful lobbying by the National Association of Street Vendors, India's central government has a policy that aims to regulate rather than prohibit street vending. This national policy also acknowledges street vending is a major component of alleviating urban poverty. Unfortunately, the ground reality is often not consistent with such policies and, more often than not, vendors are forcibly evicted. This is a small fragment of the larger, radical changes unfolding in the retail sphere.

In 2004, India's retail sector was almost entirely decentralised and 'unorganised'. Corporate entities had just 4% share of the retail sector. But within a decade the picture could be vastly different. While the total retail market in India is projected to grow at a compounded annual growth rate of 5.5%, to reach US$374 billion (Rs.16,770,000 crore) by 2015, the organised retail market is expected to grow at 21.8% and be at about US$55 billion (Rs.246,000 crore). A study commissioned by the Government of India has found that small stores and big retail will co-exist for now. But the picture will change over the next 10 years since organised big retail is growing at 30% annually while *kirana* stores are growing at 2–5% annually. Associations of chemists, hawkers, footpath vendors and traders whose businesses are being affected by the rise of big retail have formed a coalition. In August 2007 they launched a Quit Retail campaign to coincide with the 65th anniversary of the Quit India movement which marked the decisive turn in India's struggle for freedom.

Big retail chains in India offer some of the same advantages as Walmart – cheaper deals and more variety under one roof. In some cases the chainstore prices can be as much as 50% lower on essentials like fruits and vegetables. These lowest-ever prices are made possible by a large procurement network which deals directly with primary producers. This could be a boon in a country where farmers have often felt exploited by local middlemen and have lost a great deal of their fresh produce which rots due to lack of storage and transportation facilities. Thus, the corporate retail procurers see their enterprise as a win–win situation of better prices for both producers and consumers and less wastage of fresh produce. One-third of vegetables and fruits are estimated to perish in the old loose, scattered supply chains. Thus, contract farming is projected to grow with farmers getting an assured and, possibly predetermined, return. This would also mean increased investments in cold chains and other logistics for long-distance transportation of food. Of course, this increases the ecological footprint of the food that some Indians eat.

Bilateral procurement on a large enough scale also means that the wholesale price index no longer fully reflects the dance of supply–demand and prices. Anxieties about the concentration of retail muscle power edging out smaller businesses have erupted in violent protests across India. But there is a fascinating twist to the story. Large manufacturers of consumer goods, who have been squeezed for years by the overweening power of Walmart, Tesco *et al.*, in the developed world, are acting on those lessons. In India, some of them are giving matching discounts to the neighbourhood retail stores, to shore them up as an alternative distribution channel. In some cases they are also offering help to improve accounting and supply-chain management at the small retail stores.

If this happens on a large enough scale then there might be a healthy balance between the corner store on Main Street and the retail giants from the realm of Wall Street. And it is just possible that in the Indian context enough of big business will realise that it has a live stake in the vibrancy of small business. This is why most observers of these emerging scenarios are confident that big retail can spread in India without becoming a monolith that dulls competition and squeezes out other bazaar energies.

Besides given the sheer size, diversity and complexity of India's urban areas, small retailers have some clear advantages. Their overheads are low and they are closely tuned in to the needs and quirks of their assorted consumers in any particular neighbourhood. The local store also usually does instant home deliveries for orders placed over the phone, free of charge. Plus it sells on credit based purely on trust and long acquaintance rather than credit cards. And, best of all, it is just round the corner.

All this could change if urban zoning regulations and other planning policies enable large organised retailers to have a dispersed presence, with a store every few blocks. The retail giants would then operate both superstores and the shop around the corner. At least one major retailer has provided shelf-space for home-made products supplied by a women's cooperative. But fair-trade shelf space may not redress the basic imbalance between big and small. What, in this context, are the implications of large corporations digging for 'the Fortune at the Bottom of the Pyramid'.

Local multiplier and the pyramid

Orderly rows of stacks upon stacks of goods in a brightly lit box-building are almost a planet apart from the swirling, dusty, noisy bazaars that have been common in India for millennia. Yet India's first ever rural hypermart promoters felt a need to connect with tradition and so called their venture Choupal Sagar. The 'choupal' evokes ancient memories of the open meeting place of a village and 'sagar' alludes to an ocean-like limitless scale. This says something about the intentions of the creators of these hypermarts. There are clues here for deciphering how the quest for local multiplier at the base may or may not match plans made at top of the pyramid.

Choupal Sagar is a chain of rural malls created by the Indian Tobacco Company (ITC) as part of its ambitious Bottom of the Pyramid programme called 'e-Choupal'. Here a customer could pick up anything from a sewing needle or groceries to a tractor or fertiliser. Since ITC buys products from suppliers in bulk and passes on some of the discount to its customers, shopping at a Choupal Sagar tends to be cheaper than other nearby retailers. And if you are looking for a one-stop shop then the Sagar may be your only option for miles around. Unless there happens to be a Kisan Sewa Kendra nearby. This is another brand of rural malls started by the Indian Oil Company – its petrol pumps spread across India.

These are initiatives that seek to tap what management guru C.K. Prahalad has called the Fortune at the Bottom of the Pyramid. The BoP approach is largely about the Wall Street-realm businesses simultaneously finding markets and social purpose by understanding and serving the four billion people at the bottom of the global economic pyramid. In its least ambitious form, this means finding low-cost ways of selling consumer goods to the rural not-so-poor. In its more ambitious and far-sighted version, the BoP approach adds further complications in the equation between Wall Street and Main Street.

At one end, the e-Choupal enhances a more open, fairer bazaar primarily because it enables farmers to access better-quality information without ITC charging any arbitrage. The e-Choupal's village-level sanchalak, or coordinator, both houses the internet link and disseminates ITC prices as well as the wholesale market, *mandi,* prices to any farmer without any notion of membership. This enhanced openness rectifies information asymmetry, which prevailed earlier and left the farmer at a disadvantage when he arrived at the mandi.

ITC procures primary produce and sells goods and services that almost entirely come from outside that village or even region – such as tractors, synthetic fabrics, cell-phones and so on. But what about the enormous variety of other goods which, in some cases, are still locally produced? The best example of this is cotton handloom fabrics. If the growing market share of entities like Choupal Sagar, Kisan Sewa Kendra and others severely undermines the local businesses then it means that more and more of the surplus generated by primary producers will wind up at the 'top' of the pyramid. The counter-argument is that as farmers get better prices they will have more savings and will themselves go into non-farm businesses. But how the surplus flows, and where it comes to rest, is only one part of the story.

E-Choupals are also providing agricultural extension services by making scientists and researchers available to train and educate the farmers in best practices. Like better information about prices, there is a desperate need for such linkages. But how is 'best practice' to be defined? A true choupal would provide space for all competing ideas and perspectives to find equal space – then Monsanto's patented seeds and technologies would meet on level ground with traditional or modern but non-corporate systems of farming. Will the e-Choupal format permit that degree of openness? Or will ITC's legitimate need to secure its own profit bottom line cause it to push the technologies and products of its corporate partners? In principle, ITC is committed to promoting sustainable and farm-friendly practices. There are even projects for organic cultivation in the pipeline.

According to one young ITC manager, who did not wish to be identified, the e-Choupals have introduced important efficiencies such as immediate payment and accurate weightings and measures. This is a vital gain because traditional mandis have thus been compelled to upgrade the reliability of their weight and payment mechanisms. As the mandi system matches the new standards, ITC is in turn compelled to seek further ways to add value for the farmer. In such a win–win situation, said the manager, few people tend to think about the local multiplier. Farmers shopping at a rural hypermart are not likely to think in terms of their money leaving or staying in the area. They just focus on advantages in the immediate deal. 'If we as interveners want to change this situation, to what we believe is more fundamental, lasting and good, then we need to work with the people to change their consumption patterns and the choices they make,' says Ashish Panda, who managed the early stages of Timbaktu Collective's organic food venture.

This draws us into the world of interveners who are working at the very base of the pyramid to empower small producers rather than just trying to sell them something. Vijay Mahajan, a pioneer of for-profit micro-credit in India, focuses on expanding not only livelihood finance but also enhancement of skills which enables people at the base to enter conversations between different levels of the economy. SEWA's long experience of working at the base of the economy has shown that if producers and vendors of the informal economy are to link up with the formal sector they need to first build their own organisations. For instance, SEWA's apex federation of women vendors gave its members bargaining power which they did not have as individuals. Such bodies can also provide vital access to both technology and information.

How does this compare with corporate BoP ventures? When Unilever India reached into low-income markets it also created jobs and livelihoods for those selling its products. At the end of 2007 about 42,000 women were working as Shakti Entrepreneurs selling Unilever products across India. This is quite different from the broad-based empowerment of the informal sector that SEWA has facilitated. Sales by Shakti Entrepreneurs send money from the informal and unorganised sector, estimated to be about 93% of India's workforce, to top of the pyramid, in this case Unilever.

Dastkar Andhra's work offers one example of the kind of interventions that grow the multiplier at the base. A market-focused non-profit entity, Dastkar works with some of those weavers we saw earlier, marching in protest on the streets of Chirala. Most handloom weavers are being driven out of work not because there isn't a market for their goods but because they cannot access a steady supply of affordable cotton yarn. This is largely because raw cotton stopped being home-spun into yarn some 150 years ago. So, cotton that often grows in the weavers' backyard is packed into tight bales and shipped off to distant spinning mills. The yarn produced by the mills is expensive and its supply is unreliable.

So Dastkar has promoted decentralised production of cotton yarn, not by reviving hand-spinning of cotton yarn but by designing and manufacturing innovative new machinery that produces yarn at the village or small-town level. Some of this work is being facilitated by another non-profit entity, the Decentralised Cotton Yarn Trust which aims to develop skills for a uniquely Indian industrial scene. Building upon the country's craft heritage not only expands opportunities for buyers and sellers in bazaars like Chirala, it potentially gives an edge to that most basic bazaar where it intersects with global markets. However, the best-known endeavour to strengthen crafts based industries is a for-profit company called Fabindia, which began in 1960 with a single store in New Delhi. Its founder, John Bissell, was an American who first came to India as a consultant for the Ford Foundation. Almost half a century later, the company has 97 outlets across India selling cotton garments and household goods produced by craftspeople. It remains committed to its original goal to source 'hand crafted products which help support and encourage good craftsmanship'. At a time when knowledge, technology, finance and BPO services are considered the growth sectors of the Indian economy, Fabindia has managed a compounded annual growth rate of 35% and had a turnover of Rs.4.5 billion in 2007. The volume of customers has continued to grow exponentially with minimal or no advertising. Fabindia also collaborates with non-profits in a 'Shop for Change: Fair Trade' campaign.

However, in order to retain the integrity of their objectives such entities tend to draw a line to protect themselves from a market culture that operates entirely or predominantly on a money bottom line. For instance, Fabinda CEO William Bissell is reluctant to take Fabindia public. 'If there was some way of involving the weavers and skilled artisans, instead of banks and VCs, an IPO would be worth thinking about,' Bissell told the *Economic Times*. Keeping the company out of the stock market gives him the freedom not to be assessed every quarter and run Fabindia on the basis of five-year business plans which Bissell calls 'a great planning tool to borrow from socialism'.

Fabindia generates one job for every Rs.100,000 of additional turnover, and its future growth pattern is linked to retaining or improving this ratio. That's a benchmark most other business would find difficult to match. On a smaller scale, hundreds of non-profit entities, like Timbaktu Collective, have played a similar role in bridging the space between small, often artisan, producers and distant customers. This partly explains why there is now a global buzz about 'social entrepreneurship'.

Interestingly, the one person who is most famous for promoting activist-oriented entrepreneurs traces his inspiration back to India. Bill Drayton, the founder and head of Ashoka Innovators, named his ambitious undertaking after the third-century-BC Indian emperor. Ashoka was a brutal conqueror who was transformed by Buddhist ideals and went on to become a builder of large-scale public services. Founded in 1980, Ashoka Innovators supports both individual social entrepreneurs and group enterprises across the world on the basis that everyone is a potential 'changemaker'.

But can such change-making micro-endeavours resolve the imbalance of power between Wall Street, Main Street and beyond? No, they can't, says Timbaktu Collective's Bablu Ganguly, himself a former Ashoka Fellow. Over 30 years in both political activism and social entrepreneurship have shown Ganguly that micro-entities that successfully combine social, ethical, ecological and commercial objectives serve as inspirations but they won't become the norm as long as a money bottom-line mind-set dominates and big players enjoy outsized advantages.

For example, in 2008 the US based agro-industry giant Cargill Inc. showed best-ever returns even when farm prices were falling. That's not merely because Cargill is a behemoth with an annual revenue of $120 billion. Its complex operations extend across several spheres – grain trading, chartering of cargo ships, structuring derivative investments for hedge funds. Being multi-dimensional gives Cargill such a detailed view of several different sectors that it can leverage both money and knowledge in ways that few can match.

At the other end of the line is half the world's workforce, engaged in some 3 billion micro-enterprises. According to the New Economics Foundation, 67% of Britain's 3.7 million businesses are a one-person show. There are another 1.1 million micro-enterprises that employ nine or fewer workers. Many of these 'Low-Flying Heroes', as the NEF calls them, make real progress in tackling poverty, renewing neighbourhoods, building social capital, economic inclusion and making communities green and sustainable. By contrast only 32,000, or less than 1%, of Britain's businesses employ more than 50 people. Out of these only about 1,200 companies are registered on the Stock Exchange and yet this is the segment of the economy that gets the most media attention and political backing. This general picture would be true for most countries.

Stuart Hart, who heads the Base of the Pyramid Learning Lab at Cornell, argues that this reality can be altered by linking the informal and formal economies in productive and mutually beneficial partnerships. In a book titled *Capitalism at the Crossroads*, Hart documented case studies of successful enterprises, at the top of the pyramid, innovating new business models by involving those at the Base of the Pyramid (BoP) as co-creators. What Hart calls a 'Great Leap Downward' is urged upon corporations as a way of getting a lead in the large-scale 'disruptive innovation' that is becoming inevitable as pressures for environmental sustainability intensify.

This approach has spawned a new breed of angel investors such as the Acumen Fund. Though it is itself a non-profit entity,

Acumen supports transformative businesses that tackle the poverty of the 'bottom billion'. Acumen's objective is to invest $100 million and reach at least 50 million people. Others, like India's first-ever micro-venture capital fund Aavishkaar, aim to reach those who are not quite at the bottom but still disadvantaged. Aavishkaar's mission is to provide 'micro-equity' to incubate innovative projects among those who fall through the cracks of both conventional investment and philanthropic investing. There are plenty of opportunities for businesses that need an investment of $200 million or $2 million but little for those in between. Vineet Rai, founder of Aavishkaar, says his mission is to serve those left out.

Popularisation of the Bottom of the Pyramid approach has certainly boosted the prospects for such initiatives. Though C.K. Prahalad has been criticised for urging businesses to seek a 'fortune' among the poor at the base, his emphasis on the creation of transparent markets has made a vital contribution. In boardrooms it has increased acceptance of the reality that many market relations are opaque and unfair. 'Opportunity for the majority' and 'business for the benefit of all' are now commonly espoused goals. Prahalad seeks to democratise commerce by creating opportunities for productive work at the base of the economy.

However, for millions of people, the lack of finance or business opportunities is a distant hurdle. Their more immediate problem is absence, or denial, of basic democratic *rights*. In India there are villages rich in natural resources which have neither electricity nor a properly functioning elementary school nor a healthcare centre but now have to live with a paramilitary presence in their midst. The police force is installed by state governments in order to evict people who refuse to sell or relinquish their ancestral lands for a mining operation, a factory, a dam or a special economic zone.

Such power struggles are the most obvious face of conflict in the many zones between Wall Street, Main Street and beyond. But there are sub-surface tensions that are altering the terrain for everyone. Multiple visions of a transition to a different market culture are being driven as much by ethical concerns as survival anxieties across the spectrum.

NEW RULES FOR A GLOBAL AGORA

Late in 2007 the United Nations Special Rapporteur on the right to food, Jean Ziegler, condemned the increasing use of crops to produce biofuels as a crime against humanity. He called for a five-year ban on the practice until technological advances enable agricultural wastes, such as corn cobs and banana leaves, to be used for biofuels. Manufacturers of bio-fuels howled in protest. The Food and Agricultural Organisation refused to take sides and called for more studies to determine links between biofuels, food security and environmental sustainability. Meanwhile, as staple foods became both scarce and more expensive in 2008, food riots broke out across the world, in Indonesia, India, Uzbekistan, Mozambique, Namibia, Zimbabwe, Morocco, Austria, Hungary, Mexico, Peru and more. While bad weather and poor harvests took some of the blame, biofuel manufacturers and commodity speculators emerged as the darkest villains.

Agriculture and biofuels are likely to present society, bazaars and the market with the most painful muddles. After all, even the most passionate proponents of unfettered market forces are unlikely to advocate that millions be allowed to starve while the logic of supply and demand turns more and more food into fuel. But precisely what new rules will enable the global agora to optimise technology and natural resources to ensure not just food but 'well-th' for all?

Voices heard in this chapter are a fraction of the energies arising in response to this question. Multiple answers are blowing in the wind but they seem to be spinning around two poles. One is the need to restore power to actual producers and define value in tangible goods and services that induce well-being – rather than paper wealth of the kind that Wall Street revels in. Correspondingly, the other pole is the need to rein in speculation and financial jugglery so complex that the pursuit of wealth endangers both wealth and well-being all the way from Wall Street down to the grassroots.

Wall Street as the hub of loosely regulated financial jugglery and daringly risky speculation was declared dead in mid-September 2008 by its own paper of record – the *Wall Street Journal*. Even before the implosion, many in the vicinity of Wall Street were losing sleep as ground reality and market trades seemed to spin further and further apart. For instance, cotton traders in the US woke up one morning in August 2008 and found that cotton prices had suddenly, inexplicably, soared overnight. Global cotton stocks stood as they were, no sudden disaster had hit cotton supplies, but the 'market' for cotton was in hyperdrive. Cotton merchants blamed the price distortion on speculators who had pumped billions of dollars into cotton trading.

Record-high oil prices in 2008 raised such deep fears in the US that folks from different levels of the economy joined hands in a coalition called 'Stop Oil Speculation Now'. This coalition brought together diverse industries, labour organisations and citizens' groups who lobbied the US Congress to restore 'reasonable financial controls and transparency' which had earlier been eliminated by 'big speculation market players'. At the peak of the oil frenzy the number of 'paper barrels' traded by speculators was estimated to be 22 times the barrels actually bought and delivered.

These developments might expand the space for exploring possibilities that have otherwise been limited to political activists. For instance, the Washington-based Institute for Local Self-Reliance (ILSR) has for years run a New Rules Project which serves as a clearinghouse for information about what kinds of market rules and public policies would empower those on Main Street and beyond. Essentially this means that

Americans recommit themselves to the founding ideals of their republic, most of all the inalienable right to liberty. The author and activist David Korten, who coined the term 'mindful markets', invokes this right to urge that people liberate themselves from failed ideas and institutions. We cannot be truly free as long as Wall Street in its old mode dominates, argues Korten, who is the author of *A Post Corporate World: Life after Capitalism.*

While this tension with Wall Street has deep cultural roots in American life, work like Korten's has so far remained on the fringes. But, post meltdown, far more people are willing to rebel against the absurdity that a mess-up of accounting entries on Wall Street can cause the real economy to collapse even though nothing has in fact changed in terms of willing workers with needed skills, requisite physical infrastructure and natural resources. What such groups and individuals, across the world, have always known is that market culture fundamentally depends on the political choices we make. It is firstly about identifying the ends and then seeking the means.

For instance, Michael Pollan, author of the *Omnivore's Dilemma*, suggests that it is not enough that Americans have voted with their forks to make organic food a $15 billion industry in that country. Americans will also have to vote with their votes to alter policies in a wider sense. Otherwise, argues Pollan, the genius of industrial capitalism lies in taking its failings and turning them into exciting new business opportunities without addressing the root cause of a problem.

This partly explains why agribusiness corporations distanced themselves from the findings of the International Assessment of Agricultural Science and Technology for Development (IAASTD) – even though it reflected the consensus of 4,000 interdisciplinary scientists and other experts from across the world. In April 2008 the IAASTD released a collaborative report which appealed to all nations, and global business, to urgently reconsider intensive industrial agriculture because it is accelerating environmental degradation and widening the rich–poor gap. Social and environmental organisations across the world welcomed the report as a sign that there can now be a richer conversation about how to phase out energy-intensive, toxic agriculture and evolve new forms that are more people-friendly and eco-friendly. But Australia, Canada and the United States refused to approve the final report. Here is a stark illustration of the difficulties in crafting new rules for the global agora.

Those engaged in business-as-usual find it painfully difficult to deal with 'root causes' that are too far upstream, seem overly abstract or threaten to limit their own money bottom line. Managers who are accountable to shareholders purely in the framework of Wall Street still have little or no liberty to distinguish wealth from 'well-th'. Besides, even those on Main Street are not necessarily focused on either social justice or ecological sustainability. Defining food security through dispersed and sustainable practices rather than just stores of tradeable grain is a survival *need* that cannot be left either to business or regulators alone.

Meeting this need is fundamentally a social and political challenge for people as citizens rather than consumers and producers. So our future depends above all on deeper democratic freedoms of the kind that would facilitate conversations among many different levels of the market economy and between it and the core or love economy. Given realities of the world-as-is this may seem like a naïve hope. Some activists who are in pitched battles with a Walmart or a Cargill have told me it is absurd to suggest that they might successfully enter into a dialogue with the giants. After all, David's job is to fell Goliath not sit him down for a conversation. And yet from deep within the status quo there are challenges to the divine right of capital.

Besides, the process of re-imagining our relationship with the Earth and other humans is accelerating on many different grids. On a bright and chilly December morning in 2010, hundreds of Indian farmers gathered for a solemn ceremony

at Gandhi Samadhi, the place where the Mahatma was cre-
mated 62 years ago. Some of them had spent the previous
three months traversing hundreds of towns and villages of
India on a *Kisan Swaraj Yatra*, a Farmers' Self-reliance Tour.
The yatra's aim was to raise awareness on the issues that link
food, farmers and freedom.

On reaching the nation's capital they handed over a charter of demands to leaders of major political parties. 'Stop
treating agricultural resources like seeds, land and water
as commodities for the benefit of business corporations and
instead ensure that they are used to serve the livelihood needs
of people at large' was at the top of that list. They also want
new rules that would empower the rural economy by creating
infrastructure for farmer-led agricultural processing, storage
and marketing.

But how is this to be made possible? Demands to roll back
Intellectual Property Rights in seeds are considered absurd by
both business leaders and many powerful elected representatives. The Kisan Swaraj demand that the Indian government
cancel all agreements with Monsanto, Syngenta and other
agricultural MNCs is treated as unthinkable. This impasse
between groups of citizens and the powers-that-be is one facet
of a global reality – the crisis of democracy.

Paul Hawken calls this dispersed global phenomenon
'blessed unrest' – something so vast, varied and scattered
it cannot be called a 'movement' in any conventional sense.
There is no central secretariat, no single manifesto, no vanguard. And yet the energies of this unrest are as relentless
and unafraid as they are non-coercive. Documenting the thousands of groups and individuals that make up this 'movement'
Hawken has predicted that these strivings will prevail not by
defeating or conquering but by suffusing institutions in ways
that reverse 'centuries of frenzied self-destructive behaviour.'

While the folks at Catalpa Ridge Farm or Timbaktu Collective are more obvious leaders of this 'blessed unrest',
challengers from within the realm of finance are also living

evidence of an inspiration exquisitely expressed by the poet Wendell Berry:

> The real work of planet-saving will be small, humble, and humbling, and (in so far as it involves love) pleasing and rewarding. Its jobs will be too many to count, too many to report, too many to be publicly noticed or rewarded, too small to make anyone rich or famous.

6
WHO CARES . . . WINS!
CHALLENGING THE DIVINE RIGHT OF CAPITAL

> I am not ashamed to own that many capitalists
> are friendly towards me and do not fear me.
> They know that I desire to end capitalism . . .
> My theory of trusteeship is no make-shift, cer-
> tainly no camouflage. I am confident that it will
> survive all other theories . . . No other theory is
> compatible with non-violence.
>
> *Mahatma Gandhi in Harijan,*
> *16 December 1939*

The corporation is a child of the market. The offspring is now grappling with a troubled legacy. Is this just a new way of carrying its burgeoning self or a metamorphosis? Answers will emerge over the next decade. Meanwhile, the pressure for a more socially embedded and environmentally engaged corporation is no longer growing incrementally. The shrunken time-line for ecological reckoning has made this an imperative for survival.

In no other domain does the essence of the tussle between market and bazaar appear as starkly – and it's about power. What is really being challenged is the divine right of capital.

Is enhanced accountability and responsibility enough? How does the ferment within corporations tally with the clamour for truer democracy? What is the role of the corporation in the multi-level quest for values which could secure the future for our species?

My journey has been lit by the wonder of discovering that 'disaster capitalism' has a counterpoint, as a startling array of people – from boardrooms to village choupals – search for answers.

~

Aaron Feuerstein became famous by accident. In the winter of 1995, a fire destroyed the textile manufacturing unit owned by Feuerstein's family in a small town in Massachusetts, USA. Instead of moving his business to some low-wage, low-tax country, Feuerstein, as CEO, declared that the factory would be rebuilt in the same place. He even continued to pay his 3,000 idle workers during the reconstruction.

Feuerstein was baffled to find that these decisions turned him into a folk hero. From his point of view, these were just acts of common decency. But Feuerstein stood out because such actions were highly uncommon in the business climate of the US in the mid-1990s. ABC News declared him 'Person of the Week'. Hillary Clinton invited him to sit next to her during the President's State of the Union Address. The Columbia Business School gave Feuerstein the Botwinick Prize in Business Ethics for 1996.

The puzzled hero's reasoning was quite simple: 'I have a responsibility to the worker, both blue-collar and white-collar,' he told the magazine *Parade*, 'I have an equal responsibility to the community. It would have been unconscionable to put 3,000 people on the streets and deliver a deathblow to the cities of Lawrence and Methuen. Maybe on paper our company is worthless to Wall Street, but I can tell you it's worth more.'

Feuerstein did not seem to care that he looked like a fool to many conventional corporate managers. The fundamental difference, he said, 'is that I consider our workers an asset, not an expense.' He also did not see profit for shareholders as the *purpose* of his business enterprise.

What others perceived as largesse was to Feuerstein just sound *leadership* and an investment in Malden Mills' workers and the community of a 300-year-old mill town. The workers returned the trust by operating out of makeshift sheds and doubling production within a few weeks. 'Our people became very creative. They were willing to work 25 hours a day,' Feuerstein recalls. From the vantage point of Main Street, and bazaars with social moorings, Feuerstein is a role model. From Wall Street's perspective Feuerstein was an annoying, paternalistic moraliser and a bad manager because he couldn't stay focused on profits. When Malden Mills filed for bankruptcy in 2002 the critics were quick to say, 'Aha! We told you so.' It did not matter that the company's financial troubles were unrelated to the alleged benevolence towards workers and local community.

Curiously enough, when businesses driven purely by monetary profits run aground the model itself is not called into question. By contrast, an article in the magazine *Capitalism* titled 'Greed Makes the World Go Round' welcomed the fall of false-hero Feuerstein and in the same breath lamented the frequent media vilification of Jack Welch, as a ruthless, profit-minded, self-aggrandising CEO.

This caricatured contrast of hard-hearted efficiency versus humane 'bumbling' was always a smokescreen. In this chapter we will explore some initiatives that attempt to clear the air. Why have the world's leading finance companies declared that 'Who Cares Wins' and begun integrating environmental, social and governance issues in their analysis? And if such criteria are being applied why has runaway greed brought down global finance? Is it, after all, only a minority of idealists who see profits as the means, rather than the purpose, of business?

A hundred years ago, when Mohandas Karamchand Gandhi proposed a metamorphosis of capitalism into 'trusteeship', it seemed at best absurd and, at worst, an offence to the proletariat. Three converging trends now glimmer in the spreading light of the political transformation dramatically launched by Gandhi and carried forward by Martin Luther King, Nelson Mandela and many others. Firstly, a new kind of leader has emerged who is trying to locate business within the wider needs and challenges of society. Secondly, there is pressure for greater accountability to human communities and ecosystems in traumatic, even fatal, distress. Thirdly, there is a renewed challenge to the supreme rule of capital, or at least to money as the only bottom line. Underlying all these developments is the audacious question: What comes first, society or business?

Amy Domini, a pioneer in the sphere of socially responsible investing, has first-hand experience of a new kind of owner of capital. These are people who believe that 'there is a difference between making money and stealing money from our children, our neighbours, our natural environment'. Exploring this shift will take us back to that mother question – how broadly is self-interest being redefined? Feuerstein defined his own commercial self-interest to include the well-being of his workers and local community. Ray Anderson of Interface Corporation defines his business's self-interest to include the well-being of planet Earth.

These energies may seem completely at odds with the reality that Naomi Klein has described as 'disaster capitalism'. Klein's book *The Shock Doctrine* documented how some corporations are relentlessly pursuing profits by privatising public goods and violating basic democratic rights. For instance, as the Indian economy grows, the struggle over land and natural resources is becoming painfully bitter and violent – with local residents often pitted against *both* big government and big business. This situation cannot change unless we first reject old adages like 'the business of business is business' and 'the rising tide will lift all ships'. As Domini says, 'It hasn't, it won't, and it cannot without a rewriting of the definition of success.' So far the dominant model of success has been driven by a set of rules that give primacy to making money for the few owners. But it is precisely those rules that are now challenged, tweaked and redeployed to make business itself a powerful force for social change. More and more people are openly wondering about what kind of business culture will foster economic democracy. Can the bottom line be grown to include more than money profits? But let us start by looking at why the term 'corporate social responsibility' has been called an oxymoron.

MORPHING THE CORPORATION

Some time in the 1990s an episode of the Calvin and Hobbes cartoon strip showed the irascible Calvin running a lemonade stall on his front lawn and charging $15 a glass. Along comes his classmate and *bête noire* Susie Derkins.

> An outraged Susie: '15 bucks a glass?!'
>
> A sanguine Calvin: 'That's right! Want some?'
>
> Susie (yelling, flailing her arms in exasperation): 'How do you justify charging 15 dollars?'
>
> Cool Calvin: 'Supply and demand.'
>
> Susie (pointing to the absence of any customers): 'Where's the demand?! I don't see any demand!'
>
> Calvin: 'There's LOTS of demand.'
>
> Susie: 'Yeah?'
>
> Calvin (scowling and fist-thumping): Sure! As the sole stockholder in this enterprise, I DEMAND monstrous profit on my investment! And as President and CEO of the company, I DEMAND an exorbitant annual salary!

And as my own employee, I DEMAND a high hourly wage and all sorts of company benefits! And THEN there's overhead and actual production costs!

Susie: But it looks like you just threw a lemon in some sludge water!

Calvin: Well, I have to cut expenses SOMEwhere if I want to stay competitive.

Susie: What if I got sick from that?

Calvin: 'Caveat Emptor' is the motto we stand behind! I'd have to charge more if we followed health and environmental regulations.

Susie (walking away in disgust): You're out of your mind. I'm going home to drink something else.

Calvin (flailing his fist after her): Sure! Put me out of a job! It's you anti-business types who ruin the economy.

Calvin, growling and fuming, abandons his lemonade stall going inside to demand of his mother: 'I need to be subsidized.'

This animated spoof was a pungent depiction of how millions of people across the world view big business. Some time in 1999, the UK supermarket chain Tesco, itself a major corporation, actually ran tests on its pies to determine which ones were best for flinging! They were responding to a flurry of protests in which pies were landed on the faces of corporate chiefs like Bill Gates and even the economist Milton Friedman. 'We like to keep abreast of what the customers are doing, and that's why we have to do the testing,' said a Tesco spokesperson. She went on to recommend the custard tart as best for protestors since it 'gives total face coverage'.

Such wacky expressions of anger and frustration are merely the extreme end of a broad spectrum of anti-corporate feeling. Similar signals have come through on various frequencies. In 2002 a survey commissioned by the World Economic Forum found large businesses at the bottom of the list of trusted institutions. When the public relations firm Richard Edelman Inc. conducted research among thought leaders in the US, Europe and Australia, it found that NGOs dominate firms in terms of public trust on issues relating to the environment, human rights and health.

Global Finance magazine dripped irony in a 2000 cover story titled 'Corporate Angels' which depicted Niall Fitzgerald, the then CEO of Unilever, with a golden halo and fluffy white angel-wings. 'There is something magnificently perverse about the concept of the "socially responsible" corporation,' said the accompanying editorial. 'After all, multinational corporations have worked long and hard for their reputation as environmental and social pariahs.'

'What is it about the modern corporation that makes joining it feel like we're making a Mephisto bargain for our soul?' asked David Batstone, author of *Saving the Corporate Soul.* Himself an entrepreneur, Batstone offered a simple answer to his own question: enough corporations make false promises and violate trust. Ray Anderson, the founder and CEO of the US flooring giant Interface, put it more dramatically: 'I am a plunderer of the earth and a legal thief [and] perverse tax laws, by failing to correct the errant market, are my accomplices.'

Joel Bakan's book and documentary *The Corporation* offered a far more searing indictment by describing the corporation as a psychopathic creature incapable of recognising or acting upon moral reasons to refrain from harming others – particularly when the benefits of choosing the harmful course are greater than the costs. As an illustration of this, Bakan offered the case of how General Motors put its Chevrolet Malibu car on the market, knowing that it was likely to explode in the event of a rear-end collision. When victims of one such explosion sued General Motors, evidence produced in court showed that the company opted for a weaker design because it saved them $6.19 per car. The jury found General Motors guilty of morally reprehensible behaviour which both violated applicable laws and put profits above public safety. It awarded the accident victims compensatory damages totalling

$107 million and punitive damages of $4.8 billion – the total amount later being reduced to $1.2 billion.

The victims of a far more famous case, at Bhopal in India, did not come out as well as this. On the night of 3 December 1984, a runaway chemical reaction in one unit of Union Carbide's pesticide factory triggered a gas leak which killed about 4,000 people within days. Another 11,000 people died slowly over the next few years. Tens of thousands more are still suffering from ailments caused by the toxic exposure. Several investigations into the accident held Union Carbide responsible for gross negligence and dangerous forms of cost-cutting. To make matters worse, medical relief operations were severely impeded by Union Carbide's refusal to fully divulge technical details about the cocktail of chemicals that leaked that night, presumably because there were business secrets at stake.

Bakan and other researchers of such incidents have argued that these are not managerial lapses but an inevitable consequence of the basic purpose of a corporation, to maximise profits. Several generations of business school students have indeed been brought up on the mantra: 'maximise the medium-term earnings per share'. However, our story begins by observing that 'maximise' has always been understood and acted upon in many different ways. And now there are new pressures pushing for a redefinition of both 'profit' and 'maximisation'. Let us take a bird's-eye view of both the dark and light sides of the legacy, as well as the winds of change.

~

The earliest corporations took shape in Western Europe during the 16th century when royal charters where given to merchants and traders for creating an assortment of public facilities and services – ferry services, canals, water systems, toll roads, bridges, colleges and later railroads. During the 17th and 18th centuries the British and Dutch East India Companies turned trade into an instrument of empire building.

In a study of how the East India Company shaped the modern multinational, Nick Robins has described this process as 'a corporate revolution, designed to acquire the riches of an entire people for the benefit of a single company'. Adam Smith's dream of a free market was a direct attack on the excess concentration of power that monopolies like the East India Company enjoyed.

There are now more than 79,000 corporations with operations in more than one country, and they, in turn, have more than 790,000 affiliates around the world. Some critics have described the modern global corporation as the most powerful, non-military, instrument for concentrating power and wealth ever devised. There is no dispute about the fact that corporations now have a gigantic financial, political and ecological footprint. What is in dispute is the net worth of their contribution to the quality of life to the world as a whole.

Corporations are being challenged from two different vantage points. One view rejects the corporation as an inherently exploitative agent of imperialism. The other view holds that corporations are given a licence to operate on the expectation that they will produce wider social good. This second critique is now rapidly gathering momentum as a wide range of people struggle to actively reconnect the corporation with the social purposes, they believe, it was originally intended to serve.

Corporate social responsibility has been called an oxymoron because many of the corporations that adopt cutting-edge *voluntary* social responsibility practices also lobby for trade and investment rules that have the side-effect of fostering inequity and curtailing freedoms and opportunities of smaller entities in the bazaar spaces. The conundrum is succinctly described by Halina Ward and Bernice Lee of the International Institute for Environment and Development:

> ... the dogma is that trade and investment liberalization will bring overall benefits *if* the right policies are in place at the domestic level to ensure that it does so. But business lobbying often undermines efforts in developing

countries to strengthen social or environmental protection, and it is businesses (though not necessarily the same ones) that provide the financial resources for the corruption that undermines efforts to improve democratic governance in many parts of the world.

A much sharper critique has been made by David Korten, author of *When Corporations Rule the World* and *The Post Corporate Word.* Korten lists the many different kinds of capital that corporations tend to deplete. Social capital is depleted when corporations break up labour unions, drive down wages and foster job insecurity. Human capital is depleted when employees are made to work in hazardous or stressful conditions. The Earth's natural capital is depleted by over-exploitation of forests, fisheries and mineral deposits, careless dumping of wastes and marketing of toxic chemicals. Society's institutional capabilities are depleted when corporations oppose environmental and other regulations essential to the long-term health and viability of society, in order to protect their short-term profits. Even business capital is depleted when managers are forced into a short-term view in running their own operations.

Increasing pressure to make corporations more accountable is partly a response to successive waves of scandals. In 2001, senior executives of several corporate giants – including Enron, WorldCom, Adelphia, Tyco and Xerox – confessed to, or were prosecuted for, wronging investors. Joseph Stiglitz took pains to point out that the amount of money misappropriated by executives of Enron and WorldCom alone was greater than the GNP of many countries. More recently, there has been public outrage about bonuses claimed by Wall Street money managers, even as their firms went into a tailspin and shareholders were losing money.

Aaron Feuerstein is among those who have been surprised by the public outrage at such disclosures. He saw it as 'a natural evolution that arose from accepting the idea that ethical values should not be considered in a business'. This has not been a lone voice. John S.R. Shad, chairman of the US Securities and Exchange Commission from 1981 to 1987, worried about these issues as well. In 1987, Shad made a donation of $30 million to support a Harvard Business School (HBS) programme on ethics. At that time, in only one-third of MBA schools in the US was Ethics a required course. HBS was not one of them, and Shad's donation triggered quite a furore among the faculty. Economist Amitai Etzioni, who was part of that highly charged debate, recalls that the reactions ranged from distrust to outright hostility. One economist argued that the business school's job was to teach science not ethics. Another pointed out that the students were adults who could and should get their ethics education at home or at church.

The idea of having not one separate course but integrating the ethical dimension in all business courses seemed most threatening of all. As Etzioni wrote later:

> A member of the marketing department mused that if [this] policy were adopted, his department would have to close because much of what it was teaching constituted a form of dissembling: selling small items in large boxes, putting hot colors on packages because they encourage people to buy impulsively, and so forth. A finance professor was also concerned about its effects on his teaching. Students later told me that they learned in his course how you could make a profit by breaking implicit contracts.

Later, Etzioni taught the ethics course at HBS for two years and found that it was treated as a minor requirement to be gotten out of the way as quickly as possible. 'Ethics, they told me repeatedly, were something a corporation simply cannot afford,' Etzioni recalls. 'Only if being moral bought the corporation "good will" – with a value that could be calculated and demonstrated – should the corporation take ethical considerations into account.'

A survey of graduates at the world's top 13 business schools, commissioned by the Aspen Institute in 2002, concluded that a B-school education weakens the ethical frame of the students. The study tested the views of students at three points – when they first joined, at the end of the first year and on graduating. The number of those who believed that max-imising shareholder value was the prime responsibility of a corporation increased from 68% at the entry point to 82% by the end of the first year.

However, the students were only being faithful to a legal and structural reality. The concept of fiduciary responsibility makes it binding on all corporate executives to give primacy to earning profits for shareholders – within the framework of the law. This was the basis of Milton Friedman's famous exhortation that 'the business of business is business'. It fol-lows that any preoccupation with clean air, clean water, uni-versal healthcare or education – which gets in the way of the money bottom line – violates that fundamental responsibility. It is in this sense that the corporation is the quintessential child of the market. It is an embodiment of what the American economist Duncan Foley has called 'Adam's Fallacy' – the idea that the economic sphere, the money-making sphere, can and should be kept separate from the social and moral sphere.

So why have the world's leading financial institutions jointly committed themselves to the view that 'Who Cares Wins'? In search for answers let us take a detour into the past, to the mansion of G.D. Birla in New Delhi. It was here, on 30 Janu-ary 1948, that Mahatma Gandhi was shot dead at point-blank range.

Long shadow of trusteeship

It was not on a whim that the ascetically inclined Mahatma Gandhi accepted the hospitality of G.D. Birla, one of India's early industrialists. The struggle against imperial power had ended six months earlier with the departure of the British and the birth of independent India. Challenging the concentration of money power was next on Gandhi's agenda. Born into the *baniya*, merchant, caste Gandhi had an instinctive grasp of commerce and valued the openness of the bazaar. He was an honorary member of the Mumbai-based Indian Merchants' Chamber. What he opposed was brute force whether it flowed from the barrel of a gun or power gained by concentration of money and resources.

Gandhi's vision of 'trusteeship' was essentially a call to embed commerce in ethics and social responsibility. Gandhi *asked* of Birla and other capitalists what the Communists and Socialists were keen to *force* upon them. But with a crucial difference: Gandhi's vision of 'trusteeship' would *socialise* property rather than nationalise it. Then owners of capital would naturally, willingly, orient their entire operations to directly serve their workers, consumers and society at large. Gandhi was drawing both on Indian tradition and Western influences like the Quakers who promoted industrial humanism, worker-owned companies and cooperatives. Curiously enough, the contemporary movement for socially responsible investing has its roots in the struggle against racial discrimination that Gandhi inaugurated a century ago in South Africa.

The refusal of some Americans to invest in 'sin stocks' – namely, guns, gambling and alcohol – is a tradition that goes back to the 18th century. The Interfaith Center on Corporate Responsibility (ICCR), based in Manhattan, is an extension of that legacy. This is an international network of 275 Protestant, Catholic and Jewish institutional investors who together manage portfolios worth more than \$110 billion. The ICCR cut its teeth on the anti-apartheid movement in the 1980s. It mobilised shareholder activism to pressurise leading American corporations to either limit or close down their operations in South Africa. Apart from making a substantial contribution to the eventual collapse of apartheid, this mobilisation also forged the tools that aided the now much wider phenomenon of socially responsible investing.

Traumatic events have also played a vital role in boosting the rise of socially responsible investing. Leading British businesses responded to inner-city racial riots in UK by creating a non-profit organisation called Business in the Community (BITC) in 1982. The catastrophic *Exxon Valdez* oil spill off the coast of Alaska in 1989 led to the formation of Ceres, the Coalition for Environmentally Responsible Economies, which includes environmentalists, social investors, churches and public-interest groups. Technical knowledge of the environmentalists combined with the insights of social investors to form a code of principles for environmentally sound business practices. The Ceres code is now endorsed by 80 publicly traded companies – with close to $150 billion in combined assets – including General Motors, Coca-Cola, Gap, Bank of America and McDonald's. Similarly, Hurricane Katrina triggered a shift towards greening at many companies, most notably at Walmart.

The European Union now defines corporate responsibility as behaviour that 'goes over and above legal requirements, and is adopted because businesses deem it to be in their long-term interest to integrate economic, social and environmental performance management'. Human rights, drug pricing and labour standards, which once had a 'none of our business' status within the corporate world, have come aboard and seem to here to stay. For instance, the World Bank's Business Partners for Development projects encourage the joint participation of civil society groups, business and government participation in projects funded by the Bank. The UK's Ethical Trading Initiative has forged a voluntary partnership of NGOs, trade unions and business to improve the ethics in corporate supply chains. London-based BITC enables corporate executives to engage with ground realities in different corners of the world through a programme called 'Seeing Is Believing'.

Big-brand names have bent over backwards to counter criticism and enhance their corporate social responsibility (CSR) ratings. For instance, Starbucks, the coffee retail giant, attempted to alter its image as an exploiter of third-world farmers by starting a preferred supplier programme to attract and reward farmers committed to socially and environmentally responsible farming. The London Stock Exchange installed an online disclosure tool through which companies can provide details about a wide range of social, environmental and governance issues. This gives institutional investors a unified source of information. Among the topics covered are health and safety issues and supplier relationships. Most major global companies now produce social or environmental reports. But according to the International Business Leaders Forum there are probably less than 3,000 major companies that systematically and strategically address corporate responsibility issues through their entire operations. The bad news is that by the close of 2010 the UN Global Compact had 8,000 companies, spread across 135 countries, in its network, whereas UNCTAD estimates that there are at least 79,000 transnational companies with about 790,000 affiliates. It is a hopeful assumption that this mass of transnational companies will follow the example of the top few thousand.

Moreover, how do the more responsible corporations remain competitive at the regional, national and international level? The search for viable pathways to 'Responsible Competitiveness' maybe growing but the concept of corporations as public servant is still far from being a universal principle. Allen L. White, one of the co-founders of the Global Reporting Initiative, has argued the corporation cannot be transformed from a private value generator to a public benefit generator without altering its genetic code: 'For all the intense CSR activity during the last decade, the locus of such activity has been in the outer ring – on elements most removed from core genetics. It thus should come as no surprise that CSR has limited effect on fundamental behavioural change.'

Of course, the task outlined by White is a sub-set of the larger, still more daunting, challenge of reworking the relationship between society and market. Gandhi's confidence in the concept of Trusteeship was based on his faith that humankind can rise to the civilisational challenge of checking brute force with 'soul force', of fostering a more humane balance between cooperation and competition, individual 'self' and collective 'common' good. This striving is being driven by restless individuals but finding expression through institutions both in the realm of spirit and material bean-counting.

Faith in business

'Is there an alternative to global capitalism?' This is not a question you expect to find being debated at the heart of The City, London. Yet such a debate is reverberating from the high dome of St Paul's cathedral. There is a long and complex history of interface between the theologians of this house of worship, which dates back to 604 AD, and the merchants and financial wizards who have surrounded it. What matters to our story is that for 300 years, since Christopher Wren's masterpiece cathedral came to dominate the cityscape, matters of 'faith' and 'fortune' have been kept in separate compartments. Why, then, is this centre of ecclesiastic power attempting a new kind of engagement with not just its immediate neighbours but with capital everywhere?

The search for an answer took me to a rather heavenly address – Amen Court in Ave Maria lane in the shadow of St Paul's. That is the home of Canon Dr Edmund Newell, an economic historian and then Chancellor of St Paul's. He was also director of St Paul's Institute which is grappling with the ethical challenges facing business, finance and global economics in the 21st century. The outcome is a neutral forum for debate where all sides can be heard. For one such interaction, Dr Newell brought together Muhammad Yunus, founder and director of Bangladesh's famous Grameen Bank, Professor John Kay, an Oxford economist and Dr Rowan Williams, the Archbishop of Canterbury. Why, asked Yunus, does the business of making money recognise people's desire for self-gain but not their simultaneous willingness to share with others?

This core concern about broadening the definition of self-interest underlies what *Fortune* magazine has called a 'groundswell' of activism, mingling spirit and business. The initiative at St Paul's is one facet of a growing trend on both sides of the Atlantic. The Fifth Avenue Presbyterian Church in Manhattan, for example, has an initiative called 'Faith@Work' which urges business people to become 'points of distribution' for God's love in the marketplace.

In 2000 the Alliance of Religions and Conservation collaborated with the World Wide Fund for Nature, UK, to urge religious organisations to adopt the following checklist in order to ensure that their investments are consistent with their values:

- Does the faith organisation have an ethical investment policy and is its portfolio compatible with this?

- Does the organisation's bank have a policy regarding ethical banking?

- Develop a statement of ethical investment principles on human rights and environment with reference to urgent issues such as forestry, toxics and climate change

Apart from these institutional initiatives, there is also significant ferment at the individual level. For example, Aaron Feuerstein is a devout Jew who has often said that the ideals of his religious heritage played a major role in his business decisions. Ben Cohen and Jerry Greenfield, founders of the famous Ben & Jerry's Ice Cream in the US, have lamented the fact that most companies try to conduct their business in a spiritual vacuum:

> Just because the idea that the good you do comes back to you is written in the Bible and not in some business textbook doesn't make it less valid. We're all interconnected. As we give we receive . . . it's absurd to think that just because spiritual connection isn't tangible or quantitatively measurable, it doesn't exist.

Marc Gunther's book *Faith and Fortune: The Quiet Revolution to Reform American Business* showed that, while attempts to bridge the divide between spirituality and work are not entirely new, the current burst of energy in this sphere is partly a response to the trauma of September 11. 'The recognition that life is short – that it can be taken away in an instant – intensified people's desire to do meaningful work, work that makes a contribution to society.' Therefore the term 'faith' is no longer restricted to traditional devoutness. It covers those who have a simple conviction that people are good and business can be reconfigured to make the world a better place. Tensions between spiritual values and the compulsion to produce short-term profits have not evaporated. But infusing spiritual and ethical values has demonstrated practical benefits. Many companies find these values a good basis for building networks of long-lasting, win–win relationships with workers, partners and communities.

More and more talented people are looking for work in companies that have demonstrated high ethical standards. Offering more money is not enough to retain such talent. Many of these individuals are also seeking a more direct link between their role in the marketplace and their role in society. 'The real game in the business world of the ecological age is running a business or a career so as to make a contribution to the community, the nation, and even to the planet as a whole,' says Gifford Pinchot, business consultant and author of *Intrapreneuring*. In this context, true business competence is equated with products or services that not only satisfy the needs and wants of customers but also reduce pollution, regenerate natural habitats and help the less fortunate. It is possible that this new culture will best suit those who are not quite *driven* by the need to accumulate and inclined to live simply, regardless of how much money they have. The incentives, adds Pinchot, are quite compelling: 'The old status system is hard on the heart. Living for the larger self through a strategy of frugality and service opens up the heart to the glory of creation all around us. The gift is repaid manifold.'

This partly explains why major corporations, such as American Express, Verizon and Forbes, became sponsors of Spirit in Business (SIB), which was born out of a dialogue with the Dalai Lama on competition in 1999. For about seven years, SIB served as a network linking business people who believe that a lack of spiritual values is deepening the crisis in public leadership, global governance and business integrity which in turn is degrading both consumer and investor confidence. But in due course the founders of SIB concluded that the word 'spirit' was triggering religious associations and preventing the network from engaging in a meaningful dialogue with many senior business leaders. So the SIB logo has been put into suspended animation and new group called Global Leaders Academy pursues the same agenda with more emphasis on emerging insights from neurosciences which validate the potential for transforming individual and institutional behaviour. Leaders of this network believe that a profound and potentially paradigm-shifting transformation is unfolding in the world of business.

Micro-finance pioneer Muhammad Yunus pursues similar goals without any overt reference to spirit. Social business entrepreneurship is neither charity nor 'do-gooding,' says Yunus. It is a way of making capitalism a more complete set of ideas and practice. The problem, he adds, is that the theory and institutional structures of the market still don't work in favour of social business entrepreneurship on the scale that is required. For instance, asks Yunus, why can't the old-style stock market which stands in front of St Paul's Cathedral in London be matched with a different kind of stock market on the other side, 'where people will come to invest money to do good to other people and there will be rating agencies to find out which other organisations, which other entrepreneurs were doing good to people.'

Some representatives of the orthodoxy are not only unim-
pressed by Yunus's vision but actually a bit horrified. Professor John Kay, on the other side of that debate at St Paul's, was
quite clear that:

> Not only do I not think business has the obligation to do
> good, I don't think it has the right to do good. I am very
> frightened of the idea of the people who run large cor-
> porations, you know, regarding it as proper or legitimate
> for them to engage in their own particular conception
> of what a good society might be – that is a job for other
> people.

As an economics professor at Oxford and author of a book
called *The Truth About Markets,* Kay was being faithful to
the gospel of the market as it has been preached for almost
two centuries. A sharper, more nuanced response to Yunus's
exhortation was provided by the Archbishop of Canterbury.
It is not that difficult to outline the market values that would
underlie a good society, urged the Archbishop:

> Trust, obviously. Inclusion – that is, drawing an ever-
> increasing number of people in to have their place at
> the table. Patience – the systematic refusal of short-term
> solutions, short-term perspectives. And, fourthly, a con-
> sistent refusal once again to think that economic man is
> a definition of any real being on the face of the globe . . .
> The New Testament in general, never mind just the Gos-
> pels, seems to work with a model of human community
> in which the prime determinative vision is 'All gifts are
> given so as to be given again'. The second thing which
> the Gospels in particular say pretty bluntly is: acquisi-
> tiveness kills, literally as well as spiritually.

The Archbishop was not indulging in a spiritual fantasy.
Varying shades of these principles are being applied by
socially motivated businesses. Above all, such businesses are
attracting the interest of people in the mainstream. Take, for
instance, Gary Hirshberg, the CEO of Stonyfield Farm yoghurt
company, an organic produce enterprise committed to 'healthy

food, healthy people and a healthy planet'. By the late 1990s Hirshberg found himself being invited to attend roundtable meetings with CEOs of some of the largest corporations in America. He was fascinated by how:

> these people spend most of their time at these luncheons asking me questions about my little $30 million business. The fact that I'm even at the table is a statement in itself. But the fact that they're asking the questions is an even more important statement about the changing role of socially responsible companies in the business world. Mainstream corporations are recognizing that we're on to something – that it's to their competitive advantage to take the needs of people, not just their own profits, into account.

Scepticism about a 'values-led business' is alive and well, but there is clearly more elbow room for the idea of 'caring capitalism' now than there was when Ben & Jerry's Ice Cream was set up back in 1978. To them it seemed perfectly natural that business has a responsibility to the soil in which it is planted – its immediate community and the Earth. To business consultants and investors their socially preoccupied perspective looked crazy. 'The pundits said our business couldn't survive if we were going to focus energy on helping to solve social problems,' Cohen and Greenfield recalled 20 years later.

Growing Ben & Jerry's, from an initial investment of $12,000 into a multi-million-dollar business, was one of many success stories that established that there are enough customers who, given a choice between products of equal quality, would opt for one made by a company that shares their values. This was a far more all-encompassing approach than conventional philanthropy. A values-led business, Cohen and Greenfield wrote, 'seeks to maximize its impact by integrating socially beneficial actions into as many of its day-to-day activities as possible.'

Many such innovators are linked through the San Francisco-based Social Venture Network (SVN), an international association of successful business and social entrepreneurs dedicated to changing the way the world does business. Founded in 1987, the SVN not only provided a nurturing ground for such entrepreneurs, it also became instrumental in getting these ideas more space in the public discourse. By the late 1990s, case studies of socially responsible companies were included in college textbooks, business books and business school classes both in the US and Europe.

Proponents of this approach take pains to point out that they are not 'business softies'. Socially responsible business is not about hesitating to make money or just giving away what you earn. It is about *how* the money is made every day. Peter Barnes, one of the pioneers of this sphere, explains the difference in terms of biology. 'The dominant DNA is to make profits first and foremost but our genes are different,' Barnes would tell incoming employees at his company Working Assets. 'Giving back to the world isn't something we think about after we make a profit – it's part of our cost of doing business. It's a cost we pay up front. Our mission is to out-compete companies who don't pay this cost, and thereby not only survive, but eventually change corporate DNA.'

But to what extent have things really changed? After all Ben & Jerry's was sold to the behemoth Unilever in 2000 for an estimated $350 million. It is not clear how much of the original social entrepreneur culture of Cohen and Greenfield has transferred to Unilever. In any case, what are the options for those who have that 'dominant DNA' and work within the complex structure of corporations? The universal, rather secular, concerns articulated on the platform of St Paul's or by Spirit in Business find resonance with many in the corporate world. But how does it translate into action that seems viable in the flow of existing operations?

While obstacles are daunting, motivations seem to be equally strong. First of all, enough individuals are ill at ease with making a 'Mephisto bargain'. Plus there is the need to heal the divide between the personal life and professional life. As Cohen and Greenfield found over the years,

> people running those big companies were wonderful, caring people. They had social values. They cared about social problems and the state of our society and the world. In their private lives, they made donations and volunteered their time to organizations that help disadvantaged people.

This is in essence the rupture between the bazaar, where commerce as an adjunct of civic life anchored in values deeper than material exchange, and the market where the sharp, crisp measurability of money rules supreme. Can this individual angst by itself be an agent of transformation? Perhaps not, but for over two centuries some form of this angst has energised and driven many revolutions and revolts. The collapse of the Russian and Chinese revolutions marked the end of one kind of revolt against the power of capital. What are some of continuing forms of that struggle?

CHALLENGING THE 'DIVINE RIGHT OF CAPITAL'

'Can it be believed', asked Alexis de Tocqueville, 'that the democracy which has overthrown the feudal system and vanquished kings will retreat before tradesmen and capitalists?' At the close of the 20th century it was commonly believed that this question had been decisively answered. Liberal democracy would now be defined by the rule of the market dominated by capital. And yet the 'divine right of capital', as Marjorie Kelly has called it, does face an assortment of challenges.

A co-founder of the American journal *Business Ethics,* Kelly draws a parallel between the divine right of kings under which the interests of the aristocracy were paramount, and the divine right of capital under which the investors' interests are paramount. The narrow focus on maximising shareholder value is seen as a violation of both democratic and market ideals – since it isolates money-making from the social and environmental base that actually enables business to exist in the first place. Kelly, herself the owner of a small business, is among those who treat the publicly owned corporation as a potentially democratic instrument that has been subverted by a 'corporate aristocracy' to facilitate great concentrations of wealth.

In the US the wealth gap is now at its widest since 1929. The wealthiest 10% of households are estimated to hold about 90% of financial assets. In 2005 it was estimated that 21.2% of US national income accrued to 1% of the population. For instance, in 1968, the CEO of General Motors took home, in pay and benefits, about 66 times the amount paid to the average GM worker. In 2005, the CEO of Walmart earned 900 times the pay of his average employee.

The rallying call for greater economic democracy draws energy from the ideals of America's founding fathers. It equates liberty and equality with 'a new economic order that respects the workings of the market while reclaiming its gifts for the many rather than for the few,' Kelly wrote in her book *The Divine Right of Capital: Dethroning the Corporate Aristocracy.* This aspiration has a broad base. For example, an opinion poll by *BusinessWeek* magazine in 2000 found only 4% of Americans answering 'yes' to the suggestion that making profits for shareholders should be the sole purpose of corporations. About 95% of the people polled agreed that corporations should sometimes sacrifice profits for the sake of improving the conditions of workers and their communities. This is not just about the tussle between Main Street and Wall Street. The fundamental question is whether capital should remain dominant or can its multiplication take second place to generating social and environmental *value*?

Capital is under pressure for three different reasons. One: there have been deep fears about instability within the global casino long before the meltdown finally happened in 2008.

Two: there is the old and familiar discontent about the inequities inherent to the prevailing money system. And three, there is a growing realisation that the primacy of return on capital could prove fatal if it continues to distort the balance between the human economy and nature's ecosystems.

Until recently the concept of fiduciary responsibility, or the prudent man principle, allowed companies to exclude all social and environmental costs. There was no place for such 'externalities' on conventional balance sheets. Those unaccounted costs have now caught up with companies and the planet as a whole. The futurist Hazel Henderson, author of *The Politics of the Solar Age: Alternatives to Economics*, suggested years ago that the 'prudent man principle' should be renamed 'the prudent lemming principle,' since herd investing behaviour driven by a lowest common denominator of greed and fear creates lose–lose outcomes. This assessment, once dismissed as extreme pessimism, is now becoming accepted as an elementary truth. For instance, attempts are being made to rein in purely speculative trading in key commodities.

In June 2008 the US Congress passed a bill to limit speculators in oil after expert witnesses at congressional hearings claimed that enforcing tighter rules by the Commodity Futures Trading Commission (CFTC) could cut oil prices in half in 30 days. Even as public angst about the turmoil reached a fevered pitch, a clear distinction was being made between speculators and hedgers who buy a future contract for oil that they actually intend to buy. By contrast, speculators enter the trading floor to profit from buying and selling futures contracts. Congress acted because the volume of speculators trading in oil went from 37% in April 2000 to 71% by April 2008 – inflicting a punishing toll on all sectors of the economy. This problem has been steadily gathering momentum for about two decades.

In December 1994 when *BusinessWeek* magazine did a special report on '21st century capitalism' it referred to the international capital markets as the 'global casino' and the term has stuck. While the global GDP which reflects actual jobs, products and services stands at about $61 trillion, the sum total of financial assets that slosh about in the money markets is estimated to be about $270 trillion. According to one estimate the notional value of derivatives is in the range of $863. More than this imbalance between the value of the productive economy and the notional financial assets the term 'global casino' alludes to the increasing, and now fatal, volatility of global capital. Ironically, one of the most persistent and passionate whistle-blowers of this realm has been one of its stars – George Soros. For over two decades Soros has warned in every possible forum that the inherent instability of capital markets threatens to undermine society and democracy. Since the globalisation of financial markets has given financial capital an unfair advantage over other sources of taxation, Soros has also supported a tax on financial transactions to redress this imbalance.

Let us briefly meet some of those who were not running with the herd and instead have been busy challenging the divine right of capital from different angles.

Global casino, Tobin Tax and Jubilee

Concerns about the dangers of speculative currency trading have been around well before communications technologies enabled capital markets to go into hyperdrive. It was in 1972 that the Nobel Prize-winning economist James Tobin first proposed a 0.5% tax on currency deals. Such a tax is expected to vaporise some of the incentives for currency speculation, help to stabilise exchange rates and thus give national governments more autonomy in making fiscal and monetary policy. Since the mid-1990s, this idea has been at the fulcrum of a global activist network known as the Association for the Taxation of Financial Transactions for the Aid of Citizens (ATTAC) – which has organised some of the largest street-level demonstrations across the world.

ATTAC's network, spread over 33 countries, seeks to recapture democratic spaces that have been lost to the financial world. Thus ATTAC campaigns not merely for some form of Currency Transaction Tax (CTT) but also for outlawing of tax havens, cancellation of third-world debt and for either the reform or abolition of the World Trade Organisation (WTO). However, actually putting a CTT in place is not a simple matter. The international finance community is at best sceptical, at worst vehemently opposed. The bulk of collections under a CTT are likely to come from about 100 banks, which control most of the currency trading, with the ten biggest banks controlling over half the currency trading market. These banks see the demand for a CTT as an infringement on the freedom of capital.

Stamp Out Poverty, a coalition of international NGOs, is now working for a Currency Transactions Development Levy (CTDL). This proposal is aimed at raising funds to meet the Millennium Development Goals but does not challenge the power of global capital.

Advocates of the CTDL are emphatic about distancing it from the Tobin Tax, which aimed to alter the structure of the market. So the CTDL lacks the symbolic power of Tobin's original idea. But proponents of the CTDL, such as Avinash Persaud, President of Intelligence Capital and former head of currency research at JP Morgan, argue that it could be a significant tool for wealth redistribution. After all, in a good year the global banking sector delivers profits in the range of $100 billion, mostly out of financing of trade and arranging of capital flows. So why shouldn't the main beneficiary of globalisation make a contribution to finance initiatives that support those who are not benefitted?

In the late 1990s the inequities of global capital were also challenged by the Jubilee 2000 campaign to drop the debts of the poorest countries. Citizens from across the world joined hands to raise a storm of protest against the policies of both governments and private banks. Rock star Bono, perhaps the most famous face of this movement, helped to focus attention on an elementary question: How can we remain mute spectators while children are dying because governments spend more on servicing the national debt than on health and education? The Jubilee movement took the outrage implicit in this question from the fringes into the living rooms of millions of people in the global North, collecting 24 million signatures from 60 countries. In 2000 the G8 leaders agreed to write off $110 billion of poor-country debts.

Since then the Jubilee Movement International (JMI), as it is now known, has deepened its work on many fronts. Instead of relying on humanitarian appeals to the 'goodwill' of governments and lenders, it now aims to reform the global financial system by installing a legal framework that ensures institutional fairness. It is working to set up a new international solvency framework which would give primacy to human rights and transparency above the requirements of lenders. JMI aims to enable citizens, of poor and rich nations alike, to better monitor and control the international lending and borrowing policies of both governments and private banks. London-based Ann Pettifor, one of the leaders of this movement, sees a long hard road ahead but takes courage from the fact that over the last decade even the IMF is more willing to engage in 're-embedding' financial systems because the world's central banks are tired of bailing out private banks.

In September 2003, Pettifor predicted 'a collapse in the credit system of the rich world, led by the US, leading to soaring personal and corporate bankruptcies'. In August 2006 Pettifor noted the fall in house sales in Florida and California and saw it as a sign of 'canaries in the deep vast coal mine of US credit' that would cause a tsunami-scale financial crisis to inundate the global economy. At the time Pettifor was ridiculed in the financial press as a prophet of doom fruitlessly preoccupied with distant, possibly imaginary, dangers.

Pettifor was unperturbed. She saw these responses as an inevitable outcome of strict adherence to a theory of fantastic, always self-adjusting and self-regulating, markets that could be relied upon to act efficiently. As the bailouts of banks got underway in 2008, starting with Bear Sterns, Pettifor saw bankers and economists alike jumping to tackle symptoms rather than the disease – namely, the debt-based money system and a profound imbalance of priorities. Thus, instead of helping debtors, the bailouts helped creditors, banks rather than actual homeowners, the world of finance rather than that of workers or industry. Consequently, Pettifor warned in January 2009, a severe and prolonged global recession becomes inevitable. Thus, Pettifor featured as a finalist for the Revere Prize for Economics given by the *Real-World Economics Review*.

Pettifor is one among several critics of the prevailing money system who, until recently, were dismissed by much of the mainstream media as cranks. Peter Challen, a key activist of the Christian Council for Monetary Justice (CCMJ) in the UK, is quite happy to be called a crank. Like his mentor E.F. Schumacher, Challen enjoys reminding people that a crank is a small bent instrument that starts a revolution! What formations like the Christian Council for Monetary Justice and the Forum for Stable Currencies (FSC) seek may not be revolutionary but it would certainly disrupt the prevailing system of banking. The core premise of such activist groups in UK is that interest-bearing money created by private banks is one of the major obstacles to economic democracy. According to the FSC, the total share of money issued by government free of interest has gone down from 31% in the late 1960s to about 3% at present.

Since virtually all money is now created by private banks, this amounts to an 'unjust monopoly' which benefits private banks and their shareholders at the cost of the general public. Issuance of credit and money is the fundamental responsibility of the state, says Challen, because it represents the productive and trading capabilities of a society. Since it is people's trading liquidity, it follows that money should remain a public utility. Instead, commodity money becomes a curse that gravely endangers stability and undermines fairness. Therefore, such monetary reform groups are lobbying in the British Parliament for an expansion of government-created, interest-free, money. Quite apart from these efforts to push for new legislation they are expanding the critique of the prevailing money system through a weekly gathering, known as the London Global Table. After the meltdown they have intensified efforts to demand that financial transactions must be backed by real assets rather than shady repackaged instruments.

Yet another challenge to the 'right' of capital to earn interest comes from the rise of Islamic banking over the last 25 years. Islam's key insight is that investing capital is legitimate only when the investor shares in the risk. Earning an unconditional profit, simply for parking your capital with someone, is thus deemed to be *haram*, a sin. A true Muslim must engage in commerce on the basis of risk-sharing, fair dealing and equity. There are now more than 250 Islamic banks operating across the world, handling an estimated \$200 billion. Most major Western banks have offered Islamic banking services to devout Muslims since the mid-1990s.

In 1999, Dow Jones launched an Islamic Index, a screen that allows devout Muslims to select stocks that are deemed *halal*, or righteous. Companies that deal in alcohol, pork, gambling or interest-bearing loans are excluded from the index. By 2007 Dow Jones's services to Islamic investors included 70 indexes based on the advice of an independent Shari'ah Supervisory Board. Islamic financial services offered by conventional banks have been described as '*halal* windows on *haram* palaces'. But there are also a range of international institutions, both financial and academic, that grapple with such challenges. For example, the Institute of Islamic Banking and Insurance (IIBI), a leading academic and research institute, promotes the implementation of Islamic banking and insurance.

Interest-free lending is not unique to Islamic banking. The Danish JAK Members Bank has operated on this basis since

1931. JAK is an acronym for the Swedish words for land, labour and capital. Since it is a cooperative bank owned by its 33,000 members, borrowers pay only for administration, information and for the development of the interest-free system. Such endeavours are based on a basic truth that was famously expressed by Francis Bacon: 'Money is like muck, not good except it be spread.'

Champagne glass syndrome

This proposition is accepted by an increasingly wide range of people. Many of them will say 'I'm not a socialist', but then go on to add that economic power must be dispersed more widely. If this is indeed both a moral and practical imperative, asks Muhammad Yunus, why are 60% of the world's people still getting only 6% of global income? He calls this the champagne glass syndrome with two-thirds of human beings stuck in the stem of the glass – living on less than Rs.100 ($2) a day, virtually invisible on the radar screens of the global economy. That's why Yunus makes it his 'business' to work with those who live on just Rs.15 (30 cents) a day. Micro-finance was never quite 'philanthropy' or 'humanitarian aid' but its expansion into a for-profit sector has created both dilemmas and excitement. Let us go straight to the villages of southern India for a sample of how inclusion as business is taking shape.

Kamalamma's story is the stuff of legend in countless reports by aid agencies and global non-profit organisations. The 30-something Kamalamma runs the only tea shop in Kadlur, a village in southern India. Customers squat on the packed-mud floor, beside an earthen wood-fired stove, on which a pot of tea is on over-boil. Kamalamma serves the tea in tiny wafer-thin plastic cups which hold some four sips of the hot sweet brew. That's just about the quantity that most of her customers can afford to buy.

Kamalamma is the beneficiary of a loan for Rs.15,000, which in 2006 was equivalent to about $365. She used the loan to buy a buffalo and earn a living by partly selling its milk and using the rest as raw material for the tea business. In September 2006, when I met Kamalamma, she was comfortably paying back the loan and its 6.6% interest. The interest is low because it is calculated on a declining basis and the tea-shop cash flow allows her to repay in weekly instalments which are collected from her home by the local area bank.

Kadlur's tea shop was the quintessence of what brought a dozen European and American investors for a study tour in villages of southern India. They were all familiar with the global success of non-profit micro credit. But now a new kind of venture capital firm was urging them to 'Invest good. Do well' because international aid and charity is never going to create widespread prosperity. In 2007 micro-credit, both in profit and non-profit mode, was said to be reaching a 100 million people across the world. Some estimate that it needs to reach one billion people. A socially embedded joint venture by Netherlands-based Goodwell Investments and its Indian partner Aavishkaar seeks to reach some of those one billion people. This is why they invited existing and potential investors to see how it works on the ground in villages like Kadlur. All the visitors appeared to be troubled by one question: how is it okay to make a profit out of the poor?

Wim van der Beek wrestled with this question himself before setting up Goodwell. As an international tax partner in PricewaterhouseCoopers, van der Beek was deeply familiar with corporate wealth generation. But he was more interested in looking for ways to use his skills to generate 'well-th'. So he quit, went looking for new pathways and struck up a conversation with Yunus about redefining entrepreneurship – perhaps even the workings of capital.

Just days before van der Beek led that study tour to the villages of Karnataka, Yunus was declared the winner of the Nobel Peace Prize for 2006. Yunus had started out, three decades earlier, with a somewhat similar restlessness that now afflicted van der Beek. Yunus's turning point came in 1974, when he was troubled by the incongruity of teaching elegant economic theories, at the Chittagong University, while Bangladesh was being ravaged by a famine.

Yunus set out to do something immediate, even if it helped only one person. He went to the nearest slum and made a list of things that trapped people into poverty: 'I was shocked to discover a woman in the village, borrowing less than a dollar from the money-lender, on the condition that he would have the exclusive right to buy all she produces at the price he decides. This, to me, was a way of recruiting slave labour.' So Yunus took the equivalent of US$27 out of his own pocket and gave personal loans to 42 people so they could escape from the money lenders. That gesture led eventually to the formation of the Grameen Bank in 1983 and banking was never the same again.

Grameen altered the notion of who is bankable. It proved that the poor almost never default on a loan. But this was because Grameen worked more like a community than a bank. It invested not in projects but in people – in women and their households rather than men with stand-alone projects. 'I'm not interested in the past of my borrower but only in her future,' Yunus would say. So Grameen defined its business as 'inclusion', which meant that it gave people a fresh start through a loan, no collateral asked for.

When Yunus picked up the Nobel at Oslo he was accompanied by nine elected representatives, all women, of the seven million borrowers-cum-owners of Grameen Bank. Yunus's companions on the trip to Oslo were, at some point, like Kamalamma in Kadlur. Over 23 years Grameen has made loans for a total of about US$7.59 billion at a repayment rate of 99%. Initially dependent on donor money, it became self-reliant in 1995. Its internal survey shows that 58% of Grameen borrowers have risen above the poverty line. Among other things micro-credit has ensured that the poor could make a livelihood from activities other than agriculture.

Yunus earned the title 'Father of Micro Credit' not merely by steering Grameen as a community-oriented business but in making it possible for others to do so. For instance, back in 1989 when young Udaia Kumar wanted to set up a micro-credit institution in the southern Indian state of Andhra Pradesh, no one in the banking establishment would hear him out. It was a $34,000 loan from Grameen that allowed him to start SHARE, now one of the largest micro-lending entities in India. By the late 1990s micro-credit had arrived at the centre-stage of the global discourse on poverty alleviation and elimination. The United Nations observed 2005 as the Year of Microcredit. Giant pension funds like TIAA-CREF, in the USA, and APP, in the Netherlands, are investing in micro-credit. When major international banks launched micro-credit programmes Yunus reasserted that 'micro-credit is about poverty, it's not a business, it's not about making money'. So does micro-credit, both for profit and non-profit, in any way challenge or morph the divine right of capital?

Before looking for answers to that question it is important to first note the many grades and shades of micro-credit. According to van der Beek, the Grameen model represents micro-credit '1.0' and is fundamentally a human rights initiative focused purely on poverty alleviation. Commercial entities are engaged in micro-credit '2.0' which is more of a business development mechanism treating the poor as clients with untapped skills. And then there is micro-credit '3.0', which is about innovating an assortment of services to ensure financial inclusion. For Van der Beek, and many like him, micro-credit is simultaneously a poverty alleviation initiative and a business with a social and financial bottom line.

For instance, by a modest estimate there are 260 million people in India below the poverty line. It is also estimated that about 45% of Indians do not have access to commercial banking. By the end of 2006 only about 4–6 million Indians had access to micro-credit from the total of about $220 million in circulation in this sector. The estimated requirement is for about \$11.6–25 billion. ICICI Bank has estimated that the demand for loan officers in micro-finance institutions could create jobs for about one million people. Even the rapid expansion in philanthropy cannot meet those needs. So why not create avenues for investors who are also committed to financial inclusion?

Scepticism and objections fly at this question from opposite ends. Conventional banks are not designed to even think about 'inclusion' and certainly not to deal with millions of small-change clients. At the other end of the spectrum is the discomfort of those who have built micro-credit institutions as a community-driven and community-nurturing mechanisms. Let us take the bank's side of the story first.

Moumita Sen-Sarma is a regular commercial banker who says she stumbled upon micro-finance when she was appointed to handle the newly formed micro-credit department at ABN AMRO, India, in 2003. Reconfiguring ABN AMRO systems to deal with micro-finance was a journey into choppy uncharted waters. All the usual banking parameters – governance, transparency and sound business model – seemed terribly inadequate. At one level there was tension between the bank staff's corporate culture and the seemingly unprofessional entrepreneurial style of NGOs. But Sen-Sarma and her colleagues also worried about causing 'mission drift' if they imposed external performance pressures on their micro-finance partners at the ground. This tension was resolved by staying focused on the social agenda. But ABN AMRO was not in this purely for the social bottom line or enhanced corporate social responsibility ratings. Experience in the micro-credit sector fed into servicing corporate clients aiming to reach markets at the base of the pyramid. Plus the micro-credit division is in itself profitable.

This is what enables Washington DC-based MicroVest to work at the interface of capital markets and people it describes as the 'entrepreneurial poor'. MicroVest serves as a capital-mobilising intermediary for micro-finance institutions (MFIs) across the world. It also aims to build capital markets for the micro-enterprise system as well as to support self-sustaining financial institutions that serve the poor. MicroVest was founded by three major non-profits, CARE, MEDA and Seed Capital Development Fund. Its work is based on the assessment that MFIs are the best route to sustainable economic development because they generate competition which drives down interest rates. MicroVest therefore favours securitisation of micro-finance loans as a means of enhancing the efficiency by which capital is disbursed to MFIs and thus enabling investors to view micro-finance as its own asset class. So how do the double-edged dilemmas of micro-credit look from MicroVest's vantage point? Matthew Speh, MicroVest's young investment officer, explained it rather succinctly to the study tour group brought together by Goodwell: 'Our big concerns are the legal infrastructure and protection for investor rights. Mission drift would include forcing debt on clients.'

Oikocredit is a much older and larger entity in this field. An offshoot of the 'social gospel' of the World Council of Churches, Oikocredit sticks close to the Latin meaning of credit – which is 'believing'. Its work is premised on giving people a chance by believing in them in a wider sense than just seeing them as 'creditworthy'. Then there is MicroPlace.com, an eBay company which enables people to 'Invest Wisely, End Poverty' with just a few clicks on their website. It encourages the 'everyday investor', someone with as little as $100. MicroPlace then channels those funds to micro-enterprises across the world. Tracey Pettengill Turner, its founder, came out of the Stanford Graduate School of Business and learnt the ropes by working at the Grameen Bank in Bangladesh.

What looks like a booming new asset class to many seems like a dark-edged fad to some veterans who have spent over three decades grappling with the complex muddles of how to spread the benefits of development more widely and fairly. Such critics are particularly disturbed by the tendency to treat micro-credit as a poverty-removing magic potion. Vijay

Mahajan, the pioneer of for-profit micro-credit in India, has himself taken the lead in identifying fatal flaws. 'The poor don't just want loans, they want economic security,' says Mahajan. That includes safe harbours for savings, affordable and reliable insurance services, inputs such as artisanal raw materials, marketing linkages along with a variety of agricultural and business development services.

In any case, all those who can get micro-credit are not capable of, or interested in, becoming mini-entrepreneurs. Among the poorest of the poor most people have no wish to be self-employed or entrepreneurial. They crave steady wage-employment. Even those that are more enterprising can remain stuck at the level of Kamalamma's tea shop, unless they also have access to business and technical training matched by supportive infrastructure such as better roads, affordable and reliable supply of energy, water and other natural resources.

Some equity investors are already moving towards engaging with these backup systems essential for making micro-credit work more meaningfully. But, as van der Beek says, this is a realm for the 'patient capital' of social investors who are satisfied with 8–9% return. The market for micro-finance is unlimited and not because the rich are going to make money off the poor, says Vineet Rai, founder and CEO of Aavishkaar. There is money to be made because of scale not because of high interest rates. When micro-lending happens at interest rates ranging from 18% to 28% it can easily look usurious. However, many of those borrowers were otherwise dependent on lenders, who sometimes charged 100% interest or even more. By contrast, an 18% interest rate applied on a declining basis, is a substantial benefit. Rai also urges critics to factor in higher overheads. Processing a thousand micro-finance loans of Rs.10,000 each is far more time- and labour-intensive than lending a million rupees to one person.

So does micro-finance in any way challenge the divine right of capital? One answer is a tentative and qualified 'yes'. In its early stages micro-finance overturned conventional rules of capital by making community bankable – since it stood on the shoulders of the purely social phenomenon of village-level self-help groups based on mutual trust and cooperation. Those credit societies circulated local savings, money that was already in the community. However, it is unlikely that such community-based structures can withstand the inflow of global finance into micro-lending.

International financiers are willing to enter this domain and bear the risk of lending because there is now an established record that the poor almost always repay loans. For them financial 'inclusion' means drawing more and more people into the conventional functioning of capital by challenging the very concept on which SHGs built their strengths. For example, one former Citibank executive asked a proponent of community-based micro-credit: 'If I do not need my neighbour's help to get a loan, why should I perpetuate the model of social groups for others? Is that fair?'

This question carries two major assumptions. One that individuals wielding capital on their own, outside of community structures and approvals, are more free; and, two, that structures of conventional capital when ruled by such stand-alone individuals are more efficient. But if you look at the social and cultural realities of the SHG in the wider context of both the financial and ecological crisis then these assumptions look rather fragile.

For example, Myrada, a self-help organisation in Karnataka, has found that loan repayment behaviour changes rapidly when individuals move out of self-help groups (SHGs) and into the conventional domain of capital since the system they encounter outside retains none of the values they have thrived under. Rohini Nilekani, who has supported micro-finance as a philanthropist and also served on the board of an MFI called Sangamitra, observes that SHGs have fostered a form of 'social stickiness' that empowers people in a wide variety of ways. And yet the premise on which such formations were built, and became a success, is constantly under pressure from the outside. Perhaps because, as Nilekani suggests, 'when cultur-ally and socially un-embedded money comes, it comes at a cost to the process of social empowerment that may be impos-sible to explain'.

Events of 2008 have somewhat deflated the excitement about 'financial inclusion' by raising a rather elementary question. Why become part of a chronically unstable global financial system? Instead, it is worth exploring if the world of old-style capital may benefit from adopting the values of those sought to be 'included'. As Nilekani provocatively mused: 'What if Wall Street financiers had *had* to be part of a social group that they were accountable to in a closed system, with-out the ability to externalise their costs, just like a good old SHG, perhaps things would be different today.'

Besides, as Vijay Mahajan has pointed out, strong locally anchored banking institutions that truly serve the base by remaining embedded in the productive economy need not be afflicted by the contagion at the top. For instance, when the Asian currency crisis hit Indonesia in 1997, most of its banks suffered a huge erosion of deposits, and were hit by a high number of loans being defaulted. It was the Unit Desa or rural division of Bank Rakyat Indonesia that continued to thrive through the crisis. There was not only an upsurge in deposits but also a slight increase in its 98%-plus repayment rate. That is because people in the rural economy were largely dealing among themselves, so the effect of currency depreciation and inflation did not affect them much, wrote Mahajan.

In any case, what grassroots proponents of inclusion actu-ally seek is not absorption into global capital flows but greater economic effervescence with an overall increase in actual well-being. For some, such as Myrada, the key objective is to pro-mote an assortment of livelihoods. Savings and credit schemes are operated only as a means of ensuring that people's self-reliance and pride are not undermined. As Al Fernandez of Myrada says, micro-credit in itself has limited utility in the absence of crucial inputs like soil and water conservation, diversification of agriculture and non-farm enterprises, market linkages and so on. These concerns remain outside the ambit of those micro-finance entities that become mini-replicas of conventional banks – concerned primarily, or entirely, with the rate of outgoings and repayments.

These underlying contradictions eventually churned up the perfect storm in India's micro-finance sector. In July 2010 SKS Micro-finance became the first such company to be listed on India's stock market. But within weeks of a successful, over-subscribed IPO the offices of SKS and various other micro-finance institutions, in the southern Indian state of Andhra Pradesh, were under attack by irate mobs. Those indulging in vandalism accused the MFIs of charging usurious interest rates and even held the lenders responsible for a spate of suicides among borrowers. The MFIs, while denying charges of usury, blamed various political parties for inciting the acts of vandalism.

A cascade of events, including a government order restricting the activities of MFIs, soon brought large chunks of this sector into deep crisis. In December 2010, even as proponents of for-profit micro-finance worked with policy-makers to salvage the situation, there were pervasive fears that a domino effect could bring down most MFIs across India.

None of this came as a surprise to veterans particularly those who, like Fernandez, nurtured the SHG model of micro-finance for over 25 years. It would not matter that valuations became more important than values, wrote Fernandez in December 2010, if the associated promises had indeed materialised. Induction of venture and private capital into MFIs, while raising risks for borrowers, was also expected to increase the benefits. As competition increased, interest rates should have come down. They did not.

'It was the dreariness of making the rich even richer that made me look beyond corporate banking and I felt hugely fortunate when it seemed that in micro-finance we had probably discovered a game changer,' said Sen Sarma, after many years of heading micro-finance at ABN AMRO. She never expected micro finance to work like a silver bullet but nevertheless she was disappointed to find it reduced to serving as just another lucrative 'asset class'. In hindsight, Sen Sarma said, 'If only we hadn't overlooked the fact that a vast majority of people still see profit as the only currency for measuring success, we could have anticipated this "distortion".'

At the beginning of 2010 for-profit micro-finance could claim to promote financial inclusion even if it never posed a challenge to the divine right of capital. At the dawn of 2011 it seemed more likely that micro-finance had become another way of reinforcing the champagne glass syndrome.

Besides, at present, the bulk of micro-credit enables old-style, ecologically unviable, growth. As the pressures for sustainability mount this is bound to change. But will 'sustainability' merely be added on as means of ensuring *sustained* profits or will it change the rules of the game?

Crafting a triple bottom line

The encounter with 'deep ecology' at Schumacher College was a trifle traumatic for Peter Head, a veteran civil engineer. He could sense that the staff ecologist, Stephen Harding, was trying to be as gentle as possible. But the unvarnished simplicity with which Harding lays out the facts has a dizzying effect, like the terror of lurching over a precipice. It made Head look back on three decades of his own work, plus his role then as CEO of the civil engineering multinational Maunsell, and feel 'pretty awful'.

The Business Sustainability courses at Schumacher College are designed to simultaneously serve as shock therapy and a safe zone for exploring 'doable' options. For example, Peter Head absorbed the grim news from a deep ecology perspective and then got back to the drawing board determined to 'concentrate on improving where we are now, rather than just lamenting. Every project can change that to some extent.'

Above all, he said when I met him in 2001, the spell at Schumacher College gave him links into a network that's enormously intellectually stimulating.

Back in 2000, few people in the City were talking about sustainability or holistic sciences. But London First had just set up a Sustainability Council and Head was picked to lead it. Plus he was gripped by the book *Natural Capitalism* and was hungry to learn more. At the same time Head noticed an evocative new term cropping up within corporate boardrooms and even during discussions with senior officials at the British Treasury. That term was 'triple bottom line'. This catchy term was coined by a man who has spent a good part of his life grappling with the tricky and wondrous ways in which words limit or grow what we are able to think.

John Elkington first 'spot-welded' the term 'environmental excellence' while working with the United Nations in the mid-1980s. Linking environmental concerns to excellence in business was far more effective than making individuals or companies feel guilty about their environmentally bad behaviour. At that time mainstream business literature on excellence made no mention of environmental performance. Elkington has a graduate degree in environmental studies, from University College London, and was so deeply influenced by James Lovelock's Gaia theory that he named one of his daughters Gaia. In 1987, Elkington and his team launched an environmental and business consultancy company called SustainAbility – long before the word came into common usage or became a buzzword.

After the United Nations Rio Earth Summit in 1992 'sustainable development' became a global mantra. Governments and businesses alike now accepted that current patterns of industry and consumption are unsustainable. To enable business brains to make sense of sustainability, Elkington and his colleagues came up with the term 'triple bottom line' (TBL). Initially it referred to 'People, Planet, Profit'. Later Elkington changed the 'Profit' to 'Prosperity'. The concept was not entirely new but coining the term simplified and enlivened the debate around these issues.

Elkington and his colleagues were also driven by the disturbing realisation that a lot of activism 'tends to shut people down by winding them even more tightly into their current mind-set'. Back in the 1960s when he learnt weaving, Elkington had been struck by the way in which a chemical mordant is used to open up fibre, making it ready to absorb dyes. Likewise, the TBL became a literal and symbolic way of helping people open up to new ideas in a fertile rather than threatening way.

Elkington's book *Cannibals with Forks* (1998) sketched the details of the concept and took on the mega-question: can corporate capitalism become sustainable? Can the notion of profit be redefined? He also optimistically argued that the force of circumstance and mounting public pressure would compel corporate 'cannibals' to reform. He predicted that TBL thinking would eventually transform accounting which in turn would comprehensively alter how business is done.

Early converts, and the merely curious, met for the first ever Triple Bottom Line Investing Conference in Rotterdam in December 1999. Since then, the conference, conceived and organised by the Amsterdam consultancy firm Brooklyn Bridge, has become a major annual feature. It works on the principle that 'the world will benefit when economy supports well-being'. Such events expanded space for the view that generating shareholder value is no longer enough. Companies must generate benefits for all stakeholders by adding *societal* value.

Of course, to those who believe that 'the business of business is business' this sounded rather heretical. On Wall Street, during discussions for an IPO in 2001, Peter Head found his concerns about a triple bottom line brushed aside as irrelevant. However, the heresy has continued to seep into the innards of business life – moving from the realm of social activism – where it was incubated by people like Elkington, Amory

Lovins, Paul Hawken and many others – to the heart of the global marketplace. Through the Sustainability Unit of London First, Head introduced a triple-bottom-line index for that metropolis. This index shows that, while London has made significant economic and social progress, its environmental bottom line is poor. Virtually all major global corporations now at least claim to work for environmental sustainability. Some have set standards above those mandated by law.

Of course the actual nitty-gritty details of triple-bottom-line reporting, analysis and strategy are quite complicated. Sometimes the link of cause and effect is notoriously difficult to establish. Plus, three-dimensional accounting adds more work and complexity to day-to-day management. As the director of a major German pharmaceutical company told me, tracking the company's performance on a triple bottom line is a pain in the neck. It is tempting, said this executive who asked to remain anonymous, to just not bother even if it means that the company looks out of step with the times. But here is an illustration of why companies find it harder to ignore such pressures.

In 1998, ABN AMRO received a letter from the global NGO Friends of the Earth (FoE) asking why the bank was financing a project in Wisteria, New Guinea, which was damaging the environment and violating human rights. The letter landed on the desk of Herman Mulder, who was then heading risk management at ABN AMRO's headquarters. Had the letter come from Friends of the Earth alone it would just have been filed, Mulder told me in an interview. But this letter also carried signatures from 800 shareholders of ABN. So the matter was investigated and all the allegations turned out to be true. 'We agreed that the violations were shameful,' said Mulder. 'We then decided to disassociate with the project. But FoE said don't do that, instead make your client accountable. We also acknowledged that FoE had brought new dimensions to our definition of risk management.'

Interestingly, at about the same time, ABN lost a big new project because it stood by higher environmental standards. This led to sharp divisions within the bank. Like others in a similar hot seat, Mulder realised that lone rangers would not be able to hold out against such pressures. So he worked with the International Finance Corporation to bring together 12 large global banks to agree on social and environmental standards that all would follow. The result was the Equator Principles, a benchmark for the financial industry to manage social and environmental issues in project financing. Forty-one major international banks are now signatories to the triple-bottom-line approach of the Equator Principles.

Most of these international norms were driven by environmental activists working in tandem with, initially, just a few companies. For example, the Global Reporting Initiative was founded in 1997 by the US-based Coalition for Environmentally Responsible Economies (Ceres) and Tellus Institute, with the support of the United Nations Environment Programme (UNEP). It is now probably the most credible multi-stakeholder process for setting standards on sustainability reporting guidelines. Similarly, the Carbon Disclosure Project (CDP), an independent not-for-profit organisation launched in 2000, succeeded in creating both monitoring structures and dialogue within the business world on tackling climate change. CDP now provides a coordinating secretariat for institutional investors with combined assets of over \$57 trillion under management.

Momentum for change accelerated when data emerging from such initiatives revealed that companies that lack response plans to cope with climate change and other environmental crises are rapidly falling behind industry standards. And then, in 2004, 18 of the world's leading financial institutions, with a total of over US\$6 trillion under management, got together and declared that 'Who Cares Wins'. This process in turn led to the United Nations Principles of Responsible Investment (UNPRI), launched at the New York Stock

Exchange in August 2006. The signatories of these principles, including 200 institutional investors who together have over $9 trillion under management, are committed to integrating environmental, social and governance (ESG) issues into their investment policies and engagement strategies.

Meanwhile, Peter Head has come a long way from being shaken up by the teachings of Deep Ecology at Schumacher College. In 2008, he was designing the world's largest sustainable development project at Dongtan in China. Head is now a director of Arup, the global engineering firm charged with designing a city for half a million people which will be self-sufficient in both energy and food. Interestingly, Arup has no external shareholders. It was founded in 1946 and is owned in trust on behalf of its staff. Some of Arup's more famous projects include the structural design for the Sydney Opera House and the route of the Channel Tunnel rail link.

The life and work journeys of such individuals are both being driven by and directing the larger trends. For instance, the seemingly quirky rejection of 'sin stock' by some Puritan investors has today morphed and grown into the much wider phenomenon of the socially managed portfolio. But can investment portfolios really be used to build a better world and how? Are these adjustments just oriented to securing sustained returns on capital or ecological sustainability and prosperity for all?

Put your money where your morals are: Socially Managed Portfolio

The offices of Loring, Wolcott & Coolidge are just what you might expect of a venerable Boston investment firm. There's finely polished wood, gleaming leather and an air of old-world elegance. A surprising setting for a meeting with a radical. Yet this is where Amy Domini called me for an interview in the summer of 2003. The second surprise was that Domini is no fire-breathing activist. Instead I found a soft-spoken, gentle missionary with the patience for slow change. How did the young woman who started out as a photocopy clerk in a stock-broker's office in 1973 become a pioneer of socially responsible investing?

It was shortly after she became a stockbroker in 1975 that Domini noticed that some of her clients often expressed investment preferences over and above the need to earn money. One woman directed Domini not to buy her stock in a particular paper company because it was responsible for deforestation. The same client was also saying 'no' to stocks in nuclear power companies. Another client said to Domini, 'Don't ask me to decide what matters more – women's rights, the environment, or South Africa. They all matter.' Having come of age during the Vietnam War, Domini herself had a nagging sense of having sold out and 'become a cog in the military–industrial machinery'. But, she confessed, this had bothered her less and less as the money got better and better. Then one day she felt sick at the prospect of urging her clients to buy stock in an armament company whose stock price was about to rise dramatically because of new government contracts.

Like countless others, Domini had run smack into the stress of leading a double life – a personal life anchored in caring for family, for community and a work life of scrambling for superior investment results in a social and moral vacuum. The irony of it all, as Domini puts it, is that

> these two worlds are occupied by the same people. When at home, they care, and when at work, they care. But what they care about in each locale is at conflict with what they care about at the other. As a result, they work long days to achieve a goal that jeopardises all that they hold dear when at home.

Gradually, Domini started integrating ethical concerns with investment decisions. For a start she had to become indifferent to ridicule. In the early 1980s, the idea that brokers and bankers should screen firms on any criteria other than money gains was treated as absurd. But Domini doggedly persisted in asking why it wasn't possible to make money while also ensuring that you were keeping the air clean and environment safe? She was convinced that investors can add a caring element at the fulcrum of two worlds – the world of finance and the world of commerce. After all, in the late 1960s, students at several major American universities had demanded that their university withdraw investments from any company that was engaged in the Vietnam War. In 1972 the Church of the Brethren divested all investments in corporations producing weapons. There was already the Pax World Fund, set up in 1971, which put together investment portfolios with no stocks in armaments, liquor or tobacco companies.

Domini went on to set up a string of enterprises that became the leaders in what is now called socially responsible investing, or SRI. These included the Domini Social Index, Domini Social Equity Fund, Domini Social Investments, as well as Kinder, Lydenberg, Domini Research & Analytics. The success of these ventures won Domini the distinction of being called the 'Founding Mom' of SRI. Her ability to combine investment discipline with social concerns put her on *Barron's* list of the 30 people who changed the face of finance over the 20th century. She was the only woman on that list. In 2005 *Time* magazine included Domini in its list of the world's 100 most influential people.

When the Social Investment Forum in the US conducted the first survey of this domain in 1984, it identified a total of about $40 billion of assets involved in some form of socially screened investing. By 1995, this figure had jumped to $639 billion – which was then roughly 1 in every 10 dollars under professional management in the US. By 2003, social investing assets were at about $2.16 trillion, in the US alone. The global estimate for such investing is now about $3 trillion. Even more significant is that between 1995 and 2003 the SRI sphere grew 40% faster than routine investing.

Ironically, the rise of this phenomenon can partly be credited to the TINA doctrine. When government seemed less willing to protect either labour or environment or respond to other social concerns, rights seekers made an instrument out of shareholder activism. Socially responsible investing aims to balance out the power of the purely money-profit-driven market. As Domini wrote:

> Lenders put whole nations into bankruptcy to repay a loan they never should have made; investors demanding cheaper raw materials stand by as peasants are seized and chained to work the pipeline. These actions are immoral. Yet they happen every day on my behalf. An amoral financial services industry sees maximising shareholder return as such a noble endeavour that it must take not just precedence, but an exclusive position of power.

However, the big push for SRI has not depended on this kind of passionate desire to put your money where your morals are. The exponential growth of SRI is being driven by the increasing number of people who see cause-based investment as a practical necessity – even a survival imperative. This includes eco-regeneration projects that may offer slow and low monetary returns. Others are deploying SRI methods simply as a form of risk management and asset protection.

Many SRI investors tend to see conservation of natural resources and the switch to low-carbon growth as a survival imperative – not altruism. But some do take a moral stand on the need to respect the sanctity and dignity of all humans – and will thus insist on high labour standards. Similarly, some take a position on keeping certain functions and services *out* of the market and outside the profit motive. For example, such people will not invest in private prisons.

At the most activist end of the spectrum, SRI investors directly intervene to alter a company's priorities and operations. Proxy-based shareholder activism is one instrument but great emphasis is also placed on dialogue. Domini has found that such direct communication with management often helps both sides to find reasonable first steps for addressing complex issues which were otherwise not on the corporate agenda.

For example, an SRI fund advocate may ask a company why its suppliers are running sweatshops. The company might first reply that it can't possibly monitor thousands of suppliers but go on to work out a methodology for solving such problems in its supply chain.

Such direct engagement with social and ethical values fosters the impression that SRI challenges the primacy of monetary profits. But virtually all SRI funds promise value on all three bottom lines. For instance, the Calvert Group cites a study of 300 companies which showed that those with a superior environmental performance also showed higher money profits. The Domini 400 Social Index shows that over two decades social investment mutual funds have maintained returns that are above average in the financial sector as a whole.

Why, then, does the perception persist that you have to sacrifice some money profit in order to serve the planet and people bottom lines? Domini puts this down partly to the macho culture on Wall Street:

> The stakeholder screening process is an almost universally overlooked tool on Wall Street. The feminist in me attributes this to a hangover 'macho' attitude on Wall Street by which it is somehow considered soft to use the vocabulary of socially responsible investing. But the results speak for themselves, and the performance of the Domini 400 Social Index cannot be denied.

SRI came out of the niche stage with the setting-up of the Dow Jones Sustainability Index in 1999 and of FTSE4Good index in 2001. 'What started as a fad for idealists has now become a mainstream idea, even the world's largest and second largest pensions funds are at it,' lamented *The Economist*. In UK the Pensions Act has been modified to make it mandatory for the trustees of institutional pension funds to state what social, ethical or environmental factors they have taken into account. The listing requirements on the London Stock Exchange were changed in favour of a more expanded definition of 'risk' to include social and environmental issues. A survey by the Control Risks Group, an international business risk consultancy, has found that social and ethical issues have become more important within the City of London with 71% of those surveyed stating that awareness of these issues has risen dramatically.

Changes in the composition of ownership could also further deepen the SRI phenomenon. In the USA and Western Europe pension funds, mutual funds and insurance companies now collectively own the majority of shares in key markets and their investment horizons should be long-term. As Simon Zadek, the founder of AccountAbility, points out:

> The real owners of capital in today's markets are you and me, the intended beneficiaries of the pension funds, mutual funds and insurance companies. The responsibility of institutional investors must be to meet our intrinsic interests, which go far beyond near-term returns since we have long-term needs and depend on the long-term vitality and health of our societies, economies, communities and the natural environment.

The bad news is that pension funds, mutual funds and insurance companies continue to manage these funds with short-term criteria and old habits are hard to break. However, a growing body of data and analysis might help institutional investors to better understand and incorporate non-financial considerations. Back in 2003, a survey by the WEF showed that 70% of CEOs and CFOs expect to see increased interest in environment, social and governance (ESG) issues by mainstream investors in the future. This is largely due to how social mobilisation has raised the dangers of 'reputational risk'.

One of the most famous illustrations of this was the showdown between GlaxoSmithKline (GSK) and the South African government over alleged intellectual property rights violations in relation to Aids drugs. South Africa had opted to buy drastically cheaper generic drugs from Indian and Brazilian manufacturers. When GSK took South Africa to court, a coalition of global human rights organisations mounted an effective campaign which alerted shareholders of GSK that the company's insistence on enforcing its intellectual property rights would in this case endanger millions of lives and stick investors with a 'reputational risk of biblical proportions'. Eventually GSK pulled out of the case and launched a revised programme of access to essential drugs at lower cost.

And yet, as the *Who Cares Wins* report noted in 2004, most mainstream investors ask little or nothing about social responsibility. Or, as the head of investor relations at one company pointed out, 'no one cares unless there's a financial risk or short-term exposure'. But events just might overtake this orthodoxy. There was a time when Phil Angelides, the California State Treasurer, was considered an odd one out when he argued that 'As fiduciaries, we must take it upon ourselves to identify the emerging environmental challenges facing the companies in which we are shareholders, to demand more information, and to spur needed actions to respond to those challenges.' The red alert on climate change expanded the space for this definition of fiduciary responsibility. For example, the Investor Network on Climate Risk in the USA is headed by the Connecticut State Treasurer Denise Nappier. This network has filed shareholder resolutions with two dozen corporations calling for disclosure of financial risks from global warming.

Domini enjoys these advances but is a hard realist about the downside: 'Heck, at the end of day Shell is still an oil company. I can't understand why we're still using petrol!'

And yet Domini's inspiration is a story about the little girl who saw thousands of starfish washed ashore and quickly started throwing them in the water so they wouldn't die. Her mother discouraged her, saying, 'it won't make a difference'. The girl stopped for a moment, looked at the starfish in her hand, and said, 'It will make a difference to this one.'

Can the sum total of trends triggered by individuals like Domini and Angelides usher in a new form of prosperity where the measure of wealth is so multi-dimensional that the divine right of capital fades into history? The most powerful motivation for this possible shift comes from the expanding realisation that we are simultaneously in the place of that girl and the starfish. As Nial Fitzgerald, one-time CEO of Unilever, has famously said, 'Sustainability is here to stay or we may not be.' But why, then, do people like Angelides find themselves caught in the crossfire?

Orthodoxy strikes back

In 2005 the California State Treasurer Phil Angelides came under attack for using California's $300 billion in state pension funds to demand governance and ethical reforms from corporations. Angelides was accused by the state's Republican Party for putting a social agenda ahead of profits in the management of the California Public Employees' Retirement System, better known as CalPERS. Under Angelides's leadership, CalPERS, the largest public pension fund in the US, pulled out of tobacco stocks, installed human rights screens and emphasised environmental stewardship.

It did not seem to help that CalPERS had maintained a 13.5% return in a period when other large pension funds earned about 11.6%. Yet the American Enterprise Institute alleged that CalPERS was abusing the public trust in a serious and grave manner by prioritising non-financial criteria. State pension funds in New York and Connecticut were similarly hauled up by David Hirschmann, senior vice president of the US Chamber of Commerce, for attempting to advance the social investment agenda of organised labour.

Tim Smith, of Walden Investments in Boston, was actually sued for defamation by Cintas Corporation for statements he made about sweatshop labour abuses at the company's annual general meeting. While the matter was eventually settled with no monetary damages, the case against Smith – a respected leader of corporate reform, a former director of the Interfaith Center for Corporate Responsibility and a recipient of the Aaron Feuerstein Spirituality and Business Award – sent out a clear message. It was seen as part of a swelling counter-attack which was not just about control over more than \$3 trillion institutional funds. It was a move to stem the tide of social and ethical values impinging on the management and multiplication of capital. The fears of the orthodoxy are not unjustified.

'Our ultimate purpose is to reengineer the DNA of Wall Street,' explained Matthew Kiernan, the founder and chief executive of Innovest Strategic Value Advisors which grapples with the devil in the details of SRI. Innovest is founded on the assumption that the process of changing corporate behaviour depends on reliable and rigorous information on the social–environmental areas which have otherwise been completely opaque to financial markets. Innovest provides that information. Yet even Innovest does this by keeping its research firmly focused on those factors that contribute most to financial outcomes. Environmental, social and governance performance is given importance not in terms of intrinsic survival implications or ethical worth but as tangible indicators of management quality and long-term financial performance. However, this has not prevented the concept of triple-bottom-line reporting from being dismissed as 'a licence to obfuscate'. It has been argued that there is no significant correlation between social responsibility and profitability. Innovest has contradicted these claims by analysing 60 research studies over six years to find that 85% showed a positive correlation between CSR and profitability.

Leaders of the SRI sphere tend to lap up the criticism as a signal of their having arrived at centre-stage. It's a sign of being taken seriously by their ideological opponents. However, the criticism that moves the movement forward is more about mechanics than ideology. For example, George Soros supports the motivation behind socially responsible investing and yet remains sceptical. As he said in our conversation during his visit to India in 2007, even the most rigorous measures of social and environmental performance cannot match the clarity of measuring the money bottom line. It's an apples and oranges mismatch.

Valid comparisons between companies are even harder to make. How do you match hundreds of data points which inherently lack the one-dimensional crispness of measures like return-on-investment and earnings-per-share? Thus, at least one critique has argued that the TBL is actually just a 'good old-fashioned single bottom line plus vague commitments to social and environmental concerns'. But are the dangers of 'TBL-wash' sufficient ground to reject the concept and its related mission? All but hardened market fundamentalists tend to say 'no'. As Soros put it, a company that at least claims to meet a higher benchmark of responsibility is better than one that is brazen about damaging people and planet.

The important thing, for now, is that the multi-dimensional bottom line has altered the political economy of business and opened up spaces. It has expanded the freedom of what a corporation can do without slipping into the category of soft, fuzzy and suspect. Global giants like AT&T, Dow Chemicals, Shell and British Telecom all speak the language of TBL – at least in their press releases. Most major accounting firms now offer services to companies wanting to measure themselves on the other two bottom lines. This process has also gathered speed thanks to international benchmarks created by voluntary forums like the Carbon Disclosure Project, Global Reporting Initiative, Global Compact and so on.

Back in 2001, Elkington anticipated that thousands of companies that were in denial about the imperative for sustainable development would soon end up on the couch, mourning models that once served them well. Looking at SustainAbility's client list it can seem as though major corporations have leapt over the couch and gone straight to a drawing board to design new parameters. Some are indeed looking for new models.

But on a day-to-day basis most companies appear to be are just coping with the friction between emerging values and the old-fashioned one-dimensional bottom line. Denial about the imperative of sustainability may be a thing of the past. But what lies beyond denial? Just how much freedom is there to make course corrections? On that note let us return to the core questions with which this chapter started. Is enhanced accountability and responsibility enough? How does the ferment within corporations tally with the need for truer and deeper democracy?

Beyond denial

Late in 2007, soon after being appointed to the I.G. Patel Chair at the London School of Economics, Nicholas Stern was in India to make a pitch for low-carbon growth with a triple bottom line. 'But is that enough?' asked Anand Mahindra, CEO of Mahindra and Mahindra. Sharing a platform with Stern at a public meeting in Mumbai, Mahindra raised the bar and called for a 'triple top line' where sustainability would be woven into the design stage of all business models. Mahindra even invoked Mahatma Gandhi's foresight that modern industry and consumption threatens to strip the planet like locusts. And then he revealed a painful paradox.

His company's contribution to low-carbon growth, said Mahindra, would be to produce a hybrid version of its popular four-wheel-drive vehicles – a 'guilt-free SUV', as he called it. But carbon emissions are just one part of the SUV's extra-large eco-footprint. Can, or should, the company give up manufacturing SUVs in order to promote sustainability? Most companies that have embraced the idea of sustainability are caught in similar or worse dilemmas. The result is a jumble of contradictions with a bare glimmer of possible new models.

For the moment, most corporations are largely readjusting how they carry themselves and thus are simultaneously good and bad, depending on what part of their operations you examine.

For example, before becoming infamous for the world's most disastrous oil spill in 2010 British Petroleum (BP) was perceived as a leader in fighting climate change. Even though lax maintenance of its pipelines led to a major oil leak in Alaska, BP tended to fare well on CSR ratings.

Walmart pays low wages and inadequate healthcare coverage for its employees. Plus, its big-box mega-stores are hubs of unsustainable production and consumption. And yet, since 2005, Walmart has embarked on a number of potentially far-reaching environmental initiatives. In India, the Tata group of companies has been a pioneer of social responsibility. It created a Tata Index for Sustainable Human Development in 2000 to enable its companies to monitor and measure their performance on social responsibility. Yet several of the Tata group's companies are caught in bitter, in some cases violent, conflicts with local people over acquisition of land for new projects.

Clearly there is no simple or sure way to assess the net social worth of a particular corporation. But that is not a deterrent to mapping the overall place of corporations in society. As the British activist Deborah Doane puts it,

> The future of the ethical corporation will depend on a more courageous look at the limitations of the market; and a bold attempt to define what type of society we want and how best business can serve that end, rather than the other way around.

Enhanced accountability and responsibility are a good starting point only if they clear the way for a deeper shift – realigning economy and ecology, market and society at a more fundamental level. This is beginning to happen in companies that are no longer focused on minimising negative impacts but instead asking what kind of businesses the world needs in the 21st century. Take, for instance, the Tomorrow's Company report crafted jointly by a team of leaders from global businesses and NGOs in mid-2007.

Coming within months of the *Stern Report*, Tomorrow's Company was particularly significant because its starting point was to acknowledge that the market has failed to tackle long-term challenges of sustainability – hence the escalating threat of global warming, the depletion of natural resources, persistent poverty and human rights violations. The status quo is not an option, wrote the co-chair of the Tomorrow's Company process, Nandan Nilekani, who was then CEO of Infosys. The objective of the exercise, initiated by a UK-based not-for-profit research organisation called Tomorrow's Company, was to create a future for business that makes equal sense to staff, shareholders and society. For the compilers of the report this meant unfurling the 'full creative potential of the market'. This would only happen, they argued, when governments, companies and citizens at large worked to create effective frameworks of regulation and incentives in the short term. Only then could companies compete on equal terms, to deliver innovative goods and services that are compatible with environmental and social objectives.

Still more importantly, the Tomorrow's Company team went on to call for a shift in priorities at three levels: redefining success, embedding values and creating frameworks. Success would then depend not on juggling performance on several different indexes but the degree to which the environmental, human and financial aspects of companies' work were fully aligned and integrated. Embedding values in this way means that the company must rigorously *apply*, in actual practice, what it espouses in public – even in difficult situations.

'This is not about philanthropy or companies being seen to be "doing good". These are actions that serve the long-term interests of any company,' said the report. Since this approach would expand the space in which companies operate, it would provide them greater impact and influence over a longer time-scale. This exercise was a reaffirmation of the view that corporations are licensed to operate to serve society. 'So it's up to us to work with governments, NGOs, academic experts and others to make sure we work within a system that delivers progress and helps to resolve the world's most difficult issues,' said Sir Mark Moody-Stuart, Chairman of Anglo American and a member of the team.

Although Tomorrow's Company went much further than *Who Cares Wins,* it could still be dismissed as a mere statement of intent. Yet the report did mark an important watershed. Firstly, it was a joint endeavour in which representatives of leading global companies such as ABB, Anglo American, BP, Ford, Infosys, KPMG, McKinsey and Standard Chartered worked with major global NGOs such as the Amnesty International Business Group, the International Institute for Sustainable Development, SustainAbility and others.

Secondly, it signalled the acceptance of a long-standing activist critique. For instance, the New Economics Foundation's Transforming Markets programme has extensively documented how and why the market cannot deliver sustainable development without higher forms of accountability and new forms of regulation. The Tomorrow's Company approach took this forward by reaffirming that there is no substitute for realigning the relationship of society and business. It was partly building on recent precedents. For example, in 2004, Cisco Systems, Hewlett-Packard, Microsoft, Dell, IBM and Intel set up a supply-chain working group to implement the Electronics Industry Code of Conduct which they had recently adopted. The move was a response to a study by the Catholic Agency for Overseas Development (CAFOD) titled 'Clean Up Your Computer' which criticised the poor labour conditions in factories making computers for these companies. There is also strong consensus in favour of regulation in some areas – notably to curb bribery in international trade, carbon emissions, and public disclosure of sustainability performance. Optimists believe it is a matter of time before the concerns of labour also come under this umbrella.

Tomorrow's Company also nudged towards a rebranding of CSR from 'doing well by doing good' to a more ambitious engagement with solutions for mega global problems like climate change, poverty and inequality. But doesn't this raise the bar higher than even those supporting this framework are immediately able to tackle? For instance, David Vogel, professor of business ethics at the University of California, has pointed out that if the American home furnishings giant Home Depot is really keen to improve forestry practices, it would have to go beyond its own operations and demand, or at least support, legislation requiring all forests in the US to be managed in a more sustainable manner. If Starbucks is to deeply improve the conditions of coffee producers, then it would need to support an international agreement to stabilise coffee prices. Interface, the carpet giant that is undertaking an ambitious shift to sustainability, would have to not just make greener carpets but support regulation that makes sustainable practices mandatory.

Such steps would begin to alter the operations of the market in a more fundamental way than any one company's social or environmental engagements. Until then, even though assorted positive trends are rapidly unfolding, the everyday life of corporations is still governed by a market ethos that is either hostile or indifferent to a broader non-monetary basis for assessing value. Let us defer the deeper question until the next chapter and focus here on looking at the promise of change and its limits within the old frame.

A decade ago information about social and environmental impacts of corporations was missing in annual reports. We are still far from getting full and reliable disclosure but a much larger volume and quality of such information is now available. The UK-based Corporate Responsibility (CORE) Coalition, which has pushed for these changes, continues to work at many levels to ensure that the definition of fiduciary duty is expanded *by law* to make it more balanced and inclusive of various dimensions. A still more radical demand is for Foreign

Direct Liability, which would make British companies legally accountable for damage they do in other countries.

Such changes would expand opportunities for what Doane has called 'the ethical minnows' that are currently under mammoth pressure to show short-term gains within the stock market. Like the Nobel Laureate Muhammad Yunus, Doane favours entirely new avenues of finance – such as alternative stock markets based on a social return on investment. 'But over the long run, our ultimate goal would be to transform markets in such a way as to not need "niche" businesses like Fair Trade,' says Doane.

Elkington sees an inevitable drift in this direction as many great corporations are blown away by 'Schumpeterian' gales of creative destruction. 'These will roar with new force as the Western world struggles to adapt to new demographic, economic and political realities,' says Elkington. Corporations, he points out, are inhibited by fears of cannibalising their own markets or dilution of earnings. By contrast the open multi-layered and seemingly chaotic babble of the marketplace is ideal for innovation and constant re-engineering.

However, this can happen only if the rules of the marketplace are geared towards equity and constantly monitored to remove systemic injustices. As Amy Domini herself points out, so far neither CSR nor SRI has altered the fact that

> Exxon is still paying $5 an acre as a lease on which they earn or 'steal' millions ... In Mexico the poor person has fallen below subsistence level because the papaya he could earlier just pluck and eat is now behind a fence of an agro-industrial farm.

This brings us to the critical limits to the market for virtue. The main constraint, as David Vogel has written, is the market itself. In his book *The Market for Virtue*, Vogel shows that proponents of CSR err when they assume that because some companies are behaving more responsibly this pattern can repeat itself on a larger scale. That is because, while there is a place for more responsible companies, 'there is also a large place for their less responsible competitors'. After all, investors did not exit from Halliburton because of its role in US the invasion of Iraq. By contrast, in 2004 Costco's earnings exceeded Wall Street's expectations and yet its share price fell by 4% because the company was deemed to be over-generous in its payment to workers.

Plus there are tens of thousands of global businesses that are not brand-dependent and relatively invisible compared to the large corporations. Many such companies are resistant to censure and the competitive compulsions of the market tend to drive them to lower and lower social and environmental standards. These are the kinds of units that supply to big brand names and have come under increasingly rigorous monitoring from their buyers on issues like child labour, working conditions and environmental standards. For instance between 2002 and 2004, General Electric alone performed 3,100 audits on its suppliers. But there is stiff resistance among the smaller companies to voluntarily pay higher wages, or allow the formation of unions. And in most corners of the world the surplus of work-seekers over employers keeps the advantage firmly in the hands of owners of capital.

Similarly, in 1985, the international chemical industry responded to Union Carbide's fiasco in Bhopal by setting up a code called Responsible Care which set health, safety and environmental standards. But the code relies on self-reporting and observers have given it mixed reviews. In any case this code and other forms of enhanced responsibility have not helped the victims of the Bhopal gas tragedy. In February 2008, about 60 survivors of that toxic leak marched the 800 km from Bhopal to Delhi in order to draw the world's attention to how basic promises of healthcare and full compensation have been repeatedly broken by the Indian government, Union Carbide, and now Dow Jones, which bought Union Carbide. The protestors also reminded the world that, even though 20,000 have died due to the toxic gas leak and 120,000 still suffer from ailments, no one has gone to jail for the negligence.

Proponents of CSR have argued that, in situations where local laws, or governance structures, are lax, the onus of maintaining humane standards must fall on corporations. But such voluntarily enhanced corporate responsibility is valuable only as one component of greater economic democracy. It cannot be a substitute for the deepening and widening of democratic institutions – from the most local form of government to parliaments and courts of law. The battle against usurpation of public goods for narrow private gain cannot be won even in socially embedded bazaar spaces – it will also have to be fought on the floors of legislative bodies, in election booths and other institutions of democracy.

For instance, the Halliburton Company's role in driving US foreign policy towards war in Iraq was not even nominally curbed when Innovest gave it the lowest possible rating of 'CCC'. Likewise eco-friendly packaging of a McDonald's hamburger does not alter or undo the damaging agricultural production systems that produced the meat. Whether the US should be making war in Iraq or what types of agriculture are best for the future of our species and the planet are not questions that either individual companies or conglomerates of investors can decide. These decisions require collective processes in which each of us responds as a citizen more than as a consumer or investor.

Yes, there are 'market forces' inducing companies to be better corporate citizens but these forces alone are mostly inadequate for the scale of change that is needed. As Jeffrey Hollander, founder of the eco-products company Seventh Generation, puts it, 'Market forces, when they work often produce cheaper and more innovative solutions to social and environmental problems, but that in and of itself will not provide an acceptable solution to the problems we face.'

In this context, SRI funds may have to consider if their insistent claims about earning equal or greater monetary returns are not counter-productive. Vogel has argued that SRI funds might actually have more impact on corporate social and environmental performance if they supported investment in companies that earn less to foster innovations that have far-reaching consequences for people and planet. So far the idea that investors should forego some monetary benefits in favour of dispersed social and environmental gains is anathema. That is precisely the 'goody-goody' ethos from which the SRI community tries to distance itself. But they do so because they do not feel free to challenge the core principle behind the divine right of capital. The idea that money must primarily earn more *money* is still regarded as both sacred and sound science.

What, then, is the role of the corporation in the multi-level quest for *values* which could secure the future for our species? Those who ask this question are grappling with various paradoxical 'unfreedoms'. For instance, on a social platform the head of a corporation might acknowledge that the shift to sustainable modes is still dangerously slow. But he or she is often not *free* to take his company away from manufacturing and aggressively marketing the props of unsustainable lifestyles, as long as there is demand for those goods. The hard truth is that, as long as financial markets reward and punish companies primarily on the basis of money profits, they will continue to extract value from the planet and labour at unsustainable rates. A stark illustration of this reality was provided by Richard Bookstaber, who became a whistle-blower on Wall Street at the height of the sub-prime crisis. If you are a risk manager, Bookstaber said in an interview, 'all you care about is the risk to your institution. If all the world is self-destructing, but we're making money, I've done my job . . .'

At the ground this can even include collusion in slave labour. In 2007 *Bloomberg Markets* magazine reported that hundreds of thousands of workers toil without pay in Latin America, producing timber, gold and the charcoal used to make steel for major companies – including General Motors, Kohler, Toyota

and Whirlpool. When such reports appear, many of the impli-
cated companies tend to suspend purchases from the tainted
sources. But, argues Domini, this offers no solace: 'We and
they were all eager to take advantage of savvy competitiveness until we were faced with exposure.'

In 2010 the BP Deepwater oil spill in the Gulf of Mexico
drew attention to staggering imbalances of power between
people and environment on the one hand and corporations on
the other. Zygmunt Plater, a professor at Boston College Law
School, lamented the 'complacency, collusion, and neglect'
displayed by agencies that were supposed to regulate the
oil industry, as well as by corporations that promised safety
along with profit. Plater had served as chairman of the State
of Alaska Oil Spill Commission's Legal Task Force after the
Exxon Valdez oil spill. 'Twenty years later' he wrote in the *New
York Times*, 'we still don't have the liability and accountability structures needed to rectify and deter the harms that are
imposed upon the public by risky private actions.'

This reality persists not because enough investors actively
intend to do harm but because they remain silent about a
market culture which demands that managers are ruthless in
the pursuit of money profits.

Stronger human rights monitoring alone will not alter these
realities. It will take what John Mackay, co-founder of Whole
Foods, has called 'a deep, fundamental reform in the essence
of business'. So how do the proponents of this radical vision
live with the slow incremental improvements? They relentlessly badger, bully, persuade and transform from within.
Fundamentally, this is an endeavour based on the assumption that altering the genetics of capital and the corporation is
not an all-or-nothing proposition. Challen, retired priest and
monetary reformist, sees it as a challenge of 'learning to slay
giants without slaying or flaying people and altering mindsets
without affronting the dignity of those who differ on the fundamental flaws in our economic system'.

Nick Robins, who heads HSBC's Climate Change Centre of Excellence, suggests that we might live with a combination of 'tactical optimism and strategic despair'. Tim Smith at Walden Investments in Boston puts it like this:

> If you're a person of faith you don't take it as a personal failure ... You have to celebrate victories otherwise you'll go mad ... but if you get carried away with that you're fooling yourself. We need both fans who applaud the good achievements and those who look at the continuing problems – I walk down that tightrope every day.

7
NATURE BATS LAST
EARTH AS HOME OR MARKETPLACE

> **While it is unwise to believe in any one environ-**
> **mental projection of the future, it is important**
> **to bear in mind that nature bats last and owns**
> **the stadium.**
>
> *Hawken, Lovins and Lovins,*
> **Natural Capitalism**

Climate change is merely one signal of the collapsing conver-
sation between humans and the rest of nature. As the scram-
ble to restore this dialogue intensifies, the crisis is also seen
as a bonanza of business opportunities.

But economy remains at war with ecology. Regardless
of how many white flags we wave, Gaia's mechanisms will
respond only if our actions are aligned with its inherent self-
correcting, self-protecting systems. Tweaking business-as-
usual is not enough. There is urgent need for reorienting the
equation between the human economy and nature's economy.

This challenge surpasses anything that has come up ever
since our ancestors first gathered in agoras and choupals. It
calls for a quality of introspection and innovation which may
be impossible with a homocentric view of reality. Here we jour-
ney into the life and work of just a few people who have a more

inclusive vision – and dare to craft a new operating system for markets.

~

A few weeks before Katrina and Rita ravaged the gulf coast of the US in 2005, the city of Mumbai was submerged by a freak deluge. The skies dumped about 37 inches of rain in and around India's financial centre over just 24 hours, leaving more than 800 people dead and thousands of homes and offices inundated. Residents of Mumbai fumed about bad urban planning which resulted in excessive waterlogging. There were just stray murmurs linking the deluge to climate change.

At the same time a new cheap-fares airline was running a powerfully emotive advertisement on television. It depicted the life of a rural craftsman and his little son's fascination with aircraft amid a life of bare basics, bullock-carts and bicycles. The son grows up to be an urban professional and sends his father an air ticket to come and visit him – thanks to fares so low that more and more people are flying around. The film went on to capture the elderly man's delight at his first-ever plane ride. Its closing scene, as father and son embrace in an arrivals lounge, was crafted to leave many viewers misty-eyed.

That ad was not just tapping into filial love and loyalty. It was essentially a celebration of the democratising promise of market competition. That is partly why more people now have access to services that once only the rich could afford. By itself this expansion of opportunity is an achievement. But the dreams it triggers have a dark underside. More air traffic, like more cars, means more carbon emissions, further imbalances in the Earth's atmosphere and thus more and more human-induced *natural* disasters.

At that time, in 2005, the deluge in Mumbai was stoically accepted as an act of God. Two years later climate change was grabbing headlines. A cover story in one news magazine presented a near-future scenario by showing Mumbai harbour's famous landmark, the Gateway of India, partially inundated by sea water. Meanwhile the cheap-fares airlines are doing roaring business. To their typical, upwardly mobile, customer any argument against more people flying is both unfair and undemocratic.

Prosperity for all within ecological limits threatens to become the 21st century's utopia or fantasy. Consuming more is now so tightly coupled with both 'progress' and fun that *impending* doom may not be sufficient incentive to deter consumption, just as the long-term risk of cancer does not deter some people from smoking or chewing tobacco. But what if the market culture changed in ways that served everyone's needs and wants while also bringing our species back into sync with nature? This may seem impossible, and yet some people are engaged in precisely such a bid to reconfigure the prevailing market culture.

Once again, the primary impetus has come from the social sphere – from those anchored outside the market but now working in the hope of transforming both commerce and patterns of demand. Lester R. Brown of the Washington-based Earth Policy Institute has outlined a 'Plan B' because business-as-usual, which is Plan A, has led us into an economic crisis and the brink of ecological collapse. Jonathan Porritt, veteran leader of the British Green Party, has mapped the contours of change in a book called *Capitalism as if the World Matters*. Others are making a case for a natural capitalism that crafts a new equation between the needs and wants of the human economy and the ecosystems which enable us to live at all.

There was a time when these energies flourished on the fringes of society, as wishful fancies of idealists who had little or no role in either government or business. This has changed over the last ten years and somewhat dramatically since 2006 when climate change reached the red-alert stage. In January 2007 an unprecedented coalition of blue-chip US companies and environmental lobby groups drew up a plan to cut greenhouse gases by 10–30% over 15 years. This was just one of innumerable signals that business-as-usual is no longer viable. Since then some of the largest companies in the world have announced what the Worldwatch Institute called 'breakthrough environmental initiatives'. These include Citigroup, Goldman Sachs, McKinsey & Company and Walmart. This could be taken as evidence of magical market forces turning a crisis into business opportunity and thus catering to the needs and wants of people at large. But a meaningful Plan B requires deeper change than tweaking of business-as-usual can provide. It means looking for answers to some tough questions.

Firstly, what resources and areas of life are best left altogether outside markets? For instance, should water be a saleable commodity? Can the sky be *owned*? And, if yes, then by whom? Where should commons end and markets begin?

Secondly, is a *natural capitalism* possible and, if so, what would it look like? This depends on whether current challenges to the divine right of capital have substance or turn out to be a mirage. Can *value* be liberated from the dominance of the price mechanism? Because the real cost of what we consume or destroy cannot be known by monetising the losses. As Paul Hawken, co-author of *Natural Capitalism*, asks, 'How do we decide the value of a 700-year-old tree? We need only ask how much it would cost to make a new one. Or a new river, or even a new atmosphere.'

The intrinsic value of the natural world, its right to exist irrespective of usefulness to humans, is fundamentally an ethical matter that cannot be resolved by markets. Reducing living systems to mere factors of production diminishes all life. However, even those who know this are now compelled to think in terms of 'ecosystem services' and look for market mechanisms to salvage or save them. Such is the overpowering nature of the prevailing market culture. Markets for a variety of ecosystem services are already worth billions of dollars and expected to grow exponentially. Proponents of these methods argue that ecosystem markets offer win–win deals to everyone – from forest-dwelling tribal people, to farmers and industrialists. But behind these glimmering opportunities is a dark paradox.

Is the Earth our home or is it one large marketplace?

LIVING SYSTEMS IN CHAOTIC RETREAT

Images of our blue planet floating luminously in the infinite blackness of space defined the 20th century. None of our ancestors had ever seen this portrait. In the 21st century the same image is used to convey divergent aspirations. An inter-national credit card company uses a dazzling picture of the blue sphere and its wispy white cloud drifts with the tag-line 'the world in your hands'. This is an invitation to consume more and do it with ease anywhere in the world. Environmental groups posit the same shimmering image of our only home to urge more people to join 'the race to save the planet'.

The first inducement sees the Earth essentially as a marketplace. The second treats the Earth as a precious home and sacred gift to be nurtured. From the latter point of view the buying and selling functions of life are secondary or even incidental. Of course, these divergent outlooks do not exist in neat compartments. Most people relate simultaneously to both images. You can enjoy the world as marketplace and also lose sleep over the staggering damage to our habitat – one polluted river at a time, one dying coral reef at a time, one eroded ton of topsoil at a time, one songbird at a time, one melted glacier at a time . . .

For the first time in the Earth's existence, the total flows and movements of materials by one species exceed natural planetary flows. Excess carbon is merely one element of a much larger imbalance. For instance, the amount of lead that humans now put into the environment is 300 times more than what natural sinks can absorb or dissipate. Similarly, we put 23 times more zinc and 38 times more antimony than the environment can cope with. This trend was inaugurated by the industrial revolution in the 18th century and has gone into hyperdrive over the last 50 years. But it was only in last decade that individuals, companies and nations have begun tracking their 'ecological footprint'. Designed by the Ecological Footprint Network, this is a measure of the sum total of materials consumed by a product or a person. For example, a 9 lb laptop computer is produced by processing 40,000 lbs of materials. This still leaves out its impact on the Earth's sinks for pollutants

The human economy's impact on the Earth increased by 150% between 1961 and 2000. The Ecological Footprint Network has estimated that it was some time in the mid-1980s that humanity's burden on the Earth crossed the planet's carrying capacity. Created in 1993 by Mathis Wackernagel and William Rees, the Ecological Footprint is a measure of the sum total of materials consumed by a product or a person. This measure is now widely used by governments, communities and businesses to monitor ecological impacts and to plan for the future. Exponentially expanding patterns of consumption, more than rising population, are responsible for imbalance. For example, Europe's share of the world population declined from about 9.5% in 1961 to about 7% in 2001. But, in the same period, Europe's use of world biocapacity rose from 10% to 19%. At the UN's 1992 Earth Summit in Rio de Janeiro, the world's nations agreed that existing patterns of production and consumption are unsustainable and called for 'sustainable development'. But in the decade after Rio, the ecological footprint of the 27 wealthiest nations increased by 8% per person, while in middle- and low-income countries it shrank by 8% per person. The wealthy 25% of humanity now has a footprint as large as the entire biologically productive surface area of the Earth.

The WWF's periodic Living Planet Reports have become a grim record of what Paul Hawken has graphically described as 'living systems in chaotic retreat'. With the human economy consuming over 20% more than nature's ecosystems can replenish, the most basic needs of life, breathable air and drinkable water, are fast dwindling. Laws and policies to stem environmental degradation have been multiplying across the world since the mid-1970s. But in 1995 the Intergovernmental Panel on Climate Change (IPCC) declared that the Earth's sinks are so severely over-stretched that we are hurtling headlong towards disaster. This panel of 2,500 scientists called for total carbon emissions to be reduced by 60% of what they were in 1990. Despite worldwide acceptance of these findings and recommendations, by 2001 the global carbon emissions stood at 15% *more* than they were in 1990 and are still rising.

This suicidal anomaly persists because our awareness of dangers to Earth as home is at odds with the compulsions of life as commerce. For instance, the conversations and concerns evident at the 1992 Rio Earth Summit were partly undermined by the setting-up of the WTO just three years later. The agreements at the Earth Summit were based on the effective authority of governments to implement rules in favour of the public good. The WTO structure weakened the regulatory power of states in the interests of freer movement of goods and capital, with only cursory attention to ecological concerns.

Ten years later, reviewing the damage since Rio, a report by environmental activists from 12 countries showed how many WTO provisions contradict the spirit and in some cases the letter of the Rio conventions and other environmental accords. Moreover, while the WTO's rules are binding and enforceable by trade sanctions, environmental treaties tend to be non-binding and provide for voluntary dispute resolution. The WTO was created to serve the needs of the global marketplace by creating an even playing field between foreign and domestic producers to expand the sum total of global trade. What the

Earth as home needs is an up-to-date trading system capable of creating an even playing field between environmentally sound and environmentally destructive production. Instead, 'everywhere, the playing field is skewed, to allow an extractive economy to enjoy massive advantages,' wrote the activist authors of *The Jo'burg Memo: Fairness in a Fragile World.*

Many such activists are not anti-trade. What they clamour for is a reduction, and gradual elimination, of environmentally damaging subsidies worldwide – on a sufficiently large scale to give an equal chance to sustainable production. But doing this would mean giving primacy to Earth as home. At present, the global market is treated as *the* overarching system of the 21st century. In reality it is just one function of human society which in turn is a sub-set of the biosphere. This is why human-induced climate change is not merely a 'market failure': that is, an inefficient allocation of resources; it is a manifestation of the possibly fatal divergence between nature's efficiency and how efficiency is defined by human production systems.

Convergence is possible. Then the use of renewable resources would match their rate of regeneration and pollution emissions would be limited to the assimilative capacity of the biosphere and atmosphere. But the compulsion for constant growth and powerful incumbents in the world-as-marketplace present some tough obstacles.

Resistance by incumbents is expressed through rather ambitious spin-doctoring. For instance, the American coal sector has crafted CARE – Coalition for Affordable and Reliable Energy. 'Technology Makes Electricity from Coal a Clear Choice' declared an advertisement by CARE. It went on to claim that coal-based electricity is so reliable, affordable and increasingly clean that it can enable Americans to maintain their quality of life for centuries to come.

But the toughest incumbent resistance has come from the world's largest oil company. Long after global consensus on the need to cut carbon emissions Exxon stood in opposition by arguing that fossil fuels are not to blame for climate change.

The most profitable oil company in the world, with a net income of $40 billion in 2008, Exxon has insisted that there is no business case for sweeping changes in the global economy. Even though other oil giants, notably British Petroleum and the Royal Dutch/Shell Group, endorsed the 1997 Kyoto Protocol and begun investing in alternatives, Exxon insisted that fossil fuels need to be made more efficient not replaced.

This position has become harder to maintain after the Intergovernmental Panel on Climate Change issued a red alert in 2006. But the tilt began about five years earlier when Munich Re, the German insurance company, announced that damage caused by weather disruptions and pollution is rising alarmingly. This echoed findings by the United Nations Environment Program's (UNEP) Finance Initiative. In the same year, 2002, Innovest Strategic Value Advisors estimated that as much as 15% of the total market capitalisation of major companies may be put at risk by climate change. These are the realities that led to a cascade of companies signing up for the Carbon Disclosure Project. By 2005 the Association of British Insurers (ABI) found itself in the same corner as environmental activists – pleading with the G8 leaders for urgent measures to control greenhouse gas emissions.

While these trends are significant, they do not explain the depth of the home-versus-marketplace divide. We need a deeper view of the conflict before seeking possible answers.

COMMONS AND MARKETS

Market value of ecosystems

On a blistering summer day in 1920, Rabindranath Tagore was travelling in a, then rare, motor car across rural Bengal. A defect in the car forced Tagore to stop frequently and refill water in the vehicle. In village after village of a drought-affected countryside, strangers came forth to share their limited supply of water and refused to accept payment or reward. Tagore, who won the Nobel Prize for literature in 1913, later wrote:

> In a hot country where travellers constantly need water, and where the water supply grows scanty in summer, the villagers consider it their duty to offer water to those who need it. They could easily make a business out of it, following the inexorable law of demand and supply. But the ideal which they consider to be their *dharma* has become one with their life. To ask them to sell it is like asking them to sell their life. They do not claim any personal merit for possessing it. To be able to take a considerable amount of trouble in order to supply water to a passing stranger and yet never to claim merit or reward for it seems absurdly and negligibly simple . . . but that simplicity is the product of centuries of culture; that simplicity is difficult of imitation. In a few years' time it might be possible for me to learn how to make holes in thousands of needles instantaneously by turning a wheel, but to be absolutely simple in one's hospitality to one's enemy or to a stranger requires generations of training

Like his friend Mahatma Gandhi, Tagore was a distressed observer of the steady evaporation of this cultural wealth accumulated over countless generations. As Tagore's car neared Calcutta, during that hot summer journey, water had to be paid for even though it was more abundant and easier to supply as 'progress flowed in numerous channels in all directions'.

Since then, more and more water has gone over from the realm of home to market, from gift to commodity. It is now a large-scale business opportunity. For example, World Water is a multinational company that ships fresh water across continents and oceans. Its mission is to provide 'quality potable water to those in need, regardless of race, ethnic origin, nationality, political or religious beliefs so long as it is economically viable – returning a reasonable profit'.

But what is a reasonable profit? Even if we leave aside this imponderable, there is a more fundamental question: should water and other commons be turned into commodities? Within the dominant market culture the answer is 'yes'. Yet counter-energies persist.

Travellers in the more environmentally denuded parts of rural India are sometimes astonished to suddenly come upon a thick cluster of trees. Often this is an 'oran', a traditional commons that has somehow miraculously survived into the present century. It remains lush green because a local community still manages it – either as a sacred grove or as a collective resource which is harvested on the basis of strict rules that ensure its natural regeneration. Such commons preceded and later surrounded the market in all societies across the world. Private property has co-existed with commons, which according to Roman law covered wildlife, grasslands, water and the sea shore.

Right up to the last century some societies, particularly indigenous peoples, remained organised around commons and reverence for Mother Earth or, as one South American tribe calls her, 'Pachamama'. At the turn of the present century an estimated 100 million people still depended directly on forests and other commons for their basic survival needs. But increasingly such communities find themselves excluded from forests and their traditional, often biologically rich, habitats. As a report by Friends of the Earth has noted,

> These lands are progressively being handed over to logging, tourism and private park management companies. They are also being reserved for a new breed of company that establishes 'carbon parks' – a new and lucrative avenue intended to offset the carbon dioxide emissions of rich fossil fuel addict consumers in the North.

While activist groups such as Friends of the Earth fight for the *rights* of communities to retain their commons, there is now a powerful counter-view that it is more effective to put a market *price* on those commons. This approach converts the indigenous people, who see themselves as offspring of Mother Earth, into 'clients' of the ecosystem.

However, the contemporary struggle for commons is not just about woods and lakes; it is about reframing the *idea* of commons. Peter Barnes, co-founder of the Friends of the Commons, suggests that a modern definition of commons would be 'the sum of all we inherit together and must pass on, undiminished and more or less equally, to our heirs. And here I include non-human as well as human heirs.' This definition encompasses the countless irreplaceable processes of the biosphere and atmosphere and their sinks. In other words, the sum total of the Earth's capacity to recycle water, oxygen, carbon and everything else we excrete and exhale or just throw away.

Even this eminently common-sense definition must contend with the fact that for over three decades the term 'commons' has been in disgrace within the Western world. This view dates back to 1968 when the biologist Garrett Hardin wrote a vastly influential essay called 'The Tragedy of the Commons'. Hardin focused on those cases where virtually unmanaged free spaces are overused and depleted by individuals or groups. However, Hardin overlooked the fact that many societies across the world evolved elaborate norms and customs that successfully nurtured commons in sustainable ways. The Worldwatch Institute's *State of the World* report for 2008 documented numerous situations where community management of resources is still effective. The real tragedy of commons, according to the Ecological Footprint Network, occurs when individual resource users hog the benefits and leave the costs to be borne by society at large.

It is true that, as modern markets and monetisation of local economies took place, traditional structures of nature husbandry collapsed in many societies. Conventional market wisdom deems this to be 'proof' that private property regimes are a more robust mechanism than community-based bazaar structures. But this is because for almost 300 years the market has become a process of privatising public goods in ways that undermined other models. During the same period industrial growth has been viable largely because both government policies and market forces colluded in drawing resources from and dumping wastes into commons, usually without paying either a full fee or a penalty.

Thus innovators like Peter Barnes argue that the time has come to restore the balance between the market and the commons:

> Within the market part of the system are the things we mostly manage for the short-term monetary gain of a property-owning class. Within the commons part of the system are the things we manage, or *should* manage, for the long-term enhancement of all living beings ... The commons precedes the market, is the source of most that enters the market, and the sink for all that leaves ... the commons is the pond in which the fish of private property swim.

Seeing commons as a pond is powerful because it presents both markets and commons as dynamic, living systems which constantly interact. It is precisely the nature and norms of this interaction that are now being renegotiated. But the process is often stymied by a conflict between inalienable rights and commercial interests – between those who see the Earth more as home than marketplace and those who see 'marketisation' as the most reliable basis for allocating resources.

For instance, in North America NAFTA allowed Sun Belt Water, a California-based company, to sue the government of British Columbia claiming billions of dollars in damages because the government refused to let the company export Canada's fresh water in supertankers. But the United Nations Committee on Economic, Cultural and Social Rights has established water as a fundamental social good not merely a commodity. This means that the 145 countries that have ratified the International Covenant on Economic, Social and Cultural Rights are obligated to ensure access to clean water as a basic human right. The World Health Organisation has endorsed this move as vital for achieving the Millennium Development Goal of halving the number of people without access to water and sanitation by 2015.

Conflicts over water are becoming both frequent and embittered. This is partly because the quality and quantity of accessible fresh water is declining while global consumption has been doubling every 20 years. The demand for water is growing twice as fast as growth in population. Since the 1990s the World Bank and other international agencies have come to see privatisation and markets as the key to addressing this deepening crisis. At the start of this century about 7% of the world's population was served by privatised water systems. By 2015 it is estimated that 17% of the world's population will depend on private, for-profit water-supply systems.

Olivier Barbaroux, the president of Vivendi's water business, does not question that water is a gift from God. But, he points out that God forgot to lay the pipes. Proponents of privatisation argue that this is the most reliable, efficient way to deliver water to the thirsty. But what about those who are thirsty but cannot afford the market price of water which includes an 'appropriate profit' to the entrepreneur? Clearly water is too crucial to human well-being to be treated as just another commodity.

However, some of the strongest arguments in favour of respecting water as commons are ecological. Governments and private companies have been alike in treating rivers and lakes virtually as plumbing systems rather than delicately balanced elements in the web of life. From this perspective, water flowing into the sea or remaining in a wilderness lake looks like a wasted resource because it is not serving the human economy. But this is a short-sighted, and distorted, understanding of efficiency. Ecologically sound mechanisms of water maximisation yield a higher level of efficiency by providing sustained benefits for countless generations without damaging habitats.

A commons approach also makes a clear distinction between *water trading* and *water sharing* between different regions. Blue Gold, a study by the San Francisco-based International Forum on Globalisation, noted that commercially traded water exchange tends to leave out those who lack purchasing power. Besides, importing water for only those who could afford it reduces the urgency and political pressure to find real, sustainable and equitable solutions to water problems throughout the world. By contrast, if water is treated as a commons it could be shared on a short-term basis along with strict timetables and conditions to make the receiving region water-independent in due course. Such sharing of water would encourage the restoration of local water systems. However, social activists across the world fear that once privatisation of the world's water is accepted as the most 'viable' solution, it would deter such non-profit systems of water transfer from happening.

But then there are efforts which try to save and regenerate commons by creating markets for ecosystem services. For example, an enterprise called Ecosystem Marketplace starts with the premise that environmental services have suffered because they have been taken for granted. Ecosystem Marketplace aims to be a 'one-stop-shop of timely and transparent information on the emerging markets and payment schemes for ecosystem services'. The assumption is that, if there is reliable and realistic information on prices, regulation, science and other related issues, then eventually markets for ecosystem services will be at the core of the global economy and help to save the planet.

Such services are made possible by increasingly sophisticated work at the interface of ecology and economics which has produced a nuanced understanding of the links between natural habitats and the human economy. Such analysis helped New York City to save billions of dollars and secure its future water supply. In 1997 the city government of New York recognised that its drinking water supply is inextricably linked to the state of the Catskill Mountains and agricultural practices in the region. Instead of investing an estimated 6 billion dollars in new water filtration plants, to cope with the increasingly polluted water, the government invested just $320 million in buying land in the Catskills to prevent development and paying farmers to minimise water pollution.

The USA now also has a system of 'wetland credits'. A company that needs to destroy a wetland habitat can buy such credits from a mitigation bank which in turn uses those funds to restore wetlands in another region. More than 400 'wetland banks' throughout the US handle more than $3 billion per year in transactions, and there are more than 70 species conservation banks which trade an estimated $370 million in species credits each year.

These trends have been boosted by the UN's Millennium Ecosystem Assessment (MEA), launched in 2001. This is an international programme designed to gather and analyse scientific information on the health of global ecosystems. The MEA, which completed the first round of its work in 2005, found that two-thirds of the ecosystems it reviewed are being used unsustainably and thus being degraded. The MEA shifts the focus away from the intrinsic value of natural habitats towards identifying and measuring the critical economic services contained in those ecosystems. This enables ecosystem services to be measured in terms of a conventional money bottom line.

Whether emissions trading and ecosystem pricing will secure the Earth as home is now a matter of bitter dispute. Those who favour such market methods find the pure ecological arguments romantic and unrealistic. A California-based citizens' group called Friends of the Commons counters this criticism by saying that

> The real utopians are those who believe the market can
> continue unbridled forever. This dream has great allure,
> but it's a dangerous fantasy. The reality is that, without

> a healthy commons, the market (and much else) won't
> survive the 21st century.

Friends of the Commons are advocates of free exchange based on appropriate legal and institutional protections to firstly recognise and protect commons. Working out optimum forms of property rights could ensure equity in ways that mere monetisation of ecosystem services cannot. But this implies an entirely new understanding of both commons and property. 'The distinguishing feature of the assets in the new commons is that they'd be held in trust for everyone equally, and for future generations,' says Barnes.

What Friends of the Commons hope to do is expand the cognition of markets – which have otherwise been eco-blind. But there is a catch. Such 'assetisation' of commons is meaningful only within a framework that defines growth as production *plus* regeneration and restraint. For instance, carbon trading could become meaningless if it does not alter the scale and nature of human production systems in relation to the biosphere. Herman Daly, the father of ecological economics, evokes the imagery of the Plimsoll line which is painted on ships as a safety measure. A ship is at risk of sinking when it is so heavily loaded that its Plimsoll line vanishes below the water surface. Merely moving the cargo around won't help save that overloaded ship. So, Daly urges, a global recognition of the finitude of the biosphere is now the Plimsoll line that the sum total of human enterprise must respect.

But how is this to happen? At present the accelerated search for solutions is based on the assumption that the market, as we know it, is the best mechanism for both aggregating information and efficiently allocating resources. This conventional wisdom has not been dented by acknowledging climate change as the greatest market failure of all time. This severely curtails the range and speed of options that can even be considered. The case of Lake Gatun offers several hints about this conundrum.

Lake Gatun, in Panama, is a water body of enormous strategic value to the global economy. For 90 years this man-made lake has supplied the 52 million gallons of fresh water that each ship needs in order to traverse the multiple locks of the Panama Canal. But the Gatun's water is dwindling. This is largely because economic growth in its watershed area has taken the form of logging as well as slash-and-burn agriculture on an unprecedented scale. The only way to provide the shipping canal with fresh water is to restore the commons that sustain it – a massive reforestation of the Gatun's watershed. But who is to pay for planting those trees and keeping them in place? The Panamanian government, which now ostensibly controls the canal, is already neck-deep in debt.

So, John Forgach, a Brazilian environmentalist-cum-investment banker, is trying to broker a deal for companies that depend on the canal to invest in the reforestation of Gatun's watershed. But Harvard-educated Forgach, who is Chairman of ForestRe, a specialist insurance company, also knows that the Panamanians could actually get far more for their lovely fresh water by shutting down the canal, bottling the water and selling it. Running the canal is a crazy waste of fresh water, Forgach told *The Economist*.

At present shutting down the Panama Canal seems absurd because it is considered vital for the efficiency of global trade. But this notion of efficiency excludes the human and ecological cost of the fresh water in the locks of the canal. It excludes the fact that the Panamanians are not free to make other uses of that water and are, in a sense, subsidising global trade. The ecosystem services of the Gatun watershed may now be more fully valued as investors engage in afforestation. But this eco-friendly activity will still obscure the total costs of long-distance trade links. Besides, as Forgach said, 'Valuation is only ever part of the answer.'

A more rational pricing system, one that tells the full truth about costs, is still barely in infancy. Meanwhile, fundamental anomalies persist. The Earth as commodity remains at odds with Earth as gift and home. For instance, citizens' groups in the USA have launched a 'think outside the bottle' campaign to demand efficient public systems that provide safe drinking water so that people do not have to buy bottled water. But across the world the sales of bottled water are projected to keep growing exponentially.

Yet it is not just poets who are distressed that the inexorable law of demand and supply has overwhelmed that simplicity which, as Tagore said, is difficult of imitation.

Who owns the sky?

Peter Barnes's fascination with the inner workings of capitalism began in childhood. He grew up poring over Standard & Poor's and Moody's reports to do some number-crunching for revised editions of his father's book *Your Investments*. Leo Barnes, an economist who specialised in stock market analysis, also encouraged his son to have an understanding of ratios, trends and cycles and the impacts of public policies. This knowledge helped when Peter found himself driven to make the world a little bit fairer.

After taking a graduate degree in history from Harvard University, Barnes worked as a journalist for many years. But since the market seemed mightier than the pen he decided that going into business was one way of making the world a fairer place. So he co-founded a solar energy company that designed and installed solar heating systems. The business found an ideal niche in San Francisco where it installed solar water heating systems in apartment buildings with ingenious finance mechanisms which gave the owners a positive cash flow immediately.

Later Barnes co-founded Working Assets, a socially screened money fund, whose purpose was *greentapping* – diverting money within the market to good uses. This venture was founded on the conviction that it is possible to create market pressure on companies not to support oppressive regimes, ignore environmental rules or pay appallingly low wages. Working Assets went on to issue a special credit card called 'Plastic with Purpose', and later provide a long-distance phone service. Every time a customer made a call, Working Assets donated 1% of their charges to non-profit groups. After a while, the company also sent information about important pending votes in Congress along with its phone bills. In short, it used the market to achieve social goals and, on the side, make a profit.

But 'after 20 years as a capitalist, I decided to hang up my cleats,' says Barnes. By then he had learned a great deal: 'I'd found that while markets can be cruelly limiting, they can also be exciting and liberating. You can even use markets to protect the environment and make society more democratic, if that's your inclination.' But, in order to make this happen, Barnes realised, the operating system of capitalism needs to be debugged and upgraded. Barnes traced the source of all these 'bugs' to a narrow definition of shareholder value which causes private assets to be maximised at the expense of common assets. For example, Barnes noticed that when an executive of DuPont was asked why his company did not do more to protect the environment the answer was: 'Any company that doesn't respect shareholder value doesn't do anyone any good.'

That's true, thought Barnes, 'but aren't we all shareholders in something larger than a single corporation – and don't we have to protect *that* shareholder value, too?' So what mechanisms will protect the Earth on behalf of all people? Suppose, for a moment, that all the critical ecosystems in the world – the oceans, the atmosphere, forests, rivers, watersheds and so on – were owned by one large holding company, called perhaps Gaia Inc. with each person on Earth owning one share each. Each ecosystem could be managed by a separate company which would collect a scarcity rent for limited use of that particular ecosystem.

Such mechanisms would empower the commons sector – one that conventional economics has ignored and neglected. In societies across the world this sector was eliminated by what Barnes likes to call Capitalism 1.0, a system that privileged capital, joint-stock companies and governments. A new operating system for markets, 'Capitalism 3.0', would empower the commons, lengthen the private sector's time horizons and offset its inequities by strengthening people's rights as citizens.

This world-view rests on a razor's edge. On the one hand, it reveres air, water, forests and fauna as gifts – as an inheritance that is priceless and immeasurable. But in order to be protected and regenerated these gifts must now also be dressed up as property because otherwise they are not measured or valued by contemporary markets and thus destroyed. In Capitalism 1.0 whoever managed to get control of the priced 'asset' reaped dividends. Capitalism 3.0, as envisioned by Barnes, would claim those 'assets' on behalf of all citizens – not out of greed but in order to protect and pass them on, undiminished, to future generations.

For instance, Barnes reasons, if we limit emissions into the sky, markets will see the sky as scarce. If the sky is a hugely valuable asset, who should own it? Is there a way *all* of us can own it, a way all of us can benefit from this valuable shared inheritance? Since the sky is a sacred trust, the proper entity to own it is a trust. Thus the concept of a Sky Trust is a radical conjunction of market mechanism and non-market values. Barnes is playing with a fruitful paradox: life does not depend on markets in quite the same way that it depends on air and water but we can't manage without markets. The problem is that markets are efficient at determining the price of a thing someone owns but a lousy system for measuring or even acknowledging intrinsic value. In the case of the sky, Barnes argues, 'the very incalculability of intrinsic value is what makes it necessary to create an artificial value markets *can* understand'.

Essentially, this is an endeavour to marry the technical efficiencies of the market with the social strengths of commons. That's a daunting task. For instance, in the USA there is probably only one law – the Endangered Species Act – that gives precedence to permanence over transience and puts a species' right to survive above capital's right to short-term profit. But there is a catch because a species has to be on the brink of extinction for the law to apply.

While the market is 'populated by aggressive, profit-maximising robots, armed with property rights, money, lawyers and lobbyists,' says Barnes, the commons are institutionally threadbare. Governments have a generally bad record as custodians of commons. Therefore the first object of the Sky Trust is to assert that neither governments nor corporations can be allowed to own the sky. Government ownership strengthens the machinery of state power whereas the purpose is to strengthen ownership by families and communities.

The Sky Trust, a non-profit organisation set up by Barnes, is a private-sector mechanism for reducing US carbon emissions with minimum economic pain and maximum social equity. In its full form, the Sky Trust would be a not-for-profit federally chartered institution for preserving the mix of gases in the sky. Its trustees would be accountable not only to citizens alive today, but also to citizens yet unborn.

Applying the 'polluter pays' principle the Trust would charge fossil fuel companies for the 'right' to put carbon into our sky. As consumers, Americans would pay more for burning fossil fuels but, as sky owners, they'd get money back. Those who burn less carbon would come out ahead. Dividends would be paid on a per capita basis, including children.

Barnes visualises the Sky Trust initially issuing permits for 1.3 billion tons of carbon, which is the level of carbon emissions by the US in 1990. The market would then set demand-driven prices for those carbon permits. Without a Sky Trust, those higher prices for 'using' the sky would go straight into the pockets of fossil fuel companies. With a Sky Trust, every

American woman, man and child would receive a dividend that might exceed $1,000 per person per year. MIT's Joint Program on the Science and Policy of Global Change has esti-mated that the dividend from such a trust could be as much as $4,900 per year for a family of four.

The Sky Trust builds on a powerful institutional precedent. The Alaska Permanent Fund was founded in the 1970s on the premise that Alaska's oil wealth is a common inheritance that must be equally shared by its people, not appropriated by either the government or private corporations. Jay Hammond, then Alaska governor, argued that if the wealth from the oil went to the state it would be squandered on government pro-jects or tax breaks to businesses. Instead, the Alaska Perma-nent Fund gives the state's citizens a dividend on the basis of one person, one share. Alaskans received their first dividend cheques in 1982 – when the annual return was about $1,000 per person. By 2000 the return was approximately $1,800 a year. Apart from this, in two decades, the fund has evolved into an economic engine that brings more money to Alaska's people than any industry. In 2005 the Fund itself was valued at over $30 billion.

In 2008 the Irish government announced a plan to create carbon permits, not to regulate individual consumption, but instead to share revenue from carbon trading among all citi-zens. With such a scheme, a petrol company would need to acquire sufficient permits in order to do business. Those per-mits would then be bought from Irish citizens who would get a payment for the use of the sky. Higher prices of fossil fuels would create an incentive for people to adopt low-carbon life-styles while the revenue sharing would ensure that the poor are not disadvantaged since the rich – who tend to have higher emissions – would pay more.

Since Barnes first proposed the Sky Trust the idea has taken on a life of its own. A study by the Congressional Budget Office has shown that, of all cap-and-trade systems that could be deployed to reduce carbon emissions, the Sky Trust would be the easiest to implement, have the most positive effect on household incomes and result in the lowest overall cost to society. Some of the Sky Trust's principles were embodied in the McCain–Lieberman bill, called the Climate Stewardship Act, which aims to reduce greenhouse gas emissions. The Corporation for Enterprise Development, a Washington DC-based non-profit that aims to expand economic opportunity, has launched a Sky Trust initiative. This version provides for parents investing their children's dividends in tax-free Individual Development Accounts. These savings could be withdrawn by the grown children for higher education, vocational training, first home purchase or starting a small business.

After languishing on the sidelines for years, after 2007 the idea of a Sky Trust began featuring in much of the media coverage about how to halt climate change. *Newsweek*'s Jonathan Alter called it a 'win–win–win for the economy, the taxpayer and the environment'. Just a few years ago the clamour for capping carbon emissions, mostly by those in the bazaar spaces, was rejected as anti-market, anti-growth. Today 'cap and trade' has become big business because it turns carbon into a commodity.

Since 2009 many supporters of a cap-and-dividend approach have been backing a bipartisan bill introduced by Senators Maria Cantwell and Susan Collins. Known as the Carbon Limits and Energy for American Renewal (CLEAR) Act, this bill seeks to set up a mechanism for selling 'carbon shares' to fuel producers and return most of the resulting revenue in checks to every American.

And yet the leap from 'cap and trade' to 'cap and *dividend*' is likely to prove quite demanding. Not only does it assert the power of commons over the power of state and private companies, it also invokes a broader definition of 'self-interest'.

Thus most reformers, who favour broader sharing of dividends, also challenge John Maynard Keynes's exhortation that we must continue to pretend that 'fair is foul and foul is far, for foul is useful and fair is not'. As Barnes says, what Keynes

overlooked is the part about getting from greed to gentility.
The objective is not to attain, the real or imagined, bliss of
the Kalahari hunter–gatherer bushman but a market culture
based on a fuller range of human aspirations. Transforming
capitalism is not about changing human nature, Barnes tirelessly reminds us. It's about inserting new code into the current operating system so that property rights and boundaries
are defined more creatively.

One way of doing this is to design fiduciary relationships
that preserve common assets while delivering benefits to a
much broader class of beneficiaries. This means that the state
will have to assign and protect common property rights with
as much vigour as it now nurtures the market. Then the state
would become not a usurper of commons but an instrument
in balancing commons and the market. Barnes is at pains to
clarify that he is not trying to change the fundamental calculus
of the market or even do away with that sector that thrives on
short-term profit maximisation for the few. He sees that sector as being important for productivity, creativity, vitality and
freedom. The problem begins when we confuse the calculus of
the market with the calculus of society itself.

Introducing the possibility that this can be altered is the
first and most significant contribution of innovators like
Barnes. The next requirement is both patience and dogged
persistence in working towards that goal. These are sufficient
conditions for attracting still more innovators who, over the
coming years, will fine-tune the details and evolve these aspirations into actual institutions – one step at a time toward
reverence for the commons as well as legal precedents and
supportive bazaar structures.

As Barnes says in his more imaginative moments:

> In the 21st century I envision, there'd be a large common
> sector populated by thousands of trusts . . . They'd act as
> protectors for various commons – as proxies for exter-
> nalities that markets currently ignore. They'd have prop-
> erty rights, management, money and beneficiaries – in

short, as much power as the corporations that populate the market. The primary engine of productivity would still be profit-maximising corporations and the market, but this engine would now be tempered by automatic balancing mechanisms, like the governors in James Watt's steam engines. There'd also be a kind of common property that disperses income equally – as well as private property that disperses income unequally.

NATURAL CAPITALISM

Ray Anderson, the CEO of Interface Inc., who passed away in 2011, had been known to address gatherings of business leaders by greeting the audience as 'fellow plunderers'. After all, there isn't a company anywhere in the world that is fully sustainable. It's not our fault, Anderson quickly comforts. The first industrial revolution was itself fundamentally flawed. So it is time to move on to another and better industrial revolution. And this time, Anderson pleaded, let's get it right.

There was a time when this kind of talk may have sounded offensive to Anderson himself. Back in 1992, when the term 'sustainable development' first made headlines, Anderson was among the millions who had no clue what this might mean. Paul Hawken remembers business people walking out of a public gathering when he said that unless enterprises became restorative 'we business-people will march the entire human race to the undertaker'. Hawken, himself a successful entrepreneur, was speaking at the prestigious Commonwealth Club in California. He had touched a raw nerve by pointing out that most chief executives of Fortune 500 corporations probably could not name five edible plants, five native grasses, or five migratory birds within walking distance of their homes, 'yet it is with the hands and minds of these CEOs that the environmental battle is being waged and lost'.

Hawken and Anderson's paths crossed in 1994. Hawken had just published a book, *The Ecology of Commerce,* which made the case for why and how business needs to learn from nature and its 3.8 billion years of rigorous testing. Hawken was building on E.F. Schumacher's appeal that *nature* is *capital* and drawing on his own experiences of the logjam between ecologists and businesspeople.

One buyer of Hawken's book was so moved by its content that she handed it to her mother – who happened to be a sales manager at Interface, and she, in turn, forwarded the book to her CEO. It was a time when Anderson was feeling utterly at a loss about a new kind of customer who was asking if Interface had eco-friendly carpeting. In response to these pressures, the company's research division had set up a task force to craft an environmental policy. The company was already complying with all the existing environmental laws and regulations. So what more is there to do, Anderson wondered. Hawken's approach to combining commerce and ecology was a bolt from the blue. Anderson was struck by the serendipity of that book landing on his desk at just that moment. Reading it, he later wrote, felt like 'a spear in my chest that remains to this day'.

First of all, Anderson was dumbfounded by how little he knew about the environment and the impacts of the industrial system: 'A new definition of success burst into my consciousness, and the latent sense of legacy asserted itself. I got it. I was a plunderer of Earth, and that is not the legacy one wants to leave behind. I wept.' A few weeks later Anderson went before that task force of his engineers and sales staff and declared a course correction for Interface which 'surprised me, stunned them, and galvanised all of us into action'.

An industrial engineer who graduated from Georgia Institute of Technology, Anderson founded Interface in 1973 and built it into one of the world's largest manufacturers of interior furnishings, particularly carpets for offices. Interface grew into a billion-dollar business with 26 factories in six countries and customers in over 100 countries. His company's products drained the Earth's resources and sinks in innumerable ways. For example, its non-biodegradable carpets required exponentially bigger dumping grounds after wearing out and being discarded.

The Ecology of Commerce not only alerted Anderson to grim facts but also provided a framework in which to understand the structural flaws that cause the human economy to violate the laws of nature. Changing this became Interface's 'mid-course correction', which was later also the title of a book Anderson wrote. Initially, many of his peers thought he had gone crazy. Some friends sent him books that dismissed Hawken's thesis as doomsday alarmism. Anderson carefully considered the full range of views and decided to live on the sharp edge of a paradox. If you accept the foot-draggers' assessment, what now sounds alarmist will come true. If you accept the alarmists' assessment and act accordingly, the foot-draggers' prediction will come true. So Anderson focused his attention on the top of what he began to visualise as 'Mount Sustainability' and started climbing. The goal: a zero eco-footprint. Fellow travellers on this journey included not only Hawken but Hunter and Amory Lovins from the Rocky Mountain Institute. Gradually, Interface became one of many companies seeking to drop out from the ranks of plunderers. The temptation to produce without waste and toxicity was obvious enough. If there was any surprise it was the money to be made from climbing up Mount Sustainability.

Nature is capital

Amory Lovins is famous for walking into a home or office or hotel and, at a glance, seeing the thousands of dollars being lost because of inefficient lighting or heating and cooling systems. Lovins's own home, amid the chilly Colorado Rockies, has no furnace but its ingenious design keeps it warm enough to grow bananas indoors. Virtually all the heating and cooling depends on the sun, working in sync with plants and water storage devices. For over two decades Lovins has demonstrated the wonders of technologies and architectural features working in tandem to conserve energy and more.

A Harvard- and Oxford-educated physicist, Lovins started out as an expert on energy efficiency but is now regarded as a senior statesman of the green movement. He has been a MacArthur Fellow and holds a string of honorary doctorates. In 2000 *Time* magazine picked him as a 'hero for the planet'. In his youth Lovins was deeply influenced by E.F. Schumacher's *Small is Beautiful* and has since learnt that size matters in quirky ways. For example, in some industrial projects there are enormous savings to be had from replacing small pipes and big pumps with big pipes and small pumps. The hallmark of Lovins's inventiveness is a whole-systems approach where devices are intricately interlinked to serve multiple purposes. This is based on the key insight that closed-loop production systems eliminate both waste and toxicity, often while also conserving energy. Since this enables companies to do more, and better, with less resources, it also enhances money profits.

But Lovins is intrinsically a visionary not a gizmo inventor. Like Hawken, Lovins has relentlessly emphasised that piecemeal deployment of more eco-friendly devices will ensure neither sustainability nor equity. There is no substitute for fundamentally reprogramming the reward system of commerce in favour of a holistic social transformation. For instance, he emphasises that an innovation like the hydrogen-powered Hypercar, designed by the Rocky Mountain Institute, becomes meaningless if it simply joins the millions of vehicles already stuck in traffic jams. His solution for traffic jams is, naturally, not more freeways but a radical transformation of land use patterns and economic activity – so that fewer people have to travel long distances every day.

But how is this to happen? What kind of market culture, what modes of commerce, will bring about these shifts? Hawken and Lovins's experience showed that the answers lie in the 'next industrial revolution' and a new kind of capitalism, one that 'behaves according to the proper value of natural and human capital'. So in 1999, the same year that all of them contributed to a special 25th anniversary edition of *Small is Beautiful*, Hawken and Lovins collaborated in writing *Natural Capitalism: Creating the Next Industrial Revolution*; what they presented was not a how-to manifesto but rather a philosophical framework for how humans relate to the natural world and draw on its resources. Its aim was to serve as one step towards creating a new operating system with which to produce goods and regenerate the depleted biosphere.

'Natural Capitalism' could easily be dismissed as an oxymoron if it was understood as a variant of the prevailing capitalism which undervalues both natural and human capital because it is focused on a narrow definition of capital – money and the means of production. To prevent this confusion Hawken and Lovins started by making a distinction between *commerce* and capitalism. After all, commerce and free exchange have been around for millennia. The challenge of our times is how to heal the rupture between ecology and economy – forge systems of exchange that better balance the needs of humans with the needs of the wider ecosystem. Hawken scorns the sceptics who immediately fear that this aspiration will suppress innovation, cause stagnation and unemployment: 'That is what the unimaginative declare because they have no idea what they would do in a system that wasn't based on acquisitiveness, aversion and delusion. People have to change their values in order for the system to change.'

Operationally, Natural Capitalism is an approach based on four broad principles. Firstly, a whole-system design mentality that fundamentally changes facilities, production processes and products to radically increase the productivity of natural resources. Secondly, shifting production to biologically inspired patterns – or biomimicry – in which closed materials loops eliminate waste and toxicity. Thirdly, move to a solutions-based business model that delivers value as a continuous flow of services rather than just sale of goods. This would reward both the provider and the customer for doing more and better with less for longer. Fourthly, reinvest in natural capital or eco-regeneration

The first step towards a new operating system based on these principles is proper valuation of ecosystems. The second step is to simultaneously reject heavy-handed government regulations while building a more rigorous understanding of just how and why markets become dysfunctional or are misapplied. Essentially, Natural Capitalism aims to extend the sound principles of the market to all sources of material value, not just to those that by accidents of history were first appropriated into the market system. Then all forms of capital would be prudently stewarded – precisely what trustees of financial capital now do for money. However, these are necessary, but insufficient, measures.

Markets can fulfil their promise only if we are clear about their true purpose – namely, to allocate scarce resources efficiently *over the short term.* Merely adding more items to the list of scarce resources is not enough. There is need for efficiency to be defined in longer time-frames. Natural Capitalism is an approach that enables businesses and individuals to capture the profit potential inherent in rectifying current market flaws. But there are powerful obstacles to this approach within the current market dispensation. For example, at the close of the 20th century the US market typically required roughly tenfold higher returns for saving energy than for producing it. This distortion made it 'cheaper' for consumers to opt for buying more energy rather than investing in efficiency. So, most people would not buy an efficient light bulb because, upfront, it costs $15–20 dollars while an ordinary bulb sells for 50 cents. But actually that 50 cent bulb is more expensive in the long run because the efficient bulb not only saves on electricity consumption it lasts almost 13 times longer and keeps a ton of CO_2 out of the atmosphere. As the Lovinses and Hawken pointed out, even perfectly accurate prices are useless without markets that offer a level playing field where all options can contend fairly at honest prices.

At the time that *Natural Capitalism* was being written, in the late 1990s, there were no significant markets for saved energy or 'negawatts'. Lovins and Hawken campaigned to turn electricity saved by reducing inefficiencies into a fungible commodity – one that is subject to competitive bidding, arbitrage, secondary markets, etc., just like markets in copper, wheat and sowbellies. By 2005 some utilities companies in the US were deploying 'negawatts' as a commodity. For example, an electricity company 'A' may pay another company 'B' to save electricity in B's territory and sell those 'negawatts' to A. One particular company in the northwest of the US sold electricity in one state but efficiency in nine states.

Such markets in resource efficiency are crucial to ensure the success of anti-waste regulations. For example, the Rocky Mountain Institute has shown that it is not enough to make depletion and pollution expensive through taxes on emissions: 'People won't be able to respond very imaginatively to that price signal unless there's also a marketplace where their potential losses from the taxes can be turned into someone else's profit.'

Natural Capitalism became one of many 'boats' that were lifted by the rising tide of unrest about market fundamentalism and old-style government regulation. The first Triple Bottom Line Investing Conference was held at Rotterdam at just about the same time that *Natural Capitalism* arrived in bookstores in late 1999. About the same time, the principles and experiences of the Natural Step process, designed by Dr Karl-Henrik Robèrt, a Swedish research oncologist, became available to a wider audience with the publication of *The Natural Step for Business: Wealth, Ecology and the Evolutionary Corporation*.

The Natural Step is an approach based on the conviction that solving environmental problems comes naturally to people once they can understand and define the issues for themselves. The process depends on four system conditions. One:

nature cannot withstand a systematic build-up of dispersed matter mined from the Earth's crust (e.g. minerals, oil, etc.). Two: nature also cannot withstand steady accumulation of persistent compounds made by humans (e.g. PCBs). Three: nature cannot cope with a systematic deterioration of its capacity for renewal (e.g. harvesting fish faster than they can replenish, converting fertile land to desert). Four: it follows that, if we want life to continue, we must not only use resources more efficiently but also promote economic justice. Poverty compels the poor, for short-term survival, to destroy resources that we all need for long-term survival. Interface's website credits The Natural Step with providing it the compass and tools to shift from linear industrial processes to cyclical ones where resources, wastes and services are in a closed loop.

The Natural Step became the basis of action for many companies not because it offered a ready-to-install blueprint but because it is based on a pedagogy of consensus and shared discovery. It enabled companies to explore, in their own unique circumstances, how economy, equity and ecology could be seamlessly merged with innovation, strategic planning and the compulsion to show financial results.

At about the same time, the term 'biomimicry' was also being more widely recognised. *Biomimicry: Innovation Inspired by Nature*, written in 1997 by Janine Benyus, a life sciences writer, made a powerful case for a new science that studies nature's models and then deploys this understanding to design products or processes that solve human problems – for example, solar energy cells inspired by leaves. Biomimicry is a new way of viewing and valuing nature based on the premise that, over 3.8 billion years of evolution, nature has learned what works and what lasts.

All these works together provided a vision and a framework for what is otherwise a piecemeal shift towards recycling and eco-friendly technologies. When *Natural Capitalism* was translated into Chinese, in 2001, the mayor of Shanghai bought copies for every administrative department of the city's government. Sweden's largest refiner and retailer of gasoline, OK Petroleum, lobbied for higher carbon taxes once it saw itself not as a petroleum business but as a clean energy company. Since it was thinking long-term, the company lobbied for taxes on carbon emissions, rather than on the quantity of energy consumed. In the US, DuPont discovered that taking back the spent sulphuric acid it had sold, purifying and reselling it turned out to be cheaper than creating the product from scratch.

Today there is much greater acceptance for the view that the future belongs to companies that are agile, alert and green. Lovins's prediction that early adopters will enjoy a huge competitive advantage has served as a powerful incentive for change. Interface's experience is just one piece of evidence. Interface's adventure up 'Mount Sustainability' has been guided by five 'R's: Reduce, Reuse, Reclaim, Recycle and Redesign. Within two years of its shift towards sustainability, Interface implemented new designs in its production cycle. The aim is to eventually put only compostable and non-toxic materials back into the biosphere. At some point Interface also hopes to do without petrol, by switching entirely to renewable sources of energy. It also aims to comprehensively abandon linear practices and shift to cyclical ones – as happens in nature. It now defines waste as anything that does not provide value to its customers.

In 1994 Interface was sending about six tons of carpet trimmings to the landfill every day. By 1997 it was sending none. The amazing thing is that these new production systems require one-seventh as much materials and just one-tenth of the capital, compared to the old ways. These efficiencies eventually contributed to over a fourth of Interface's operating profits and helped it ride through a recession. Between 1995 and 2006 Interface saved $336 million through waste elimination activities. In the same period water intake per square metre of carpet came down by 81% in modular carpet facilities and 41% in broadloom facilities. It reduced greenhouse gas emissions by 60% while growing the business by 50%.

In the summer of 2007, when I met Anderson, he estimated that Interface is about 45% of the way to its ultimate goal of a zero footprint by the year 2020. Interface is not alone in this journey. Collins & Aikman Floorcovering, another American company, has also based its competitive strategy on footprint reduction. In the mid-1990s this company began converting old carpet and PVC waste into carpet backing for a new product line called ER3 because it is environmentally redesigned, restructured and reused. The lowered costs raised functionality and gave the company double-digit growth in profits.

In New Zealand, EcoCover used biomimicry principles to develop a biodegradable mulch mat made from 'upcycled' shredded waste paper bound with fish paste. The product, a substitute for black plastic sheeting, reduces the need for chemical garden care, conserves water, improves soil, and diverts fish waste and waste paper from landfills. The Worldwatch Institute has estimated that corporate R&D spending on clean energy technologies reached $9.1 billion in 2006. Venture capital and private equity investment in clean energy increased tenfold between 2001 and 2006. Walmart is now working to ensure that all the seafood it sells in North America is caught through sustainable practices.

In May 2008, the US-based giant private equity firm Kohlberg Kravis Roberts & Co. entered into a partnership with the Environmental Defense Fund (EDF) in order to improve the environmental performance of dozens of businesses it owns. Interestingly, the deal is based on a creative commons approach which will ensure that business tools created as a result of this partnership are shared with other companies, including rivals of Kohlberg Kravis Roberts. Similarly, Interface has created a consulting arm to share its innovations and help other companies to shorten their learning curve.

Much of this innovation is not so much 'Natural Capitalism', in a revolutionary sense, but natural within old-style money-bottom-line capitalism which is driven by a perpetual quest for new technologies and innovation. For about 300 years such advances have taken place in the context of capitalist accumulation. But, as the economist Duncan Foley highlights, the process of technical innovation and improvement in productivity does not depend on 'the social relations of capitalism and the antagonistic laws of the market'.

This is the crux of a dispersed quest for a 'progressive capitalism' or 'sustainable prosperity'. Across the world some of the most innovative business models are being created by non-profit or quasi-commercial enterprises. For instance, Light Up the World (LUTW) aims to bring a safe source of light at night to the billions of people around the world who are still without electricity. This network is developing an affordable rural, off-grid lighting system that combines solar photovoltaics and light-emitting diode (LED) technology.

In India, one radical post-fossil-fuel strategy – known as 'Banking on Biomass' – combines renewable energy technologies with new forms of ownership and social relations. This vision for a regenerative economy, primarily crafted by civil engineer K.R. Datye, combines market exchange with new forms of collectivity – private ownership with empowerment of commons. Once again, the Banking on Biomass approach originated in the bazaar spaces and is based on the lessons learnt from community-based water sharing and land regeneration experiences. These grassroots initiatives challenge the oppressive hierarchies of traditional community structures and forge new kinds of collectives based on equity, sustainability, participation and the openness required to ensure accountability.

Banking on Biomass and simple living

The Banking on Biomass approach, above all, promotes a voluntary culture of equating prosperity with non-wasteful simplicity. Datye's blueprint, published in 1997, called for maximising renewable resources and for 'thrift'-based consumption which provides a higher standard of living for all Indians, not just a segment of the population, without the waste that has been built into the affluence of earlier developed countries. But such a shift cannot happen with top-down policy-making by government. It requires social acceptance of thrift-as-resource-maximisation, as opposed to thrift-as-frugality. The Banking on Biomass approach rests on the assumption that both the existing market culture and the role of the state can be morphed in ways that creates incentives for regeneration from the local to regional and national level – thus ensuring that both production and consumption match the carrying capacity of the biosphere and atmosphere.

However, concepts like Banking on Biomass remain on the fringes while 'market forces' are aligned with a version of growth that involves increasing consumption without accounting for the full costs. This definition of market forces is considered more 'natural' than the centuries-old practices which combine abundance, comfort and pleasure with a clear and voluntary definition of 'enough'. Therefore, despite pitched grassroots struggles and micro-successes of the Banking on Biomass approach, the process of economic 'reforms' in India has meant dilution of environmental norms in order to push industrial growth. In the process local communities have usually been denied participation in decision-making and in many places been brutally displaced. Penalties stipulated by law are rarely implemented and mechanisms for redressal remain weak.

This rough-shod model of industrial growth has often been justified on the grounds that India must first experience a high level of affluence and then work for simplicity and sustainability. From this vantage point it seems only natural, and correct, that a Voluntary Simplicity movement is emerging in the US. For instance, the Simple Living Network provides Americans with tools, tips and links for a conscious, simple, healthy and restorative lifestyle. Triggered by Duane Elgin's book *Voluntary Simplicity*, this network is anchored in the belief that the world can be a better place if we all take more responsibility for what we consume and how we live.

~

But do all these energies add up to help us resolve, or even creatively grapple with, the tension between Earth as home and Earth as marketplace? There is, of course, no single or clear answer to this question. Several possible answers are jostling for space amid bitter contradictions. Quite unsurprisingly, this is most starkly manifested at the world's largest retailer – Walmart. It all began with Hurricane Katrina in 2005.

Stunned by the scale of devastation, and predictions about its frequent repetition, Walmart set a course to make 'sustainability sustainable'. Walmart now runs a Personal Sustainability Project to help its 1.3 million employees define sustainability in practical terms to ensure that they can have *enough* for now without harming the future. This is done by asking participants to themselves identify some element of their life that seems unsustainable and then work out a way to fix it. Resulting changes can range from not printing a paper receipt at the ATM to biking instead of taking the car to work. Employees are then expected to spread the message to Walmart's multi-million weekly customers. This voluntary approach is based on positive psychology and aims to alter the impression that being eco-friendly must involve sacrifice or denial of the good life.

But how does Walmart remain faithful to its 'lowest prices ever' motto and still provide products in ways that are eco-friendly or at least less eco-hostile? In this case there are two clear, and sharply conflicting, answers. One is that it can't be done. Walmart's model is so fundamentally unsustainable that no amount of tinkering will fix it. However, it is the second answer – a tentative 'maybe it can be done' – which is inspiring what looks like daredevilry to some and arrogant stupidity to others.

Adam Werbach, lifelong environmentalist, lost friends and clients when he decided to work for Walmart. Werbach became president of the Sierra Club at the age of 23 and has spent many years condemning Walmart as a 'new breed of toxin'. So why did he decide to design and operate the Walmart Personal Sustainability Project? Werbach's justification is that the environmental movement, within which he grew up, is not suggesting solutions that are as big as the problems. Being inside Walmart gives him a chance to make sustainability matter to its customers – who happen to be 90% of the US population.

Above all, the Personal Sustainability Project creates spaces for questions and challenges. For instance, one senior manager who was inducted into the programme asked the management to explain why a meal of pizza and soda in the company cafeteria cost $2, while salad and water cost more than $5. According to Werbach, the price of the healthy food was lowered in all Sam's Clubs within a week.

Werbach has entered into this venture knowing full well that Walmart could use him as 'greenwash'. According to a report in *Fast Company* magazine, one of Werbach's wealthy supporters even offered to fund the work to spare him the indignity of a Walmart cheque. But Werbach declined because he wanted the kind of access that an unpaid outsider would never have. However, he is not alone. Environmental Defense now has an office in Bentonville to work more effectively with Walmart. Amory Lovins advises the company as does Elkington's SustainAbility. The National Resources Defense Council worked with Walmart to facilitate an unprecedented jump in the sales of compact fluorescent light bulbs.

Walmart's stated goal is now zero waste and 100% renewable energy. But, while it opens a few energy-saving stores, it also opens hundreds of its conventional energy-guzzling and waste-generating stores every year. This is partly why many in the environmental movement feel that old colleagues who are trying to turn Walmart green are deluded betrayers. By implication, that view can easily extend to the customers of Walmart, who are mostly low-income Americans running households on a tight budget.

This takes us back to the beginning – the tricky matter of respecting rising aspirations while fostering a culture of *enough*. Hawken offers a sage view:

> if we think of SUV owners as careless, non-thinking despoilers of the commons, we are further in the hole, because then we are marginalising – if not demonising – our fellow human beings. Not a strong basis for change. This world is riddled with ignorance. You can blame people who knock things over in the dark, or you can begin to light candles.

Having lit quite a few of these candles, Ray Anderson was always utterly confident that society will succeed in reinventing commerce because 'people are brought together by higher purpose'. By 2007, when I met him at the Tallberg Forum in Sweden, Anderson had moved on from his 'fellow plunderer' opening line. He greeted the global forum at Tallberg by saying: 'I am an industrialist and a businessman and as competitive and profit-minded as anyone you know.' But his goal changed to one of competing to be the first to have a zero eco-footprint. Anderson saw the framework changing steadily as the recognition grows that externalities cannot be ignored and the key problem of economics now is not the gap between what we have and what we want but what the Earth can sustain.

These upbeat stories are not meant to obscure the fact that the attempted transformation is a maddeningly difficult struggle on a day-to-day basis. Plus, much of the excitement around 'carbon-free capitalism' hopes to turn climate change into a huge business opportunity without having to reconsider, let alone challenge, the political economy that created the problem in the first place. Therefore, government and 'market forces' continue to collude to produce some stark inequities.

In 2008 *Time* magazine reported that the US Federal Government budgets about $5 billion per year to cover research and tax incentives for renewables and energy efficiency – while it spends an estimated $12 billion *every month* on the war in Iraq. Meanwhile, the US oil industry still enjoys tax breaks of about $18 billion a year. According to one estimate quoted in *The Economist*, American oil companies receive preferential treatment from their government worth more than $250 billion a year.

In effect, the sky has already been claimed by governments and private companies as buying and selling of carbon credits accelerates. In 2008, about 70% of carbon permits were estimated to be changing hands off the public exchanges, in direct transactions between firms or financial institutions. Though carbon trading is booming in Europe, there has been no major reduction in emissions. Meanwhile, banks, traders and exchanges are making handsome profits – in a sense by selling the sky, or at least its sinks for carbon. Some economists, including Joseph Stiglitz and Gregory Mankiw, have called for a carbon tax instead – on the grounds that it would be more transparent and less vulnerable to lobbying by industries trying to win higher caps for themselves.

In this context, the odds of 'cap and trade' regimes giving way to 'cap and dividend' are rather slim. For most business people the divide between economy and ecology is too firmly entrenched as a *given*, to be challenged. As Richard Sandor, founder of Chicago Climate Exchange and the European Climate Exchange told the *Wall Street Journal*: 'I am a capitalist who runs a business and has to deliver value to shareholders . . . I consider myself to be an environmentalist, but I divorce those sentiments from my day job.'

Changing this reality is an epochal process and a struggle without clear counter-poles – at least not of the kind that existed in the Cold War face-off between capitalism and communism. Amory Lovins is among those who believe that the absence of a counter-pole will work in favour of a positive transformation. 'Polarisation is the false construct we inherited from Descartes. Webs of relation, not simplistic polarities, are the reality,' Lovins told me in our meeting at Schumacher College. Perhaps this approach comes naturally to Lovins because of his Buddhist and Taoist affinities. Hawken has similar moorings. After all, says Hawken, the human condition has not changed much over several millennia. So the core question is actually not how to save the Earth, but how to alleviate suffering.

Of course, caring about the suffering of others is a personal, ethical and social ability. Similarly, imbuing commerce with a capacity to care is not a 'management' issue; it is fundamentally about the values and purpose that give meaning – to individual lives and thus build civilisation. This is why Werbach has urged that philanthropic initiatives should measure their effectiveness by changes in public *values* rather than by what things or species they succeeded in protecting.

Transforming values is much more likely to create a groundswell for lowering eco-footprints than either 'command and control' variety of regulation or the free-market orthodoxy which expects the drive for profits to provide all the answers. But there is a catch. The shift in values depends on more people being sufficiently confident and thus feeling free to question and to challenge the given order. It also requires a certain faith – the kind that moved Ray Anderson to visualise the pioneers like lighthouses guiding those still out there on the stormy sea: 'The value of what we are doing, outside of its impact on my own company, is that when things come crashing down and people look for a model we will have a model ready.' And yet even Anderson never ruled out the possibility of ecological collapse.

Survival and hope in a fratricidal war

The emergence of biofuels offers a perfect illustration of a possibly fatal conundrum. Biofuels are presented as a classic example of how market forces throw up solutions. But do they? Demand for alternatives to petrol has accelerated the clearing of native habitats to grow crops for biofuel – ironically increasing carbon emissions. Meanwhile, ethanol now has its own lobbies. So spokespersons of the Renewable Fuels Association insist that 'ethanol production and use is a responsible way to address the environmental, energy and economic challenges the world faces today'.

Among other incumbents clinging to their 'market share' is the coal industry. At the end of 2007 the International Energy Agency announced that the demand for coal, which dipped at the end of the 20th century, has again been rising. In the US, 150 new coal-fired electrical plants are proposed over the next decade. In China a coal-fired power plant goes online almost every week! Emissions from these plants alone are expected to nullify gains made in other sectors. The World Coal Institute has predicted that three decades from now coal will still provide about 39% of the world's electricity. This prediction is accompanied by the assurance that there have been advances in clean coal technologies and new technologies are expected to take the industry towards a 'zero emissions' future. Greenpeace, among other environmental groups, rejects these claims because emissions and wastes are not actually avoided, but just transferred from one waste stream to another.

This once again illustrates that you cannot depend on supply and demand alone to provide optimum allocation of resources – at least not if the returns are sought simultaneously in social, environmental and money terms. Also that pure market, by itself, won't foster the kind of deeper conversations that are urgently required – that go beyond aggregation of information to reflection and negotiation about values and objectives. The need and willingness to act beyond money profit may be more widely expressed now than 10 years ago but the money bottom line still firmly rules the global economy. For instance, illegal loggers, cattle ranchers and a growing number of soy producers continue their slash-and-burn advance into the rainforests of the Amazon. This destruction is driven by a simple, stark truth. As the market price for soy and beef rises, so do the incentives for destruction. Even ambitious efforts by the Brazilian government to prevent deforestation are thus undermined. These realities certainly dwarf efforts made by people like Forgach to promote innovative conservation-cum-livelihood mechanisms in the bazaar spaces.

In 2010 the State of Sustainability Initiatives Review showed that markets for sustainable products have grown over the previous five years and are expanding much faster than those for conventional products. Meanwhile, there is disagreement on the implications of climate negotiations concluded at Cancun in December 2010. One view is that a pragmatic formula has been found and a small step has been taken to cut emissions. The opposing view, articulated among others by Indian activist Sunita Narain, is that Cancun legitimises the right of the Western nations to continue polluting because it allows them to make a voluntary pledge. Al Gore told Reuters: 'I'm a little depressed about Cancun. The problem is not going away, it's getting steadily worse.'

A deadly combination of factors is at work. The law lacks the machinery to be effective, market forces are still creating as many, or more, incentives for destruction than conservation, and civil society initiatives are too small or too late to make enough of a difference. Thus 'carbon commerce' could boost growth of greener energy systems and leave the human economy at war with ecology in a wider sense. According to one estimate, UK's biggest polluters are likely to reap a £6 billion windfall from mostly free carbon allowances without encouraging development of clean energy.

We have to look between the lines for combinations of good and bad news. China's Ecological Footprint, having quadrupled in the last four decades, is now second only to the United States. An equivalent of more than two Chinas are needed to provide for the country's resource consumption and to absorb its waste. But the average ecological footprint of the Chinese, at 1.6 hectares, is still well below the world average of 2.2, and a fraction of the 9.6 hectare footprint of the average US resident. More significantly, China's rating on the UN Human Development Index, such as years of life expectancy, adult literacy, and per capita GDP, has grown while its footprint has remained relatively moderate by comparison.

Meanwhile, car manufacturers in India are competing vigorously to produce small cars so cheap that even lower-income families, now using two-wheelers and public transport, will become car owners. Tata's Nano, the first of these low-price cars, has been hailed by stock markets, media and people at large as a brilliant innovation. Environmentalists and others who have questioned the wisdom of adding more carbon-spewing automobiles to India's already clogged roads have been dismissed as both anti-people and anti-progress.

Again, the whodunit of the hurtling environmental disaster is complicated. No one – neither corporations nor environmental groups, nor economists nor members of parliament – has a ready-made template for addressing the basic, life-and-death question: what are the optimum ways of organising and facilitating mobility for a billion-plus Indians over the next 10 or 50 years?

Awareness of this question is still a mere dot on the horizon. Deep and diverse conversations that attempt to address it are far from mature. Both in corridors of elected power and on trading floors, solutions are being sought within the old frame of values and assumptions about human motivation. But the voices of those who challenge both the market and governments, as we know them today, are filtering through. A wider range of values are pulling or stretching the old box from the outside, while some are pressing against its limits from within. At the heart of this foment is a nascent cultural renaissance driven by the awareness that the future of our species depends on seeing ourselves as a wider community of beings – knowing that the welfare of the parts depends on the welfare of Earth as home.

For instance, Thomas Berry, a priest, poet and eco-theologian, has called for a new framework of human systems based on 'Earth Jurisprudence' – a value system that celebrates humility, generosity, patience and restraint. This involves a voluntary curtailing of our freedom in nature in order to survive and plenitude for all.

These values get more airtime than ever before, but that does not impress the Kondh tribe in eastern India. The Kondh find these values quite lacking in the companies that plan to extract bauxite by destroying their forests and a sacred hill. When the Kondh lost their case against the British mining company Vedanta Resources, in India's Supreme Court, the UK NGO ActionAid joined forces with them by deploying absurdity and satire. ActionAid filed an application with the governing body of St Paul's Cathedral asking for the demolition of the famous London landmark, in order to explore mining possibilities below it. This proposal was the protestors' way of asking Vedanta's investors to consider whether making money by desecrating a sacred site of the Kondh, as well as the habitat that provides their food and clean water, was any less outrageous.

Do the Kondh have the freedom to live by their creed of Earth as home or must they join the rest of us in treating the Earth as a marketplace with a set of ecosystem services and commodities? Whichever way you answer this question, it is not just the future of the Kondh that is at stake. Kondh versus Vedanta is a proxy for the core conflict between the Earth's ecology and the human economy. As in the epic *Mahabharata*, this is a fratricidal war that can have no victors.

'To see the momentum of loss is to want to close one's eyes,' Hawken wrote some years ago. But, he added, this is the one thing that is certain to get us deeper into trouble. Thus, there is precious merit in the diverse, even seemingly conflicting, ways of engaging in the search for answers, regardless of the dangers ahead. Hawken's expression of this faith is both poetic and practical:

I believe in rain, in odd miracles, in the intelligence that allows arctic birds to find their way across the Earth. In other words, I don't believe I know or understand the means whereby this Earth and its people will transform. I don't know how human culture will long endure. I am comforted by this ignorance, this vast possibility of what I don't know.

EPILOGUE

Back in the winter of 2001, while the rubble of the WTC was still being cleared and the air was heavy with fear, Edgar Cahn carried a rather basic question into a gathering of the Social Venture Network. He recited T.S. Eliot's poem about the stranger who comes in from the desert and asks, 'What is the meaning of this city?' 'Can we say,' asked Cahn, 'that this is a community; or do we merely dwell together to make money from each other?'

India's philosophical traditions recognise this as a *yaksha prashna* – a fundamental question which lures us to the depths of our consciousness. What, for instance, would we have to renounce in order to be both happy and wealthy? This was one of the questions asked by the God of Death, disguised as a yaksha or Earth spirit, to the warrior prince Yudhishthira in the epic *Mahabharata*. Yudhishthira's answer, 'renounce desire to become wealthy', is less important than the question itself.

Cahn, and other protagonists of these stories, may or may not change the course of market culture in the 21st century. But they will be remembered for asking fundamental questions and persistently attempting to bring down barriers that constrain our imagination. The meltdown of 2008 has made these voices sound ever more urgent, intense and *rich*. They build on the wealth of learning, or decoded messages, gleaned in the transition from Menatay to Wall Street, from free exchange to free market.

First and foremost, there is wider acceptance that neither the *idea* nor the mechanisms of the market are laws of nature. Both are human constructs than can morph to a higher level. We are in the midst of unbundling the good of bazaars, with their freedom of exchange, from the mangled remains of a narrow and self-destructive version of the market. Just as communism was defeated not by military force but by life and the human spirit, so also now the free-market orthodoxy is giving way to conscience and the longing for a fuller freedom.

A broader definition of self-interest is being driven as much by practical survival imperatives as moral restlessness. This may seem like a delusion to those who have observed the proliferation of gated communities within which affluent people build enclaves of comfort and security. But some of the same people now realise that, if climate change accelerates, there will be severe limitations to buying your way out of danger.

Sheer creativity is forging new connections between money, motivation and innovation. A jolt has been delivered by the greed and foolishness in money markets, causing the productive economy to double up in pain. In 2009, the World Economic Forum at Davos, otherwise a celebration of the free market, witnessed reflections on values, hubris and greed. Down south, at Belem in Brazil, its counterpart gathering of activists at the World Social Forum, witnessed renewed passion and zeal for all-encompassing reform and a new regime to govern the international movement of capital. Some proposed solutions were fairly conventional – such as an overhaul of credit-rating agencies and reducing incentives for excessive risk taking. More radical demands included an international tax on financial transactions, which makes the wealthy finance global public programmes, along with abolition of 'nefarious structured products' such as some types of derivatives and collateralised-debt obligations, as well as an end to speculation in commodity markets and a shift of international monetary reserves away from the US dollar.

These proposals are bound to trigger bitter squabbles between those who defend the restoration of business-as-usual in the old market culture and those who see the need for a profound transformation. And yet the ground beneath these familiar scuffles has shifted. The financial crisis has exposed fundamental weaknesses in the intellectual under-pinning of Western economic dominance. It has undermined 'the confidence of Asians in the probity of Wall Street, long admired and imitated by Asians as the icons of financial excel-lence, dynamic innovators and paragons of integrity,' wrote Andrew Sheng, former chairman of the Hong Kong Securities and Futures Commission.

Besides, as Paul Volcker said towards the end of 2010, it is no longer possible to treat the financial mechanism as being, on its own, so sensitive and efficient that 'economic growth will be placed at risk by sensible and needed regulatory intervention.' And yet the proposition that regulation hurts growth has powerful proponents. For instance, in the immedi-ate aftermath of 2008, Lloyd Bankfein, the chief of Goldman Sachs, accepted the desire for wholesale reform of the regu-latory regime as both natural and appropriate, but opposed imposition of measures designed to protect us from the 100-year storm. If you took risk completely out of the system, he warned, it would be at the cost of economic growth.

But the current crisis is only superficially about risk man-agement in the financial sector. It is more fundamentally about the limitations and intrinsically self-destructive nature of a market culture that depends on greed and fear as *drivers*. Perhaps this is an excellent time for deeper and wider reflec-tion. For instance, those who looked upon a phenomenon like Time Dollars as a 'do-good' activity on the fringes are now eager to look for more ways of mobilising human energy than conventional money allows. Even more importantly, the inno-vators tend to be hopeful without being delusional.

Cahn, for instance, is quite clear that the banking system and its supportive economy continue to function like a religion – geared to making people believe the system will work if we can just keep on creating new product lines. So why does Cahn feel that we are more ready than ever before to face the fundamental questions? Because he has become more confident that a tectonic shift to reweave family, community and commerce is already happening by osmosis; it does not require a cataclysmic collapse of the prevailing system.

Some hope, and others fear, that the pendulum is swinging towards socialism. However, it is far more likely that the current crisis will become the final resting place of the false contest between private ownership versus state ownership. The loudest message from the meltdown on Wall Street is that private ownership driven by market forces based on narrow self-interest can make as big, or worse, a mess as centralised government ownership and control made in some places.

As a consequence some core values are shining through – a wider definition of accountability, deeper transparency and multi-dimensional participation that prevents excessive concentration of power with its command-and-control behaviour patterns, be it in the hands of governments, corporations or individuals. Above all, there is a renewed surge to protect and create true commons – mechanisms that democratically secure and nurture public *goods* and resources rather than allowing them to be fenced in for a few to enjoy or profit from – be it minerals in the Earth's crust, fish in the sea, the sky's sinks or the internet.

But this restlessness for greater freedom of opportunity and more equity is now overshadowed by dire survival issues. For instance, the Northwest Passage which European traders were seeking four centuries ago now exists because enough ice has melted on the northern coast of Canada. That thinning ice, which might prove useful for shipping and trade, is a signal of cascading losses that require more and more people to respond first as citizens of the global agora rather than as producers and consumers, buyers and sellers.

~

So what has this exploration taught me in the ten years I have been on the road? Primarily, it has reconfirmed a basic intuition – that pessimism is for better times. The only hope of overcoming the many dangers that our species has spawned lies in our ability to face and acknowledge our fears without being overwhelmed. This realisation has also given me a deeper respect for what I do not know, and thus a renewed sense of wonder about the onward journey. For instance, in February 2009, Rohini Nilekani happened to ask Ray Anderson why the pace of change towards more ecologically sound forms of production and consumption is so frustratingly slow. 'I don't know,' replied Anderson, 'but it's good to remember that once someone has moved over to this side, there is no going back.'

Of course, I have been cautioned by my activist friends about exaggerating the importance of individuals or even the trends documented here. They fear that I am falling prey to facile optimism. After all, they say, the seekers and adventurers of these stories – and thousands more who are not even mentioned here – cannot match the scale of crisis both in our market culture and in our systems of production. Indeed, such critics can draw support from historical evidence. It was just 50 years ago that no less a man than Franklin D. Roosevelt fought the practices of the 'unscrupulous money changers' which he said had been 'indicted in the court of public opinion, rejected by the hearts and minds of men'. If history repeated itself, why should the future be different? And yet there is a catch in this line of reasoning.

As one of my mentors, Dhirubhai Sheth, puts it – this pessimism is rooted in 20th-century theories of change which were based on the notion of irreconcilable dichotomies. This may no longer be true because there is no absolute centre or locus of power. As these stories have shown, both conscience and pragmatic perception are energising a wide variety of efforts for reform. Sheth, a veteran political scientist and one of the founders of the Centre for Study of Developing Societies in Delhi, advised me not to worry about which of these efforts were mainstream and which were on the fringes, but to focus on pondering over the essence of human striving in our times. Sheth then reframed the Yaksha Prashna: 'Is wealth creation now the civilisational goal? Is freedom to be defined largely in terms of producing and using money?'

On this note let us return to the image of Bill Gates rummaging about inside Pandora's Box which was empty of all else but hope. 'Humanity's greatest advances are not in its discoveries – but in how those discoveries are applied to reduce inequity,' says Gates. He is putting his hope on this happening through a combination of factors – democracy, strong public education, quality healthcare, broad economic opportunity.

Gates's trajectory may well come to represent the core dilemmas of our time. Many are struggling to reconcile their benefits as affluent consumers and owners of capital, with outrage about inequity and injustice they witness as citizens and as social and moral beings. This is partly what shifted Gates from being a cheerleader for capitalism to a crusader for 'creative capitalism'. However weak and riddled with holes this idea might be, it still marks a dramatic movement from the fundamentalist dogma that market forces, if lightly regulated, will provide plenitude for all.

Gates's unfolding journey is part of a much larger trend of 'philanthrocapitalism' outlined in a book by Matthew Bishop and Michael Green. This is an entrepreneurial results-oriented approach to solving the world's big problems by tweaking and reapplying familiar business models. Since most philanthrocapitalists have become immensely rich through the prevailing free-market model, they tend to overlook or remain in denial about its systemic flaws. There is a growing concern that as 'venture philanthropists' acquire a disproportionately large influence over media, government and private companies, their approach could scuttle serious rethinking about the interface between society and market, civilisation and commerce. As Michael Edwards, head of the Ford Foundation, has pointed out, 'No great social cause was mobilised through the market in the 20th century.'

Besides, as Amy Domini tirelessly reiterates, there is a basic conflict between making the highest possible profit for the few that have investments and building the most liveable world for the many that inhabit it. She is convinced that if civilised people continue to define monetary rewards to investors as the reason for commerce, the future we hope for cannot be realised. Why then is Domini optimistic? Because she perceives the context for a seismic shift:

> This is not about bad people; it is about bad systems. We have an answer: use the strength of the investment industry to build a better world. We can reach out and touch the dangers . . . The planet is shrinking, and there isn't much time left.

Whether conversations in and about socially embedded bazaar spaces can be pathfinders for this seismic shift depends largely on how we understand freedom. At the institutional level, even market fundamentalists accepted that some regulation was essential in the way that traffic lights ensured smoother flow of traffic. But the essence of what is at stake here is more subtle and it might help to draw on Karl Polanyi's key insight. It is only when we commit ourselves to creating and ceaselessly guarding a more abundant freedom for *all*, wrote Polanyi, that we can be liberated from the fear that either private wealth or state planning will turn against us.

Therefore the cutting edge of emerging conversations is not about regulation or the ideal size of the state. It is about democratic values and the place of commerce in civilisation.

As an illustration of the challenges, and darkness, ahead, let us return to our starting point – the vicinity of Wall Street. There was a valiant effort to secure Ground Zero, the site of the fallen World Trade Center, for a memorial *sans* commerce. It failed. As plans to replace the lost towers with a memorial plus office complex went ahead, one activist noted that the dead could not compete with reverence for lost construction.

Such dark choices are not new. They have repeatedly surfaced in the journey of civilisation. Thus the most tenacious innovators and seekers have set their gaze on a transformation of epic proportions and several of them invoke the imagery of the *Bhagavad Gita*. It is only in an apparent sense that the forces of escalating consumption and destruction are arrayed against the forces of frugality, simplicity and restoration. At a deeper level, as the Song Celestial tells us, these elements are not 'out there' but manifest within each of us as competing and fluid urges. Who we are is not static.

After all, Yudhishthira was the very embodiment of righteousness and good conduct, but in a moment of weakness he gambled away not only his kingdom and his liberty but also committed his brothers and wife to servitude. Why, then, does Yudhishthira remain an epic hero? Because he suffered the consequences and went on to seek a higher freedom which comes from mindful exercise of one's passions.

A market culture beyond greed and fear will necessarily be anchored in a civilisational ethos that seeks freedom from limitless wants. It will ensure universal freedom of opportunity but celebrate with more gusto the freedom to be oneself, the freedom to give, freedom to keep areas of life entirely outside the marketplace.

Two and a half millennia ago a prince was born into a life of complete freedom from want. He could have, as other kings in his time did, used that resource to annex other kingdoms. Instead, he walked away to seek a higher freedom, and is remembered today as the Buddha. The path of right livelihood, along with that of the innovators and seekers you have encountered here, could be dismissed as inaccessible to most human beings. Then again, these images can be a lure to further quests, beyond barriers of habit that shrink and curtail what we think is possible.

SOURCE NOTES

Prelude

Details about the summertime gathering place at Menatay, before the arrival of Europeans, were mostly taken from information displayed at the National Museum of the American Indian located in the Alexander Hamilton US Custom House at One Bowling Green, a few blocks from Wall Street. A plaque outside the museum records that, while many kinds of goods were exchanged here, such as the bright copper of the Great Lakes, sparkling mica of the Carolina highlands, shining shell beads, stone tools and golden maize, the gatherings were essentially about wider human contact: 'when the smell of wildflowers perfumed the air, they travelled for trade and adventure, meeting here to exchange goods, share knowledge, give thanks, and show respect to the spirits'.

1. 'It was on 11 September 1609.. . .'. Josef Berger and L.C. Wroth, *Discoverers of the New World* (New York: American Heritage Publishing Co., 1960). Hudson recorded in his journal that the natives were 'very loving people'. When the Indians thought Hudson was afraid of their bows and arrows, 'they broke them in pieces and threw them into the fire'. Other works referred to for this period include: Carl Carmer, *The Rivers of America Series: The Hudson* (New York: Farrar & Rinehart [later Holt, Rinehart & Winston], 1939); Ted Morgan, *Wilderness at Dawn: The Settling of the North American Continent* (London: Simon & Schuster, 1993).

2. '. . . the fall of Lehman Brothers'. Their filing for bankruptcy on 15 September 2008 has come to be seen as the crucial event that sent glo-

bal financial markets into freefall. The *Wall Street Journal* has recorded that as the week that Wall Street died.

4. Rohini Nilekani is a Bangalore-based journalist, author and philanthropist. She is founder and chairperson of Arghyam, a non-profit organisation whose mission is 'Enough water, safe water . . . always and for all.' At the time she was also chairperson of Akshara, a non-profit working on primary education. The villager being quoted is Premkumar Sharma, better known as 'Premji'.

5. 'Can civilisation survive when only the commercial . . . ?' Jeremy Rifkin, *The Age of Access*. Rifkin is an economist and the founder as well as president of Foundation for Economic Trends based in Washington DC.

7. 'Yet we find an astonishing variety of "unfreedoms" persisting . . .'. Amartya Sen, *Development as Freedom*.

1. The need to gather

9. 'The Market is a good that's become a God . . .'. David Jenkins in a lecture for course titled 'Market: From Master to Servant', at Schumacher College, February 2001. Jenkins retired as Bishop of Durham.

9. '. . . a self-regulating machine that can itself ensure the equilibrium of economic activities . . .'. Oskar Lange in Fernand Braudel, *The Wheels of Commerce* II: 224. Lange, an economist, described the market as the first computer mankind ever had.

10. '. . . John Poindexter of the Iran-Contra scandal fame, masterminded a futures market in terrorism . . .'. Lead for the story in Steve Fraser, *Every Man a Speculator: A History of Wall Street in American Life*. Details from Noah Shachtman 'The Case for Terrorism Futures', *Wired* magazine, 30 July 2003.

11.'Doc Searls, the editor of the Linux Journal, liked to explain why . . .'. 'Why Markets Will Once Again Consist of People', speech by Searls at the 50th anniversary celebration of the Gottlieb Dutteiler Institute, Lucerne, 25 September 2000.

12. 'Markets are conversations' is first in the 95 theses of the Cluetrain Manifesto which was first posted on the internet and later appeared as a book. Rick Levine, Christopher Locke, Doc Searls and David Winberger, *The Cluetrain Manifesto: The End of Business as Usual*.

13. Details about origins and characteristics of early bazaars are partly from Lewis Mumford, *The City in History: Its Origins, its Transformations and its Prospects*: 70-71, 149. For the transition from bazaar to market, I depended substantially on Mumford and on Fernand Braudel's three-volume study on *Civilization and Capitalism*, particularly Volume II.

In a chapter titled 'From Marketplace to Market Economy', Mumford described liquid capital as

> a chemical solvent: it cut through the cracked varnish that had long protected the medieval town and ate down to the raw wood, showing itself even more ruthless in its clearance of historic institutions and their buildings than the most reckless of absolute rulers.

Describing the replacement of the concrete market place of the mediæval town with the abstract transnational market, Mumford noted that, earlier, concrete goods changed hands between visible buyers and sellers who operated on the same moral norms and met somewhat on the same level: 'here security, equity, stability, were more important than profit'. By contrast, the abstract market was about people at greater distance:

> engaged in monetary transactions for which the goods themselves served, rather, as counters: the purpose of such transactions was profit, and the accumulation of more capital, to be sunk in other enterprises of increasing magnitude. Customary morality, corporate standards, traditional evaluations all served as brakes upon speculative enterprise (*The City in History*: 412-13).

Other sources for this period included: Shepard Bancroft Clough and Charles Woolsey Cole, *Economic History of Europe* (Boston, MA: D.C. Heath & Company, 1967): 50; James Masschaele, *Peasants, Merchants, and Markets: Inland Trade in Medieval England, 1150–1350* (New York: St Martin's Press, 1997): 58; C.A. Bayly, *Rulers, Townsmen and Bazaars: North Indian Society in the Age of British Expansion, 1770–1870* (Cambridge, UK: Cambridge University Press, 1983).

A tattered social fabric

14. 'Londoners once held their breath waiting for . . .'. Peter Watson, *A Terrible Beauty*: 383-86.

15. 'Through the 1930s an average of about 18.2% of American workers were unemployed . . .'. Robert J. Samuelson, 'Great Depression', in *The Concise Encyclopedia of Economics: Library of Economics and Liberty*; Paul Kennedy, *The Rise and Fall of Great Powers* (Random House, 1987): 282-83.

17. 'These moves marked a rejection of the "Let us Alone" philosophy . . .'. Leo Huberman, *Man's Worldly Goods: The Story of the Wealth of Nations* (New York/London: Monthly Review Press, 1936). Huberman notes that in 1770 the French Physiocrat, Mirabeau gave the following advice to the ruler of the state of Baden:

> Ah, Monseigneur, be the first to give to your states the advantage of a free port and a free fair, and let the first words read on setting foot in your territory be your loved and revered name, and beneath it these three noble words: Freedom, Immunity, Liberty! . . . Your states will rapidly become the privileged habitation of men, the natural route of trade, the meeting-place of the universe (143-44).

Hayek and Polanyi: free market versus freedom

18. This section is inspired by conversations with Nick Robins and particularly his article 'Three Wise Men', *Resurgence* magazine, December 1998. Details are also drawn from Watson, *A Terrible Beauty*. Robins headed the socially responsible investing division of Henderson in London for many years. He currently heads HSBC's Climate Change Centre of Excellence. He is also author of *The Corporation that Changed the World: How the East India Company Shaped the Modern Multinational* (London/Delhi: Pluto Books/Orient Longman, 2006).

18. 'This view had deep roots in Western Europe . . .'. Albert O. Hirschman, *Rival Views of Market Society:* 43.

19. 'Therefore, Hayek argued . . .'. F.A. Hayek, *The Road to Serfdom.*

20. 'First of all, Polanyi's reading of history . . .'. Karl Polanyi, *The Great Transformation.* Polanyi identified three common operating principles in virtually all societies prior to the late Middle Ages: reciprocity, redistribution and householding. Householding referred to primary production for village subsistence needs and day-to-day use values. These values or principles were sanctioned and enforced by custom, magic, religion and law. Two millennia earlier Aristotle had elaborated this argument in detail in his *Politics*.

Fernand Braudel offered a balancing view on these matters: 'What is certain is that alongside the "non-markets" beloved of Polanyi, there always have been exchanges exclusively in return for money, however little' (Braudel, *The Wheels of Commerce* II: 228) The 'great transformation' of the 18th and 19th centuries put those money-driven exchanges and their related cultural ethos at the core of the economy. This ethos soon took over society itself and by the end of the 20th century came to be treated as the only path to 'progress' and prosperity.

The philosopher Ivan Illich extended Polanyi's cultural critique of capitalism by celebrating the 'convivial tools' of organic societies and the perennial wisdom of vernacular cultures. William Grieder drew extensively on Polanyi in his critique of globalisation in his book *One World Ready or No: The Manic Logic of Global Capitalism* (London: Simon & Schuster, 1997). Herman Daly, the pioneer of ecological economics, regards *The Great Transformation* as a foundational work. This influence is clearly visible in Daly's efforts to build a 'steady state' economics 'for the common good'. (See Chapter 2 for details.)

21. 'When the 19th-century British poet and painter William Blake . . .'. See also Christopher Finch, *The Illustrated History of the Financial Markets* (New York: Abbeville Press, 2001). A 1791 painting by the British artist William Hick portraying the miserable conditions inside an English bleach mill is included as an illustration of why Blake raised a lament about 'Satanic Mills'. But the caption adds: 'Despite such expression of sincere disgust, however, factories such as this helped make Britain the wealthiest nation of the early modern period.' This is a representative of a commonly held view that the horrors of the industrial age can and should be overlooked because of the explosion of wealth, opportunity and comfort they facilitated for some.

23. 'Half a century later ethical investing expert Nick Robins . . .'. Nick Robins, 'Three Wise Men', *Resurgence* magazine, December 1998. Robins wrote:

> The roots of today's crisis in the global economy can now be seen in Hayek's partial vision. Hayek had a deep distrust of democracy, which for him was only a means to an end, one which must be circumscribed by law so that it does not impinge on economic liberty. Later in life, Hayek's anti-democratic bias would harden into bizarre proposals for limiting the right to vote to those over the age of forty-five, a system which would have taken political freedoms back hundreds of years.

'The Market 'R' Us'

Sources for history and working of Wall Street: Walter Werner and Steven T. Smith, *Wall Street* (New York: Columbia University Press, 1991); Charles R. Geisst, *Wall Street: A History* (New York: Oxford University Press, 1997); Steve Fraser, *Every Man a Speculator*.

24. 'In the case of the US it has been suggested that . . .'. A.O. Hirschman, *Rival Views of Market Society*: 134.

25. 'The economist Milton Friedman . . .' was given the Nobel Prize largely for his work on monetary policy which gave rise to terms like 'money matters' and 'only money matters'. In the last quarter of the 20th century his ideas had a deep influence on the monetary policies of central banks in many countries.

25. 'Business writer Robert Kuttner has described . . .'. Robert Kuttner, *Everything for Sale*: 37.

25. 'Even John Maynard Keynes had twisted the knife . . .'. Paul Ormerod, *The Death of Economics* (London: Faber & Faber, 1994): 7.

26. Michael Lewis, 'The End of Wall Street', www.portfolio.com, December 2008. See also www.portfolio.com/news-markets/national-news/portfolio/2008/11/11/The-End-of-Wall-Streets-Boom.

26. 'It helped that the New York Stock Exchange had mounted a public relations campaign . . .'. Fraser, *Every Man a Speculator*: 580-81.

26. 'Wall Street's rehabilitation did more than revive confidence . . .'. Fraser, *Every Man a Speculator*: 586-88. This ideological phantasm, as Fraser called it, became *the* medium for discovering freedom and truth, with the Stock Exchange becoming a 'postindustrial version of the New England town meeting'. Wrote Fraser: 'Day traders traveling down the information superhighway saw themselves as freedom loving guerrillas, brash, fearless types who refused to defer to the men in pinstripe suits.'

28. 'Tough Love means withholding help . . .'. Edgar Cahn, *No More Throw-away People*: 40.

28. The net worth of the median American household actually dropped during the roaring Nineties. The real after-tax income of the middle 60% of Americans was less in 1999 than it was in 1977. In the same period the share of wealth held by the top 1% of the population went from 19.9% to 40%. Even in Britain income disparities were worse by 1997 than they had been for 40 years. ('Does inequality matter?', *The*

Economist, 16 June 2001.) According to one estimate, the percentage of Americans owning shares went from 10% in 1980 to 60% in 2008 (Chyrstia Freeland, 'US facing four consequences of lost pensions', *Financial Times*, 13 October 2008). See also Polly Toynbee and David Walker, *Unjust Rewards* (London: Granta Books, 2008).

Goddess TINA versus Open Society

30. 'These worries resonated within segments of the American establishment . . .'. The 20th Century Fund was founded by the American businessman Edward Albert Filene who was convinced that markets alone are not conducive to a stable and growing democratic nation. Interestingly, Filene's life was partly shaped by a visit to India in 1907 where he discovered village credit societies in a village near Calcutta. Filene went on to become the father of the credit union movement in the US. Among the progressive thinkers of his time, Filene promoted many ideas that were revolutionary in the early 1900s. For instance, he instituted profit-sharing plans for his employees and other fringe benefit programmes.

31. 'We are in a country that was founded on . . .'. Paul Hawken in an interview with Sarah van Gelder, *YES! A Journal of Positive Futures*, Summer 1999; www.yesmagazine.org.

32. 'Soros's articulation of the malaise was precise and clinical . . .'. George Soros, *The Crisis of Global Capitalism*; George Soros, *Open Society: Reforming Global Capitalism*. Over-emphasis on individual preferences undermines the importance of collective needs. Wealth, Soros wrote, is never truly private because it impinges on the interests of others. Therefore the concept of private property needs the theory of perfect competition to justify it. But since there never really is perfect mobility and perfect knowledge, 'property carries with it not only rights but also obligations towards the community' (George Soros, *The Age of Fallibility: Consequences of the War on Terror*: 133).

See also: Joseph E. Stiglitz, 'A Fair Deal for the World', review of George Soros's *On Globalization* in *New York Review of Books*, 23 May 2002. Michael T. Kaufman, *Soros: The Life and Times of a Messianic Billionaire* (New York: Vintage Books, 2002).

The *Wall Street Journal* dismissed Soros's assessment that the financial system is fatally bedevilled by wild instability and offered a counter-view straight out of the textbooks;

> The system has an inherent resilience thanks to a steady
> flow of feedback and adjustment – what in biological systems

> is called homeostasis. To be sure, this resilience can be made
> even stronger by prudent public policy, such as the Fed's
> recent, moderate lowering of short-term interest rates (*Wall
> Street Journal*, 8 December 1998).

The Economist declared Soros a 'great and a good man' whose tragedy is that he craves recognition as a great thinker. It also criticised Soros for not making concrete and coherent suggestions about what should be done. While it ridiculed Soros's philosophy of reflexivity, *The Economist* did not mention a word about his critique of Market Fundamentalism ('A Tract for the Times', *The Economist*, 5 December 1998).

33. 'Market fundamentalism, said Sakakibara...'. Presentation by Eisuke Sakakibara at the Foreign Correspondents' Club, Tokyo, on 22 January 1999.

33. Sen's empirical work helped to counter the dogma of the 1980s and 1990s that if governments and civil society would just leave the free market alone it would work for everyone. The falsehood of this claim was starkly demonstrated by Sen's famous study of four famines where the food was available but people went hungry because they could not afford to buy it. As Peter Watson has noted:

> Sen's analysis was startling, partly because, as he himself
> said, it was counterintuitive, going against the grain of common sense, but also because it showed how the market could
> make a bad situation worse. Apart from helping governments understand in a practical way how famines develop,
> and therefore might be avoided or the effects mitigated, his
> empirical results highlighted some special limitations of
> the free-market philosophy and its ethical base (*A Terrible
> Beauty*: 651-52).

In choosing Sen, the Nobel Award committee was also seen to be making amends for its choice in the previous year. The 1997 Nobel for economics had gone to Robert Merton and Myron Scholes, for the complicated formulas that were used at Long Term Capital Management (LTCM), a high-powdered hedge fund deemed to have the magic touch for getting positive returns with zero risk. Within months of collecting their Nobel, LTCM teetered on the brink of insolvency – in part triggered by the South Asian crises – and was rescued by the government.

34. 'Forbes doing a cover story called "Peace, Love, Software"...'. *Forbes* cover story, 10 August 1998.

35. 'It struck Roddick that she was probably . . .'. Anita Roddick, 'Currency of the Imagination', *Resurgence*, November/December 2007: 245.

36. '. . . there is not just one market model Joseph Stiglitz . . .'. *The Times* (London), 24 July 2002.

36. 'A constructive market model would require . . .'. Joseph Stiglitz, *The Roaring Nineties: Seeds of Destruction*. The Glass Steagall Act of 1933 prevented banks from both lending money and selling securities. The ideas behind Glass Steagall, wrote Stiglitz:

> went back even further, to Teddy Roosevelt and his efforts to break up the big trusts, the large firms that wielded such economic power. TR and the Progressives of the early twentieth century were alarmed not only about the concentration of economic power but about its impact on the political process. When enterprises become too big, and interconnections too tight, there is a risk that the quality of economic decisions deteriorates, and the 'too big to fail' problem rears its ugly head . . . When banks failed, the taxpayers paid the price through publicly funded bailouts (*Roaring Nineties*: 159).

37. 'Is there an Alternative to Global Capitalism?' A debate at St Paul's Cathedral, 15 September 2004. Speakers: Professor John Kay, Dr Rowan Williams, Professor Muhammad Yunus.

Post-meltdown rummaging in Pandora's Box

38. Paul Volcker, former chairman of the US Federal Reserve, had issued warnings about intractable problems below the favourable surface of the US economy. In 2004 Volcker identified a darkness that surpassed anything known in the past and lamented that 'no one is willing to understand this and do anything about it . . . We are skating on increasingly thin ice' (*The Economist*, 9 September 2004).

Free-market theory always provided for market volatility, but its fundamental claim was that within a certain bandwidth of turbulence markets cohere to find equilibrium. Some of the sharpest evidence to the contrary has been garnered by a new branch of scholarship, 'econophysics', which combines physics and economics. This interdisciplinary approach has undermined claims about the miraculous powers of the market to self-correct and allocate resources efficiently. See Philip Ball, *Critical Mass: How One Thing Leads to Another*: 279-80.

38. Robert J. Samuelson, 'Wall Street's Unraveling: How Greed and Fear Collapsed the Market's Business Model', *Newsweek*, 17 September 2008; www.newsweek.com/id/159334/page/1.

38. Edmund L. Andrews, 'Greenspan Concedes Error on Regulation', *New York Times*, 23 October 2008.

40. 'Barack Obama's promise to grow the American economy from the bottom up . . .'. David Korten, 'Beyond the Bailout: Agenda for a New Economy'; www.yesmagazine.org/article.asp?ID=3050.

David Korten, a former Ford Foundation executive and author of *The Post-Corporate World: Life after Capitalism,* is a thought-leader for activists who seek to align economic values and institutions with the imperatives and opportunities of the 21st century.

41. Grameen started by making loans, for a total of $50,000, to groups of immigrant women in New York's borough of Queens. It plans to offer $176 million in loans within New York City, and later expand to the rest of the US. The bank, which started in 1976 with an initial loan of $27 to 42 women in Bangladesh, has since lent $6.5 billion in loans to $7 million people in that country. In the US, about 28 million people have no bank accounts and 44.7 million have only limited access to financial institutions (Daniel Pimlott, 'Bangladesh bank offers loans to US poor', *Financial Times*, 16 February 2008).

41. Bill Gates's Speech at Harvard Commencement, 7 June 2007.

42. Raghuram Rajan and Luigi Zingales:

> The greatest danger for the market democracy today is not that it will lapse into socialism, but that it will revert to the relationship system, suppressing competition under the excuse of reducing risk. But we cannot avoid this by preaching a hands-off attitude for the state. Not only will we risk leaving the necessary infrastructure underdeveloped so that the market works poorly and access is limited to the privileged few, but we will also leave the market overexposed to the political backlash from the inevitable market downturn (*Saving Capitalism from the Capitalists*: 313).

Raghuram Rajan is the Joseph Gidwitz Professor of Finance at the University of Chicago's Graduate School of Business and Director of the American Finance Association and associate editor of the *American Economic Review*. Luigi Zingales is Robert C. McCormack Professor of Entrepreneurship and Finance at University of Chicago's Graduate

School of Business and a research fellow at the Center for Economic Policy Research.

42. John K. Galbraith used to talk about two parts of the economy – the 'market system', with its thousands of small and traditional proprietors, and the 'industrial system', consisting of a few highly organised corporations. Braudel's monumental study of civilisation and capitalism drew attention to a third sector 'that lowest stratum of the non-economy, the soil into which capitalism thrusts its roots but which it can never really penetrate'. Spontaneous links between supply, demand and prices are a base for capitalism but not its home base. This is still another layer which Braudel called 'the zone of the anti-market, where the great predators roam and the law of the jungle operates' (*The Wheels of Commerce* II: 229-30).

Chapter 2

45. 'It is market fundamentalism . . .'. George Soros, *On Globalization:* 15.

46. 'We no longer want to have this autistic science . . .'. 'A Brief History of Post Autistic Economics Movement', www.paecon.net/HistoryPAE. htm.

47. Tony Lawson is a leading critical realist, best known for his penetrating critiques of mainstream economics, and author of *Reorienting Economics* (London: Routledge, 1993). He has run the Critical Realist Workshop at Cambridge for many years and co-founded the Cambridge Social Ontology Group – which has the aim of pursuing social ontology, the systematic study of the nature and basic structure of social reality. According to its website:

> The Cambridge realist workshop has been meeting regularly on Monday evenings since 1990. The realist emphasis originated with the common perception of a group of Cambridge economists that modern economics pays too little attention to the nature of material it aims to illuminate. In consequence, an early workshop objective was to assess how method can usefully be adapted to insights into the nature of social material. Once instituted the workshop quickly broadened its themes and now encompasses almost any sort of discussion in the field of methodology or the philosophy of science. Its emphasis is pluralist and critical. A concern with relevance remains central however (www.econ.cam.ac.uk/ seminars/realist/about_the_workshop.htm).

48. 'Economics, which was becoming an ever more abstruse . . .'.
Michael Lewis, *Liar's Poker*: 24-25.

49. '. . . fair is foul and foul is fair . . .'. Keynes quoted by Schumacher in
Small is Beautiful.

Virtue of vice

50. Details about relevance of Mandeville are from: E.J. Hundert, *Bernard Mandeville and the Discovery of Society* (Cambridge, UK: Cambridge University Press, 1994); A.O. Hirschman, *Rival Views of Market Society*: 39, 38, 41, 43, 46; and Marcel Mauss, *The Gift*. Mauss saw the 18th century as marking a shift toward material utility and away from the pursuit of pleasure, and the 'good', as ends in themselves: 'The victory of rationalism and mercantilism was required before the notions of profit and the individual were given currency and raised to the level of principles. One can date roughly – after Mandeville and his Fable des Abeilles – the triumph of the notion of individual interest' (*The Gift*: 73-75).

51. 'By this interest we must govern him . . .'. Hume quoted in Hirschman, *Rival Views of Market Society*: 39

52. 'Naturally, there were challengers . . .'. Hirschman has noted that Burke

> was an intense admirer of Adam Smith and took much pride in the identity of views on economic matters between himself and Smith. His 'age of chivalry' statement, so contrary to the intellectual legacy of Smith, therefore signals one of those sudden changes in the general mood and understanding from one age to the next of which the exponents themselves are hardly aware. Burke's lament set the tone for much of the subsequent romantic protest against an order based on the interests which, once it appeared to be dominant, was seen by many as lacking nobility, mystery, and beauty (*Rival Views of Market Society:* 46).

'Invisible Hand' steals Smith's thunder

53. 'Adam, Adam, Adam Smith . . .'. Stephen Leacock, *Hellements of Hickonomics* (New York: Dodd, Mead & Co., 1936): 75. Quoted by Amartya Sen in *On Ethics and Economics*: 21-22. This section draws on: Ian Simpson Ross, *The Life of Adam Smith* (Oxford, UK: Clarendon Press, 1995): 163-64, 419-20; David Denley, 'Northern Lights: How

Modern Life Emerged from Eighteenth-Century Edinburgh', *The New Yorker*, 11 October 2004; Duncan K. Foley, *Adam's Fallacy: A Guide to Economic Theology* (Cambridge, MA: The Belknap Press of Harvard University Press, 2006).

Sen to Smith's Rescue

55. 'John Stuart Mill By a mighty effort of will . . .'. Quoted by Sen in *On Ethics and Economics*: 16-28. Sen has pointed out that the traditional dichotomy between 'egoism' and 'utilitarianism' is misleading in several respects. For example, 'actions based on group loyalty may involve, in some respects, a sacrifice of purely personal interests, just as they can also facilitate, in other respects, a greater fulfilment of personal interests . . . The mixture of selfish and selfless behaviour is one of the important characteristics of group loyalty, and this mixture can be seen in a wide variety of group associations varying from kinship relations and communities to trade unions and economic pressure groups' (*On Ethics and Economics*: 19-20).

Sen's *Poverty and Famines* (1981), which fired the academic world, was a report for the World Employment Program of the International Labour Organisation (ILO). Sen did the study while he was professor of political economy at Oxford and a Fellow of All Souls. This report was a study of four major famines: Bengal (India) in 1943, Ethiopia in 1972–74; Sahel in 1973 and Bangladesh in 1974. Sen also played a key role in shaping the concept of United Nations path-breaking annual Human Development Reports and Human Development Index.

In *Economics for Common Good* Mark Lutz credits Sen with attempts to:

> liberate normative economics from its utilitarian past. He attached the label *welfarism* to the conventional practice to represent value in terms of individual utility. Ever since, the cutting edge of modern welfare economics has been centered on his work, attempting to express well-being in a manner that bypasses utility and focuses instead on alternative conceptualizations, including such hitherto ignored aspects as rights and freedoms.

57. 'For instance, Alan Greenspan now says that human nature . . .'. Daniel Gross, 'Margaret Mead in a Pinstriped Suit: Alan Greenspan discovers that human beings are . . . irrational!' (17 September 2007; www.slate.com/id/2174082). This material is from an article Gross wrote in *Slate* based on the interview he did with Greenspan; the full interview appeared in *Newsweek*.

In the late 1980s, the political philosopher Francis Fukuyama became a celebrity by heralding the triumph of capitalism through his book *The End of History*. But soon after that Fukuyama went on to expound the importance of civil society, trust and other virtues for the creation of prosperity in a book called *Trust* (Francis Fukuyama, *Trust: The Social Virtues and the Creation of Prosperity* [New York: Free Press, 1995]).

The Self and Noogenesis

58. The Global Consciousness Project website explains the project as follows:

> Scientists and engineers from various disciplines have designed software that reads the output of random number generators and records a 200-bit trial sum once every second, continuously over months and years. The data are transmitted over the internet to a server in Princeton, NJ, USA, where they are archived for later analysis. The purpose of this project is to examine subtle correlations that appear to reflect the presence and activity of consciousness in the world. The scientific work is careful, but it is at the margins of our understanding. We believe our view may be enriched by a creative and poetic perspective. Here we present various aspects of the project, including some insight into its scientific and philosophical implications . . . (noosphere.princeton.edu).

Those machines, known as Random Event Generators, electronically flip 200 coins each second and record the random patterns that emerge. It has been observed that when major world events occur, like the 9/11 terrorist attack or the Indian Ocean tsunami, these random event generators display patterns that should not exist in truly random sequences. Scientists working on the GCP are themselves mystified and uncertain about how to read this data. They step cautiously, struggling to remain within the accepted boundaries of *science* while constantly skirting the margins of their own understanding to explore if and how all of life and consciousness may be interconnected.

As if this were not enough of a challenge to our familiar sense of the 'real', here is a detail that puts us deeper into the twilight zone. The GCP recorded a deviation from random behaviour some minutes *before* the first plane dashed into the WTC and before millions of people were glued to their televisions in horror!

59. Teilhard de Chardin, *The Phenomenon of Man*.

59. Cyber Consciousness by Jean Houston (www.absolutemagazines. com). Houston is one of the founders of the Human Potential Movement and author of the numerous books including: *The Possible Human: A Course in Extending Your Physical, Mental, and Creative Abilities* (Tarcher, 1982; 2nd edn 1997); *The Search for the Beloved: Journeys in Mythology and Sacred Psychology* (Tarcher, 1987); *A Passion for the Possible: A Guide to Realizing Your True Potential* (HarperCollins, 1997).

60. In his 1988 book *After the Crash: The Emergence of the Rainbow Economy* (UK: Green Print), Guy Dauncey made the link between Chardin and Aurobindo's vision. Dauncey, a writer and consultant on community economic development and a member of the UK Green Party, identified seven shades or core values for the Rainbow Economy: purple, for spiritual values; dark blue for planetary values; pale blue for economic values; green for ecological values; yellow for values of personal creativity and fulfilment; orange for local community values; and red for social values.

61. Marilyn Ferguson, *The Aquarian Conspiracy: Personal and Social Transformation in the 1980s* (Los Angeles: J.P. Tarcher, 1980): 406. Notions of 'self' and related behaviour are constantly shaped by broader social trends. For instance, Alexander Astin, professor of higher education at UCLA, has been collecting data on the attitudes of young people for over 40 years. He has asked thousands of first-year college students in the US what is important to them in life. In the late 1960s about 80% of students said they felt it was essential to develop a meaningful philosophy of life. By the late 1990s this number had declined to 40%. Meanwhile, the number of those who feel it is essential to be financially well off rose from about 40% to over 70%. For more details see Tim Kasser, *The High Price of Materialism* (Cambridge, MA: MIT Press, 2002); Jonathon Porritt, *Capitalism as if the World Matters*.

61. Richard Dawkins, 'Our big brains can overcome our selfish genes', *The Independent*, 2 September 2002.

62. Details about Ashoka and Bill Drayton are from David Bornstein, *How to Change the World: Social Entrepreneurs and the Power of New Ideas* (New York: Oxford University Press, 2004).

Oikonomia versus chrematistics

63. Story about Thales is from Herman Daly and J.B. Cobb Jr, *For the Common Good: Redirecting the Economy toward Community, the Environment, and a Sustainable Future*.

Ecology and economy

64. Thomas Moore, chapter on 'The Economics of Soul' in *Care of the Soul* (London: Harper Perennial, 1992): 190.

64. Daly and Cobb, *For the Common Good*: 138-39.

65. Mark Lutz, *Economics for the Common Good*: 58. 'Two Meanings of Economic', in Karl Polanyi, *The Livelihood of Man* (Burlington, MA: Academic Press, 1977).

Polanyi identified an 'Economistic Fallacy' which confusingly melded two different definitions of the term 'economic'. One is the scarcity definition which sees economics as the process of making choices about alternative ways to utilise perpetually insufficient means. Two, there is a substantive definition which is not limited to maximising utility and grapples with the multi-dimensional interactions between people. It also takes into account competing human urges – greed as well as generosity, craving and contentment.

65. Robert Kuttner, *Everything for Sale*: 59-60, 65.

Lester Thurow, a former dean of the MIT Sloan School of Management and author of several books including *Dangerous Currents* (London: Random House, 1983) has lamented that instead of adjusting theory to reality, reality is adjusted to theory. He went on to suggest that accepting the conventional supply–demand model of the economy is rather like believing that the world is flat, or that the sun revolves around the Earth. The science writer Philip Ball has noted that some economists have even asserted that to include the noise of real life in their models would be to insult the intelligence of the market. In such theory-building the model predictions were rarely compared against hard data. See Philip Ball, *Critical Mass: How One Thing Leads to Another*: 244-25.

Early signs of an economics with better cognition: historical lineage

68. 'Mr Gandhi, what do you think of *modern* civilisation?'. E.F. Schumacher, *Good Work*: 62.

68. Humanist economics 'stands in stark and fundamental contrast to the ways of the prevailing mainstream discipline . . .'. Mark Lutz, *Economics for the Common Good*: 100.

In the abstract oppression of wealth, Sismondi wrote:

> Often the tyrant and his victim do not know one another by name, do not inhabit the same country, do not speak the same language. The oppressed knows not where to carry

> his prayers, or his resentment; the oppressor, far from being
> a hard man, is perhaps generous and feeling; he takes no
> account of the evil he does. He submits himself to a sort of
> fatality which seems at this time to govern all the manufac-
> turing world. It is this fatality that, in spite of the promise
> of liberty, of equality, overwhelms with frightful oppression
> millions of human creatures.

Sismondi was the first to attempt a macro theory of under-consump-
tion based on the distribution of income between the owners of capital
and workers. Quite simply, he argued that a more equal distribution of
benefits would mean a more steady expansion of markets. Quoted in
Mark Lutz, *Economics for the Common Good*: 264-65.

69. Even John Stuart Mill, who wrote the definitive text of classical economics, was sharply critical of the dehumanising effects of a system that
leaves distribution to ruthless competition. Mill hoped for the demise of
the laissez-faire approach: 'Peace be with its ashes when it does expire,
for I doubt much if it will reach the resurrection.' Though he spent most
of his working life as an employee of the East India Company, Mill cherished the vision of a cooperative society in which workers would render
capitalist employers obsolete by the setting up self-governing enterprises (Lutz, *Economics for the Common Good*: 62).

69. John Ruskin, *Unto This Last* (New York: Wiley & Sons, 1988 [1864]):
17-18. A paradoxical figure, Ruskin tended to seek comfort in mediæval
feudalism and was suspicious of liberty and democracy. Nevertheless,
his advocacy of humanist systems of production and livelihood has made
him one of the forefathers of today's fair trade movement and ethical
investment activism.
Gandhi read Ruskin in 1903, and five year later, during his first term
in jail, he paraphrased *Unto This Last* in Gujarati and published it as a
booklet titled *Sarvodaya,* literally meaning 'the welfare of all'. 'I believe
that I discovered some of the deepest convictions reflected in this great
book by Ruskin,' Gandhi wrote, 'and that is why it so captured me and
made me transform my life.' The opening paragraph of *Unto This Last*
conveyed the essence of both Ruskin's critique and Gandhi's emerging
world-view.

> Among the delusions which at different periods have pos-
> sessed themselves of the minds of large masses of the human
> race, perhaps the most curious – certainly the least credita-
> ble – is the modern . . . science of political economy, based on
> the idea that an advantageous code of social action may be
> determined irrespective of the influence of social affection

> ... The social affections, say the economist, are accidental
> and disturbing elements in human nature; but avarice and
> the desire of progress are constant elements.

70. J.C. Kumarappa, *Economy of Permanence* (India: Sarva Sewa Sangh Prakashan, 1984).

72. 'The counter-economist and futurist Hazel Henderson credits Schumacher . . .'. Hazel Henderson, *Politics of the Solar Age*: 174. Schumacher's work was also carried forward by his younger colleague, James Robertson, who later posited the vision of a SHE future, namely 'Sane Humane and Ecological'. The Oxford-educated Robertson spent several years in the British civil service before devoting himself full-time to the work of crafting a *New Economics*. His book *The Sane Alternative* challenged the then commonly held belief that the prevailing model of industrial-economic growth could ensure perpetual prosperity. Robertson characterised this as 'a dangerous masculine fantasy – exploitative, elitist and unsympathetic'.

73. When I met Daly at his office at the University of Maryland in 2003, I found him a disappointed man. He lamented that mainstream economics is still waiting for the price mechanism and markets to solve everything. Growth is still the major goal without taking into account the carrying capacity of the planet's ecosystems. Some of Daly's ideas are also drawn from Lissa Harris, 'Wealth of Nature', www.gristmagazine. com, 10 April 2003.

A new economics

74. Others at the first TOES were: Manfred Max-Neef, the Chilean economist who went on to co-author the basic texts of New Economics; James Robertson, a civil servant, was among the promoters of TOES along with Jonathon Porritt, one of the founders of the British Green Party; George McRobbie, who along with Schumacher had co-founded the Intermediate Technology Development group back in 1965; and Paul Ekins, at that time a musician who later went on to become a professor of economics.

75. Paul Ekins (ed.), *The Living Economy: A New Economy in the Making*.

Back in the 1980s the term 'New Economics' could easily be confused with a conventional economist. In the middle of the 20th century the term had referred to the ideas and prescriptions of Lord Keynes. On the TOES platform staple economic problems, like unemployment and unstable prices, appeared as a backdrop. The main focus was on alarm

signals flashing at centre-stage – potentially catastrophic disruptions of
the biosphere, decimation of local economies, failure of development
benefits to trickle down fast enough or far enough and thus deepening
poverty.

In *Wealth Beyond Measure*, Paul Ekins, Mayer Hillman and Robert
Hutchison argued that the global economy need not depend on endless
multiplication of people's wants and thus consumption. They visualised
an increasing role for the conscience and compassion of individuals
without unrealistically idolising these traits or exaggerating them out of
all proportion – just as greed has been.

From this vantage point economy in the 21st century is envisioned
as a multi-level one-world system, with autonomous but interdependent
component parts. Starting with individuals and households this system
would simultaneously serve the needs of exchange at local, national
and international levels. The point is to ensure that each larger unit is
geared to enabling the smaller units within it to be more self-reliant and
conserving. But this cannot be done without re-examining and redefining basic economic concepts, such as: wealth creation and capital accumulation; efficiency and productivity; dependence, interdependence
and self-reliance.

For instance, needs and wants can be equally respected without
making a fetish out of insatiable wants. An economics of enough is visualised not so much as a matter of change by legislation but rather as
a fluid social and cultural process of the kind that is giving rise to the
voluntary simplicity movement in the USA. Naturally, this opens a Pandora's Box. Individual lifestyle choices are complex enough; how is the
ecologically optimum size of the human economy to be determined? The
New Economics stream does not offer any ready-made answers. Rather
it pushes for a greater valuation of the natural world and placing some
fundamental questions at the centre-stage of public life. Notably this:
do living things have a right to exist independently of their usefulness
to human beings? Can our species claim the right to reorder the rest of
nature purely for its own convenience? (*Wealth Beyond Measure*: 33).

75. New Economics Foundation is a registered charity funded by individual supporters, public finance, businesses and international grant-
giving bodies.

NEF's theoretical new economics programme aims to build a framework for a new economics that promotes real well-being (rather than
financial wealth), environmental sustainability and social justice. This
framework will incorporate the latest thinking from the different
branches of (alternative) economics and the social sciences with the aim
of drawing out the practical policy implications. Where gaps or conflicts

between these ideas exist, NEF aims to promote academic debate and research by raising the profile of the issues through hosting discussions and other events' (NEF Website; www.neweconomics.org).

NEF has promoted Time Banks, a particular kind of community currency, in UK. It has also designed sustainability indicators which measure aspects of life that were earlier inadequately accounted for or never measured at all. In collaboration with Friends of the Earth and the Centre for Environmental Strategy (University of Surrey) NEF developed the Index for Sustainable Economic Welfare for the UK. NEF has also worked at the local level, in Britain, helping communities to use indicators in ways that make a difference to their quality of life. In 2003 *The Economist* referred to NEF as 'the most innovative and eclectic think tank in the field today'.

76. In the middle of 2008, hundreds of political and social organisations from across the world issued a Global Call to Action to Demand a New Economic System. Their petition, titled 'Enough, Never Again', put forth three demands. One: there must be fundamental structural changes to transform the global economic and financial system so crises like this never happen again. Two: global economic structures and policies must put people's needs first by respecting and promoting human rights as well as social and environmental justice to ensure decent jobs, sustainable livelihoods, essential services such as health, education, housing, water and clean energy. Three: greater democratisation, which gives people greater control over resources and the decisions that affect their lives (www.ggjalliance.org/es/node/31).

Post-Autistic Economics Network

77. Aaron Ross, 'SHARE's long-awaited alternative Ec 10 class finally takes shape', 10 February 2003; www.harvardindependent.com/ViewArticle.aspx?ArticleID=8569. See also www.thecrimson.com/article/2009/10/29/economics-course-ec-10.

78. 'Post Autistic Economics Network and Post Autistic Economics Review'; www.paecon.net.

78. Kurt Jacobsen and Donald MacLeod, 'Fired up for Battle', *The Guardian*, 9 September 2003.

79. 'Plus the debates within . . .'. Edward Fullbrook, 'I just discovered the PAE movement', on PAE website, 21 November 2001 and in email interview.

While the PAE is a 'movement', its proponents take pains to be perceived as independent of any broader non-academic movement. This is not easy.

> The hegemony of neoclassical economics in universities is an extremely powerful and ubiquitous political force in today's world, so trying to dethrone it is ultimately a very political pursuit, but the road to that dethronement runs through academic institutions and customs . . . The fact-value distinction can be transcended by the recognition that the investigator's values are inescapably involved in scientific inquiry and in making scientific statements, whether consciously or not. This acknowledgement enables a more sophisticated assessment of knowledge claims (Edward Fullbrook, in an email interview).

It is not clear just how much traction the post-autistic agenda is gaining among economists at large. But the reformers are encouraged by the fact that textbook publishers are looking out for PAE textbooks. This is inevitable because enrolment in conventional economics classes is dropping and thus affecting textbook revenues. In other words, says Fullbrook, 'market forces are working against neoclassical economics'. This explains why Marglin's complementary course at Harvard attracts students. 'I'm trying to provide ammunition for people to question what it is about this economic [system] that makes them want to go out in the streets to protest,' says Marglin.

80. Steve Keen, *Debunking Economics: The Naked Emperor of the Social Sciences*. For interview with Keen on Post Autistic Network's website, see www.debunking-economics.com/Talks/Keen_YaleER_PAECON_ Interview.html.

80. Deborah Campbell, 'Post-Autistic Economics', Adbusters, September/October 2004; www.adbusters.org/metas/eco/truecosteconomics/ post-autistic.html.

81. Details on Richard Thaler; www.fullerthaler.com and www.weforum. org/s?s=Richard%20H.%20Thaler.

82. Steve Marglin's views are from my email conversation with him and from his book *The Dismal Science: How Thinking like an Economist Undermines Community*.

From Gross National Product to Gross National Happiness

87. Details about Genuine Progress Indicators are from my interactions with Jonathan Rowe and Mathis Wackernagel while they were at Redefining Progress in San Francisco; from discussions with people I met at the first international conference on Gross National Happiness held in Bhutan in 2004; from interviews with staff of GP Atlantic; and www.gpiatlantic.org/conference. Andrew C. Reykin, 'A New Measure of Wellbeing from a Happy Little Kingdom', *New York Times*, 4 October 2005.

Eduardo Porter, 'All They Are Saying Is Give Happiness a Chance', *New York Times*, 12 November 2007.

> The normative emphasis on minimization of self-concern and self-interest is usually construed as turning away from the world as it is and rejection of development or positive change. This view is far from accurate. In our opinion minimization of self-concern is an important step in the process of constructing a happier web of human relationships and of transforming Man into a less intrusive and destructive force in our natural and human environment. Man is just a sentient being, among other forms of existence. The assumption that man is on top of the chain of beings is a false comfort, considering the mysterious web of inter-dependent relationship that is now being confirmed through scientific studies. Reality is not hierarchical but whole, circular, enclosed system. Sustainable development and environmental care is in the interest of every being every day, not just in the interest of future generations alone.

'Values and Development: Gross National Happiness', keynote speech given by Lyonpo Figmi Y. Thinley, Chairman of the Council of Ministers Royal Government of Bhutan, at the *Millennium Meeting for Asia and the Pacific* in October 1998.

Failure of market idea or just another market failure

93. Full text of Stern Committee report; www.hm-treasury.gov.uk/sternreview_index.htm.

93. 'The "revenge of Gaia" is no longer a bizarre . . .'. James Lovelock, *The Revenge of Gaia: Why the Earth Is Fighting Back – and How We Can Still Save Humanity* (London: Penguin Books, 2006).

94. Quotes from Ekins and Marglin are from email conversations with them.

95. 'INET is counting on . . .'. This means changing the incentives that govern the profession. At present successful academics are those who get papers published in a handful of prestigious journals – which tend to have little room for the kind of questioning that the INET seeks to nurture. As its website says: 'At a time when much of the contemporary discourse appears closed and polarized the Institute seeks to expand conversations in ways that draw in a wider range of people – with particular emphasis on absorbing insights from other intellectual disciplines, both in the natural and social sciences.' See also www. ineteconomics.org.

95. 'More mainline economists . . .'. *Inside Job* is a 2010 feature-length documentary about the financial meltdown of 2008 directed by Charles H. Ferguson.

96. 'For example, a decade ago . . .'. This is partly because the dialogue at Cambridge included key figures such as Dominique Strauss-Kahn, Managing Director of the International Monetary Fund, Lord Adair Turner, Chairman of UK's Financial Services Authority and Simon Johnson, professor at MIT and former Chief Economist of the IMF.

96. 'Alan Greenspan, Chairman . . .'. Friedman's citation credited him with propagating the delusion that an economy can be accurately modelled using counterfactual propositions about its nature. His simplistic model of money was also credited for encouraging 'the development of fantasy-based theories of economics and finance that facilitated the Global Financial Collapse'. Summers, as US Secretary of the Treasury, was largely responsible for the repeal of the Glass–Steagall Act, which since the Great Crash of 1929 had kept deposit banking separate from casino banking. He also helped Greenspan and Wall Street torpedo efforts to regulate derivatives.

97. Reference to Kropotkin, Darwin and blind Pelican is from Lewis Hyde, *The Gift*: 92.

Chapter 3

98. '. . . the notion that it [money]'. John Kenneth Galbraith, *Money: Whence it Came, Where it Went*.

99. Joe Dominguez and Vicki Robin, *Your Money or Your Life: A Guide for Transforming your Relationship with Money and Achieving Financial Independence* (Viking Penguin, 1992). The book offered readers a nine-step programme for transforming their relationship with

money. See also www.civicreflection.org/online_tools/resource_library/mtm_archive.

'Our work is powerful because aligning money and values results in more caring relationships, more volunteerism, more ethical and socially responsible investing, more philanthropy, more functional families, and a variety of related individual and social benefits.'

100. 'Perhaps money like sex . . .'. Thomas Moore, *Care of the Soul*: 191.

The Buddhist philosopher David Loy writes that:

> . . . money symbolizes becoming real, but since we never quite become real we only make our sense of lack more real. We end up in infinite deferral, for those chips we have accumulated can never be cashed in. The moment we do so, the illusion that money can resolve lack is dispelled; we are left more empty and lack-ridden than before, being deprived of our fantasy of escaping lack. We unconsciously suspect and fear this; the only answer is to flee faster into the future. This points the fundamental defect of any economic system that requires continual growth to survive: it is based not on needs but on fear, for it feeds on and feeds our sense of lack (David Loy, 'The Repression of Emptiness Today', *Buddhist Ethics and Modern Society* 31 [1991]: 297).

Joseph Schumpeter put it in more technical terms: money is a mere credit instrument, 'a claim to the only final means of payment, the consumer's good' (J.A. Schumpeter, *History of Economic Analysis*, quoted by Braudel, *The Wheels of Commerce* I: 476.

100. 'We printed our own money . . .'. Paul Glover, www.ithacahours.com.

101. The Bia Kud Chum, has been operating in the Pomprab District of Thailand since 2000 and is equal in value to the Thai baht but cannot be exchanged for the official Thai currency. The notes come in denominations of 1, 5, 10 and 20. The word *bia* means seedling and alludes to the endeavour being like small seedlings which grow into large trees. The aim is to nurture and expand the local economy by encouraging the buying of local products.

The richly coloured Bia notes evoked excited curiosity at a workshop held in 2003, in Hyderabad, during the Asia Social Forum (ASF), the regional platform of the World Social Forum, where they were presented in a show-and-tell fashion by young Thai activists. The Bia representatives were there to share lessons about their creative adventures in the realm of community currencies. The Bia is part of our move towards self-reliance, explained Pornpita Kiangphukiew who spoke for the Thai group: 'This is a response to the loss of intimacy and relations within community, because of the race for making money.' The emergence of the Bia in Thailand signals the fledgling presence of community currencies across Asia, including Hong Kong, Indonesia, Japan, Korea and Papua New Guinea.

From the conventional economists' point of view the Bia is useless since it buys nothing in the national economy of Thailand, not even a bus ride out of the village to Bangkok or anywhere else. But, says Pranomporn Tetthai, a member of the Bia Kud Chum working group:

> That is exactly the point! We are trying to reduce the number of things villagers buy from outside the community and encourage the support of locally produced goods and services . . . Our agricultural income [from the sale of jasmine rice] will still be in baht. Therefore, we will still have baht for necessary expenses such as hospital care. However, for local goods and services we can reduce our expenses by exchanging in Bia (quoted in Lietaer, *Future of Money*: 204).

Interestingly, the Bia has emerged in the context of a wider civil disobedience movement for revival of Thailand's traditional local whisky brews.

See also James Hookway, 'When it comes to cash, a Thai village says, "baht, humbug" ', *Wall Street Journal/Mint*, 8 January 2009.

101. Mashi Blech was heading the Time Dollar programme at Elderplan, an HMO in Brooklyn, when I met her in 2001. Elderplan's Time Dollar endeavour is one of the earliest and most successful of such schemes. She is currently director of the Time Bank team at Visiting Nurse Service, a non-profit home healthcare agency in New York.

102. 'The real cost of money . . .'. Edgar Cahn and Jonathan Rowe, *Time Dollars*: 25.

Monetary innovation: mutual aid and free money

103. Details about different kinds of objects that have served as money are from Braudel, *The Wheels of Commerce* I: 442-43 and Galbraith, *Money Whence it Came*: 6.

103. 'But interestingly the word "money" . . .'. Keith Hart, *The Memory Bank*.

104. 'The process by which banks create money . . .'. Galbraith, *Money Whence it Came*: 18. Galbraith notes that by the early 1800s in England

the triumph of the moneyed classes was complete. But in the USA it remained one of the 'sharpest challenges. In one form or another, this challenge was to dominate American politics for the first century and a half of the Republic. Only the politics of slavery would divide men more angrily than the politics of money' (*Money Whence it Came*: 44).

By the mid 18th century each of the American colonies had their own currency. Later some colonies were reluctant to surrender this function to the newly formed federal government. Eventually all the states agreed, under the Constitution of the United States of America, to give up all their currencies by 1789. The function was taken over by chartered banks which then had a virtual monopoly over printing money (Geisst, *Wall Street: A History*: 9). These banks, such as the Bank of North America, the Bank of New York, the Bank of Massachusetts and the First Bank of the United States, were thus highly profitable. They were also the first American public corporations and thus the first to raise capital by issuing shares on the fledgling stock market on Wall Street (Werner and Smith, *Wall Street*: 80).

John Adams declared that 'every bank bill issued in excess of the quantity of gold and silver in the vaults represents nothing, and is therefore a cheat upon somebody' (Galbraith, *Money: Whence it Came*: 28-29).

105. 'Bryan saw himself as Main Street's "David" . . .'. Though he never made it to the White House, William Jennings Bryan was a vital presence on the American political scene at the turn of the century. In retrospect Bryan is mostly remembered for taking up the case of the 'anti-Darwin' side in the historic Scopes Trail in 1925, just before he died. The Scopes case dealt with whether Darwin's, allegedly anti-Christian, theory of evolution could be taught in American schools. Ironically, Bryan was a fiercely passionate progressive who campaigned successfully for many egalitarian policies and laws. In his own lifetime Bryan was best known for fiery speeches like the one titled 'Cross of Gold'. The year was 1896 and Bryan was a 36-year-old Congressman making a bid for the Presidential nomination at the Democratic Party's convention. Bryan denounced the 'idle holders of idle capital' and rallied support for 'the struggling masses' and the 'broader class of businessmen'. The central theme of his speech was the *money question* and the insistence that the right to issue money is a function of government. Bryan argued that this is as much a part of sovereignty as the power to make penal statues or levy taxes and thus cannot be left to private individuals. Bryan described the gold standard, and its restrictive money supply, as an evil that oppressed the working folk. Hence the famous last phrase of

his speech: 'You shall not press down upon the brow of labor this crown of thorns, you shall not crucify mankind on a cross of gold.'

105. 'What frightened them . . .'. Steve Fraser, *Every Man a Speculator*: 11.

L. Frank Baum's book *The Wonderful Wizard of Oz* has been read as an allegory for many of the same concerns – with Dorothy and her friends representing the simple farming folk while the wicked witches of Oz represent financiers.

> Farmers usually lived in debt to banks for the mortgages of their farms and sometimes for the equipment and even the seed for planting. They borrowed in gold notes and had to repay their debts in gold notes, but the price of gold increased over the course of the century as the price of their commodities dropped. At harvest time they received less money for their produce; yet they had to pay the bankers in gold notes, which were ever more costly. They wanted more money put in circulation, and one way to do that was by the free coinage of silver. The Populist farmers of the West and the South wanted silver as well as gold currency. With more currency around, they believed they would be less at the mercy of bankers and politicians from the cities (Jack Weatherford, *History of Money*: 175).

106. 'Complexity cloaks chaos'. Richard Bookstaber, *A Demon of Our Own Design: Markets, Hedge Funds and the Perils of Financial Innovation* (New York: John Wiley, 2007).

Details about history of money reform efforts are from Margrit Kennedy, *Interest and Inflation Free Money*; Bernard Lietaer, *The Future of Money*; and Thomas Greco, *The End of Money and the Future of Civilization*. See also www.reinventingmoney.com and www.monetary.org/amacolorpamphlet.pdf.

110. 'Grassroots innovators see the chaos in the global financial system as a huge opportunity . . .'. As global financial turmoil looked more and more like the perfect storm there were reports about investors bypassing Wall Street and other big money centres in favour of private electronic liquidity and trading networks – which rely more closely on information about tangible value. 'Such insights into the use of information and trading networks, including local currencies, barter networks, craigslist.com, freecycle.com and people-to-people lending as on prosper.com, are part of the emerging information-rich Solar Age economies now superseding the earlier fossil-fueled Industrial Age' (Hazel Henderson, www.ethicalmarkets.tv).

'What's up doc?' How Michael Linton created LETS

112. On the ferry-ride to Vancouver Island to meet with Michael Linton, I was browsing at the on-board book stall and stumbled on a book that put a whole new significance on the biographical detail that Linton is a Scotsman. The small paperback book was a celebration of the many Scots whose inventions and discoveries make up the modern world. This includes many of the things we blissfully take for granted: John Napier of Edinburgh invented logarithms in 1614; Joseph Black discovered carbon dioxide in 1754; James Watt of Glasgow invented the steam engine in the 1760s; Adam Smith laid the foundations of modern economics in 1776; Thomas Graham laid the foundations of physical chemistry in 1829; the pneumatic rubber tyre was invented in stages by Robert William Thomson and John Boyd Dunlop; Alexander Graham Bell invented the telephone in 1876; John Logie Baird transmitted the first television picture in 1926; Alexander Fleming developed the first antibiotic in 1928; Robert Watson-Watt invented the forerunner of the radar in 1935.

In 1979 Linton became an instructor in the Alexander technique, a form of movement training which aims to free the body of harmful tension. He was fascinated by the basic premise of this technique: 'Don't just do something, stand there.' Linton interpreted this to mean that there is often merit in allowing inconsistencies to emerge and resolve themselves. This inspired Linton to re-read *Small is Beautiful*. Additional nourishment came from Ivan Illich's *Deschooling Society* and George Bernard Shaw's *Woman's Guide to Socialism and Capitalism*.

Linton and Yacub, *Open Money*, www.openmoney.org/top/omanifesto. html.

For Linton's most recent writing in 2008, see Michael Linton, Money 2.0 at emoney.typepad.com/blog/paper_session_1_alternative_monies.

> A LETS is a membership association in which each member has an account. All accounts begin with a balance of zero. When a member sells something to another member, his or her account receives a credit (plus); when a member buys something, his or her account receives a debit (minus). A credit causes an account balance to increase, while a debit causes an account balance to decrease. Accounts are allowed to have negative as well as positive balances ... This is a system of strict reciprocity. Of course, as in any system, there will always be some who will default on their obligations: they will fail to provide the amount of goods and services they committed themselves to when they incurred debits (by buying). These defaults should be recognized at some point and written off. Thus there is no need for a

central authority or coordinating committee that must make
decisions about the amount of credits in circulation. However, the only thing to be decided is the maximum amount
of debit balance that should be allowed on each particular
account to minimize the risk of default and the amount of
potential loss. In usual practice, account balances remain
well below that maximum amount . . . The primary role in a
mutual credit system is that of the *registrar* or *accountant*,
which is strictly nonpolitical. The duties of the registrar are
to record the transactions as reported by the members, and
to update the members' account balances (Thomas Greco,
Money: 183-84).

Take the example of the Tofino LETS which was grappling with these
growth pangs and survival struggles in 2001. Tofino is a small town on
Vancouver Island, with a resident population of just 1,200 people but
is visited by about 250,000 tourists every year. However, near Tofino
there is settlement of the indigenous people of that island, which has
a high unemployment rate. Inspired by LETS adventures elsewhere on
Vancouver Island, a few people launched the Tofino LETS, also known
as Coast Dollars. Tofino LETS spread word about itself by posting col-
ourful notices urging people to 'Do It Local: Do it with Coast Dollars'.
The notice, which carried a sketch of a whale leaping out of the blue
ocean, informed people where they could get Coast Dollars and where
they could spend them. In all 20 businesses were listed as places that
accept the local currency. These included a couple of restaurants, a
sailing charter company, a bike repair shop, video and other entertain-
ment providers, and even a 'Growlies Pet Mart'. The Tofino Coast Dollars operate through Smart Cards.

One of the founders of Tofino LETS, James Rogers, dropped by to
meet with Linton and Ernie Yacub while I was visiting them in 2001.
When I asked him how it was going, Rogers said candidly that the Coast
Dollars had not yet gone beyond the point of being 'just a pain in the
ass'. Rogers lives in Tofino and runs a organic grocery store as well
as a cooperatively owned coffee shop, that has 70 members. Watching
Rogers looking low and despondent, Linton smiled knowingly and said
confidently, 'Exetation energy'.

'What does that mean: "exetation energy"?' said the already exasperated Rogers. 'This is why you guys are not making sense to many
people.' Utterly unperturbed, Linton replied, 'Critical mass is a more
accurate term but the point is that mass is not enough.'

'Sure,' said James, *'activity* is the issue . . . but Jerry, a sailor, and
I both aren't the people who can go door to door to raise business for
community currencies. Jerry and I are planning to go on a retreat to

figure it out, i.e. reflect on why it's not working. We're going to give it another month to see if there's light at the end of the tunnel!'

The problem, as James explained further, is that the Coast Dollars pile up with the member businesses. His own organic products grocery store accepts 15% of payment in Coast Dollars and even pays its staff partly in the community currency. But the staff are not able to spend all of their community currency.

Michael insisted that this would change when more businesses accept the Coast Dollars. Then people might even 'buy' the Coast Dollars, in exchange for conventional cash, from others who have an excess of Coast Dollars. But arriving at that level of activity requires that more people become aware of its possibilities. As long as only a few businesses are part of the community currency, it will find it difficult for the currency to survive, let alone thrive. As Rogers said, it needs more people like his friend Warren who sells solar panels and insists on taking part payment in Coast Dollars. Similarly, there's John who fixes bikes and Paul who does handiwork around town – both taking part payment in Coast Dollars.

So while Tofino LETS is not quite poised to take over the local economy it does keep bubbling as a micro-community. But Rogers's dream is a time when five or six businesses begin to act as community currency flagships, thus bringing it into the everyday life of more people in Tofino. 'It could still take off,' said Rogers, 'even if we do throw in the towel now it doesn't mean it will never take off . . . We know that it can be made to work.' But he warns that if you just look at the data no one would feel encouraged to take this on.

Linton's vision of the future includes a mechanism he calls Community Way. This is meant to be a tool for locally based fundraising and economic development that marries the mainstream economy with the world of community action, voluntarism and complementary currencies. Community Way Dollars would be a complementary currency issued by businesses and donated to schools, organisations and projects of their choice. The issuing businesses would then accept Community Way Dollars (CW$) as part-payment for their products or services. Even individuals could support projects and causes of their choice by exchanging conventional money for CW$ – which they would then spend in any of the participating shops, restaurants, etc. If there are enough participating businesses then they could also use CW$ to make payments to each other – or as part of the pay-packet to their staff.

Linton's promotional pitch is that Community Way would be both good for business and quality of community life:

> For business, this is a simple and cash-free way to increase
> sales, strengthen the local economy, and secure customer
> recognition and loyalty. Since the CW$ are as good as cash
> at participating businesses, people can help without losing
> purchasing power, and by shopping locally, they vote for the
> community they want. The transactions can be recorded
> through Smart Cards, ledger forms, voice mail or email, with
> the accounts being maintained by a community currencies
> service provider.

121. 'A moral, fiscal, political gridlock'. Ralph Nader, in the Foreword to
Edgar Cahn and Jonathan Rowe, *Time Dollars*.

Time Dollars: Edgar Cahn's vision of co-production

121. This section is based on meetings with Edgar Cahn in 2003 and
a continuing conversation by email, as well as his books *Time Dollars,
No More Throw-away People* and other writings to be found at www.
timedollar.org.

Members of this Time Dollar programme can use their credit points
to buy, among other things, home-delivered meals, movie and theatre
tickets, bus rides to Atlantic City casinos, cushions, pillows, a heat wave
massager, an illuminate magnifier reader and so on. The Time Dollars
also come in handy to pay for such things as computer classes, safe driving lessons for elders, walking clubs and even lessons in how to live with
Arthritis.

> The non-market world, within its realm, functions more effi-
> ciently than the market world . . . What would it take to pro-
> vide the full range of services that a family provides to raise
> a child? We know that feminist groups costed out the market
> value of a mother/housewife to be, in 1980 dollars, $66,000.
> Neither families nor the government can afford to buy those
> services at that price. One study on the value of the informal
> support provided by family, neighbors and friends computed
> an annual value of $196 billion when that labor was valued
> at only $8 per hour (Cahn, *No More Throw-away People* and
> interview with author).

Stan Hall, one of Cahn's colleagues, is a maths teacher at a high
school in an inner city neighbourhood of Washington DC. Many of his
students live in grinding poverty and have trouble staying on the right
side of the law. As Hall sees it the youth in these parts of DC are one of
the most disenfranchised segments of the American population. Hall,
who is himself an African American and once served in the US Navy,

has seen countless good young people just drift towards a life a crime by default rather than an evil bent of mind. He realised years ago that in the absence of social intervention that first, often causal and petty, criminal act can grow into a serious career in crime. Accepting this reality as a given fact of life has made prisons a big business in the USA, which is in a sense the market solution to the problem.

However, people like Stan Hall devote themselves to preventing the growth of the prison population. In the case of inner-city youth this is partly being done through the creative process of Youth Courts where cases are heard by former offenders, themselves teenagers. The most powerful incentive of this process is an almost magical improvement in self-esteem because the convicted juveniles don't go to prison but instead wind up doing community service or jury duty – and they earn Time Dollars along the way.

Youth Courts have existed for many years all over the USA but followed the conventional adversarial system. Cahn worked to create mechanisms which ensure that the jury is not there primarily to ascertain guilt or innocence but instead engage with the young person and his or her parents. So convicted offenders are then made to do jury duty for eight weeks. An adult still presides over the hearing but the questions are asked by a teenager. The focus therefore is on listening to the accused with sympathy, rather than focusing on guilt. This allows for moving on towards constructing the future.

Among its long-term goals the Time Dollar Institute lists:

- The creation of a society where decency and caring are rewarded automatically

- This can be done by providing 'practical alternatives to the zero sum dynamic that pits self-interest against altruism, individual achievement against equity and human being against human being'

- The promotion of a new currency 'that combines market incentives and psychological rewards in order to tap the ultimate wealth of all individuals and their time, in order to meet critical social needs'

- To nurture and rebuild the core economy of family, neighbourhood and social networks which in developed countries have been weakened and depleted. This means partly finding ways to encourage and celebrate the vital tasks of raising a family, being an informed citizen and just caring for others

- Work can be redefined in similar ways in the developing countries, while recognising their vastly different circumstances (www.timedollar.org).

Great innovation or crazy idea?

130. Like the Bia in Thailand, there is the Tlaloc mutual credit system in Mexico, the Commonweal Service Dollar of Minneapolis, Toronto Dollars in the St Lawrence neighbourhood of Toronto, and an explosion of diverse forms of complementary currencies across Japan.

Mexico's Tlaloc mutual credit system is named after the Aztec rain god. This currency takes the form of cheques which have to be endorsed by each user by signing on the reverse side. The credits exchanged are reported to a coordinator who maintains the record on computer. (Lietaer, *Future of Money*: 202). The members of Tlaloc and Bia keep in touch and learn from each other's gains and failures. The Commonweal Service Dollar of Minneapolis is a currency in which community service volunteers are paid. Participating organisations issue what they call a 'Hero Card' to each volunteer on which their hours of service are lodged and then eventually fed into the volunteer's account on a Hero Card electronic network. Every hour of work earns ten Commonweal Dollars. The scheme, launched in 1997, works because some shops and service providers accept a part-payment for goods and services in Commonweal Service Dollars. See www.stable-money.com/commonweal.htm and also www.le.org.nz/tiki-index.php?page=CommonWeal.

Similarly, the St Lawrence neighbourhood of Toronto has a coalition of businesses that participate in the Toronto Dollars scheme which has a little over a hundred member companies and voluntary groups. These include some food vendors and restaurants which accept 100% payment in Toronto Dollars. Japan is undergoing a virtual explosion of diverse forms of complementary currencies, including LETS and Hours. Lietaer has noted with due fascination that in the sphere of healthcare many Japanese people prefer Hours-based services instead of those supported by the conventional yen. It turns out that services under the Hours system bring a higher quality of caring than the professional market-transaction variety.

130. Bernard Lietaer, keynote speech at LETSLINK UK Complementary Currencies Conference, 16 October 1998.

Then there is Raam NL, issued by an organisation made up of disciples of Maharishi Mahesh Yogi, the Indian spiritual guru who once inspired the Beatles and is now based in Holland. The currency is named after the Hindu God Lord Rama and is fully backed by equivalent euro deposits in the Fortis bank. Each Raam NL is worth €10 or about Rs.580. According to one report, about 167 shops in 45 Dutch cities and villages accept the Raam NL. It is also accepted in the Maharishi Vedic City, Iowa, USA.

The website of a network called Appropriate Economics carries reports on both modern and traditional forms of local money spread across Asia, Africa and Latin America. There is also a web-based *International Journal of Community Currency Research* (IJCCR), which serves as the hub for scholarly and activist debate. The IJCCR's e-group buzzes with questions and shared reflections by community currency innovators from across the world.

In Minneapolis Commonweal Inc., a company launched by Joel Hodroff, a solar-energy entrepreneur and business-barter consultant, issues service dollars. The scheme was born out of Hodroff's observation that many businesses have a problem with over-capacity. There are empty seats in movie theatres, empty tables at restaurants and grocers are stuck with rotting food. Hodroff's Hero Card mechanism helped to simultaneously solve this business problem and benefit time-rich but cash-poor volunteers. The Hero Card programme was a semfinalist in Harvard University's Innovations in America Government Award in 1999.

> Volunteers can spend their service credits in the real economy at outlets that have agreed to be in the system. Effectively volunteers receive discounts such as a 25 percent discount on computer classes at Open University, a 20 percent discount on gifts at the Mall of America, a 25 percent discount on auto repairs, and a 50 percent discount on bowling. When time dollars are spent, they are canceled. There is something in it for the firm accepting them. They gain at least some cash from the discounted sale, they have a reduced advertising bill, and their customer base and civic goodwill increases.
>
> The card carries two currencies at once and can pay in both currencies at once in one transaction. It is also discreet, since nobody can detect whether the customer has paid in cash or partly in Commonweal Dollars. The card deducts a 5% transaction fee for every transaction. Of this four fifths goes to the company, one tenth to a sponsoring organization like Oxfam and one tenth to a volunteer organization. Thus the business is self-funding and independent of grants from government or charities. The benefit authorities have zero-rated the C$Ds earnings, but as at 2001 the IRS had not decided on taxability of C$Ds.

> By 2000 they had 72 merchants and 2000 volunteers and 43 neighborhood organizations involved. Its diverse partners and impressive endorsements include government, neighborhoods, businesses, community-based foundations, a community bank and individual citizens (www.stable-money.com/commonweal.htm).

There are also (Greco, *Money*: 113-15):

- Toronto Dollars

- Friendly Favors, a voluntary World Wide Web-based association of people who acknowledge one another by awarding 'Thank Yous'

- Equal Dollars, a currency unit used in a community exchange project of Resources for Human Development (RHD), a large Philadelphia-based non-profit social service organisation

- The Global Trading Network, in South America, which began on the outskirts of Buenos Aires 'with the organization of a single "barter club" in an outlying sector of Buenos Aires in 1995, the social money movement, as it is called in Latin America, has exploded into a socioeconomic phenomenon involving hundreds of thousands of people in at last nine South American countries'

For more details see *International Journal of Community Currency Research*; www.uea.ac.uk/env/ijccr.

Information about complementary currency systems in Asia, Africa and Latin America: www.appropriate-economics.org.

Eric Helleiner, Thomas Princen, Michael Maniates and Ken Conca (eds.), 'Think Globally, Transact Locally: The Local-Currency Movement and Green Political Economy', in *Confronting Consumption* (Cambridge, MA: MIT Press, 2002): 258.

Bernard Lietaer was born into a business family, in the town of Flanders, Belgium, during the Second World War. He was educated at University of Louvain and got an MBA degree at Sloan School, MIT in 1969. Before these degrees, at the age of 19, Lietaer hitch-hiked to India, from where he came away transformed for life, determined to be a 'karma-yogi' (www.lietaer.com).

131. WIR: amid the economic chaos of the Great Depression, most people were not concerned about dying forests and rivers. Among the few who did worry about such matters were two middle-class entrepreneurs in Switzerland: Werner Zimmerman and Paul Enz. As unemployment soared in the early 1930s, Enz founded a horticulture cooperative that

aimed to promote the 'physical and ethical recovery of the whole nation' in ways that would also ensure 'protection of the wage-earning woman and mother'. Zimmerman wrote about ways of saving the depleting forests and increasingly polluted rivers.

In 1934 these two men brought together a group of 15 people and launched the *Wirtschaftsring-Genossenschaft* or 'Economic Mutual Support Circle', which came to be known simply as WIR. In German 'wir' means 'we', thus implying community, as opposed to 'ich', the German for 'I'. Thus *Wirtschaftsring* alludes to a business circle and also contains the Swiss ideal of holding together as a community while protecting the interests of the individual. WIR emerged as a ray of hope in dark times by promoting local industries and trades through a system of exchange and mutual help. The founders' aim was to enable people to find satisfying work, make fair earnings and build a sustained prosperity.

The WIR immediately attracted members not only from the commercial middle class but also farmers, civil servants and white-collar workers. This is how it worked. People paid some conventional cash into the account, and after having been credited a bonus of 5% could go shopping within the WIR ring. The interest-free WIR-credit enhanced purchasing power and this in turn stimulated the slow turnover of goods. Its interest-free nature also stifled any tendency to hoard WIR credits. As membership grew, to over 1,000 within the first year, community-level volunteers began working for the WIR ideal which in turn further boosted the active exchange of goods and services.

Today WIR defines itself as a cooperative self-help organisation of trade, industry and service businesses of the middle class. Lietaer describes WIR as 'a Swiss example of a complementary currency run by and for a community of individuals and small business people'. It is interesting for three reasons. First, it is the oldest continuous system in the modern Western world. It was founded in 1934 by 16 members in Zurich, and has continuously grown in both number of participants and volume of business for over 60 years. Second, it illustrates that complementary currencies make sense, even in the most conservative and hard-nosed capitalist country with one of the highest standards of living in the world. Finally, it is a system that has grown to a respectable size: 'It operates in four languages and owns its own bank building, as well as six impressive regional offices' (Lietaer, *Future of Money*: 168). One WIR franc is the equivalent to one Swiss franc but is not convertible.

131. Lietaer has also been lobbying for a commodity-based currency that could be called TERRA. This proposal builds on work done by Jan Tinbergen, the winner of the first Nobel Prize for economics, and other

economists including Nicholas Kaldor and Albert G. Hart in the 1960s. They proposed the creation of 'bancor', an international commodity reserve currency (CRC) which would work in such a way that a fall in the prices of primary commodities would not depress demand for manufactured goods or cause a fall in investment in the primary sector.

Lietaer cautions that any private initiative on a CRC today would have to ensure open market access for all regardless of size or place of origin. One possibility is that:

> A specialized business entity called the Countertrade Alliance would issue this 'currency' in exchange for deposits of inventories of the goods in the basket. It would also be in a position to pay back Terras on request in national currency against a small fee, by delivering the corresponding raw materials to existing commodity exchanges and thereby transforming them into conventional national currency when needed. The commodity exchanges involved would be the same ones as those used for commodity futures trading today (*Future of Money*: 256).

See also Jan Tinbergen, Albert G. Hart and Nicholas Kaldor, 'The Case for an International Commodity Reserve Currency' (UNCTAD, 1963). reprinted in *Essays on Economic Policy II*. Vol. IV: *Collected Economic Essays of Nicholas Kaldor* (New York: Holmes & Meier, 1980 [1st edn 1964]).

Chapter 4

Competing compassionately: the freedom to cooperate

135. 'As long as we treasure the freedom . . .'. Amartya Sen, *Development as Freedom*: 25.

136. Sander Tideman spent over a decade working for ABN AMRO Bank. For some part of this period he was a vice-president based in Amsterdam. He was also the Bank's chief representative in China for some time. After he quit ABN AMRO, Tideman became an independent management and development advisor. He has multi-dimensional links in the world of business, social activism and spiritual practice. Details about Tideman are from several meetings with him and from Sander Tideman (ed.), *Enterprise and Development in the 21st Century: Compassion or Competition. A Forum Discussion with H.H. the XIV Dalai Lama* (The Netherlands: Dalai Lama Visit Foundation, 2000). Tideman wrote in this report:

> ... It seems that we have all agreed that in the real world
> – where it is always 'business as usual' – other norms pre-
> vail, norms that tell us that we can only achieve happiness
> on the basis of material wealth and security. We fear that
> delving into questions of spirituality or philosophy distracts
> us from reality, absorbs valuable time (for 'time is money'),
> making us as vulnerable as social outcasts – all liabilities in
> our quest for financial security.

Tideman has co-founded the Global Leaders Academy: www.
globalleadersacademy.com/gla-community.

136. Reference to the game of tennis is from Fred Matser, a former
real estate professional who heads the Fred Foundation, in Amsterdam, which supports projects that harmonise development with the
environment.

The old form of the game, said Matser:

> ... reflected nature, the cycle of life, coexistence, joy, crea-
> tivity, variation and things like that. And what did *we* make
> of it? We made of it a competitive game in which the person
> who is the first to break that cycle is rewarded with a point!
> (*Enterprise and Development in the 21st Century*).

138. 'One could be the best at bringing . . .'. Dalai Lama quoted in *Enterprise and Development in the 21st Century*.

138. 'When it comes to making the rules . . .'. George Soros, interview in
New York Review of Books, 14 January 1999.

Compassion or competition: a dialogue with the Dalai Lama

139. 'I want to have the biggest company . . .'. Eckart Wintzen in *Enterprise and Development in the 21st Century.*

140. Hazel Henderson quoted from *Enterprise and Development in the
21st Century.*

142. Dee Hock and the promise of 'chaordic' organisations. Hock's
ideas have been shaped by his idols – Marcus Aurelius, Lao Tse, Francis Bacon, Thomas Jefferson, Gandhi, Goethe, Einstein, Shakespeare,
Milton and Montaigne. Hock is reluctant to take too much credit for the
success of Visa: 'It's the organisational concepts and ideas that were
essential. I merely came to symbolize them.'

142. M. Mitchell Waldrop, 'The Trillion-dollar-Vision of Dee Hock: The corporate radical who organised Visa wants to dis-organise your company'; www.fastcompany.com, October 1996.

145. Dee Hock, 'The Birth of the Chaordic Century: Out of Control and into Order', speech at *State of the World Forum*, San Francisco, CA, 26 October 1998.

> By Chaord, I mean (1) any self-organizing, adaptive, non-linear, complex organism, organization or system, whether physical, biological or social, the behavior of which harmoniously blends characteristics of both chaos and order, (2) an entity whose behavior exhibits observable patterns and probabilities not governed or explained by its constituent parts, (3) an entity characterized by the fundamental organizing principles of nature (Dee Hock, 'An Epidemic of Institutional Failure', keynote at the *Organization Development Network Conference,* New Orleans, LA, 16 November 1998).

In the mid-1990s Hock went in search of people who shared his worry about institutional failure. In the process he met hundreds of people – 'inner-city leaders, scientists, corporate CEOs, indigenous peoples, authors, communications experts, army generals, environmentalists, politicians, economists, philosophers, and a great many less specialised people of exceptional wisdom'. The result was the Chaordic Alliance which then morphed into the Chaordic Commons – a global network of individuals and organisations who are committed to pioneering organisations that enable equitable sharing of power and wealth, improved health, and greater compatibility with the human spirit and biosphere.

The work of the Chaordic Commons encompasses: new forms of governance; innovative models of business; emerging concepts of citizenship; new models for ownership, investment, and philanthropy; new approaches to public–private partnerships and multi-stakeholder alliances; dynamic approaches to collaboration; new forms of leadership; generative models of organisational learning and change; and new, more global architectures of relationship in every field. The Chaordic network includes entrepreneurs, educators and communications professionals, financiers, philanthropists and researchers and scholars in diverse fields. People in the public, private and non-profit sectors are participating – and they come from around the world (www.chaordic. org).

Earning empowerment: are cooperatives skill relevant?

148. The Rochdale Principles (weaversway.coop/index.php?page=rochedale_principles):

1. Open, voluntary membership. Membership in a cooperative society should be voluntary and available without artificial restriction or any social, political, racial or religious discrimination, to all persons who can make use of its services and are willing to accept the responsibilities of membership.

2. Cooperative societies are democratic organisations. Their affairs should be administered by persons elected or appointed in a manner agreed to by the members and accountable to them. Members of primary societies should enjoy equal rights of voting (one member, one vote) and participation in decisions affecting their society. In other than primary societies the administration should be conducted on a democratic basis in a suitable form.

3. Share capital should only receive a strictly limited rate of interest.

4. The economic results arising out of the operations of a society belong to the members of that society and should be distributed in such a manner as would avoid one member gaining at the expense of others. This may be done by decision of the members as follows: a) by provision for development of the business of the cooperative; b) by provision of common services; or c) by distribution among the members in proportion to their transactions with the society.

5. Cooperatives should deal openly, honestly and honourably with their members and the general public.

6. The ultimate aim of all cooperatives should be to aid in the participatory definition and the advancement of the common good.

7. All cooperative societies should make provision for the education of their members, officers and employees and of the general public in the principles and techniques of cooperation, both economic and democratic.

8. All cooperative organisations, in order to best serve the interest of their members and their communities, should actively cooperate in every practical way with other cooperatives at local, national, and international levels.

148. The International Cooperatives Alliance (ICA) is an independent, non-governmental association whose members are national and international cooperative organisations in all sectors of economic activity. It holds the highest level of consultative status with the United Nations Economic and Social Council (ECOSOC). Over a century after it was formed the ICA is going strong with offices in Geneva and over 230 member organisations from over 100 countries representing more than 760 million individuals worldwide. In 1946, the ICA was one of the first non-governmental organisations to be accorded United Nations Consultative Status. The ICA's members together cover virtually every field including industry, agriculture, banking, energy, insurance, fisheries, housing, tourism and consumer services. The ICA defines a cooperative as an: 'autonomous association of persons united voluntarily to meet their common economic, social and cultural needs and aspirations through a jointly-owned and democratically-controlled enterprise.'

Mondragón

149. Stephanie Vince and Greg MacLeod, 'Mondragón Pastor Made Ideas Real', *Saint* 14.5 (1997); www.gvanv.com/compass/arch/v1405/saint.html.

Mark A. Lutz, *Economics for the Common Good*: 186.

Roy Morrison, *We Build the Road as We Travel: Mondragón, A Cooperative Social System* (Toronto: Glad Day Books, 1999).

150. Mondragón Cooperatives Corporation (www.mcc.es). Trusteeship Institute (www.trusteeship.org). The Mondragón cooperatives aim to balance interests at many levels – for example, the individual with the community, the particular cooperative with the whole co-op system, the human interests of workers with the necessities of the market, the industrial process with the environment. The ownership shares in these cooperatives cannot be sold to outsiders, thus control has remained in the hands of the workers. By the late 1990s, the Caja Laboral Popular had become a large bank with hundreds of branches and assets of almost $10 billion. The MCC consists of 218 companies and bodies, half of which are cooperatives. At the end of 2003, the MCC workforce totalled 68,260 people, of which 49% were based in the Basque Country, 39% in the rest of Spain and 12% in the international field.

In his book on Mondragón titled *We Build the Road as We Travel*, Roy Morrison showed that such worker cooperatives can play a key role in the global transition away from hierarchical and ecologically destructive economic structures. This inspiration rests on the fact that the Mondragón enterprise has never been about spinning utopian webs and thus has helped to 'clarify and explain what is already in process, what is implicit in a complex reality'.

What sort of activities linked to social action does the corporation promote? From its origins, the Mondragón Co-operative Experience has been characterised by its commitment to solidarity and social responsibility in terms of the environment, with this being one of its distinguishing features. This solidarity has led, first of all, to a significant contribution to the well-being and quality of life of the communities in which our companies are located: creating direct employment, generating induced employment in other companies and promoting diversified business activity. It is significant that the Mondragón cooperative system has never been linked to the state or to any type of public administration. It is entirely the creation of groups of independent people connected by a cooperative working philosophy.

Self Employed Women's Association (SEWA)

Details are based on interviews with Ela Bhatt, Mirai Chatterjee and Reema Nanavaty.

152. SEWA responded to the pressures of globalisation with four key strategies:

- It continues to organise women into membership-based groups like trade unions, cooperatives, associations

- Within these bodies SEWA works to enhance both technical and managerial skills

- Encourages capital formation both for individual members and in collectives

- Creating social security mechanisms which ensure access to healthcare, childcare, insurance, housing and old-age benefits

The SEWA Bank is a cooperative bank and for women workers. It pumps in Rs.10 million each day into the hands of the poorest among the women workers in the city of Ahmedabad. Similarly, SEWA has built a federation of 110 cooperatives of 20,000 workers providing services and making products. SEWA has built its own Academy that educates the workers as workers, as women, as citizens and as social change agents. SEWA has built 11 associations at local district levels that provide economic and social support services to the poor women workers. Over three decades SEWA has built 18 such economic institutions of the poor women workers among which SEWA Bank is the most significant, well known and trend-setting.

SEWA works on an integrated approach. The women workers are organised into local, village-level producer groups or collectives. This brings collective strength, action and bargaining power. The next logical step is to federate these village producer collectives – so that they compete in the market on a collective basis; access technical inputs, product and design development; and avail credit collectively. This helps sharing of costs, and again, being poor, collective action brings strength and better bargaining power. Also, in a village workers can organise on the basis of trades. There can be multiple groups of workers in a village.

159. 'What is given away feeds again and again, while what is kept feeds only once and leaves us hungry.' Lewis Hyde, *The Gift*: 21

Gift economy

161. 'They (the disciples) are thinking . . .'. Lewis Hyde, *The Gift*: 117.

161. This section draws on Marcel Mauss's *The Gift* and Lewis Hyde's *The Gift: Imagination and the Erotic Life of Property*. Both drew on anthropological studies and religious texts and folk fables from across the world to explore the nature of gifts exchange and its intersection with market exchange. Mauss's research revealed fairly enlightened societies in a state of 'perpetual economic effervescence' where, in some cases, goods and services circulated without sale, purchase or speculation (Mauss, *The Gift*: 70). Hyde's enquiry included gifts as material objects and talents, such as 'a gift for music' or 'a gift for painting'. He speaks of gift exchange as an 'erotic' commerce: 'opposing *eros* (the principle of attraction, union, involvement which binds together) to *logos* (reason and logic in general, the principle of differentiation in particular). A market economy is an emanation of *logos*' (Hyde, *The Gift*: xiv).

Hyde makes vital observations about the difference between gift and charity:

> The recipient of a gift should, sooner or later, be able to give it away again. If the gift does not really raise him to the level of the group, then it's just a decoy, providing him his daily bread while across town someone is buying up the bakery. This 'charity' is a way of negotiating the boundary of class. There may be gift circulation within each class, but between the classes there is a barrier. Charity treats the poor like the aliens of old; it is a form of foreign trade, a way of having some commerce without including the stranger in the group. At its worst, it is the 'tyranny of gift,' which uses the bonding power of generosity to manipulate people (Hyde, *The Gift*: 138).

162. The Maori believed that: 'Give as much as you receive and all is for the best' (Mauss, *The Gift*: 69).

> Some gift systems tended to mimic the natural world. For instance, food is perishable. So failure to share it, hoarding or letting it rot, was equated with destroying the essence of food both for oneself and others. This is why avarice was seen to interrupt the action of food which, when properly treated, is always productive of more (Mauss, *The Gift*: 55-56).

Gifts are a class of property whose value lies only in their use and which literally cease to exist as gifts if they are not constantly consumed,' wrote Hyde. 'When gifts are sold, they change their nature as much as water changes when it freezes, and no rationalist telling of the constant elemental structure can replace the feeling that is lost (Hyde, *The Gift*: 21).

As repositories of the ancient values of relationship-centred gift exchange, the Brahmins refused to engage with the commodity-centred transactions of the market. The *dana*, gifts, they received were neither a favour nor charity. Instead the *dana* was a reaffirmation of the interdependence of strictly defined castes with their separate social economic functions. Thus, Mauss observed:

> In a national economy with towns, markets and money, the Brahmin remains faithful to the economy and morality of the old Indo-Iranian shepherds and other aboriginal peasants of the great plains. He maintains the dignity of a nobleman in taking offense at favors towards him (*The Gift*: 57-59).

162. Romila Thapar, *Ancient Indian Social History: Some Interpretations* (India: Orient Longman, 1978).

That is why many cultures evolved market exchanges but kept them at arm's length. At the turn of 19th and 20th centuries Western ethnographers studied the Kula, a form of ceremonial exchange, practised by the people of the South Sea Islands near New Guinea. Bronislaw Malinowski, who studied these practices over many years, recorded that if there was any impropriety in the manner of giving gifts the people would say scornfully that it was done like a *gimwali* or market transaction. 'Again, market exchanges, so long as they are peripheral, are perceived but not discouraged, present but not obtrusive, perhaps irritating but not disruptive,' wrote Malinowski, quoted in David W. Tandy, *Warriors into Traders: The Power of the Market in Early Greece* (Berkeley, CA: University of California Press, 1997): 116.

166. '... the sentimentality of the man with the soft heart calls to us because it speaks of what has been lost'. Hyde, *The Gift*: 140.

166. As Hyde puts it, 'In a free market the people are free, the ideas are locked up' (Hyde, *The Gift*: 82-83).

As Gifford Pinchot, an expert on innovation management puts it, 'Antelope meat called for a gift economy because it was perishable and there was too much for any one person to eat. Information also loses value over time and has the capacity to satisfy more than one. In many cases information gains rather than loses value through sharing. While the exchange economy may have been appropriate for the industrial age, the gift economy is coming back as we enter the information age' (Gifford Pinchot, 'The Gift Economy: Not all economies are based on maximizing personal gain – some are founded on giving', *Business on a Small Planet* IC#41 [Summer 1995]: 49).

168. Howard Rheingold, *Smart Mobs: The Next Social Revolution* (New York; Perseus Books, 2001).

Source war

170. This section draws on an interview with Richard Stallman in 2001, an email exchange with Eric Raymond in 2003 and the following books and articles: Linus Torvalds and David Diamond, *Just for Fun: The Story of an Accidental Revolutionary*; Eric Raymond, *The Cathedral and the Bazaar: Musings on Linux and Open Source by an Accidental Revolutionary*. Kropotkin's quotation as well as Raymond's are from Eric Raymond, *The Cathedral and the Bazaar*: 63-64.

170. 'Hacker' is an appellation of honour. According to Eric Raymond, a hacker is 'an enthusiast, an artist, a tinkerer, a problem solver, an expert' (Raymond, *The Cathedral and the Bazaar*). Richard Stallman has written:

> The use of 'hacker' to mean 'security breaker' is a confusion on the part of the mass media. We hackers refuse to recognize that meaning, and continue using the word to mean, 'Someone who loves to program and enjoys being clever about it.' ... hacking means exploring the limits of what is possible, in a spirit of playful cleverness. Activities that display playful cleverness have 'hack value' (Richard Stallman, *Free Software Free Society: Selected Essays* [Boston, MA: Free Software Foundation, 2002]: 15. See also Steven Levy, *Hackers: Heroes of the Computer Revolution* [New York: Delta, 1984]).

172. 'But I knew that at the end of my career . . .'. Stallman, *Free Software Free Society*: 17.

173. GNU is a recursive acronym which stands for 'GNU's Not Unix'. Torvalds calls this a typical 'computer science in-joke'. Unix was then the standard operating system on which most computers ran and by the early 1980s this had become a proprietary software. The aim of the GNU project was to create *free* software which, even if it was not technically superior to Unix, would have social advantages. That is, it would allow users to cooperate and have, as Stallman says, 'the ethical advantage of respecting the user's freedom' (Stallman, *Free Software Free Society*: 22).

173. The Free Software Foundation and its copyleft mechanism the General Public Licence (GPL) became the fulcrum of free software development in the 1980s. Raymond has written that:

> For many years the FSF was the single most important focus of open-source hacking, producing a huge number of tools still critical to the culture. The FSF was also the only sponsor of open source with an institutional identity visible to outside observers of the hacker culture. It effectively defined the term 'free software', deliberately giving it a confrontational weight (which the newer label 'open source' just as deliberately avoids (*Cathedral and Bazaar*: 83).

174. 'The GPL is wonderful in its gift of letting anyone play . . .'. Torvalds and Diamond, *Just for Fun*: 195.

176. 'If you don't let money enter the picture, you won't have greedy people'. Torvalds and Diamond, *Just for Fun*: 87-95.

176. '(Sure, it's going to happen, but it's never been my goal.)'. Torvalds and Diamond, *Just for Fun:* 151 (brackets in original).

176. Tim Berners-Lee, 'The World Wide Web: Past, Present and Future'; www.w3.org/People/Berners-Lee.

The W3 Consortium, made up of several teams including MIT's new Computer Science and Artificial Intelligence Laboratory (CSAIL), European Research Consortium for Informatics and Mathematics (ERCIM), and Keio University in Japan, serves as the standard-setting body that ensures there is agreement on openly published protocols. About 400 organisations are members of the Consortium. For more information see www.w3.org.

177. Joshua Quittner, 'Tim Berners-Lee: From the thousands of inter-connected threads of the Internet, he wove the World Wide Web and created a mass medium for the 21st century'; www.time.com/time/time100/scientist/profile/bernerslee.html.

179. 'I'm not against making money . . .'. Stallman, *Free Software, Free Society*: 63.

179. Red Hat and Torvalds. Torvalds and Diamond, *Just for Fun*: 228.

180. 'What part of ten million dollars don't you understand?' Torvalds and Diamond, *Just for Fun*: 166.

180. Lawrence Lessig's quotes are from his Introduction to Stallman, *Free Software, Free Society*: 10-11. Lessig is an authority on cyber-law and teaches at Stanford University. While on the faculty of Harvard Law School, Lessig founded the Berkman Center for Internet and Society at Harvard and initiated its Open Law project.

181. 'Provided, adds Torvalds, playing it safe is more important . . .'. Torvalds and Diamond, *Just for Fun*: 230

181. 'The owner(s) of a software project are those who have the exclusive right, recognized by the community at large, to re-distribute modified versions.' Raymond, *Cathedral and Bazaar*: 89.

182. Rishad Aiyer Ghosh, 'Cooking-Pot Markets: An Economic Model for the Trade in Free Goods and Services on the Internet'. A longer version of this text was first published in *First Monday*, the peer-reviewed journal of the internet, in 1998. See www.firstmonday.org/issues/issue3_3/ghosh. Ghosh is one of the founders and current managing editor of *First Monday*. He has worked as analyst, journalist and researcher. He is Program Leader at the International Institute of Infonomics, University of Maastricht, where he researches non-monetary economic activity with a focus on free/open-source software.

Is it a paradigm shift?

183. O'Reilly has suggested that what we are witnessing is 'a dynamic migration of value, in which things that were once kept for private advantage are now shared freely, and things that were once thought incidental become the locus of enormous value'. To more passionate proponents of the open-source ethos these dynamic shifts can sometimes seem like a fall from grace. But some, like O'Reilly, have argued that on the whole these processes create more value for all, provided there is a balance 'in which we as an industry create more value than we capture

as individual participants, enriching the commons that allows for further development by others' (Tim O'Reilly, 'The Open Source Paradigm Shift', May 2004; www.tim.oreilly.com).

184. Malovika Rao, 'This group's really shouting Yahoo after publishing a book', 29 January 2008; www.livemint.com.

184. See www.xigi.net to 'discover the capital market that invests in good'.
Amazon does not share or distribute the software that makes it the world's largest internet bazaar for books. But Amazon has created a structure of participation that has far-reaching implications since it has connected millions of people buying, reading, rating and reviewing books in an open space; www.oreilly.com/pub/a/oreilly/ask_tim/2004/amazon_0204.html
Think of how this approach could speed up the development of cures for disease, for example . . . As the world becomes smaller, as the pace of life and business intensifies, and as the technology and information become available, people realise the tight fisted approach is becoming increasingly outmoded' (Torvalds and Diamond, *Just for Fun*: 226).
Felicity Barringer and Andrew Ross Sorkin, 'Trying to stay "ahead of curve", KKR eyes pact with green group', *New York Times*, reprinted in *Mint*, 2 May 2008; www.socialfunds.com/news/article.cgi/article2453.html.

185. Levine *et al.*, *The Cluetrain Manifesto: The End of Business as Usual*: 84. Report on Neem case, *Mint*, 20 March 2008.

189. Open Source Institute; www.opensource.org.
Open Society Institute: A Soros Foundations Network; www.soros.org.
Save the Internet; www.SavetheInternet.com.
Tim Berners-Lee, 'Long Live the Web: A Call for Continued Open Standards and Neutrality', *Scientific American*, 22 November 2010; www.scientificamerican.com/author.cfm?id=1656.

190. Dee Hock, 'The Birth of the Chaordic Century: Out of Control and into Order', speech at State of the World Forum, San Francisco, California, 26 October 1998.

Chapter 5

Cosmopolitan localism

192. 'My backyard is this fragile planet . . .'. Amy Domini, *Socially Responsible Investing: Making a Difference and Making Money* (Chicago: Dearborn, 2001): xix. Domini poses this approach as the opposite of the more common NIMBY ('not in my backyard') syndrome where communities oppose a landfill or a polluting industry in their vicinity. But how relevant is this approach? asks Domini, when 'within six hours I can travel from my home in Cambridge to the rainforest in Panama and visit with indigenous people whose language is undocumented. Or I can be in the desperately poor squalor of Port au Prince, Haiti, where illiteracy is 80% and standards of living have been dropping for 25 years. My backyard is this fragile planet.'

194. Details of the scene of farmers' market at base of WTC are from interviews with farmers at Union Square and reports found on the internet. About three years later the WTC farmers market re-emerged adjacent to the reconstruction site. Most farmers primarily spoke about needing to restore relationships with old customers they had not seen since that fateful day; www.lowermanhattan.info/news/fresh_produce_ _ old_63585.asp.

194. The International Assessment of Agricultural Science and Technology for Development (IAASTD) report was put together by panels involving more than 400 individuals from governments and civil society and broadly endorsed by 60 nations at a meeting in South Africa in April, 2008. Modelled on the highly influential work of the Intergovernmental Panel on Climate Change (IPCC), the report seeks to forge an international consensus on a new path for global agriculture that learns from the errors of the past and meets the needs of a hungry world in an environmentally and equity-conscious manner.

The study was sponsored by the UN, the World Bank, the UN Food and Agricultural Organization and UNESCO, besides other international organisations;   www.scidev.net/en/news/global-agriculture-study-calls-for-increased-resea-1.html.

195. Navadanya; www.navdanya.org. See Carlo Petrini, *Slow Food Nation* (New York: Rizzoli, 2006); www.slowfood.com.

Mass suicides: whodunit?

196.

> There are alternatives to corporations as we know them in
> Europe, Japan, and the United States. Cuernavaca, Mexico,
> enjoys a large, vibrant central marketplace in which thou-
> sands of vendors hawk their wares. They show up at the
> same place every day, and are self-organized into blocks
> that sell children's clothing, blocks that sell electrical parts,
> blocks that sell flowers, and so forth. There are no share-
> holders; no central purchasing office negotiates prices; no
> marketing department designs advertisements; no corner
> office distributes bonuses at the holiday season. Yet an
> extremely effective exchange of products takes place. Not
> only do consumers find the goods they desire, but also hun-
> dreds of individuals are able to earn a livelihood and support
> their families (Amy Domini, *Socially Responsible Investing:*
> *Making a Difference and Making Money*: 7).

Both the current tussle between Main Street and Wall Street, as well
as its historical antecedents, are quite multi-dimensional. In some ways
the tussle goes back to the pure trader aspiring for a higher status in
some societies. In Europe this was part of the larger process of commerce laying claims to greater respectability than had otherwise been
granted by most traditional societies. For example, in France it was
only after an ordinance issued in 1627 that nobles could participate
in maritime trade without losing rank. But later in 1702 French merchants insisted on being clearly distinguished from any manual workers such as an apothecary, goldsmith, furrier, wine-seller and so on. In
other words, wrote Braudel, they demanded that the status of merchant
should only be granted to those 'who sell merchandise without either
making it themselves or adding anything of their own to it' (*The Wheels*
of Commerce II: 382).

198. One of the few economists who predicted the crash of 1929 was
also the author of a book titled *Main Street and Wall Street*. William
Z. Ripley, a professor at Harvard University, showed that just because
more Americans entered the stock market in the 1920s, that did not
mean that ownership was actually passing from Wall Street to Main
Street. Owning a tiny fraction of a company's shares did not give the
folks on Main Street any say in either the companies or the economy.

198. In *Growing Prosperity: The Battle for Growth with Equity in the*
21st Century, Barry Bluestone and Bennett Harrison said that Main
Street is not merely a metaphor but also a more robust model for the

market economy. While the Wall Street model was originally conceived by economists working within the standard 'neoclassical' paradigm, during the 1980s and 1990s, its most ardent proponents have been those who make a living on Wall Street. Bluestone and Harrison trace the emergence of an implicit accord between Wall Street and Pennsylvania Avenue over this period. This *accord* was based on the assumption that if US government policies concentrated on controlling inflation and boosting savings, financial markets would work their magic and ensure economic growth.

201. 'Take the case of Billy Tiller . . .'. James Meek, 'Subsides Gap between Rich and Poor', *The Guardian*, supplement on Trade, 8 September 2003.

203. The Global Subsidies Initiative (GSI) is the next stage of the Van Lennep Program, named after Emile van Lennep, the distinguished Dutch economist and Minister, and former Secretary-General of the OECD. A collaborative effort of International Institute for Sustainable Development and the Earth Council, the Van Lennep Program focused on four sectors in its initial phase: energy, road transport, water and agriculture. Following a detailed review of subsidies applied in these sectors, its report, 'Subsidizing Unsustainable Development: Undermining the Earth with Public Funds', offered a dramatic demonstration of how subsidies serve as disincentives to sustainable development.

In December 2005 the GSI was launched to put a spotlight on subsidies – transfers of public money to private interests – and how they undermine efforts to put the world economy on a path toward sustainable development. Subsidies are powerful instruments. They can play a legitimate role in securing public goods that would otherwise remain beyond reach. But they can also be easily subverted. The interests of lobbyists and the electoral ambitions of office-holders can hijack public policy. Therefore, the GSI starts from the premise that full transparency and public accountability for the stated aims of public expenditure must be the cornerstones of any subsidy program; www.globalsubsidies.org/en/general/about-gsi.

204. Davuluri Venkateswarlu, 'Cotton Farmers' Suicides in Andhra Pradesh', study commissioned by Basix, November 1998.

M.S. Swaminathan, the father of India's green revolution, himself shifted to calling for an 'ever-green revolution'. His answer to the problem of farmers' suicides included comprehensive credit and insurance for farmers.

Professor Swaminathan specified that the rate of interest for farmers should be 4 per cent, and there ought to be a four- to five-year credit cycle in drought-prone areas. Farmers had to be made credit- and insurance-literate; barely 4 per cent of farmers participate in insurance schemes. Farmers could be insured as a group, rather than individually, with a low transaction cost and the village treated as a unit. There could be a Rural Insurance Development Fund (Darryl D'Monte, 'The Truth about Subsidies'; www.infochangeindia.org/analysis186.js).

Local Food, Global Solutions

From 6th Street Manhattan ...

208. Cary Fowler and Pat Mooney, *Shattering: Food, Politics and the Loss of Genetic Diversity* (Tuscon, AZ: University of Arizona Press, 1990). Quoted in Richard Douthwaite, *Short Circuit*: 271. In 1985 Fowler and Mooney won the Right Livelihood Award for their work on Sustainable Agriculture.

209. The ideas that informed the first two American CSAs were articulated in the 1920s by Austrian philosopher Rudolf Steiner (1861–1925), and then actively cultivated in post-WWII Europe in the 1950s, 1960s and 1970s. The ideas crossed the Atlantic and came to life in a new form, CSA, simultaneously but independently in 1986, at both Indian Line Farm in Massachusetts and Temple-Wilton Community Farm in New Hampshire. The pioneering CSA farms were influenced by Rudolf Steiner's concept of world economy and Schumacher's ideas of local production and consumption. The first two CSAs were set up in the USA in 1986. Today there are estimated to be anywhere between 1,200 and 1,700 such schemes spread across the USA. Since the mid-1990s the number of farmers' markets in the US has doubled and now stands at about 3,706. Given the scale of the American economy this is a negligible figure. In the second half of the 20th century, 1.2 million American farms went out of business.

209. In addition collectively managed community gardens are increasingly popular, with an estimated 18,000 gardens in the United States alone. Likewise, the number of farmers' markets grew 150% between 1994 and 2006, and today there are well over 4,000 in the United States ('State of the World 2008 Factsheet: Innovations for a Sustainable Global Economy').

It is estimated that a farmer is likely to get only ten cents out of a box of cornflakes that retails for $3.99, while conglomerates like Procter & Gamble or RJR Nabisco collectively spend billions on advertising and packaging to promote brand loyalty. How much value does this add to actual consumer welfare? For instance, in *Everything for Sale* Kuttner described how his local supermarket offers 150 brands of breakfast cereal not because shoppers demand that many choices but because companies like Kellogg's and Post compete with each other to grab shelf space and brand loyalty.

> In the process they add to their own overhead costs, those of the supermarket, and ultimately those of the economy. The fact that these overhead costs are roughly comparable among different food wholesalers and different supermarkets doesn't mean that consumers 'want' 150 brands of cereal; it only means that the price mechanism is not competent to squeeze out this particular inefficiency (*Everything for Sale*:15).

209. Author's interview with Howard Brandstein in 2001.

John Cloud, 'Eating Better than Organic', *Time* magazine, 2 March 2007.

The Institute for Food and Development Policy/Food First shapes how people think by analysing the root causes of global hunger, poverty and ecological degradation and developing solutions in partnership with movements working for social change; www.foodfirst.org.

212. The Japan Organic Agriculture Association runs a producer–consumer co-partnership known as the *Teikei* system. The JOAA, founded in 1971, is a non-profit voluntary organisation of producers and their consumers who are committed to the spread of organic agriculture. It runs entirely on membership fee and takes no subsidies from either government or corporations. The JOAA estimates that there are around 650 food related co-ops with 16 million members in Japan.

The JOAA was created as a response to the environmental destruction unleashed by the post-war spurt of industrialisation in Japan when the GNP was growing at the rate of 10% annually. As heavily chemical-based agriculture became the rule, consumers became alarmed about the safety of the food they were eating and thus formed groups for the promotion of organic farming. According to the Association's website, it has about 3,000 members of whom about 20% are growers the rest are consumers; www.joaa.net/english/index-eng.htm.

... to Timbaktu

215. The Timbaktu Collective is a registered voluntary organisation that was initiated in 1990, to work for sustainable development in the drought prone Anantapur district of Andhra Pradesh, India; www.timbaktu.org.

220. Colin Hines, 'Local Food, Global Solutions', *Resurgence* 210 (January/February 2002; www.resurgence.org/magazine/issue210-in-adoration-of-nature.html).

Street vendors, public markets and superstores

221. Michael Shuman currently heads the Community Food Enterprise project at the Training & Development Corporation (TDC), a non-profit think-tank based in Maine. This project, supported by the Gates Foundation and the Kellogg Foundation, builds on evidence from across the world that local ownership is a fundamental building block for long-term prosperity. Shifts in favour of local food, in particular, offer small farmers and other entrepreneurs a promising new path to economic security.

The Wallace Center at Winrock International, in partnership with the Training and Development Corporation (TDC), is working with 12 locally owned food enterprises, based abroad, to be profiled as part of *Community Food Enterprise: Local Success in a Global Marketplace.* The project, funded by the Bill & Melinda Gates Foundation and the W.K. Kellogg Foundation, is designed to highlight successful models of locally owned food enterprises from around the world; an additional ten US-based enterprises were announced earlier this year. The complete list of case studies can be found at www.wallacecenter.org/cfe.

Some books on food-related issues: Michael Pollan, *The Omnivore's Dilemma: A Natural History of Four Meals* (New York: Penguin, 2006); Gary Paul Nabhan, *Coming Home to Eat: The Pleasures and Politics of Local Foods* (New York: Norton, 2001); Ann Cooper, *Bitter Harvest: A Chef's Perspective on the Hidden Dangers in the Foods We Eat and What You Can Do About it* (New York: Routledge, 2000).

221. Author's interview with Elizabeth Ryan at Union Square farmers' market, November 2001 and later over the phone.

223. Pre-industrial Europe had a wide array of pedlars and vendors. Braudel mentions 192 specialised trades and kinds of street criers in Rome – including knife-grinders, wood-choppers, tooth-pullers, travelling cooks (*The Wheels of Commerce* II: 380).

Spread over 14 acres the Maxwell Street market served as a hub of entrepreneurship for over 800 vendors who sold a wide variety of goods

– including food, household gadgets, clothing, furniture, trinkets, toys and even music. Maxwell Street's bazaar is credited for being one of the incubators for the Chicago style of blues.

223. The National Trust for Historic Preservation in the USA has an entire programme for dealing with the decay of neighbourhood market places in towns and cities across the country.

This programme, known as the Main Street Center, aims to revitalise neighbourhood business districts through a combination of historic preservation and economic development by promoting community self-reliance, local empowerment, and the rebuilding of traditional commercial districts based on their unique assets: distinctive architecture, a pedestrian-friendly environment, personal service, local ownership, and a sense of community; www.preservationnation.org/main-street.

> Few pieces of legislation protecting workers, consumers, or ecosystems can proceed very far without opponents warning about the dire consequences for the business climate. And even if, as liberals argue, corporations benefit from well-paid workers and decent environmental regulations, few CEOs actually believe this. Consequently, most community efforts to improve the quality of life wind up scaring away major corporations (Michael Shuman, *Going Local: Creating Self-Reliant Communities in a Global Age*).

Jagriti Jyot Mahila Grih Udyog supplies snacks. Women's groups have been doing this for decades, but in this case their products have a new brand: 'Thank You Aunty' – complete with a label that explains the cottage-enterprise origins of the product. Another product line by a women's group is called 'Helping Hands' – a touch of fair trade! *Mint*, 26 March 2008.

226. According to Reema Nanavaty of SEWA, this sector, which includes petty traders, small producers, micro-entrepreneurs, domestic workers, home-based workers and casual labourers, contributes 60% of national income, about over 54% of national savings and over 40% of national exports.

For instance, an American initiative called the Apollo Alliance did focus groups among undecided, working-class voters before the 2004 Presidential elections which began with a simple question: 'how are things going?' The answers produced a depressing picture of depleted local economies, poorly paid jobs and many people working two jobs to make ends meet. The mood of the group changed dramatically when they were asked to respond to the idea of a major federal investment programme to accelerate America's transition to the clean energy economy of the future. 'We didn't have to prove to them that such a program would pay for itself; they knew it would intuitively,' Adam Werbach, who observed these groups, wrote later. 'What had been a roomful of tired and semi-depressed working folks transformed itself into a roomful of excited, optimistic Americans in a period of just 20 minutes. The energy emanating from the room was palpable' (Source: Adam Werbach's speech 'Is Environmentalism Dead?' at Commonwealth Club of San Francisco, 8 December 2004; www.grist.org/article/werbach-reprint).

For more on Decentralised Cotton Yarn Trust, see Darryl D'Monte, 'Artisanal Weavers Struggling to Survive', 9 September 2008; www.indiatogether.org/2008/sep/eco-artisans.htm.

David Korten ('Beyond the Bailout: Agenda for a New Economy', *YES! Journal for Positive Futures*, Winter 2009) outlines an essential five-part policy framework to facilitate the work of responsible businesses, investors, civic organisations and local governments engaged in growing a 21st-century economy from the bottom up.

David Korten, 'After the Meltdown: Economic Redesign for the 21st Century', November/December 2008; www.tikkun.org/magazine/tik0811/frontpage/economic.

The task before us, writes Korten, 'is to replace the culture and institutions of a twentieth-century economy designed and managed to serve financial values with the culture and institutions of a new twenty-first-century economy designed to serve life values'.

See also Andrew Simms, *Tescopoly: How One Shop Came Out on Top and Why it Matters* (UK: Constable & Robinson, 2007).

229. When Procter & Gamble acquired Gillette in early 2005 the financial press saw this as a manoeuvre to create enough bargaining clout to stand up to Walmart (James Surowiecki, 'The Customer is King', *The New Yorker*, 14 February 2005).

Local multiplier and the pyramid

233. Vijay Mahajan, 'Scaling up Social Innovation', *Seminar* 593 (January 2009).

> Grassroots financial intermediaries that address these needs do so through micro-lending, through partnering with social service agencies, through training and oversight, and through sharing risks and rewards in non-traditional ways. In many ways these are the oldest and most common forms of socially-responsible investing ... Lending circles have ancient roots. Savings banks were originally chartered for

exactly the purposes that the community development financial institutions now serve: to teach the poor how to save,
how to buy a home, and how to start a business (Domini,
Socially Responsible Investing: 25).

Michael Shuman reports that compared to banks with far-flung portfolios, those lending only to geographically restricted borrowers were
typically twice as profitable and wound up with fewer bad loans. 'One
key reason is that community banks actually know their lenders.'

Shuman also describes how some localities are discovering an
alternative to TINA named LOIS – 'Locally Owned, Import Substitut-
ing' development – which aims to move the community toward greater
prosperity through greater self-reliance.

Despite all the rhetoric about globalization, specialization,
and growing scales of production, a quiet revolution is
occurring worldwide: Economies of scale for more and more
businesses are shrinking. This revolution, if it continues,
promises to reshape the way politicians and planners pursue community development worldwide (Michael Shuman,
'Amazing Shrinking Machines: The Planning Implications
of Diminishing Economies of Scale', *New Village* 2; www.
newvillage.net/Journal/Issue2/2amazing.html).

See also, Justin Sacks, *The Money Trail: Measuring Your Impact on
the Local Economy Using LM3* (London: The Countryside Agency and
the New Economics Foundation, 2002). 'LM3' stands for Local Multiplier effect measured for the first three rounds of spending.

Stacy Mitchell, *The HomeTown Advantage: How to Defend Your Main
Street against Chain Stores . . . and Why it Matters* (Washington, DC:
Institute for Local Self Reliance, 2000).

New rules for a global agora

238. In 2007, 20% of the US corn crop went into making ethanol. By
2015, up to half of the US corn crop is expected to be used to produce
biofuels (Jikun Huang, Scott Rozelle, Bharat Ramaswami, and Uma
Lele, 'The Real Cost of Surviving', *Mint,* 21 July 2008).

239. Susanne Craig, Jeffrey McCracken, Aaron Lucchetti and Kate Kelly,
'The weekend that Wall Street died', *Wall Street Journal,* 30 December
2008.

'Cultural creatives' is a term used to describe people who actively
want to rebuild community and work for ecological sustainability. The
term was coined by researchers Paul Ray and Sherry Ruth Anderson

whose surveys, done over 20 years and involving over 100,000 Americans and 500 focus groups, indicated that approximately 23.6% are inclined to work for social and ecological transformation (Paul Ray and Sherry Ruth Anderson, *The Cultural Creatives* [New York: Harmony Books, 1999]).

241. Christopher Hayes, 'Free Traitors: Mainstream economists reconsider globalization', *The New Republic*, 8 October 2008; www.tnr.com/politics/story.html?id=3b1abc81-8d49-4641-b3c1-77f378b7a443&p=1.

www.StopOilSpeculationNow.com. Members of the Stop Oil Speculation Now Coalition included: Agricultural Retailers Association; Air Carrier Association of America along with numerous airlines; Petroleum Marketers Association of America and United Motorcoach Association.

241. Ann Davis, 'Cargill's insider view helps it buck downturn', *Wall Street Journal,* 15 January 2009.

243. Wendell Berry, 'Out of your Car, Off your Horse', in Wendell Berry, *Sex, Economy, Freedom and Community: Eight Essays* (New York: Knopf, 1994). It is also quoted by Shuman in 'Amazing Shrinking Machines'.

Chapter 6

Who Cares . . . Wins!

244. United Nations Global Compact, *Who Cares Wins: Connecting Financial Markets to a Changing World* (2004).

'I am not ashamed to own . . .'. Mahatma Gandhi, *Harijan*, 16 December 1939.

245. Details about Aaron Feuerstein are from Jonathan Rowe, 'Reinventing the Corporation', *The Washington Monthly*, April 1996; *Parade* magazine, 8 September 1996. When Malden Mills ran into trouble years later Feuerstein said an interview that he had no regrets about his actions following the fire at his mill: 'The problems we're in today are not a direct result of having acted fairly with workers and having treated them with respect. It's because we did not have adequate insurance to rebuild with the state-of-the-art equipment that would enable us to produce the best quality in the marketplace – which is what we're famous for. So we spent more money than we had and got into heavy debt. With the debt, the minute you hiccup and something doesn't go right for one year, you're in trouble. We had a tough year in 2001 and were in default on some of the interest, so our creditors put us under' (www.morethanmoney.org/articles/mtm31_after.html).

246. Radley Balko, 'Greed Makes the World Go Round', *Capitalism*, 29 December 2003; capmag.com/article.asp?ID=3436.

247. 'there is a difference between making money . . .'. Amy Domini, *Socially Responsible Investing*: 2-3.

247. 'Ray Anderson of Interface Corporation defines his business's self-interest . . .'. Ray Anderson, *Mid-course Correction*.

247. Naomi Klein, *The Shock Doctrine: The Rise of Disaster Capitalism* (New York: Metropolitan Books, Henry Holt, 2007).

Morphing the corporation

248. I found that Calvin and Hobbes cartoon strip stuck on the door of Richard Stallman's office at MIT.

249. Reference to pies and Tesco is from Naomi Klein, *No Logo: Taking Aim at the Brand Bullies* (Toronto: Knopf, 2000).
    'Entarteurs Take Note: Custard Wins Test of Best Pies for Throwing', *Wall Street Journal*, 26 May 1999.
    Pie flinging as protest has been advocated among others by the Biotic Baking Brigade which believes that 'our planet is not dying, it is being killed; and the ones doing the killing have names and faces'. The Biotic Baking Brigade is opposed to all those who undermine individual/local/regional/national autonomy, privatise industries and services, deregulate financial markets and 'hoodwink citizens into trusting "the invisible hand" of the market to protect them.' The Brigade's website offers tips from militant bakers on practical and theoretical aspects of creating 'palatable projectiles' (web.archive.org/web/20080207123817/http:// bioticbakingbrigade.org).

249. Survey for World Economic Forum was conducted by Environics and Gallup. Other reference: Richard Edelman, 'The Relationship among NGOs, Government, Media and Corporate Sector', a presentation at the Harvard Club of New York, 12 January 2002.

250. David Batstone is co-founder of Business 2.0, executive editor of the leading social ethics magazine *Sojourners*, and a frequent contributor to the *New York Times* business section, *Wired*, *Chicago Tribune* and the *San Francisco Chronicle*. He is also a tenured professor of social ethics at University of San Francisco.
    David Batstone, *Saving the Corporate Soul* (San Francisco: Jossey-Bass, 2003).

250. Joel Bakan, *The Corporation: The Pathological Pursuit of Profit and Power* (London: Constable & Robinson, 2005).

Union Carbide's official website states that approximately 3,800 people died, approximately 40 people experienced permanent disability, and approximately 2,800 other individuals experienced partial disabilities. It also implies that the accident was caused by sabotage not negligence. BBC has quoted an official estimate of 15,000 fatalities, over the last two decades, which can be traced back to the accident. In 1989, Union Carbide made a settlement of $470 million with the Government of India, which represented all claimants in the case. Though this settlement was challenged by victims it was later upheld by the Supreme Court of India. Both NGOs and journalists have documented at length how large numbers of the affected people remain without adequate medical help and other support. In 2001 Union Carbide was bought by Dow Chemicals.

India's capital Delhi alone has 1,777 industries generating hazardous wastes but the city has no chemical hazards map or effective disaster management plan. Tilak Bazaar, Asia's largest chemical market, is in the heart of Chandni Chowk, and feared to be a tinderbox.

251. At the ground the Bhopal gas leak is remembered as stark example of lessons not learnt. 'Simply put, the current culture among regulators, planners policymakers and judges, not to mention industrialists, allows a community to exercise its right to a hazard-free living and working environment only if that is economically and technologically viable for the industry, and politically expedient for the powers-that-be' (Nityanand Jayaraman, 'Wrong Question, Wrong Answers', *Infochange Agenda* 1 [December 2004]).

252. '. . . the dogma is that trade and investment liberalization . . .'. Halina Ward and Bernice Lee, 'Corporate Responsibility and the Future of the International Trade and Investment Agendas', *Perspectives,* October 2003. Ward is Director of Corporate Responsibility at the International Institute for Environment and Development (IIED) and Lee is Strategic Knowledge Manager at International Centre for Trade and Sustainable Development. *Perspectives* is a journal published by the IIED, a London-based non-profit research institute working in the field of sustainable development.

253. David Korten, *The Post-Corporate World: Life after Capitalism.*

254. Amitai Etzioni, 'When It Comes to Ethics, B-Schools Get an F', *The Washington Post*, 4 August 2002: B4. Etzioni is the author of *The Moral Dimension* (New York: Free Press, 1988).

Long shadow of trusteeship

256. Gandhi's concept of trusteeship did have an impact on the ground in India. In the 1950s, Gandhi's disciple Vinoba Bhave led a movement called 'Bhoodan' – literally, 'gift of land' – in which landowners voluntarily surrendered thousands of acres of land in favour of the landless. Gandhi's social trust theory influenced people across the world and some industrialists converted their firms voluntarily into co-ops. The most famous example of this was the Scott Bader Commonwealth in Britain. The concept of social auditing emerged from the same influences. The Community Land Trust movements in the USA, Canada and Australia also trace their inspiration to Gandhian activities in India.

Gandhi did not dismiss the importance of profit but saw it as a means not as the end purpose and it would be measured in a multi-dimensional manner. Industrialists would limit their own rewards and remuneration in a manner similar to trustees of public charities. The moving energy for this change was to come neither from legislators nor an ideological vanguard but an open, ongoing process of voluntary social-cultural transformation.

M.K. Gandhi, *Trusteeship* (compiled by Ravindra Kelkar; Ahmedabad, India: Navajivan, 1960).

By keeping its members informed about the increasing power and impact of global corporations ICCR helps religious investors to provide ethical checks and balances on a wide range of companies. Thus ICCR members have successfully put pressure on multinational energy companies to change products and practices that contribute to climate change and instead switch to renewable energy.

256. See also Paola Triolo, Martin Palmer and Steve Waygood, *A Capital Solution: Faith, Finance and Concern for a Living Planet* (UK: The Alliance of Religions and Conservation and World Wide Fund for Nature, 2000).

257. One of the ways in which Business in the Community (BITC) engages business people with wider social and environmental issues is a programme called 'The Prince's Seeing is Believing'. It invites senior business leaders to a first-hand encounter with harsh social realities that they would not otherwise experience. The programme is subtly designed to focus on problems in ways that are conducive to finding some, even if partial, solutions; www.bitc.org.uk/princes_programmes/the_princes_seeing_is_believing/index.html.

258. 'The bad news is . . .'. Letter to Stakeholders by Georg Kell, Executive Director, UN Global Compact Office, 15 December 2010.

UNCTAD figures from press release, 24 September 2008; www. unglobalcompact.org/docs/email_downloads/2010_12_15_ALs/ AnnualLetter_2011_EN.pdf.

258. Allen L. White, 'Lost in Transition? The Future of Corporate Social Responsibility', *Journal of Corporate Citizenship* 16 (Winter 2004). White is Vice President and Senior Fellow of the Tellus Institute in Boston, USA. He is also co-founder of Corporation 20/20, an initiative focused on designing future corporations to sustain social purpose.

Faith in business

259. Dr Newell was appointed as a Residentiary Canon of St Paul's Cathedral in 2001 at the age of 39 – the youngest for a century. In 2003 he was appointed Chancellor of St Paul's and Director of the St Paul's Institute. Other workshops have explored the spiritual and theological framework, and tools of ethical analysis and the understanding required to interact intelligently with our global environment.

The dialogue referred to here was part of a series, in September 2004, which was presided over by Dr Rowan Williams, the Archbishop of Canterbury. Other themes covered in this series were: 'Is Humanity Killing Itself?'; 'Environment and Humanity: Friends Or Foes?' and 'How should the world be governed?'

See www.stpauls.co.uk/page.aspx?theLang=001lngdef&pointerID=1 2494hhXmqniD2vd771NnsLnh7WBE8LM.

Or, alternatively, www.stpauls.co.uk/News-Press/Latest-News/ St-Pauls-launches-economics-think-tank.

260. Ben Cohen and Jerry Greenfield, *Ben & Jerry's Double-Dip: Lead with Your Values and Make Money Too* (New York: Simon & Schuster, 1997).

261. Marc Gunther, *Faith and Fortune: How Compassionate Capitalism is Transforming American Business* (New York: Random House, 2005).

261. Gifford Pinchot, 'The Gift Economy: Not all economies are based on maximizing personal gain – some are founded on giving', *Context: A Quarterly of Humane Sustainable Culture*, Summer 1995: 49. Gifford Pinchot and his wife Elizabeth are principals of Pinchot & Company, a consulting firm that helps large workplaces escape from bureaucracy and hierarchy to release the intelligence, creativity and integrity of the members.

264. Among other things the Social Venture Network helps people who need information about wide range of issues relating to starting and

running a socially responsible business or making socially responsible investments. It also helps to build locally networks for such like-minded people. See www.svn.org.

In 1991, the Act Now group within SVN took up the issue of automobile fuel efficiency. All the participating companies used their packaging and communications to encourage customers to write to their elected officials, expressing support for a bill that required greater fuel efficiency from all automobile manufacturers. Act Now received 300,000 postcards, which were then carried to Capitol Hill with much fanfare. Act Now also got 19 companies to sign on a statement asking the Bush government for a diplomatic solution and opposing the Gulf War. The statement, titled 'An Unnecessary War', appeared as a full-page ad in the *New York Times*. Notably, the signatories to that advertisement were not individuals but companies.

The SVN network now has spin-off organisations, such as the Business Alliance for Local Living Economies (BALLE) which has the motto 'Building Economies for the Common Good'. BALLE works on the premise that strengthened local economies will build long-term economic empowerment and prosperity. SVN also supports a network of business students across the USA (www.livingeconomies.org).

> The dominant DNA is to make profits first and foremost. Our genes are different. We take money off our top line and give it back to the world which makes our existence possible. Giving back to the world isn't something we think about after we make a profit – it's part of our cost of doing business. It's a cost we pay up front. Our mission is to out-compete companies who don't pay this cost, and thereby not only survive, but eventually change corporate DNA (Peter Barnes, *Who Owns the Sky? Our Common Assets and the Future of Capitalism*).

Challenging the 'Divine Right of Capital'

266. Marjorie Kelly, *The Divine Right of Capital*: xii-xiii.

Corporations today are governments of the propertied class, exercising power over Americans that is greater than the power once exercised by kings. They are governments that have become destructive of our inalienable rights as a people. We can end their illegitimate reign and institute a new economic government, laying its foundation on such principles as seem most likely to effect our safety and happiness. We can one day complete the design in the economic realm that the framers began in the political realm, the design of *novus ordo seclorum* – a new order of the ages.

Global Casino, Tobin Tax and Jubilee

269. In March 1999 the Canadian Parliament became the world's first legislature to pass a motion calling for a Tobin Tax by a resounding 2:1 margin with all-party support. Throughout 2000, legislatures in Brazil, UK, France and Belgium all debated the matter. A study conducted on behalf of the IMF has favoured a variant of CTT. The German Trade Union Confederation (DGB) and the AFL-CIO in the US have also supported some form of CTT. In June 2000, at the UN Social Summit in Geneva, over 160 governments agreed to undertake a study on the feasibility of a currency transactions tax. NGOs in over 20 countries have spent almost a decade campaigning for a Tobin Tax.

See also Mahbub ul Haq, Inge Kaul and Isabelle Grunberg (eds.), *The Tobin Tax: Coping with Financial Volatility* (Oxford, UK: Oxford University Press, 1996).

270. According to a report by Paddy Allen in *guardian.co.uk* on 29 January 2009, the Bank for International Settlements estimates that the assets of the world's big commercial banks are about $39 trillion. The notional value of all derivatives is estimated to be $863 trillion.

The total asset value of developed economies peaked at $290 trillion, while the global GDP is about $ 55 trillion.

By the end of 2008, there had been about $1.9 trillion total state assistance to the banking system through either direct spending or guarantees.

Eventually, only about one-third of these promises actually came through.

In 2003, leaders of Jubilee 2000 undertook an assessment of the campaign's impact. They documented how countries which have gained even partial debt relief have improved their spending on health and other social needs. But underlying this thin veneer of good news was a dark picture. The overwhelming majority of the world's poor remain deeply indebted and existing policies offer them no hope of relief.

271. Ann Pettifor is a political economist whose most recent writings can be found at www.debtonation.org. See also Ann Pettifor, 'A Debt Spiral we could have Avoided'; www.newstatesman.com/economy/2008/10/rates-debt-banks-economists.

New Economics Foundation, 'Chapter 9/11? Resolving International Debt Crises – the Jubilee Framework for International Insolvency' (2002).

For details about the insolvency framework called for by Jubilee International, see the website: www.jubileeplus.org.

- Total cancellation of the unpayable debts of developing countries

- Promoting a framework of justice and discipline for relations between sovereign debtors and international creditors

- Ensuring that the international financial activities of sovereign governments and multilateral institutions become more transparent and accountable to citizens

- Promotes environmentally sustainable policies for financing development

- Advocates the repayment of the North's ecological debts to countries of the South

- Challenges IMF-imposed structural adjustment policies which, by imposing deflationary economic policies, help to transfer assets from sovereign debtors to international creditors

- Questions IMF policies that elevate the rights of foreign creditors over those of citizens by removing policy autonomy from sovereign governments

- Calls for developing development finance policies in a more self-reliant way, with less or no dependency on foreign donors and creditors

In 1964 the Congregational Union of Scotland commissioned a report on a Christian view of wealth. The report concluded that the present system of wealth generation is fraudulent and that a nation's wealth must primarily be directed to ensuring that every citizen's livelihood is ensured. This thinking eventually gave birth to the Christian Council of Monetary Justice, a forum for Christians committed to working for monetary reform.

The idea of monetary justice is a subset of the broader concept of Global Justice, which encompasses monetary, economic, social and environmental justice. Monetary Justice requires a money system that is devoid of usurious exploitation and conducive to ensuring justice in the other three sphere. Economic justice refers to 'land and resource use befitting trustees not owners and a profound respect for the gift of the Commons'. Social justice implies the basic unit of human relations is based on equality and mutuality, and this remains the precondition for any hierarchically ordered institutions or relations that are required for effective action. Environmental justice requires us to be trustees of planet Earth by developing psyches the size of the universe, wherein our humble significance is affirmed (Peter Challen, email to author).

Objectives of the Global Justice Movement:

- Secure incomes for all, including pensions – created by new technology and new investment

- Capital ownership for all – individual capital estates provide secure income

- Public capital investment – at half the present cost

- A huge reduction in debt – personal, corporate and national

- A proper deal for women – ensures independent income

- Safeguarding the environment – sustainable resource use and thus – Peace

273. The Global Table is an open meeting held every Wednesday from 11 am to 12.45 pm in the basement cafeteria of Friends House, opposite Euston station, in London.

The Campaign for Interest-Free Money in UK was launched in 1998, by a group of people, mostly from London, who wanted to get this debate rolling. Their website describes them as 'a highly non-hierarchical, non-ageist, non-party political, inter-cultural, inter-faith, ecumenical and very, very all-inclusive activity'. Early in its existence the Campaign's members realised that the question of debt is deeply uncomfortable for some people and has thus emphasised the need to ask all to examine these questions 'in the spirit of love and respect'; www.interestfreemoney.org.

See also Margrit Kennedy, *Interest and Inflation Free Money: Creating an Exchange Medium that Works for Everybody and Protects the Earth* (Philadelphia, PA: New Society Publishers, 1995). Kennedy is a consultant in complementary currencies and travels extensively lecturing on these themes; www.margritkennedy.org.

274. For more information on Islamic Banking, see www. islamicbankingnetwork.com.

Champagne glass syndrome

274. Figures on microcredit in India, Nilah Pandian, Intellecap, presentation to *Aavishkaar-Goodwell Study Tour*, Raichur, 4 November 2006.

279. www.oikocredit.org/en/home

280. From Vijay Mahajan, *Microcredit to Livelihood Finance* (Hyderabad, India: Basix, 2005).

281. Rohini Nilekani's observations are from her correspondence with micro-finance professionals.

282. Vijay Mahajan's observations on Indonesian crisis are from his article in *Economic Times*, 31 December 2007.
      Aloysius P. Fernandez, 'Whose Risk is it Anyway?'; www.microfinancefocus.com/latest-news/Aloysius-Fernandez/microfinance-crisis-whose-risk-it-anyway.
      Interview with Sen Sarma in December 2010.

Crafting a triple bottom line

Author's interviews with Peter Head, John Elkington, and Herman Mulder.

284. Interest in the concept of a triple bottom line has been steadily growing. One indication of this is the number of Google hit figures. There were just 15,600 Google hits for the term 'triple bottom line' in August 2002. The figure went up to 69,500 in September 2004 and then leapt to 187,000 in January 2005; www.businessethics.ca/3bl.

285. John Elkington has most recently co-founded Volans: the business of social innovation – a for-profit company founded on the conviction that out of the ashes of the ongoing market crash a 'Phoenix Economy' will rise with new business models focused on social, environmental and financial challenges; www.volans.com.
      Signposts in the spread of a triple-bottom-line ethos as recorded in *Who Cares Wins*:

- The Carbon Disclosure Project called on companies to provide investment-relevant information relating to greenhouse gas mitigation

- The Institutional Shareholders Committee Principles, issued by a group of large institutional investors, calls on fund managers to take a more active approach in relation to their engagement with companies, which should include ESG issues

- The Pharmaceutical Shareowners Group works on better disclosure in the pharmaceutical industry

- The Investors' Statement on Transparency in the Extractives Sector aims at increasing the transparency of payments made by extractive-sector companies to governments and government-linked entities

- The US Investor Network on Climate Risk, a group of US State and City Treasurers and Trustees with fiduciary responsibility for some of America's largest and most influential pension and labour funds, brings greater investor focus on climate change risks and opportunities

- The UK Institutional Investors' Group on Climate Change has similar goals as the US Investor Network on Climate Risk

See also www.sustainability-indexes.com.

287. Herman Mulder was later decorated by the government of Netherlands for his leadership in the formation of the Equator Principles.

Put your money where your morals are: Socially Managed Portfolio

290. Details about Domini are from author's interview with her in 2003 and Amy Domini, *Socially Responsible Investing: Making a Difference and Making Money*.

The Association of British Insurers, whose members manage about $1.5 trillion in assets, has created guidelines for companies to report on social, ethical and environmental risks.

David Vogel, *The Market for Virtue: The Potential and Limits of Corporate Social Responsibility*: 3, 72

294. Simon Zadek, *The Civil Corporation* (London: Earthscan, 2001).

Andrew Leonard, 'Why Wall Street Should be More Like a Cockroach'; www.salon.com, 20 December 2007.

TIAA-CREF, or Teachers Insurance and Annuity Association – College Retirement Equities Fund, is one of the largest financial services providers in the world managing over $280 billion in assets – mostly the pensions of some 2.3 million teachers and academics. The CREF Social Choice Account has both negative and positive screens. It excludes companies that derive any revenues from the manufacture of alcohol or tobacco products, or from gambling; companies that derive significant revenues from producing military weapons; and electric utilities with interests in nuclear power plants. It seeks out companies that demonstrate a respect for the natural environment; strong charitable giving and employee benefits programmes; the presence of women and minorities in leadership positions; quality products and leadership in research and development; and the payment of fair wages and protection of the environment where they operate. Concerns identified in one area will not automatically eliminate the company from the portfolio.

Orthodoxy strikes back

296. Tracy Rembert, 'CSR in the Cross-Hairs: A broad counter attack against corporate reform is growing', *Business Ethics,* Spring 2005.

297. 'Our ultimate purpose . . .': William Greider, 'Could Wall Street become the vanguard of environmental activism?', 28 October 2003; www.greenbiz.com.

More recently Kiernan has said, 'The investment logic that we pursue at Innovest should be obvious to a 10-year-old child, but the tragedy is that you never have a 10-year-old with you in JP Morgan's boardroom when you need one. Every piece of research that I've seen says that when you ask Wall Street analysts, management quality is the number one determinant of a company's financial performance, yet it's the very exceptional analyst that has a systematic template, that says if I saw these 20 things in a semiconductor company, I would know it's a well-managed company . . . What we've tried to do is make it a lot more systematic and disciplined and robust.' Robert F. Keane, 'It's all about Green', *Investment Advisor,* 12 January 2008; www.advisorone.com/author/robert-f-keane.

Beyond denial

300. 'As the British activist Deborah Doane . . .'. Interview with Deborah Doane and her article 'Beyond Corporate Social Responsibility: Minnows, Mammoths and Markets', *Futures* 37 (2005). Deborah Doane is a member of the Operating and Financial Review working group on UK Company Law, and is on the Stakeholder Council of the Global Reporting Initiative. She speaks and writes internationally on a range of CSR and humanitarian issues, including at the London School of Economics, London Business School and Harvard University and has contributed to a range of national newspapers, television, radio and journals. Previously, Deborah was head of the International Humanitarian Ombudsman Project, and was a senior policy analyst with the Canadian government.

301. 'Coming within months of the Stern Report . . .'; www.tomorrowscompany.com.

303. '. . . information about social and environmental impacts . . .'. CORE represents over 100 charities, faith-based groups, community organizations, unions, businesses and academic institutions. Its steering group includes: ActionAid, Amnesty International, Christian Aid, Friends of the Earth and Traidcraft. This coalition was formed in response to the UK Government's *Modernising Company Law* White Paper, which failed to specify rules that would require companies to be more transparent and accountable to the communities and environments in which they operate.

304. '. . . critical limits to the market for virtue . . .'. David Vogel, *The Market for Virtue: The Potential and Limits of Corporate Social Responsibility*: 3, 72.

307. '. . . all you care about . . .'. Andrew Leonard, 'Why Wall Street Should be More Like a Cockroach', 20 December 2007; www.salon. com.

309. 'Tim Smith at Walden Investments in Boston . . .'. Interview with Timothy Smith, one of the pioneers in the socially responsible business movement, and as co-founder of the Interfaith Center on Corporate Responsibility he played a key role in mobilising corporate exodus from South Africa during the apartheid regime. By assisting banks and companies rethink their role, Smith helped to pave the way for Nelson Mandela and the end of apartheid. At the time that the defamation suit was filed against him Smith was Director of Socially Responsive Investing at Walden Assets Management. He was given the Aaron Feuerstein award for promoting the concept that corporations have responsibilities to society, that business can be a force for positive social change, that shareholders can demand that business leaders be ethically credible as well as good corporate citizens and that spiritual values can be linked to business practice and that business should accept the importance of all stakeholders.

'In 2010 the BP Deepwater . . .'. 'How Much Will BP Really Pay?', Room for Debate Blog, NYTimes.com, 16 June 2010; roomfordebate. blogs.nytimes.com/2010/06/16/how-much-will-bp-really-pay.

Chapter 7

Nature bats last

310. 'While it is unwise to believe in any one environmental projection . . .'. Paul Hawken, Hunter Lovins and Amory Lovins, *Natural Capitalism* (Boston, MA: Little, Brown & Company, 1999): 316.

Details about Ray Anderson and Interface are from my interview with him and his book *Mid-course Correction* as well as the Interface website.

312. Lester Brown, *Plan B 2.0: Rescuing a Planet under Stress and a Civilization in Trouble*; Jonathon Porritt, *Capitalism as if the World Matters*.

312. In January 2007 an unprecedented coalition of blue-chip US companies and environmental lobby groups drew up a plan to cut greenhouse gases by 10–30% over 15 years. This was just one of innumerable signals that business-as-usual is no longer viable. A press release by the WorldWatch Institute described many large companies as putting their political muscle where their investment capital is. Twenty-seven major corporations, including Alcoa, Dow Chemicals, Duke Energy, General Motors and Xerox, actively urged the US Congress to pass legislation regulating greenhouse gas emissions – something that would have been unthinkable two years ago. 'Adam Smith Meet Mother Earth', *World-Watch Institute*, 10 January 2008.

313. Paul Hawken, 'How do we decide the value of a 700-year-old tree?', *Mother Jones*, March/April 1997. After briefly working on the staff of Martin Luther King Jr's office in the early 1960s, Hawken co-founded Erewhon Trading Company, a natural foods wholesaling business, in the 1960s. He went on to co-found the very successful and innovative Smith & Hawken mail-order garden supply company in 1979. He is the author of several books, including *The Ecology of Commerce, Growing a Business, The Next Economy, and Seven Tomorrows*.

Living systems in chaotic retreat

314. '. . . one polluted river at a time, one dying coral reef at a time . . .'. Paraphrased from a speech by Ray Anderson at the international conference on Operationalising Gross National Happiness, Nova Scotia, Canada, June 2005.

315. The Ecological Footprint Network has emerged out of the work by Mathis Wackernagel and William Rees who developed this concept.

See 'Perceptual and Structural Barriers to Investing in Natural Capital: Economics from an Ecological Footprint Perspective', *Ecological Economics* 20 (1997); www.footprintnetwork.org.

The Ecological Footprint Network is committed to fostering a world where all people have the opportunity to live satisfying lives within the means of Earth's ecological capacity. It aims to advance scientific rigour and practical application of the Ecological Footprint, a tool that quantifies human demand on nature, and nature's capacity to meet these demands. In other words, it now takes more than one year and two months for the Earth to regenerate what we use in a single year. We maintain this overdraft by liquidating the planet's natural resources; www.footprintnetwork.org/index.php.

316. The World Meteorological Organisation and United Nations Environment Programme established the Intergovernmental Panel on Climate Change (IPCC) in 1988. The IPCC is a scientific body: the information it provides with its reports is based on scientific evidence and reflects existing viewpoints within the scientific community. The comprehensiveness of the scientific content is achieved through contributions from experts in all regions of the world and all relevant disciplines including, where appropriately documented, industry literature and traditional practices, and a two-stage review process by experts and governments; www.ipcc.ch.

Despite the increasing international sense of urgency, the growth rate of carbon emissions is still speeding up. The atmospheric CO_2 concentration in 2007 was 383 parts per million (ppm). According to *Science Daily*, 'Anthropogenic CO_2 emissions have been growing about four times faster since 2000 than during the previous decade, despite efforts to curb emissions in a number of Kyoto Protocol signatory countries. Emissions from the combustion of fossil fuel and land use change reached 10 billion tonnes of carbon in 2007. Natural CO_2 sinks are growing but slower than the atmospheric CO_2 growth, which has been increasing at 2 ppm since 2000 or 33% faster than the previous 20 years.'

'Carbon Emissions Shoot Up Beyond IPCC Projections', *Science Daily*, 28 September 2008; www.sciencedaily.com/releases/2008/09/080925072440.htm.

See also *Clean Energy Blueprint* by The Union of Concerned Scientists, The American Council for an Energy-Efficient Economy and the Tellus Institute. These institutions found in 2001 that the United States can do the following (www.ucsusa.org/assets/documents/clean_energy/blueprint.pdf):

- Meet at least 20% of its electricity needs by renewable energy sources – wind, biomass, geothermal, and solar – by 2020

- Save consumers a total of $440 billion by 2020, with annual savings reaching $105 billion per year or $350 for a typical family

- Reduce the use of natural gas by 31% and coal by nearly 60% compared to business-as-usual by 2020, and save more oil in

18 years than can be economically recovered from the Arctic National Wildlife Refuge in 60 years

- Simultaneously avoid the need for 975 new power plants (300 MW each), retire 180 old coal plants (500 MW each), retire 14 existing nuclear plants (1,000 MW each), and reduce the need for hundreds of thousands of miles of new gas pipelines and electricity transmission lines

- Reduce carbon dioxide emissions by two-thirds from business-as-usual by 2020, while also reducing harmful air emissions of sulphur dioxide and nitrogen oxides by more than 55%

317. Wolfgang Sachs *et al.*, *The Jo'burg Memo: Fairness in a Fragile World*, A Memorandum for the World Summit on Sustainable Development, Heinrich Böll Foundation, 2002: 58-59.

317. CARE's advertisement, seen in Metro Rail, Washington, 2003. CARE Energy is a coalition of scores of industry associations in the US. CARE's website says, 'The quality of the air in the US is improving even as energy use has increased. The coal-based electricity industry has a strong commitment to the environment that has manifested itself in billions of dollars invested in clean air technology and a record of exceeding government targets for certain types of emissions.'

318. Innovest, *Strategic Value Advisors* report of 18 August 2002; www. innovestgroup.com.

Exxon is a leader of the viewpoint that there is not enough evidence to show how much of the contemporary climate change phenomenon are human-induced or that the changes pose a serious threat. A corollary of this view is that it is better to focus attention on how humanity can live with climate change, rather than trying to stop it from happening. According to the *Wall Street Journal* story, Exxon spent about a $1 billion on renewable energy research in the 1980s and eventually concluded that it was not a worthwhile business. The Journal quoted Exxon CEO Raymond as saying, 'What all these people are thinking about doing, we did 20 years ago – and spent $1 billion, in dollars of that day, to find out that none of these were economic,' he says. 'That's why I feel so strongly about it – because I've been there and I've done that' (*Wall Street Journal*, 14 June 2005).

318. In June 2005, the Association of British Insurers released a report that showed that even small increases in the severity of extreme storms could increase average world-wise damage by two-thirds over the 21st century; www.abi.org.uk/default.aspx.

Commons and markets

Market value of ecosystems

319. 'In a hot country where travelers . . .'. Rabindranath Tagore, *Lectures and Addresses* (Delhi: Macmillan, 1970).

320. Just 2.5% of the world's water is fresh. Merely one-hundredth of 1% of the world's fresh water is readily accessible for human use – the rest is either frozen or deep underground.

Scientists warn that removing vast amounts of water from watersheds has the potential to destroy entire ecosystems. Lowering water tables can create sinkholes and dry up wells . . . Existing water diversions and hydroelectric projects are causing local climate change, reduced biodiversity, mercury poisoning, loss of forest, and the destruction of fisheries habitat and wetlands.

'Blue Gold: The Global Water Crisis and the Commodification of the World's Water Supply', Report of *International Forum on Globalisation*, San Francisco, 2001.

'Nature for Sale: The Impacts of Privatizing Water and Biodiversity', Report of Friends of the Earth, January 2005; www.foei.org/en/publications/link/privatization/index.html.

For example, in Canada, organisations of indigenous peoples have rallied to protect their water sources arguing that '. . . The Creator placed us on this earth, each in our own sacred and traditional lands, to care for all of creation. We have always governed ourselves as Peoples to ensure the protection and purity of Water. We stand united to follow and implement our knowledge, laws and self-determination to preserve Water, to preserve life. Our message is clear: Protect Water Now!' (The Blue Planet Project, which is an international effort begun by The Council of Canadians to protect the world's fresh water from the growing threats of trade and privatisation; www.blueplanetproject.net/english/treaty).

321. Peter Barnes, 'Capitalism, the Commons and Divine Right', Speech at the E.F. Schumacher Society, Great Barrington, USA, 25 October 2003.

325. The Millennium Ecosystem Assessment (MEA), launched by the UN in June 2001, is an international work programme designed to meet the needs of decision-makers and the public for scientific information concerning the consequences of ecosystem change for human well-being and options for responding to those changes. It will help to meet assessment needs of the Convention on Biological Diversity, Convention to Combat Desertification, the Ramsar Convention on Wetlands, and the

Convention on Migratory Species, as well as needs of other users in the private sector and civil society. If the MEA proves to be useful to its stakeholders, it is anticipated that such integrated assessments will be repeated every 5–10 years and that ecosystem assessments will be regularly conducted at national or sub-national scales; www.maweb. org/en/index.aspx.

Tina Butler, 'How much are ecosystems worth? For What It's Worth: Ecological Services and Conservation', 4 May 2005; news.mongabay. com. WorldWatch Institute, *State of the World* Report, 2008.

326.

> The real utopians are those who believe the market can con-
> tinue unbridled forever. This dream has great allure, but it's
> a dangerous fantasy. The reality is that, without a healthy
> commons, the market (and much else) won't survive the 21st
> century (www.friendsofthecommons.org).

See also www.community-wealth.org/_pdfs/articles-publications/ commons/report-barnes-et-al-07.pdf.

327. Story about Lake. Gatun: query.nytimes.com/gst/fullpage.html?res =9C03EEDD1239F937A15756C0A9639C8B63. And 'Rescuing Environ-mentalism', *The Economist*,23 April 2005.

Who owns the sky?

328. Peter Barnes, *Who Owns the Sky? Our Common Assets and the Future of Capitalism.*

Working Assets was established in 1985 to help busy people make a difference in the world through everyday activities like talking on the phone. Every time a customer uses one of Working Assets' donation-linked services (Long Distance, Wireless and Credit Card), the company donates a portion of the charges to non-profit groups working to build a world that is more just, humane, and environmentally sustainable. To date, over $47 million has been raised for progressive causes. The company also serves as a strong political force, dedicated to giving its customers the opportunity to speak out on critical public issues through its website and monthly phone bill.

329. '. . . after twenty years as a capitalist, I decided to hang up my cleats . . .'. Peter Barnes, *Who Owns the Sky*: 9-10.

> The trouble is, markets have no appreciation for intrin-
> sic value. They're blind and dumb and stunningly mind-
> less; they do what they're programmed to do with ruthless
> aplomb. That wouldn't matter if we run our lives without

> markets. But we can't. We need to communicate with markets because markets determine how resources are used. All our preachings and sermons will be for naught if we don't inscribe them on tablets that markets can understand (Barnes, *Who Owns the Sky*: 34).

'Capitalism, like a computer, requires an operating system . . . In capitalism, the operating system coordinates workers, investors, managers, and consumers all over the globe. Its code is written in many legislatures and courtrooms, a little at a time – in this regard, it's more like Linux than Windows' (Barnes, *Who Owns the Sky*: 126).

Peter Barnes, 'Capitalism, the Commons and Divine Right', speech delivered at the E.F. Schumacher Society, 2003.

331. Establishment of a US Sky Trust would be an historic event, comparable to the Homestead Act of 1862, the Federal Reserve Act of 1913, and the Social Security Act of 1935. Like the Homestead Act, a Sky Trust would create a new class of property owners – in effect giving every citizen an equity stake in the sky. At the same time, the Sky Trust would establish an independent board of trustees to manage the carbon flow through the US economy, much as the Fed manages the money flow. And, like the Social Security system, the Sky Trust would define a new formula for the movement of money within the economy. In this case the formula is: from all according to their use of a commons, to all according to their equal ownership. The trustees would have three legal responsibilities: one, to issue carbon burning permits up to a limit established by legislators; two, to receive market prices for those permits; and three, to distribute that income equally (*Who Owns the Sky?*: 63-64).

332. According to calculations by Barnes and by James K. Boyce of the University of Massachusetts, those earning more than $160,000 a year – who have bigger cars and houses and thus use more energy – would end up paying more in energy charges than they got back in dividends. Those earning less than about $45,000 would end up paying less and with some extra cash in their pockets. And those in between would find it roughly a wash, though about 70% overall would make money on the deal. The country as a whole, of course, would be much better off. The planet, too. Boyce and a pair of UMass colleagues wrote an article in *Energy Policy* magazine last year explaining how a sky trust could work in China. See also Jonathan Alter, 'A Clear Blue-Sky Idea', *Newsweek,* 14 June 2007.

333. Mark Lynas, 'If the cap fits, share it', *New Statesman,* 31 January 2008; www.newstatesman.com/200801310021#reader-comments.

Cap and dividend is a simple, market-based way to reduce CO_2 emissions without reducing household incomes. It caps fossil fuel supplies, makes polluters pay, and returns the revenue to everyone equally; www.capanddividend.org.

334. '. . . the real or imagined, bliss of the Kalahari hunter-gatherer . . .'. *Who Owns the Sky?*: 131.

Natural Capitalism

335. Ray Anderson, speech at Second International Conference on Gross National Happiness, in 2005.

336. Hawken's speech was delivered at the Commonwealth Club of California, one of the USA's oldest and largest public affairs forums which organises events ranging across politics, culture, society and the economy.
    Paul Hawken, *The Ecology of Commerce: A Declaration of Sustainability* (London: HarperCollins, 1993).

336. Ray Anderson, *The Interface Model*.

337. 'The surest way to realize the alarmists' outcome, collapse, is to accept the foot draggers' view. The surest way to realize the foot draggers' outcome, abundance, is to believe the alarmists' view that we are in trouble and have to change' (Donella Meadows, 'Managing for Life'; www.yesmagazine.org).

337. Shel Horowitz, 'Amory Lovins: Reinventing Human Enterprise for Sustainability'; www.frugalmarketing.com/dtb/amorylovins.shtml.

339. 'That is what the unimaginative declare . . .'. 'Down to Business': Paul Hawken interviewed by Renee Lertzman, GreenMoneyJournal.com, 2002. The Rocky Mountain Institute reported in 2005 that: 'About a dozen utilities have profitably sold efficiency in the territories of other utilities. (Electricity is usually a monopoly, but efficiency isn't; you can sell it anywhere you want to. Gas utilities can even sell electric efficiency in ways that change the behavior of buildings so that it becomes more economical to switch to gas?).'

> Some states and towns have been considering a law permitting them to charge hook-up fees (or issue rebates) to new buildings on a sliding scale, depending on the buildings' efficiency. (This same type of law could vary the typical 5-per cent sales tax on new cars over a range of 0–10 per cent, depending on their efficiency. Even better would be to offer rebates to purchasers of very efficient new cars,

provided they scrap their old 'Brontomobile' to get it forever off the road. Or the rebate for the efficient new car could be based on the difference in efficiency between the new car you buy and the old car you scrap) (www.rmi.org/Content/Files/AnnualReport05-06.pdf).

341. Brian Nattrass and Mary Altomare, *The Natural Step for Business: Wealth, Ecology and the Evolutionary Corporation* (Canada: New Society Publishers, 1999); www.interfacesustainability.com/step.html.

343. Interface's ReEntry programme has diverted a total of 66 million pounds of material from landfill and used it in recycling. However, the company still draws 89% of its energy from non-renewable sources of energy; www.interfacesustainability.com.

Interface's mission statement says, 'What we call the next industrial revolution is a momentous shift in how we see the world, how we operate within it, what systems will prevail and which will not. At Interface, we are completely re-imagining and redesigning everything we do, including the way we define our business . . . It's an extraordinarily ambitious endeavor; a mountain to climb that is higher than Everest'; www.interfaceinc.com/goals/sustainability_overview.html.

344. Stuart L. Hart, *Capitalism at the Crossroads: The Unlimited Business Opportunities in Solving the World's Most Difficult Problems* (Philadelphia, PA: Wharton School of Publishing, 2005): 46.

344. WorldWatch Institute, *State of the World 2008*.

344. Felicity Barringer and Andrew Ross Sorkin, 'Trying to stay "ahead of curve", KKR eyes pact with green group', *New York Times*, reprinted in *Mint*, 2 May 2008; www.socialfunds.com/news/article.cgi/article2453.html.

Nationwide, the American Solar Energy Society estimates, there are already 8.5million jobs in the clean-tech sector, which it projects could grow to 40 million by 2030 with the right policies; www.time.com/time/specials/2007/article/0,28804,1730759_1731383_1731363-4,00.html.

Light Up The World Foundation; www.lutw.org.

Banking on Biomass and Simple Living

345. The Banking on Biomass approach aims to simultaneously alter the existing market culture and role of the state. So far, argued Datye, the state has been seen as the sole representative of collective interest in both capitalist as well as socialist economies. The time has come to limit the role of the state to mediation between self-managing communities

in the allocation of resources. The idea is that all those who depend on land for their livelihood should get a certain minimum amount of water, which includes farmers, landless labourers, artisans, women, dalits, etc., irrespective of their holdings.

K.R. Datye, Banking on Biomass: A New Strategy for Sustainable Prosperity Based on Renewable Energy and Dispersed Industrialisation, Centre for Environment Education, Ahmedabad, 1997.

347. Duane Elgin, Voluntary Simplicity.

348. Danielle Sacks, 'Working with the Enemy', *Fast Company*, 18 September 2007. Werbach's consultancy firm Act Now has designed and runs the Personal Sustainability Project at Walmart. Employees who undergo this training then recruit ten volunteers each from among the other employees and help them to develop their own 'personal sustainability project'.

Between 2006 and 2007 Walmart sold compact fluorescent light bulbs to its 100 million customers. Walmart worked with the National Resources Defense Council and other environmental groups to reach its goal – which it did, in the fall of 2007. The retailer established high-performance specifications for the bulbs to ensure customer satisfaction with the quality of the lighting and to allay concerns over the amount of mercury used in the bulbs' manufacture. The result of Walmart's push is a market flush with high-performing, energy-saving bulbs that contain minimal amounts of mercury.

In energy-saving moves that will save Walmart money, Scott said the company plans to increase the fuel efficiency of its truck fleet – among the largest in the country – by 25% over the next three years and double it within ten years. 'If implemented across our entire fleet by 2015, this would amount to savings of more than $310 million a year. Compare that to doing nothing,' he said (money.cnn.com/2005/10/25/news/fortune500/walmart_wage).

350. 'The Future of Energy: The Power and the Glory', *The Economist*, 19 June 2008.

Leila Abboud, 'Economist strikes gold in carbon trade', *Wall Street Journal*, 24 March 2008.

The idea of the old-style market is firmly entrenched. For instance, Robert Stavins, an environmental economist at Harvard's John F. Kennedy School of Government, told Abboud: 'The only way we can fight climate change is if there is an opportunity for business and individuals to make a fortune off it.'

350. When I asked Amory Lovins how he apparently glides peacefully through what is a gruelling schedule, he said that he rides on the

blessing of having capable and dedicated colleagues: 'So I don't have to do much, just learn from them and get better.'

Most people who have dedicated themselves to this work are inspired by what Donella Meadows said years ago: yes, we have just enough time starting *now*! This is the driving energy that Anderson communicates both to employees of Interface and the world at large.

Conversation with Amory Lovins at Schumacher College, UK, 2002.

351. Adam Werbach, Speech to the Commonwealth Club, December 2004.

Werbach is working for a New Apollo Project for jobs and energy independence is a political solution to the problem of global warming that attempts to break from modern environmental thinking. The idea is simple: invest a massive amount of public and private capital in our clean-energy infrastructure, creating millions of new American jobs, ending our dependence on foreign oil, and reducing our contribution to global warming. We can follow the model of the original Apollo Project to reach the moon or the manner in which built the highways, or supported the development of micro-chips, or created the internet.

Survival and hope in a fratricidal war

352. Gautam Naik, 'Biofuels may hinder antiglobal-warming efforts', *Wall Street Journal*, reprinted in *Mint*, 9 February 2008.

352. www.worldcoal.org/environment_&_society.asp.

353. Tom Phillips, 'The Amazon Burns Once Again', *The Guardian*, reprinted in *The Hindu*, 7 October 2007.

353. Jake Ulrich, the managing director of Centrica, has said, 'If companies and individuals are to be made to reduce their output of CO_2, the European Trading Scheme (ETS) needs to be structured to make polluters pay. To do this, we need to eliminate the current free handouts of allowances to emit, which give big windfalls to polluters and do not encourage development of clean generation.'

Danny Fortson, 'Power firms to pocket £6bn from carbon "handouts"', *The Independent*, 2 January 2008; news.independent.co.uk/business/news/article3301065.ece.

355. Ian Mason, 'Earth Jurisprudence', *Resurgence* magazine, March/April 2008.

356. 'I believe in odd miracles . . .'. Paul Hawken interviewed by Renee Lertzman, 2002; www.greenmoneyjournal.com/index.mpl.

SELECT BIBLIOGRAPHY

Anderson, Ray C. (1998) *Mid-course Correction toward a Sustainable Enterprise: The Interface Model* (Atlanta, GA: Peregrinzilla Press).

Ball, Philip (2004) *Critical Mass: How One Thing Leads to Another* (London: Arrow Books).

Barnes, Peter (2001) *Who Owns the Sky? Our Common Assets and the Future of Capitalism* (Washington, DC: Island Press).

Bluestone, Barry, and Bennett Harrison (2001) *Growing Prosperity: The Battle for Growth with Equity in the 21st Century* (Berkeley, CA: University of California Press).

Bornstein, David (2004) *How to Change the World: Social Entrepreneurs and the Power of New Ideas* (UK: Oxford University Press).

Boyle, David (2000) *Funny Money: In Search of Alternative Cash* (London: Flamingo).

—— (2002) *The Money Changers: Currency Reform from Aristotle to E-cash* (London: Earthscan).

Braudel, Fernand (2002) *The Wheels of Commerce: Civilization and Capitalism 15th–18th Century* (3 vols.; London: Phoenix Press [1st edn 1982]).

Brown, Lester (2006) *Plan B 2.0: Rescuing a Planet under Stress and a Civilization in Trouble* (New York: Earth Policy Institute and W.W. Norton).

Cahn, Edgar (2000) *No More Throw-away People: The Co-production Imperative* (Washington, DC: Essential Books).

—— and Jonathan Rowe (1992) *Time Dollars: The New Currency that Enables Americans to Turn Their Hidden Resource – Time – into Personal Security and Community Renewal* (Emmaus, PA: Rodale Press).

Daly, Herman, and J.B. Cobb Jr (1989) *For the Common Good: Redirecting the Economy Toward Community, the Environment, and a Sustainable Future* (Boston, MA: Beacon Press).

Datye, K.R., Suhas Paranjape and K.J. Joy, (1997) *Banking on Biomass: A New Strategy for Sustainable Prosperity Based on Renewable Energy and Dispersed Industrialisation* (Ahmadabad, India: Centre for Environment Education).

De Chardin, Teilhard (1983) *The Phenomenon of Man* (London: Collins).

Domini, Amy (2001) *Socially Responsible Investing; Making a Difference and Making Money* (USA: Dearborn).

Douthwaite, Richard (1996) *Short Circuit: Strengthening Local Economies for Security in an Unstable World* (Totnes, UK: Green Books).

—— (1999) *The Ecology of Money* (Totnes, UK: Green Books).

Durning, Alan (1992) *How Much is Enough: The Consumer Society and the Future of the Earth* (The Worldwatch Environmental Alert Series; New York, London: W.W. Norton & Company).

Ekins, Paul (1986) *The Living Economy: A New Economy in the Making* (London: Routledge & Kegan Paul).

—— (1992) *A New World Order: Grassroots Movements for Global Change* (New York: Routledge).

——, Mayer Hillman and Robert Hutchison (1992) *Wealth Beyond Measure: An Atlas of New Economics* (London: Gaia Books).

Elgin, Duane (1993) *Voluntary Simplicity: Toward a Way of Life That is Outwardly Simple, Inwardly Rich* (New York: Quill, William Morrow).

Fraser, Steve (2005) *Every Man a Speculator: A History of Wall Street in American Life* (New York: HarperCollins).

Fullbrook, Edward (2004) *A Guide to What's Wrong with Economics* (London: Anthem Press).

Galbraith, John Kenneth (1995) *Money: Whence it Came, Where it Went* (Boston MA/New York: Houghton Mifflin).

Greco, Thomas H. (2001) *Money: Understanding and Creating Alternatives to Legal Tender* (White River Junction, VT: Chelsea Green).

—— (2009) *The End of Money and the Future of Civilization* (Vermont, USA: Chelsea Green).

Greider, William (2003) *The Soul of Capitalism: Opening Pathways to a Moral Economy* (New York: Simon & Schuster).

Hart, Keith (1999) *The Memory Bank: Money in an Unequal World* (London: Profile Books).

Hart, Stuart L. (2005) *Capitalism at the Crossroads: the Unlimited Business Opportunities in Solving the World's Most Difficult Problems* (New Jersey, USA: Wharton School Publishing).

Hawken, Paul (2007) *Blessed Unrest: How the Largest Movement in the World Came into Being and Why No One Saw It Coming* (New York: Viking).

——, Hunter Lovins and Amory Lovins (1999) *Natural Capitalism: The Next Industrial Revolution* (Boston, MA: Little, Brown & Company).

Hayek, F.A. (1944) *The Road to Serfdom* (London: Routledge).

Henderson, Hazel (1996) *Creating Alternative Futures: The End of Economics* (West Hartford, CT: Kumarian Press; first published in 1978 by G.P. Putnam's & Sons, NY).

—— (1998) *The Politics of the Solar Age: Alternatives to Economics* (Indianapolis, IN: Knowledge Systems).

Hirschman, Albert O. (1986) *Rival Views of Market Society* (Cambridge, MA: Harvard University Press).

Huber, Joseph, and James Robertson (2000) *Creating New Money: A Monetary Reform for the Information Age* (London: New Economics Foundation).

Hyde, Lewis (1999) *The Gift: Imagination and the Erotic Life of Property* (New York: Vintage Books).

Jenkins, David (2000) *Market Whys and Human Wherefores: Thinking Again About Markets, Politics and People* (London/New York: Cassell).

Kaufman, Michael T. (2002) *Soros: The Life and Times of a Messianic Billionaire* (New York: Vintage Books).

Keen, Steve (2001) *Debunking Economics: The Naked Emperor of the Social Sciences* (Australia: Pluto Press).

Kelly, Marjorie (2001) *The Divine Right of Capital: Dethroning the Corporate Aristocracy* (San Francisco: Berrett-Koehler).

Kennedy, Margrit (1995) *Interest and Inflation Free Money: Creating an Exchange Medium that Works for Everybody and Protects the Earth* (Philadelphia, USA: New Society Publishers).

Kohr, Martin (2000) *Globalization and the South: Some Critical Issues* (Third World Network).

Korten, David (1995) *When Corporations Rule the World* (San Francisco: Berrett-Koehler).

—— (1999) *The Post-Corporate World: Life after Capitalism* (San Francisco: Berrett-Koehler and Kumarian Press).

Kuttner, Robert (1997) *Everything for Sale: The Virtues and Limits of Markets* (New York: Alfred A. Knopf).

Levine, Rick, Christopher Locke, Doc Searls and David Weinberger (2000) *The Cluetrain Manifesto: The End of Business as Usual* (London: Pearson).

Lewis, Michael (1989) *Liar's Poker: Rising through the Wreckage of Wall Street* (New York: Penguin).

Lietaer, Bernard (2001) *The Future of Money: Creating New Wealth, Work and a Wiser World* (London: Century).

Lovelock, James (2006) *The Revenge of Gaia: Why the Earth Is Fighting Back – and How We Can Still Save Humanity* (London: Penguin Books).

Lutz, Mark (1999) *Economics for the Common Good: Two Centuries of Economic Thought in the Humanist Tradition* (London: Routledge).

MacGillivray, Alex, Pat Conaty and Chris Wadhams (2001) *Low Flying Heroes: Micro-social Enterprise below the Radar Screen* (London: New Economics Foundation).

Marglin, Stephen (2008) *The Dismal Science: How Thinking Like an Economist Undermines Community* (Boston, MA: Harvard University Press).

Mauss, Marcel (1970) *The Gift: Forms and Functions of Exchange in Archaic Societies* (trans. Ian Cunnison; London: Cohen & West [1st edn 1925, in French]).

Moore, Thomas (1992) *Care of the Soul: A Guide to Cultivating Depth and Sacredness in Everyday Life* (New York: Harper Perennial).

Mumford, Lewis (1961) *The City in History: Its Origins, its Transformations and its Prospects* (New York: Harcourt Brace).

Plant, Christopher, and Judith Plant (1991) *Green Business: Hope or Hoax?* (Totnes, UK: Green Books).

Polanyi, Karl (1957) *The Great Transformation: The Political and Economic Origins of Our Time* (Boston, MA: Beacon Press).

Porritt, Jonathon (2005) *Capitalism as if the World Matters* (London: Earthscan).

Prahalad, C.K. (2005) *The Fortune at the Bottom of the Pyramid: Eradicating Poverty through Profits* (New Jersey, USA: Wharton School Publishing).

Rajan, Raghuram, and Luigi Zingales (2003) *Saving Capitalism from the Capitalists: Unleashing the Power of Financial Markets to Create Wealth and Spread Opportunity* (New York: Crown Business).

Raymond, Eric (1999) *The Cathedral and the Bazaar: Musings on Linux and Open Source by an Accidental Revolutionary* (Sebastopol, CA: O'Reilly Publishers).

Rifkin, Jeremy (2000) *The Age of Access: The New Culture of Hypercapitalism, Where all of Life is a Paid-For Experience* (New York: Putnam Publishing).

Robertson, James (1978) *The Sane Alternative: A Choice of Futures* (Oxon, UK: James Robertson).

—— (1990) *Future Wealth: A New Economics for the 21st Century* (New York: TOES Books, Bootstrap Press).

Robin, Vicki, and Joe Dominquez (1993) *Your Money or Your Life: A Guide for Transforming Your Relationship with Money and Achieving Financial Independence* (New York: Penguin).

Sachs, Wolfgang (ed.) (2002) *The Jo'burg Memo: Fairness in a Fragile World* (Berlin: Heinrich Böll Foundation).

Schroyer, Trent (1997) *A World that Works: Building Blocks for a Just and Sustainable Society* (Boulder, CO: Bootstrap Press).

Schumacher, E.F. (1999) *Small is Beautiful: Economics as if People Mattered* (25 years later with commentaries; Introduction by Paul Hawken; Vancouver: Hartley & Marks).

—— (1979) *Good Work* (London: Jonathan Cape).

Sen, Amartya (1999) *Development as Freedom* (New York: Alfred A. Knopf).

—— (1987) *On Ethics and Economics* (Oxford, UK: Oxford University Press).

Shuman, Michael (1998) *Going Local: Creating Self-reliant Communities in a Global Age* (London/New York: The Free Press).

Soros, George (1998) *The Crisis of Global Capitalism* (New York: PublicAffairs).

—— (2000) *Open Society: Reforming Global Capitalism* (New York: PublicAffairs).

—— (2006) *The Age of Fallibility: Consequences of the War on Terror* (New York: PublicAffairs).

—— (2006) *The New Paradigm for Financial Markets* (New York: PublicAffairs).

Stiglitz, Joseph (2003) *The Roaring Nineties: Seeds of Destruction* (UK: Allen Lane).

Torvalds, Linus, and David Diamond (2001) *Just for Fun: The Story of an Accidental Revolutionary* (New York: Harper Business): 168.

Vogel, David (2005) *The Market for Virtue: The Potential and Limits of Corporate Social Responsibility* (Washington, DC: Brookings Institute Press).

Watson, Peter (2000) *A Terrible Beauty: A History of the People and Ideas that Shaped the Modern Mind* (London: Weidenfeld & Nicolson).

Weatherford, Jack (1997) *The History of Money* (New York: Three Rivers Press).

Wood, Ellen Meiksins (2002) *The Origin of Capitalism: A Longer View* (London: Verso).

Zadek, Simon, John Sabapathy, Helle Dossing and Tracey Swift (2003) *Responsible Competitiveness: Corporate Responsibility Clusters in Action* (The Copenhagen Center and AccountAbility).

INDEX

NOTE: Page numbers in *italics* refer to additional references in the Source Notes.